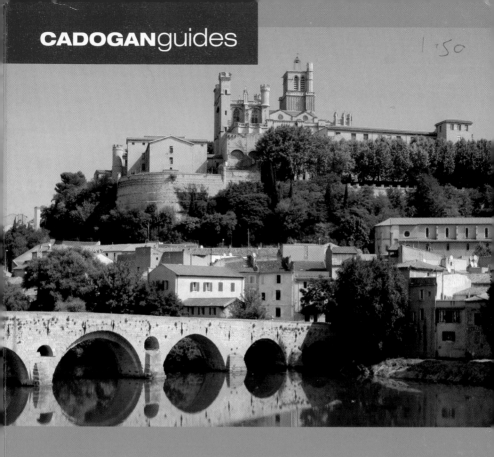

1.50

LANGUEDOC-
ROUSSILLON

*'Approaching the town from the surrounding p
you'll see its heroic hilltop skyline from miles
crowned by its soaring cathedral.'*

D1419426

Dana Facaros & Michael Pauls

About the Guide

The full-colour introduction gives the authors' overview of the country, together with suggested itineraries and a regional 'where to go' map and feature to help you plan your trip.

Illuminating and entertaining cultural chapters on local history, art, architecture, food, wine and everyday life give you a rich flavour of the country.

Planning Your Trip starts with the basics of when to go, getting there and getting around, coupled with other useful information, including a section for disabled travellers. The Practical A–Z deals with all the essential information and contact details that you may need while you are away.

The regional chapters are arranged in a loose touring order, with plenty of public transport and driving information. The authors' top 'Don't Miss' ✪ sights are highlighted at the start of each chapter.

A language and pronunciation guide, a glossary of cultural terms, ideas for further reading and a comprehensive index can be found at the end of the book.

Although everything we list in this guide is personally recommended, our authors inevitably have their own favourite places to eat and stay. Whenever you see this Authors' Choice ⭐ icon beside a listing, you will know that it is a little bit out of the ordinary.

Hotel Price Guide (*see also* p.73)

Luxury	€€€€€	€230 and above
Very Expensive	€€€€	€150–230
Expensive	€€€	€100–150
Moderate	€€	€60–100
Inexpensive	€	under €60

Restaurant Price Guide (*see also* p.79)

Very expensive	€€€€	over €60
Expensive	€€€	€30–60
Moderate	€€	€15–30
Inexpensive	€	under €15

About the Authors

Dana Facaros and Michael Pauls have written over 30 books for Cadogan Guides. They have lived all over Europe with their son and daughter, and are currently ensconced in a old farmhouse in southwest France with a large collection of tame and wild animals.

2nd Edition published 2008

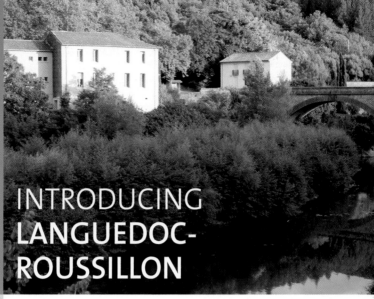

INTRODUCING LANGUEDOC-ROUSSILLON

Y ou can sail halfway around the Mediterranean coast, from Gibraltar as far as Tuscany, and you'll only find one little slice of coastline that doesn't advertise itself as a 'Costa' or a 'Riviera'. Why such humility? There's certainly no lack of beaches; Languedoc-Roussillon is lined with sand from the Rhône to the Pyrenees, and behind the sand you'll find as many bustling resorts as in any region of France.

Languedoc, perhaps, suffers a little problem of identity. Provence, the region's pampered sister across the Rhône, conjures up images of mimosa and lavender, rich *bouillabaisse* and dramatic seafront *corniches*. On the other side, everyone knows France's southwest as the land of *foie gras* and truffles and strong red wine. Poor Languedoc in the middle has its share of fatted ducks and mimosas and good fish soup and everything else; and there's at least one modest *corniche*, and enough wine, heaven knows, to sozzle visitors by the billion. What it lacks, to the despair of the regional tourism authorities, is something unique, something it can call its own.

Promotion is their job, fortunately, not ours. If we can't boil down this region into a single image or a handful of clichés, let's take it as a sweet invitation to look at the place a little more closely and find out what's really there. If you do that, you'll find it a real grab-bag, with a little bit of everything and plenty of surprises – Gothic cathedrals and space-age beach resorts, bullfights and sea-going jousts. Within the space of a day you can visit one town founded by the ancient Greeks, another with the refined air of a little Paris from the days of Louis XIV, and its lively neighbour, a brash workaday port famous for nothing but sardines.

Previous page: Béziers, pp.172–5

Opposite page: harbour, Palavas, pp.160–61; flowers

Above, from top: Olargues, p.157; dome, Montpellier, pp.127–40

Above: Les Arènes, Nîmes, pp.88–9

Opposite page: Old town, Perpignan, pp.242–9

The landscapes, too, conspire to surprise. In an area roughly the size of Wales or New Jersey, they've managed to squeeze in the best part of the Pyrenees, a swampy Rhône delta populated by cowboys and flamingos, chestnut forests and olive groves, not to mention a lost plateau where the French army does its desert training. Rolling hills covered in vines seem to stretch on forever, but when they finally run out they leave you in a dry *garrigue* country studded with ancient monasteries that could be a stage set from the Crusades.

History hasn't always been kind here. Languedoc seems to blossom only every thousand years. Once this was the richest part of Gaul; the Romans left their calling card in neatly squared masonry at the famous Pont du Gard and the great amphitheatre and temple at Nîmes. A thousand years later, after rude interruptions by Goths, Franks, Arabs and other troublemakers, it resurfaced as the land of the troubadours, one of the morning stars of early medieval civilization. Once again though, outsiders would come to spoil things. Languedoc had to be dragged kicking and screaming into what is now called France, and for centuries the French weren't very nice to it. Though the region languished culturally and economically, however, it kept up its habit of providing the unexpected – these sunny Mediterranean shores gave Protestantism its warmest welcome in France, and later on they would fill up with textile mills and help France along with its Industrial Revolution.

If that big historical clock runs right, Languedoc should be set to bloom again soon. Long one of the poorest corners of France, it has been making great strides over the last few decades. You'll sense the air of a young region, an up-and-coming one. The buzzing modern cities of Toulouse and Montpellier are not only making up for lost time, they're doing more than their share in pulling France into the 21st century. Tourism (and government planning) have transformed the once-lonely coasts; some of the biggest resorts here didn't exist 40 years ago. And the land once called France's 'culinary desert', famous for its oceans of plonk and dismal restaurants, has now smartened itself up considerably in both. Let Provence keep the clichés. This side of the Rhône is a land for discovering.

Where to Go

With its complex history, just what constitutes 'Languedoc' has always been a matter for debate. Back in the 1980s, when the government in Paris decided to decentralize some of its functions by creating new regions, they went about it in a thoroughly French way, chopping up the country more or less arbitrarily into similar-sized bits, and throwing some of historical Languedoc into a region with Catalan Roussillon. Our book covers, from east to west, the *départements* of the Gard, Hérault, Aude and Pyrénées-Orientales (Roussillon), along with Languedoc's traditional capital of Toulouse.

Languedoc shares the Rhône valley with Provence, and our side is a delightful garden of olives and vines, with only a fraction of the tourists that Provence gets – except perhaps at the magnificent Pont du Gard, one of the three most visited sights in France. This is covered in **Nîmes, the Gard and Montpellier**, along with the art town of Uzès, and Languedoc's small share of the Camargue, the Rhône delta. Here you can visit two exceptional relics of the Middle Ages: St-Gilles, with its famous statuary, and Aigues-Mortes, the port Saint Louis built to ship him and his armies off to the Crusades. Eastern Languedoc's two big cities, Nîmes and Montpellier, are eternal rivals, only 40km apart. They make an interesting pair of bookends – Nîmes with its famous Roman monuments, full of atmosphere and tradition, and dynamic Montpellier, a university city that rivals rosy Toulouse in its great enthusiasm for culture and technology.

The Hérault introduces the biggest wine-producing *département* of France, with rural delights equal to those of Provence, including wine regions like the Minervois, Pézenas, Languedoc's 'little Paris', and the Mediterranean end of the serendipitous tree-lined Canal du Midi – the most beautiful canal in the world, and a lovely spot for spending some lazy time on the water. North of Montpellier lies the haunted, austere *garrigue* country, with medieval St-Martin-de-Londres and St-Guilhem-le-Désert, as well as the small, green mountain chain of the Espinouse, now a regional park. The Hérault's coast offers long miles of open beaches, coastal lagoons full of oysters and resorts ranging from the pretty town of Agde, founded by the Greeks, to futuristic La Grande Motte and Cap d'Agde, Europe's capital of naturism.

The Aude *département* is covered in **Narbonne, the Corbières and the Valley of the Aude**; here you'll find the surprising city of Narbonne, with its magnificent cathedral, and Carcassonne, the biggest and best-preserved medieval fortress city in Europe. There's the vortex of *Da Vinci Code* madness at Rennes-le-

Above, from top:
Languedoc grapes; Place
de la Comédie,
Montpellier, p.130

Opposite page:
Garrigue landscape,
Hérault

Château, on the way to scores of spectacular castles hanging over the strange and rugged landscapes of the Corbières.

Beyond these lies **Roussillon**. The Catalan corner of France is another world, one that increasingly looks more towards Barcelona than Paris. Perpignan, the 'centre of the universe' according to Salvador Dalí, has a wealth of medieval art, and nearby is Collioure, inspiration of the Fauvist painters, on the delicious Côte Vermeille. Up in the Pyrenees, two valleys flank the Catalan holy mountain, Canigou, each with its treasures of Romanesque architecture, skiing and scenery.

For many, **Toulouse** will be the gateway to Languedoc. La Ville Rose, sitting pretty on the Garonne, may be full of medieval art and buildings, but it is also France's Space City, home to Airbus and packed full of university students who make sure it stays it one of the liveliest cities of the Midi.

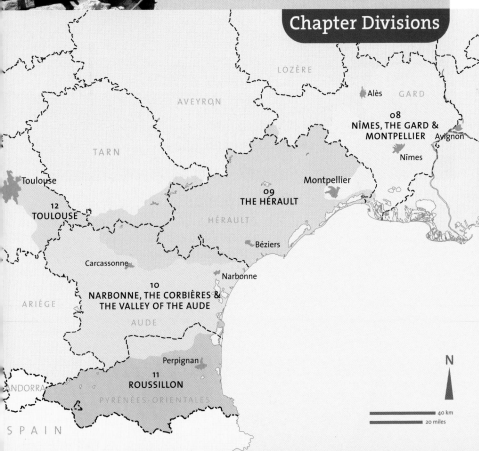

Chapter Divisions

LOZÈRE

Alès   GARD

AVEYRON

**08
NÎMES, THE GARD &
MONTPELLIER**   Avignon

TARN

Nîmes

Toulouse

Montpellier

**09
THE HÉRAULT**

**12
TOULOUSE**

HÉRAULT

Béziers

Carcassonne

Narbonne

**10
NARBONNE, THE CORBIÈRES &
THE VALLEY OF THE AUDE**

ARIÈGE

AUDE

Perpignan

ANDORRA

**11
ROUSSILLON**

PYRÉNÉES-ORIENTALES

N

SPAIN

40 km
20 miles

Above: Walled city of Carcassonne, pp.219–23

Opposite page: Cathédrale St-Just, Narbonne, pp.195–7

Land of the Troubadours

Don't ever make the mistake of thinking you're in just another part of France. Languedoc, like the rest of the south, was once a world of its own, and in the early Middle Ages this was the place to be, amid a brilliant, tolerant Occitan culture far ahead of its time.

Wherever you go, relics of this lost world lie at hand, from the delicate springtime sculpture of the 'Master of Cabestany' to the astonishing architecture of Catalan Perpignan. Landscapes of sparse *garrigue* and sandy coastline conspire to add a touch of the Mediterranean and exotic. When the French came, they added northern ideas and styles to the mix, including the matchless citadel of Carcassonne, and Gothic cathedrals in Narbonne and Béziers that would look entirely at home in the Île-de-France.

What's Roussillon?

The little corner that gives this book (and the region) its hyphenated title hasn't much to do at all with Languedoc – or even France, for that matter. Historically and culturally, Roussillon is Catalan. The French grabbed it away four hundred years ago to gain a more defensible border on the Pyrenees, but they've never really won over the Roussillonais' hearts and minds. Behind a coast lined with beaches there's an impressive little capital, Perpignan, and behind that three valleys leading up into the hills. Fortune gave the Catalans (and the French) some of the best of the Pyrenees, in fact: skiing and hiking, rugged mountain villages, unique, robust medieval art and spectacular scenery, all tugging at the skirts of the Catalans' holy mountain of Canigou.

Above: Place de la Révolution, Perpignan, pp.242–51

Right: Pyrenean gorge, southern Roussillon

Above: Ripening vines, Minervois, p.181

Wines of a Southern Sun

Not too long ago, the *vignerons* of France's biggest wine-growing region spent their free time rioting against governments that wouldn't guarantee a market for all the plonk they made. Finally, they decided instead to try and improve it. Against all odds, they did – enough so that many of the exciting new wine regions of France are right here in Languedoc. There are 22 official denominations, and, while we wouldn't recommend such velocity, you could speed through the region and sample a new AOC variety every hour or so (or, at a slightly slower pace, follow the suggested itinerary on p.15). It is Languedoc's wide range of soils and microclimates that make all this variety possible.

Under the southern sun, the best wines are red, though you'll find some surprising whites and rosés too, not to mention a strong tradition of fortified dessert wines in Roussillon.

Above: clockwise from top left: Café doorway, Sommières, p.123; Languedoc wine bottles; seafood, Bouzigues, p.165

Bon Appétit!

Provence has its *bouillabaisse*, known around the world. But so what? Across the Rhône in the Languedoc they simmer up their fish in a spicy *bourride* that is every bit as tasty. For centuries a poor and out-of-the-way place, Languedoc never was one of France's culinary stars, but, as with the wine, that's changing fast. You'll see the region's main advantage as soon as you tour one of its wonderful city markets – the basic ingredients are terrific. And it's not just about seafood; in fact Languedoc-Roussillon shows a very gratifying split personality when it comes to cooking. Look towards the sea and there are fish stews, Sète's stuffed cuttlefish, Collioure's anchovies and everything else, done up with plenty of tomatoes, garlic and olive oil. Look the other way, however, and you'll see the fine traditional country cooking of the southwest, the land of duck, *cèpes* and *foie gras*.

This page: Market produce, Sète

Water Everywhere

Sum up the Languedoc coast in a sentence? Don't even try. Instead, imagine a sort of geographer's catalogue of shorelines, where the scenery changes by the hour. It starts in the Rhône delta, with the flamingos and white horses of the glistening green Camargue. After that, the coast goes into high gear at the space-age resort of La Grande Motte, bringing in landscapes of coastal lagoons full of oysters and mussels. Next comes Sète, a major port with its thousands of sardines, and Cap-d'Agde with its thousands of naturists. Sixty miles of open sandy beaches later, it all finishes with the delicious *corniche* coast around Collioure, the Côte Vermeille.

Languedoc offers plenty of fresh water too, in the mountain streams of the Pyrenees and the Corbières, and the delightful tree-lined Canal du Midi, the perfect spot for a lazy holiday on a slow old boat.

Above, from top: River Gard, north of Nîmes, pp.96–8; beach, Palavas-les-Flots, pp.160–61; harbour, Sète, pp.163–4

Itineraries

A Wine and Culture Tour

With no less than 22 AOC wine regions and a host of lesser varieties, you can easily spend a month drinking your way across the region. If your employer objects, try this condensed version and attempt to drink Languedoc-Roussillon dry in nine days.

Day 1 Start along the **Rhône** river, where there are laid-back villages, art at **Villeneuve lez Avignon**, and three AOC wine regions to tour in a day: **Côtes du Rhone**, **Lirac** and **Tavel**. (The more famous **Châteauneuf-du-Pape** region is just across the Rhône in Provence.)

Day 2 After looking over **Nîmes** and the **Pont du Gard**, take a ride around the countryside to seek out **Costières de Nîmes**.

Days 3 and 4 Head into the heart of the Hérault, France's biggest wine-making department, and again you can experience three tiny but well-respected wine regions in a day or two: **Coteaux du Languedoc**, **Faugères** and **Saint-Chinian**. Along the way you'll pass near the evocatively medieval **St-Guilhem-le-Désert** and *grand siècle* **Pézenas**.

Day 5 Today's wine is **Minervois**, from the compact region of the same name. Attractions nearby include the tremendous medieval fortress town of **Carcassonne** and the pretty countryside around the **Canal du Midi** towards the coast.

Day 6 Spend most of this day getting to know the elegant and historic city of **Narbonne**, with a trip to the coast to sample some of the vintage from the tiny mountain area of **La Clape**.

Days 7 and 8 The Corbières will be good for two days of wine-tasting and touring. The areas between the villages of **Fitou** and **Tuchan** have some of the most interesting wine estates, and the great medieval castles of the Corbières – **Peyrepertuse**, **Quéribus** and **Aguilar** – are conveniently nearby.

Day 9 The last day of this gastronomical-cultural feast will be dessert, so to speak, among the sweet wines of Roussillon: a taste of **Maury**, and a ride through the scenic **Fenouillèdes**, and then to the coast for some **Banyuls**, and maybe an afternoon on the beach at **Collioure** or **Banyuls-sur-Mer**.

Above, from top: Pont du Gard, pp.96–8; Languedoc vines

01 Introduction | A Ten-day Medieval Mystery Tour

Above: Architectural detail, church, Carcassonne, pp.217–26

Below: Church, Colombiers, p.176

A Ten-day Medieval Mystery Tour

Day 1 Start on the Languedoc side of the **Camargue**, the Rhône delta, a romantic setting for the famous sculpture of **St-Gilles-du-Gard**, and **Aigues-Mortes**, the port Saint Louis built to send his armies off to the Crusades.

Day 2 Skirt around **Montpellier** and head for the lonely *garrigue* north of the city, to visit the evocative villages and churches of **St-Martin-de-Londres** and **St-Guilhem-le-Desert**.

Day 3 Head back towards the coast, making a stop at the great **abbey of Valmagne** on your way to two of the greatest Gothic cathedrals of southern France, conveniently located near each other at **Béziers** and **Narbonne**.

Day 4 Head north, and then west, following the route of the **Canal du Midi**; the route goes through pretty **Colombiers** and then takes in medieval relics at **Capestang**, **Quarante** and **Trèbes**, and then the mystical seven-sided church at **Rieux-Minervois** before arriving at Carcassonne.

Day 5 The full tour of **Carcassonne**'s walls and towers, as well as its medieval Cité, museums and cathedral, is good for a whole day.

Day 6 From here, the D118 south takes you into the old Cathar heartland, where you can explore the mysteries of **Rennes-le-Château**, and perhaps make a side trip to the Cathars' last redoubt, the castle of Montségur.

Day 7 Continue on south, into the Pyrénées, where the micro-region of the **Cerdagne** offers not only gorgeous scenery, but a number of unique and peculiar Romanesque village churches.

Day 8 Find your way out of the mountains down the valley of the **Conflent**, with some masterpieces of medieval Catalan architecture and sculpture at **St-Michel-de-Cuxa**, **St-Martin-du-Canigou** and **Serrabonne**, on the slopes of holy Canigou.

Day 9 Spend another day with the Catalans in **Perpignan**, home to a fine cathedral and the 13th-century Palace of the Kings of Majorca. If there's time, drive out to **Elne**, for a cloister that contains some of the finest medieval sculpture in the region.

Day 10 North of Perpignan, have a look at a strange, almost barren vortex of occult mysteries, the **Plateau d'Opoul**. From here, head into the Corbières. The most impressive collection of castles in southern France waits here, including cloudtop **Peyrepertuse** and the Cathar redoubt of **Quéribus**.

CONTENTS

Contents

About the Updater

Linda Rano has lived near Toulouse for over 10 years with her husband and two children. She writes regularly for a number of publications, mainly on tourism and the property market in southwest France.

History

O2

First, we'll try to set the terminology straight. When the Romans ruled here, they called all of southern Gaul 'Provence' at first, then 'Gallia Narbonensis'. Finally, the region between the Rhône and the Pyrenees was sorted out as 'Septimania', a name that survived up to medieval times. In the days of the troubadours almost all the south was poetically 'Provence', but the political split continued, between lands subject to the Holy Roman Emperors (Provence) and those claimed by France (Languedoc). Today, southern regionalists call the entire south of France 'Occitania' (a word only invented in the 17th century).

Roussillon, the modern *département* of Pyrénées-Orientales, followed an entirely different course of history: part of the Catalan nation since the 10th century, it was an essential part of the County of Barcelona and later the Catalan Kingdom of Aragon, until the French annexed it in 1559.

Under the *ancien régime*, the Revolution and all the regimes that followed it, these areas were smothered, politically and culturally, by France. The turning of the tide came only in our own time, with the election of the 1981 socialist government and the beginnings of regional autonomy. The old Languedoc was cut in two; the western half, including its traditional capital Toulouse, became the Midi-Pyrénées, while the rest was combined with the department of Pyrénées-Orientales to become the region covered in this book: Languedoc-Roussillon.

Just Another of Prehistory's Backwaters

Tools and traces of habitation in southern France go back as far as 1,000,000 BC. The first identifiable personality on the stage, however, is 'Tautavel Man'; a remarkable recent find in the small Roussillon village of that name has unearthed hundreds of thousands of bones of a people who rate among the very first Europeans yet discovered – from at least 450,000 BC, and perhaps as far back as 680,000 BC. Someone may have been around through all the millennia that followed, but evidence is rare; Neanderthal Man turns up about 60,000 BC (at Ganges, in the Hérault, and other places). The first evidence of the Neanderthals' nemesis, that quarrelsome and unlovable species *Homo sapiens*, comes some 20,000 years later.

Neolithic civilization arrived as early as 3500 BC, and endured throughout the region for the next 2,000 years. People knew agriculture and raised sheep, traded for scarce goods (obsidian from the islands around Sicily, for example), and built dry-stone houses; one of these has been reconstructed by archaeologists at Cambous, in the Hérault. Unlike Provence, Languedoc has few important Neolithic monuments, just a few large dolmens in the Minervois in the southern Hérault, and the exotic 'statue-menhirs' you can see in the museum at St-Pons-de-Thomières. Of succeeding ages we know more about the technology than the culture and changes in population: the use of copper began about 2000 BC, iron c. 800 BC. In both cases the region was one of the last parts of the Mediterranean basin to catch on.

The first settled villages appear about 800 BC. Who built them is a matter of conjecture; later Roman and Greek writers would call the people along the coast 'Iberians', though just about this time Languedoc was feeling the great invasion of the Celts, then spreading their control over most of continental Europe. The Celts by nature didn't much care for towns, but you will find traces of their settlements today, called by the Latin name *oppida*. An *oppidum* is a small, fortified village, usually on a hilltop, built around a religious sanctuary or trading centre. Already, more advanced outsiders were coming to make deals with the natives: the Phoenicians, the Etruscans and, most importantly, the Greeks.

In the 7th century BC, Greek merchant activity around the Mediterranean turned into full-scale colonization. The Ionian city-states of Asia Minor had become over-populated, agriculturally exhausted and politically precarious, and their citizens sought to reproduce them in new lands. The first was Massalia – Marseille – c. 600 BC. Soon Massalia was founding colonies of its own, including Agde in Languedoc. Greek influence over the indigenous peoples was strong from the start; as in everywhere else they went, they brought the vine (wild stocks were already present, but the Celts hadn't worked out what to do with them) and the olive, and also their art. The Celts loved Greek vases, and had metals and other raw materials to offer in return. Increased trade turned some of the native *oppida* into genuine cities, such as Ensérune, near Béziers.

The Romans Arrive to Wake It Up

From the start, the Greeks were natural allies of the young city of Rome – if only because they had common enemies. Besides the strong Etruscan federation, occupying the lands in between the two, there were their trade rivals, the Phoenicians (later Carthaginians) and occasionally the Celts and Ligurians. As Rome gobbled up Etruria and the rest of Italy, the area became of increasing importance, a fact Hannibal demonstrated when he marched his armies through Languedoc towards Italy in 218 BC, with the full support of the Celts (historians still argue over how and where he got the elephants across the Rhône).

When the Romans took Spain in the Second Punic War (206 BC), the coasts of what they called Gaul became a logical next step. In 125 BC, Roman troops saved Marseille from another Celtic attack. This time, though, they had come to stay. The reorganization of the new province – Provincia – was quick and methodical. Domitius Ahenobarbus, the vanquisher of the Celts, began the great Italy–Spain highway that bears his name, the Via Domitia, in 121 BC. New cities were founded, most importantly Narbo Martius (Narbonne, 118 BC), which became the capital of the quickly developing western half, reorganized into a new province called Gallia Narbonensis. Dozens of other new foundations, including Perpignan and Carcassonne, followed over the next century, many of them planned colonies with land grants for veterans of the legions. The Celts were not through yet, though. Two northern tribes, the Cimbri and Teutones, mounted a serious invasion of Gaul and Italy in 115 BC. They raided those areas continuously until 102 BC, when they were destroyed by a Roman army under Marius in Provence.

The last Celtic invasions came at a time when the Roman Republic was in disarray at home. Marius, leader of the populist faction, was only one of the generals who won political power in the capital. After his death, the new military boss of Rome was Sulla, a bloody reactionary whose tyranny inspired resistance in many corners of the empire. A general named Quintus Sertorius, who had fought under Marius, seized Spain and parts of Gaul and defeated five armies sent against him from

Rome. Sertorius held out until he was poisoned at a banquet in the Pyrenees by a subordinate named Perpenna (he must have been well rewarded; Perpignan is named for him).

Rome's internal struggles continued to be reflected in the fortunes of Mediterranean Gaul. Marseille's downfall came in 49 BC. Always famed for its careful diplomacy, the city made the fatal mistake of supporting Pompey over Julius Caesar in the civil wars. A vengeful Caesar crippled its trade and stripped it of nearly all its colonies and dependencies. Thereafter, the influence of Marseille gave way to newer, more Romanized towns, including Narbo Martius and Nemausus (Nîmes).

Throughout all this, the region had been easily assimilated into the Roman economy, supplying food and raw materials for the insatiable metropolis. With Caesar's conquest of the rest of Gaul, the Rhône trade route (which had always managed to bring down a little Baltic amber and tin from Cornwall) became a busy river highway and military route. Under the good government and peace bestowed by Augustus (27 BC–AD 14) and his successors, Gaul blossomed with an opulence never before seen. The cities, especially those of the Rhône valley, acquired theatres, amphitheatres for games, aqueducts, bridges and temples. Gallia Narbonensis participated in the political and cultural life of the empire, even contributing one of the better emperors, Antoninus Pius (from Nîmes, AD 138–61), only obscure because his reign was so peaceful and prosperous.

Archaeological digs throughout France turn up a preponderance of wealthy villas. This is the dark side of Roman Gaul: from the beginning of their rule, wealthy Romans were able to grab up much of the land, forming large estates and exploiting the indigenous population. This trend was magnified in the decadent, totalitarian and economically chaotic late Empire, when, throughout Roman territory, the few remaining free farmers were forced to sell themselves into virtual serfdom to escape crushing taxation. After AD 200, in fact, everything was going wrong; trade and the cities stagnated while art and culture decayed. The first of the barbarian raids brought Germans into the south in the 250s, when they raided Provence.

Constantine, while yet emperor of only the western half of the empire (AD 312–23), often resided at Arles in Provence. His pro-Christian policy gave the cult its first real influence in Gaul, at least in the cities; under his auspices, the first state-sponsored Church council was held at Arles in 314.

600 Years of Unwanted Guests

French historians always blame the barbarian invaders of the 5th century for destroying the cities of Gaul – as if Teutonic warriors enjoyed pulling down temple colonnades on their days off. Alans, Suevi and Vandals passed through the region, but they were in a hurry to get to Spain; the Visigoths, in the early 400s, came to stay. Though government collapsed in chaos, business went on much as usual, with the Roman landowners (and their new German colleagues) gradually making their transition to feudal nobles. The weakness of central power brought some long-due upheavals in the countryside, with guerrilla bands and vigilante justice against the landlords. The old and new rulers soon found common cause. For a while, a clique of a hundred of the biggest landowners took over administration in Gaul, even declaring one of their own as 'emperor' in Arles (455), with the support of the Visigoths.

The Visigoths soon tired of such games, and assumed total control in 476, the year the Western Empire formally expired. They had to share it, however, with the Ostrogoths, who had established a strong kingdom in Italy and seized all of Provence east of the Rhône – the beginnings of a political boundary that would last in various forms for a thousand years. When the Eastern Empire under Justinian tried to recapture Italy, the Franks took the opportunity to snatch the Ostrogoths' domain in Gaul (535). They were never able to hold it effectively and the area gradually slipped into quiet anarchy.

By now, the region west of the Rhône had come to be known as 'Septimania', for its seven important towns: Narbonne, Béziers, Agde, Elne, Maguelone, Lodève and Nîmes. Most of these, unfortunately, were only shadows of what they had been in Roman times. The Visigoths kept most of this land, the northernmost province of their Spanish kingdom, until the Arab invasion of the early 700s rolled over the Pyrenees. In 711 the Arabs destroyed the Visigothic kingdom in Spain. Eight years later they came over the Pyrenees and took Narbonne.

The next two centuries are as wonderfully confused as anything in prehistory. There is the legend of the great Spanish Caliph Abd ar-Rahman campaigning here, and a document survives in which the bishops of Agde are rebuked by the pope for minting coins with the image of Muhammad. Charles Martel, the celebrated Frankish generalissimo who stopped the Arab wave at Poitiers, made an expedition to the southern coast in 737–9, brutally sacking Agde before passing into Provence. His mission was hardly a religious crusade – rather taking advantage of the Visigothic defeat to increase Frankish hegemony in the south. The Arabs still held many fortified towns, and they are recorded as petitioning Córdoba, unsuccessfully, to help them keep the half-barbarous Franks out.

Córdoba couldn't help; the climate was too eccentric and the pickings too slim for the Arabs to mount a serious effort in Gaul. The nascent Franks gained control everywhere, and the entire coast was absorbed by Charlemagne's father, Pépin the Short, in 759. Under Charlemagne (768–814), the region seems to have shared little in the brief Carolingian revival of trade and culture, and after the break-up of the empire (with the Treaty of Verdun in 843) its misery was complete. The 9th- and 10th-century invasions were the real Dark Ages in many parts of Europe. The region suffered constant and destructive raids by the Normans, the Arabs again (who held towns in Provence until the 970s), and even the Hungarians, on their once-only western tour. They sacked what was left of Nîmes in 924.

The Beginnings of the Middle Ages

Even in this sorry period, the foundations were being laid for recovery. Monastic reformers in Charlemagne's time, men such as Benedict of Aniane (in the Hérault), helped start a huge expansion of Church institutions. The abbey of St-Victor in Marseille took the lead in this, founding hundreds of new monasteries around Occitania. Hard-working monks reclaimed land from forests and swamps, and later they sat back and enjoyed the rents, while always keeping up the holy work of education and copying books. Pilgrimages became an important activity, as at St-Gilles-du-Gard and St-Guilhem (near Aniane), getting a sleepy and locally bound society moving again and providing an impetus to trade.

The Treaty of Verdun (*see* **Topics**, p.40) had confirmed the Rhône as a boundary, and politically Provence and Languedoc went their separate ways. The Kingdom of Provence (or 'Kingdom of Arles'), proclaimed by a great-grandson of Charlemagne in 879, was little more than a façade for feudal anarchy. In 849, all of modern Languedoc fell to a new power, the County of Toulouse. In the beginning their hold was nominal at best, but under a capable dynasty of counts, all named Raymond, Toulouse gradually extended its control over towns and fiefs throughout the region.

Another result of the Carolingian collapse was the birth of a new nation in the eastern Pyrenees – Catalunya. The Catalans, who spoke a language closely related to the Occitan of Languedoc and Provence, coalesced around the County of the Cerdagne, deep in the Pyrenees, under the legendary Wilfred the Hairy, who became count in 874. In the 10th century his dynasty gained control of Barcelona, and expanded its control throughout what is now Roussillon. The Franks, their nominal overlords, offered the Catalans no help in their constant battles with the Arabs of Spain, and in 985 Count Borrell II declared Catalunya an independent and sovereign state; the Franks could do nothing about it.

Occitan and Catalan Medieval Civilization

All over Europe, the year 1000 can be taken as the rough milestone for the sudden and spectacular development of the medieval world, including Occitania. Towns and villages found the money and energy to build impressive new churches. The end of foreign raids made the seas safe for merchants. New cities were founded, notably Montpellier, in 985. In 1002 the first written document in Occitan appeared, highlighting the linguistic fault line that had grown up between the '*langue d'oïl*' of the north and the '*langue d'oc*' of the south (so called from the two words, *oïl* and *oc*, that they used for 'yes'). The great pilgrimage to Santiago de Compostela, in Spain, made what was left of the old Roman roads into busy highways once more, and along the main southern route the first of the medieval trade fairs appeared, at the new town of St-Gilles-du-Gard.

Populations and economies boomed throughout the 11th century, and the trend was given another boost by the Crusades, which began in 1095. With increased prosperity and contact with a wider world, better manners and the rudiments of personal hygiene were not slow to follow. Feudal anarchy began to look quite genteel, maintaining a delicate balance of power, with feudal ties and blood relations keeping the political appetites of rulers from ever really getting out of hand. From the more civilized East, and from nearby Muslim Spain, came new ideas, new technologies and a taste for luxury and art. As an indication of how far Occitania had come, there were the troubadours (*see* **Topics**, p.43), creating modern Europe's first lyric poetry. Almost every court of the south was refined enough to welcome and patronize them.

The growing cities began to assert themselves in the 12th century, often achieving a substantial independence in *communes* governed by consuls: Perpignan and

Nîmes both won these rights in 1198. In the countryside, successive waves of monastic reform spawned a huge number of new institutions: first the movement led from Cluny, in the 11th century, and in the 12th the Cistercians, who set up a score of important monasteries. Efficiently exploiting the lands bequeathed by noblemen made them rich, and also did much to improve the agricultural economy all round. Probably the richest corner of the south was the Catalan Pyrenees; substantial iron deposits, and the most advanced methods of smelting them, provided the capital for a Catalan trading empire based in Barcelona and Perpignan. From then on, Catalunya's rise was dramatic. For a brief time the Catalans attempted to expand northwards; under Ramon Berenguer I (d. 1076) their domains stretched as far as Carcassonne and Montpellier. By 1125 the counts of Barcelona controlled much of Provence south of the Durance; in 1137 they became kings of Aragon, which included much of western Spain. Besides its wealth, Catalunya was characterized by its unique constitution, recognizing the interests of the new middle class as well as nobles, and writing down elaborate codes of rights called *fueros* as a check on royal absolutism.

The other leading power in the region, the 'Raymonds' of Toulouse, eventually took back the Catalan conquests in Languedoc, while they contended with them for control of Provence. The strong state they built controlled everything from the Rhône to the Lot valley and the central Pyrenees – except for Carcassonne and Béziers, ruled by their allies the Trencavel family, Montpellier, a Catalan possession, and Narbonne, ruled by its independent viscounts.

The Cathars and the Rape of Languedoc

It was a great age for culture, producing not only the troubadours but an impressive display of Romanesque architecture, and an original school of sculpture in Roussillon. Perhaps the most remarkable phenomenon of the times was a widespread religious tolerance, shared by rulers, the common people and even many among the clergy. A long and fruitful exposure to the culture of Muslim Spain, as well as the presence of a large Jewish community, an important element in the towns since Roman times, must have helped. Still, such goodwill is hard to account for in medieval Europe. Like the troubadour poetry, it is an indication of just how advanced Occitan society was at its height in the 12th century.

Unfortunately, this tolerance was also to bring about the fall of the Occitan nation. Religious dissenters of various persuasions sprang up everywhere. Most of the new sects soon died out and are little known today, like the extremist 'Petrobrusians' of St-Gilles, who didn't fancy sacraments or relics; some of them favoured burning down churches and killing all priests and monks.

One sect, however, made startling inroads into every sector of society in 11th- and 12th-century Languedoc – the Cathars, or Albigensians. This Manichaean doctrine (*see* **Topics**, pp.41–2), obsessed with Good and Evil, had in its upright simplicity a powerful attraction for both industrious townspeople and peasants. In many ways it was the very picture of 17th-century English Puritanism, though without any of the Puritans' noxious belligerence towards the less perfect; this kept it in good standing with the worldly nobility, and also allowed Cathar and Catholic villagers to live peacefully side by side.

The Cathars were never a majority in any part of the south; in most places they never made up more than 10 per cent of the population. They might have passed on as only a curious footnote to history, had they not provided the excuse for the biggest and most flagrant land-grab of the Middle Ages. The 'Albigensian Crusade', arranged after the 1208 murder of a papal legate, was a cynical marriage of convenience between two old piratical enemies, the papacy and the crown of France. One wanted the religious competition stifled; the other sought to assert its old Carolingian claim to the lands of the counts of Toulouse. Diplomacy forced King Philip Augustus to disclaim any part in the affair, but nevertheless a big army of knights from the Ile-de-France went south in 1209 to burn some heretics and snatch what they might. Their leader made the difference: too smart, too brutal and too lucky, the sort of devil who changes history – Simon de Montfort. His vicious massacres at Béziers, where the Catholic population tried to defend the heretics and were incinerated along with them inside the churches, and his taking of the impregnable fortress town of Carcassonne put the fear of God into the southerners; Montfort won battle after battle and took every town he attacked, save only Beaucaire.

In a last attempt to save their fortunes, Count Raymond VI of Toulouse and King Peter II of Aragon combined to meet the northerners. With an overwhelmingly superior force, they blundered their way to crushing defeat at the Battle of Muret in 1213. Montfort soon claimed the titles of Count of Toulouse and Viscount of Carcassonne and Béziers for himself. The Languedociens continued to resist until after his death in 1218; six years later, again under the pretence of a 'crusade', Louis VIII took the matter in his own hands. Coming south with another army, he forced the annexation of all eastern Languedoc and Carcassonne, the fortress key to the Midi, in 1229. The remainder of the century saw the inexorable consolidation of French power: the building or rebuilding of great fortifications, as at Carcassonne and Peyrepertuse, begun by Saint Louis (King Louis IX, 1226–70), and the new port of Aigues-Mortes, used by Louis as base for his two Crusades (1249 and 1270).

Four centuries after the fall of the Carolingian Empire, the French once again had their foothold in the south. Languedoc was finished, its distinctive culture quickly snuffed out. If Montfort's men had been shock troops from France, the occupying force was made up of French bureaucrats and monks. The monks took charge of many village churches, replacing parish priests to keep an eye on the population. The Inquisition arrived to take care of the heretics – and of course anyone the northerners found politically suspect, or whose property they coveted. The last Cathar stronghold, the Château de Quéribus, fell to royal troops in 1255. The troubadours found less and less around them worthy of a song. One of the most famous, Folquet de Marseille, had already gone over to the side of France and bigotry. As a zealous convert and, later, Bishop of Toulouse, he became an extremely ferocious oppressor of the few surviving Cathars.

French Oppression and Religious Wars

Under French rule, the region languished both culturally and economically. For the next few centuries there is little news to report, and most of it bad. The strong hand from Paris had at least the virtue of maintaining peace. Roussillon wasn't so lucky, enduring occasional French invasions, and Languedoc suffered again in the early campaigns of the Hundred Years' War. Edward the Black Prince marched through the region, pillaging and burning, in the 1340s. Along with the disruptions of war came peasant rebellions, while crop failures brought some parts close to famine. The Black Death topped it off in 1348, taking a third of the population as it did almost everywhere else it struck.

One exception to the sorry state of Languedoc was Montpellier. Under the Catalan Kingdom of Majorca, this relatively young town became fat and wealthy from cloth and other manufacturing, while its famous medical school attracted students from across Europe. Doubting their ability to hold it much longer, the Catalans sold the city to France in 1349, though its prosperity continued.

More troubles came in the 16th century. The cultural effacement of Occitania became complete with the 1539 Edict of Villers-Cotterêts, which decreed French as the official language throughout the kingdom. The language of the troubadours was now derided by the northerners as nothing more than a *patois*, a rustic dialect. Worse, at the same time a big dose of the new Protestant heresy was floating down the Rhône from Calvin's Geneva. The Occitans received it warmly, and soon there were large Protestant communities in all the towns. Although this seems like a repeat of the Cathar story, the geographical distribution is fascinating – the old Cathar areas (like the Aude) were now loyally Catholic, while the orthodox regions of the 13th century now came out strongly for the dissenters. In eastern Languedoc (the Hérault and Gard) they attracted about half the population. Tolerance was still out of fashion, and the opening round of a pointless half-century of religious wars came with the 1542 massacres in the Luberon mountains of Provence.

The open warfare that followed across the south saw massacres and atrocities enough on both sides. Protestants distinguished themselves by the wholesale destruction of churches and their art (as at St-Gilles); churches were often converted into fortresses, as can be seen throughout Languedoc. Henry IV's 1598 Edict of Nantes put an end to the wars, and acknowledged Protestant control of certain areas (Nîmes, Montpellier, Uzès, Gignac, Clermont-l'Hérault, Aigues-Mortes, Sommières, Castres).

The French monarchy had been weakened by the conflict, but, as soon as it recovered, new measures were introduced to keep the provinces in line. Under Cardinal Richelieu, in the 1630s, the laws and traditions of local autonomy were swept away. As insurance, scores of feudal castles (such as Beaucaire) were demolished to eliminate possible points of resistance. Richelieu and Louis XIII warred against the increasing independence of the Protestant (or 'Huguenot') enclaves; in 1622 they besieged and captured Montpellier, and knocked down its walls. After that, Protestant resistance survived only in the Cévennes, where the Duc de Rohan carried out desultory campaigns until 1629. Royal control over Languedoc became complete with the failed rebellion of the Duc de Montmorency, 'First Duke of France' and royal governor of Languedoc. Richelieu beat him in battle near Castelnaudary, in 1632, and beheaded him in the main square of Toulouse.

Louis XIV's revocation of the Edict of Nantes in 1685 reawakened the religious troubles. Vicious repression saw many Protestants killed, exiled to the colonies or sentenced to the galleys. Bands of armed missionaries called 'dragons' travelled through Languedoc enforcing conversions. When Louis killed or imprisoned the best of the Protestant ministers, their places were often filled by wild-eyed millenarian fanatics. These 'prophets' led many of their followers into the 'Desert', the difficult terrain of the Cevennes, where they hid from the missionaries and royal troops and made a living the best they could. The king determined to root them out completely, occasioning the Camisard Wars that began in 1702. The 'Camisards' (so called because they had no uniforms, only plain shirts) waged guerrilla battles for years through the Cevennes and the plains of the Gard, with a little aid from the British and the Dutch; a British force briefly occupied Sète in 1710. The king's generals pursued a scorched-earth policy, while the Camisards themselves were not above the occasional pillage or massacre. One by one the Camisard leaders died in battle, or escaped to safety in Switzerland. Some of the 'prophets' made it to London, where they would be an influence on the thinking of Rousseau and of Ann Lee, founder of the Shakers.

By 1715, it was all over. In that year Louis XIV finally had the decency to expire; the repression slackened off, and such Protestants as survived were tolerated, if only just. Most of them, some of the south's most productive citizens, had already left. Louis' long and oppressive reign continued the impoverishment of the south, despite well-intentioned economic measures by his brilliant minister Colbert, who started new manufactories (Villeneuvette, near Clermont-l'Hérault), founded the port of Sète, and helped Paul Riquet build the Canal du Midi (see **Topics**, pp.44–6). That great work, completed in 1681, would help more than anything else in slowly bringing trade and industry back to the region. In the 18th century, things picked up considerably, with the beginnings of an important textile industry, largely fostered by the remaining Protestants. Silk was made around Nîmes and parts of Provence (where farmers gave up their bedrooms to raise the delicate silkworms in them), while Montpellier and Carcassonne made names for themselves in linen and cotton goods. It was a good start, though unfortunately the English and their new mechanized production would ruin much of Languedoc's cloth trade after 1800.

Apropos of nothing at all, to close out the ancien régime we'll mention a little historical sidebar – Languedoc's invasion of America. This occurred during the Seven Years' War, known in the USA as the 'French and Indian War', when the king sent the Régiment de Languedoc into what is now New York State, in 1755. They made a brave start, ambushing a British column with the help of their Native American allies, but then lost an important battle at Lake George. Later they would fight at Ticonderoga and Québec, finally surrendering at the siege of Montréal.

The Misfortunes of Catalunya

Roussillon had followed a quite different history, though the result was the same. Under Jaume I the Conqueror (1213–76), Aragon reached the height of its merchant empire, while keeping the French at bay along the castle-strewn Roussillon–Languedoc border. Before his death, Jaume decided to divide the kingdom between his two sons, leading to the brief but exotic interlude of the 'Kingdom of Majorca' and an equally brief golden age for Perpignan, its capital. The French tried to take advantage of the split, again shamelessly proclaiming a 'crusade' against the piously orthodox Catalans (the pope, who wanted the Aragonese out of Italy, had given his approval), but they were thrown back across the border in 1285.

Aragon was reunited in 1344, but its troubles were just beginning. After the Black Death in 1348, recessions and political strife led to a long and disastrous decline in Catalan commerce. The union of Aragon and Castile to form the Kingdom of Spain in 1492 was a disaster for the Catalans, meaning the introduction of the Inquisition, the gradual destruction of the *fueros* (see p.25) and a total ruin of their commerce. The long series of wars between France and Spain resulted in the ceding of Roussillon to France in 1659. Immediately, the province suffered systematic and heavy-handed Frenchification, leading to revolts in the mountain valleys that were violently suppressed. The southern angle of France's hexagon was now substantially complete; Roussillon would be treated as a conquered province for centuries.

Revolution, and Other Disappointments

The French Revolution was largely a Parisian affair, though southerners often played important roles (such as the Abbé Sieyès and Mirabeau), while bourgeois delegates from the manufacturing towns fought along with the Girondins in the National Assembly for a liberal republic. Unfortunately, the winning Jacobin ideology was more centralist and more dedicated to destroying any taint of regional difference than the *ancien régime* had ever dreamed of being. Whatever was left of local rights and privileges was soon decreed out of existence, and when the Revolution divided France into homogenous *départements* in 1790, terms like 'Languedoc' ceased to have any real political meaning.

In the beginning, southerners greeted the Revolution with wild enthusiasm. Volunteers from Marseille brought the 'Marseillaise' to Paris, while local mobs wrecked and looted hundreds of churches and châteaux. Soon, however, the betrayed south became violently counter-revolutionary. The Catalans raised regiments of volunteers against the Revolution. The royalists and the English occupied Toulon after a popular revolt and were only dislodged by the brilliant tactics of a young commander named Bonaparte in 1793.

After Waterloo, the restored monarchy started off with a grisly White Terror in Nîmes and elsewhere. After the revolution of 1830, the 'July Monarchy' of King Louis-Philippe brought significant changes. The old industrious Protestant strain of the south finally got its chance with a Protestant prime minister from Nîmes, François Guizot (1840–48); his liberal policies and his slogan – '*Enrichissez-vous!*' – opened an age where there would be a little Protestant in every Frenchman. Guizot's country-men were rapidly demanding more; radicalism and anti-clericalism increased throughout the century.

Southerners supported the revolution of 1848 and the Second Republic, and many areas put up armed resistance to Louis-Napoléon's 1851 coup. In Béziers, a rebellion led by the mayor himself had to be put down by French troops.

The second half of the 19th century saw the beginnings of a nationalist revival in Occitania. In Provence it was all cultural and apolitical: a linguistic and literary revival bound up with Nobel Prize-winning poet Frédéric Mistral and the cultural group called the Félibrige, founded in 1854. In Languedoc it was all political and unconcerned with culture, focusing on the first of modern France's agricultural movements. Markets since the 1800s had encouraged Languedoc to become one vast vineyard. Monoculture had its dangers, however: a fungus called oïdium threatened to destroy the vines in 1850 before farmers learned to control it with copper sulphate. A graver disease, phylloxera, hit in 1875, and ruined tens of thousands of vintners; the quick recovery favoured the biggest producers, who could afford the new, phylloxera-resistant American vine stocks. A huge wine boom in the 1880s was followed by an even huger bust, with competition from Algeria and Italy and changes in the laws that permitted the sale of cheap adulterated wines (made of the distilled *marc* from the wine residues, mixed with water and sugar and called *piquette*). By 1904 prices had dropped to one-third of 1890 levels.

All over the Midi, you'll see streets named for Marcellin Albert. In a time when many country districts had been brought perilously close to famine, this charismatic *vigneron* and café-keeper from the Aude began the first of modern France's agricultural movements, to stamp out *la piquette* and give growers an honest living for their labour. In 1907 the farmers went on the warpath. Albert spoke at monster meetings in towns across Languedoc, each time raising a bigger crowd; the last, in Montpellier, attracted some 600,000. Paris sent troops to occupy the region with guns blazing; scores were killed or injured, and some local officials got thrown into prison. This only inflamed the situation further. The leftist prime minister Georges Clemenceau made the mistake of including some local regiments among the force sent to put down the movement, and one of them mutinied at Béziers. Albert threatened to call a general strike, but Clemenceau invited him to Paris and tricked him into calling it off. Albert was nearly lynched when he got home, and the movement dwindled, but the farmers devoted their attention to building a strong co-operative system and keeping the political pressure up by more orthodox means; French politics would never be quite the same.

Southerners had other reasons to grumble. The post-1870 Third Republic pursued French cultural oppression to its wildest extremes. History was rewritten to make Occitania and Roussillon seem eternal parts of the 'French nation'. Parisians derided the Occitan languages as mere bastard 'dialects' of French, and children were punished for speaking their own language in the schoolyard, a practice that lasted until the 1970s. Catalan Roussillon was not even permitted political participation – the government and parties arranged to have outsiders stand for its seats in the National Assembly.

After 1910, economic factors conspired to defeat both the political and cultural aspirations of the Midi; rural depopulation, caused by the break-up of the pre-industrial agricultural society, drained the life out of the villages, and decreased the percentage of people who spoke the native languages. The First World War decimated a generation – visit any village church or war memorial in the south and look at the plaques; from a total population of a few hundred, you'll see maybe 30 names of villagers who died for the 'Glory of France'. By 1950, most villages had lost at least half their population; some died out altogether.

After the French débâcle of 1940, the south found itself under the Vichy government. German occupation came in November 1942, following the American landings in North Africa. After 1942, the Résistance in Languedoc was active and effective, most of all in the mountains: in Haut Languedoc, the Cevennes and the Pyrenees. Two months after D-Day, in August 1944, American and French troops hit the beaches around St-Tropez, and in a successful (and little-noticed) operation they had most of Provence liberated in two weeks. This inspired the Résistance to come out into the open in Languedoc, where the partisans of the upper Hérault defeated a German column sent against them, just weeks before liberation.

A Long-delayed Rebirth

The postwar decades brought many changes. The population got a good shaking. First came refugees from the Spanish Civil War in 1939; you'll find them and their descendants everywhere, especially in Roussillon and Toulouse. A bigger wave of refugees hit in 1962: the *pieds-noirs*, French settlers forced to flee Algeria after its independence. Languedoc took in 100,000 of them, a quarter in Montpellier. More recently, the new arrivals have been North Africans, concentrated in the cities.

Agriculture has been transformed. Languedoc vintners have learned their lesson; they make less wine, and much better. Their region, which only stopped losing population in about 1955, is on an upward swing once more. According to INSEE, the national statistics office, the number of inhabitants in Languedoc-Roussillon at 1 January 2006 was 2,520,000 – it was the only region in France, along with the Midi-Pyrénées next door, where the population increased more than one per cent between 1999 and 2006. So far, much of the economy is based on tourism. A typically French national planning effort of 1968 made its coastline into a growing resort region, with new holiday towns at Cap d'Agde and La Grande Motte. Now, much of the energy comes from the cities. Montpellier, inspired by its dynamic mayor Georges Frêche (1977–2004, *see* **Topics**, pp.46–8), strives to become the futuristic metropolis of the Midi; jealous Nîmes bestirs itself to keep pace, looking to Toulouse for inspiration.

An important political event was the election of the Socialist Mitterrand government in 1981, followed by the creation of regional governments across France. Though their powers and budgets are extremely limited, this represented a major turning point, the first reversal of a thousand years of increasing Parisian centralism. Its lasting effects will not be known for decades, perhaps centuries. Already a small revival of Occitan language and culture is resuming; indicators include such things as new school courses in the language, and some towns and villages changing the street signs to Languedocien or Catalan. Roussillon is just beginning to feel the great upsurge of Catalan culture that began after the restoration of democracy in Spain. Political and cultural movements such as the Bloc Català (which in 2006 became the Convergència Démocràtica de Catalunya) have sprung up to reinforce ties with the rest of Catalunya; Occitan and Catalan festivals and events are held throughout the year.

Ironically, Roussillon became something of a stronghold for the Front National . Due mostly to concerns over immigrants, Jean-Marie Le Pen's party grew in southern regions like Languedoc. Many of its voters are former socialists, disgusted by the massive corruption that socialist politicians enjoyed during the Mitterrand years. In France's tightly controlled political system, where the established parties collaborate closely to monopolize power and exclude grass-roots challenges, a vote for Le Pen seemed like the only kind of protest vote available. Today the new president Nicolas Sarkozy, with his centralist-right appeal, has drawn many of Le Pen's supporters back into the mainstream. During the first round of the 2007 presidential elections, all departments in Languedoc-Roussillon showed at least twice as many votes for Sarkozy as for Le Pen. During the second decisive round, only Aude voted for the socialist candidate over Sarkozy.

One of the biggest issues in this region has been the region itself: not only the matter of finding an economic future for it, but discussions over the size and shape, and even the name of it. Paris's bureaucrats made the current 'Languedoc-Roussillon' the queer, artificial two-headed creature it is, and they're content to leave it that way. People on the ground, and many of the politicians, are inclined to tinker. Some grumble that all the money and effort currently goes to aggrandizing Montpellier. They would like to see the region merge with the Midi-Pyrénées, thus restoring the old County of Toulouse with its natural capital. The gentlemen in Paris, who all know their medieval history well, aren't likely to let that happen. The Catalans in Roussillon have been agitating for a one-department region of their own, which would be called 'Catalunya Nord'. Paris won't like that one, either.

Georges Frêche, who took control of the regional council with his socialists in 2004, had an opinion on this subject too. He likes the region as it is, but wanted to change the name to 'Septimanie', recalling the old Roman province that roughly corresponded to the current one. After a long battle, Frêche had to give up that idea; polls showed that 95 per cent of the prospective Septimanians were dead against it. Beyond that, the old lion's increasingly erratic behaviour has been keeping Languedoc in the headlines. In 2007 he was thrown out of the Socialist Party for making numerous racist comments in the press, and everyone in Languedoc is waiting to see what he'll get up to next.

Art and Architecture

03

Despite a number of promising starts over the centuries, this has seldom been one of the great regions for art, and a difficult history has ensured that many of its best works were lost. As in so many other things, Languedoc seems doomed always to be overshadowed by its flashier sister across the Rhône, Provence. Nevertheless, there are plenty of monuments and fine museums to see. Great art and architecture native to the region neatly coincides with its two periods of prosperity: the Roman era and the Middle Ages. Real prosperity is coming back once more, and already there are signs that the region may have some surprises for us in the future.

Prehistoric, Celto-Ligurian and Roman

France as a nation is full of Neolithic monuments from the period 5000–1500 BC, but Neolithic Languedociens left few traces of their passing: just dolmens and a few menhirs in the Hérault and Gard. **Cambous**, north of Montpellier, has made a unique attempt to reconstruct life in this era, including a communal Neolithic house, with low walls and a thatched roof that resembles the traditional cowboy dwellings (*cabanes de gardians*) in the Camargue. The Bronze Age peoples who followed left fascinating 'statue-steles' – menhirs with faces – all around the coasts from Languedoc to Tuscany, as well as Corsica. You can see some around **Nîmes** (in the Musée de la Préhistoire) and at **St-Pons** in the Espinouse mountains of Hérault.

The arrival of the Celts around 800 BC coincided with an increase in trade; Greek, Etruscan and Celtic influences can be seen in the artefacts of this age (as at the **Oppidum d'Ensérune** near Béziers). The local Celts had talent for jewellery, ironwork and sculpture – and the habit of decapitating enemies and carving stone images of warriors clutching their heads. Look for them in the archaeology museum in **Nîmes**.

The Romans brought wealth and urbanization to the region for the first time, with public works such as the great **Pont du Gard**, and a smaller, little-known arcade of an aqueduct at **Ansignan**, west of Perpignan. Nothing but fragments is left of the great capital of Gallia Narbonensis, Narbonne, but **Nîmes** retains two of the most spectacular Roman relics outside Italy: the 1st-century BC Maison Carrée, the best-preserved of all ancient temples, and the Arènes, best-preserved of all Roman amphitheatres.

The Dark Ages, and the Romanesque Reawakening

Very few places in France had the resources to create any art at all during this period. The meagre attempts at churches were nearly always rebuilt later; the only things you're likely to see from Merovingian or Carolingian times are crudely carved reliefs and capitals. Many crypts are really the foundations of original Dark Age churches, and sculptural fragments will often be found set in a later church's wall.

When good times returned in the 11th century (in some places a little earlier), people began to build again, inspired by the ancient buildings they saw around them. There is a great stylistic continuity not only from Roman to Romanesque architecture (rounded arches, barrel vaults, rounded apses), but also a wealth of new forms and styles, as well as a rebirth of sculpture.

This region shows several distinct varieties of Romanesque – Provençal, Languedocien and Catalan, along with some imported styles – although the terms must be applied loosely; the enduring charm of Romanesque is in its very lack of restrictions and codes, giving architects the freedom to improvize and solve problems in original, sophisticated ways. Although parish and monastic churches were usually in the basilican form (invented for Roman law courts and used in Rome's first churches), the masons also created extremely esoteric works, often built as funeral chapels in pre-Christian holy sites (see the unique seven-sided church at **Rieux-Minervois** or the triangular one at **Planès** in the Pyrenees). Churches that could double as fortresses were built along the pirate-plagued coast in the 11th and 12th centuries; the basalt parish church at **Agde** is a striking example.

In general, churches in the Rhône valley are more ornate, thanks to a talented group of sculptors known as the **School of Arles**. The wealth of ruins around inspired them to adapt Roman forms and decorations to the new religion, complete with triumphal arches, gabled pediments and Corinthian columns. Some time in the 12th century (exactly when is a matter of dispute), Arlésien artists also created the remarkable façade of **St-Gilles-du-Gard**, portraying the New Testament – the true dogma in stone for all to see, perhaps meant as a refutation of the Cathar and other current heresies.

As you move west through Languedoc, Romanesque becomes more decorative and fanciful, befitting the land of troubadours (**St-Martin-de-Londres** and the frescoed **Chapelle de Centeilles** in the Minervois). Even when the austere Cistercians built here, as at the **Abbaye de Fontfroide** near Narbonne, the mood is much less sombre. Itinerant Lombard masons in the 12th century introduced their own form of Romanesque, characterized by blind arcading and bands of decorative stonework, especially around the apse (as at **St-Guilhem-le-Désert** and **Maguelone**). The Lombard campanile, pierced with patterns of windows, was adapted by the Catalans, especially in the Pyrenees (**Elne**). But **Uzès** has something even rarer in its Tour Fenestrelle: a round, arcaded six-storey campanile, typical of Byzantine Italy.

The **Catalans** produced many fine Romanesque buildings, as well as the finest medieval sculpture in the south. They got a head start on the French with the school of sculptors at the magnificent 11th-century abbey of **St-Michel-de-Cuxa**. Their work is characterized by precise and fanciful detail, arabesques and floral patterns, supremely elegant without the classicizing of the Arles school; more of their best sculpture may be seen at **Serrabonne** and **Elne**, the most beautiful cloister in the Midi. St-Michel itself is one of the great Catalan monuments, with an architecture that shows an intriguing mix of influences that includes the Lombards, Cluny and Muslim Spain. The Pyrenean valley of the **Cerdagne**, the heartland of Catalunya, contains a dozen interesting Romanesque churches in out-of-the-way villages, more than any other region, reflecting its early prosperity.

Catalunya also produced the vigorous and original, sometimes surreal **Master of Cabestany**. Even though his real name is unknown, he is one of the very first medieval artists with a personal style so unique that it can be recognized anywhere. In the early 12th century he even went to Tuscany to teach the Italians how to sculpt (some experts believe he really was an Italian, though others speculate he was a French Cathar). His best works in France are the tympanum at **Cabestany**, at **St-Papoul** (near Castelnaudary), **St-Hilaire-de-l'Aude** and a pair of capitals at **Rieux-Minervois**. Catalans could paint, too, though you will see little of it in Roussillon; there are rare medieval frescoes at **St-Martin-de-Fenollar**, south of Perpignan.

Although examples of medieval palaces still stand in **St-Gilles**, and **Villemagne** in the Hérault, the greatest secular architecture of the period is military, often done with surprising originality. The vertiginous castle of **Peyrepertuse** is only the most enormous example of the scores of imposing works around the Languedoc and Roussillon border. Saint Louis built the walls and towers of Carcassonne in a romantic fairytale style that has few equals, while the king's other project, **Aigues-Mortes** (1270s), is a grid-planned, square and functional modern town encased in a perfect set of walls.

Gothic, Renaissance and Neoclassical

Though Gothic elements first appeared in Languedoc as early as 1250 (**Abbaye St-Martin-du-Vignogoul**), the ogival vaulting and pointy arches belonged to a foreign, northern style that failed to touch southern hearts. Builders stuck to their Romanesque guns longer than anyone in France, and when Gothic made its final triumph it was usually a pale reflection of the soaring cathedrals of the Ile-de-France. There are notable exceptions, all built by northerners: the huge **Abbaye de Valmagne** near Montpellier, or the cathedrals of **Béziers**, **Carcassonne** and especially **Narbonne**, an unfinished, spectacular work that is the third-tallest Gothic church in France.

The Catalans, as ever marching to a different drum, developed their own brand of Gothic, where width and strength counted more than height. The best examples are in **Perpignan**. They also produced one of the greatest architects of the 15th century, **Guillem Sagrera** (d. 1454). Sagrera, born in Majorca, is a one-off, the Frank Lloyd Wright of his day, employing a great technical skill in forms and shapes never seen before or since. His greatest works are in Naples and Palma de Mallorca, but he also designed Perpignan's cathedral and the vaulting in its Salle Capitulaire.

Subjugation by the French and in the Wars of Religion made the Renaissance a non-event in Occitania outside Provence. Of painting there is very little, though the Gard shows influences from nearby Avignon and its school of painters; there is a great work of Enguerrand Quarton, the *Couronnement de la Vierge*, in the museum at **Villeneuve lez Avignon.** Architecture largely reflected styles in the north, and the best place to see it is **Pézenas**. From its golden age, when it was home to the Estates-General of Languedoc, this little town made itself a museum of the era's architecture – film directors often use its streets as a set for old Paris.

The French call this, the age of Louis XIV and all the Louis that followed, their *époque classique*, and admittedly even in the poor benighted south many fine things were done. Towns laid out elegant squares, fountains and promenades; trees were planted on a grand scale, on market squares, along the Canal du Midi and on the roads, especially in the western Aude, crossed with 18th-century avenues of plane trees. **Montpellier** has collections from their thriving faïence industries of the day (as does **Narbonne**'s art museum). Southerners went ape for organs, gargantuan works sheathed in ornate carved wood. The mother of them all is in **Narbonne cathedral**; others adorn the churches in **Béziers** and **Uzès**. Equally elaborate are the retables of many Catalan churches, lofty carved altarpieces that show the influence of the fevered, intricate Churrigueresque style of Spain (**Perpignan** cathedral, **Collioures**, **Prades**). Some of the best are by the sculptor Joseph Sunyer.

But nearly everything else is all wrong. People took the lovely churches left to them by their ancestors and tinkered so much with the architecture that it's often difficult to tell the real age of anything. New churches tend to be austere and unimpressive, though there are exceptions (the truly florid Baroque of St-Sauveur at **Aniane**). The 17th- and 18th-century *hôtels particuliers* of **Pézenas**, **Uzès** and **Montpellier**, and public buildings such as the 1683 *hôtel de ville* in **Beaucaire**, while lending a distinctive urbanity and ostentation to these cities, are rarely first-rate works of architecture in their own right, but rather eclectic jumbles with touches from Gothic, Renaissance and Baroque style-books. One provincial boy from Roussillon made it big at the court of Versailles in this tepid period: **Hyacinthe Rigaud** (1659–1743). Born in Perpignan, this painter of royal portraits was in great demand for his ability to make his subjects look lofty yet amiable, as well as for his accurate depiction of their clothes (museums in **Perpignan** and **Narbonne**). The most sincere paintings of the age are probably the naïve *ex votos* in many churches (some of the best are from sailors, as at Notre-Dame-des-Auzils, near **Gruissan**).

One architect who never lacked for work was Louis XIV's Maréchal **Sébastien Vauban**, whose forts and fortress-towns crop up everywhere; his fortress-town of **Villefranche-de-Conflent** is a perfectly preserved example of 17th-century urban design. Vauban also worked on the Canal du Midi after the death of Paul Riquet, and nearly wrecked Collioure, demolishing much of the town to perfect its fortifications.

The 19th and 20th Centuries

The French Revolution destroyed far more than it built; the wanton devastation of the region's greatest Romanesque art (begun in the Wars of Religion) was a loss matched only by the mania for selling it off in the early 20th century to the Americans – that is what happened to the sculptural work of the abbey of St-Michel-de-Cuxa, now in the Cloisters Museum in New York.

The 19th century, however, would bring a renewal of appreciation of medieval art, as well as the first reaction against the purposeful destruction of the past. The great champion of the Middle Ages, **Viollet-le-Duc** (1814–79), came to Languedoc to restore the walled Cité of **Carcassonne**, and the archbishop's palace of **Narbonne**.

In a great century for French painting, Languedoc and Roussillon contributed only a little. It seemed as if the Rhône had somehow become a barrier to inspiration. While new revolutions in art grew up one after another in the hothouse atmosphere of Provence, very little of it trickled into Languedoc. This, despite the fact that the man who started it all, **Gustave Courbet**, had a wealthy banker of **Montpellier** for a patron. One of the best collections of his works can be seen in that city's Musée Fabre. Courbet's journey to the region in 1854 contributed to the luminosity of his later work. His new style came to be called Realism – almost as if it took the invention of photography by Louis Daguerre (1837) to make the eye see what was 'really' there. 'Do what you see, what you want, what you feel,' was Courbet's proto-hippy advice to his pupils. The lesser-known **Frédéric Bazille** was a native of Montpellier. He met Monet in Paris in 1862 and, with him, was the first to paint the human figure (even nudes) out of doors, inspired by the spontaneity of photography. His career was cut short in the Franco-Prussian war of 1870 (Musée Fabre, **Montpellier**).

Impressionists, like the artists of the movements that followed, came south by the score to paint in the bright skies and dramatic landscapes of Provence. Only one movement, however, had any ties with this region: the group of painters nicknamed the **Fauves** ('wild beasts') for the violence of their colours. The Fauves used colour to interpret, rather than describe, moods and rhythms, to the detriment of perspective and detail and even recognizable subject matter. As a movement the Fauves lasted only from 1904 until 1908, but in those few years they revolutionized centuries of European art. Fauvism came to Roussillon in 1905, when Henri Matisse and André Derain settled at **Collioure** on the Côte Vermeille. None of their works can be seen there today, though Matisse lived for a while in the Roussillon mountain town of **Céret**; so, briefly, did Chagall, Picasso and Salvador Dalí, and works by all of these artists can be seen in the town's small art museum.

Roussillon itself produced a decidedly non-revolutionary sculptor, though he was one of the best-known figures of the early 20th century: **Aristide Maillol**, from Banyuls. Maillol spent much of his career in Paris, though he never forgot his home town, returning each summer to model endless female nudes on the pulchritude of local nymphets (Hôtel de Ville, **Perpignan**; war memorials and museum in **Banyuls**).

Since the Second World War, big government projects promoting tourism and urban renewal have brought a new impetus to architecture in the region. In the 1960s, the national government ordained the creation of two entirely new cities. One, **Cap d'Agde**, was a disappointment, a pastiche of a traditional town centre, surrounded by zones of tired academic planning (though today it is a very popular holiday resort). The other, though sniffed at by highbrow critics, may be one of the real triumphs of French postwar architecture. Work on the resort of La Grande Motte began in 1968. The Paris planners entrusted the job to an obscure but very well-connected architect, **Jean Balladur** (his cousin Edouard would later be prime minister). He gave them something startling, a town of glass pyramids by the sea complete with futuristic bridges and public spaces. None of the individual buildings stands out, but the ensemble is a lively, very real community, popular with residents and tourists alike.

Since the 1970s, ambitious mayors in many southern cities have embarked on more grand projects. None has been more ambitious than Georges Frêche, the human dynamo who ran **Montpellier** between 1977 and 2004 (*see* **Topics**, pp.46–8). Most of the city's showcase works are middle-of-the-road at best, though its huge new residential quarter called Antigone, designed by the Catalan neoclassicist (some say neo-Stalinist) Ricardo Bofill, has been stirring up controversy since it was begun in 1979. In **Nîmes**, Sir Norman Foster's glass and steel Carré d'Art was also beset by criticism when it opened in May 1993, but his influence has led to a heightened taste for architectural expansion in the region. New developments are being planned in Nîmes, Montpellier and other cities. The south, it seems, is no longer the architectural backwater it once was. Indeed, as Jean Bousquet, mayor of Nîmes 1983–95, declared, its cities will soon rival Paris in the race to be a metropolis for the 21st century.

Topics

04

Occitans, Catalans and Related Species

The place is Verdun, the date AD 843, and a fellow named Lothair is about to mess up European history for good. The three contentious grandsons of Charlemagne, unable to manage the Carolingian Empire peaceably, were deciding how to carve it up between them. The resulting Treaty of Verdun would be a linguistic landmark – one of the first documents issued in two new-fangled languages later called French and German. It would also determine the future map of Europe. Lothair's brothers were sensible: Louis took the east, the future Germany, and Charles the Bald got the western half, most of what is now France. Lothair must have thought he was the clever one. Besides the imperial title (of dubious value) and the imperial capital, Aachen, he took away the richest lands of the Empire: northern Italy, Provence, Lorraine and Burgundy, along with Switzerland and the Low Countries.

If Lothair had considered what he would be leaving to his descendants, he might have noticed that this random collection of territories could never be held together for long. If he had had any sense of historical necessity, he might have said: 'You two can keep all the northern bits; just let me have what we Franks know as Aquitania, the land that folks in a thousand years are going to call southern France and Catalunya.' It would have made sense even then, a more coherent possession both culturally and politically. In the later Middle Ages, it would have seemed the obvious choice. This is western Europe's nation that never was. The nation would have been called Languedoc, most likely, as that was the name in the later Middle Ages for the Occitan-speaking lands that stretched from the Atlantic to the Alps. Its capital would probably have been Toulouse. Instead, after the collapse of Lothair's and his brothers' kingdoms, the Occitan-speaking peoples south of the Loire and their Catalan cousins got centuries of balanced feudal anarchy with no real overlord. Real power became fatally divided between two ambitious rivals, the County of Toulouse, and the new Catalan County of Barcelona, later the Kingdom of Aragon.

The Occitans didn't mind; the relative freedom gave them the chance to create their open, advanced civilization of poetry and tolerance, a March crocus heralding the blossoming of medieval Europe. The Catalans learned to sail and trade, and built themselves a maritime empire in the Mediterranean. Unfortunately, their lack of co-operation doomed the former to a brutal French military conquest followed by the near-extinction of their language and culture. The Catalans, at least those south of the Pyrenees, would later suffer the same fate at the hands of Spain.

The great castles of Languedoc and Roussillon – Quéribus, Carcassonne, Salses and the rest – are the gravestones of the Lost Nation, the sites of defeats that marked its gradual, inexorable assimilation by the power of Paris and the north. Today, if you visit them in the off season, the only other car in the car park will be likely to have a white Spanish tag with a 'B' for Barcelona. You may see the inscrutable Catalans – culturally much more alive than the poor Languedociens – picnicking in the snow at Peyrepertuse in December, or at Salses furtively taking voluminous notes on the guided tour. Catalans abroad, even when encumbered by children and small dogs, often have the raffish air of spies or infiltrating *provocateurs*; it's part of their charm. Here, they're on a real mission, piecing together the memorials and cultural survivals of a forgotten world – forgotten by everyone else, maybe, but a dream that the Catalans and France's Occitanian malcontents will never let die.

The Cathars

...because we are not of this world, and this world is nought of ours, give us to understand that which Thou understandest, and to love that which Thou lovest.

Cathar prayer

Dualism, as the philosophers call it, has always been with us. The Greek Gnostics saw Good and Evil as contending, independent forces that existed forever. Good resided somewhere beyond the stars; Evil was here and now – in fact creation itself was evil, the work not of God but of a fallen spirit, identifiable with Satan. Our duty on earth was to seek purity by refusing to have anything to do with creation. In the 3rd century AD, a Persian holy man named Mani took up the same theme and made quite a splash, and his teachings spread gradually back into the West, where the earliest Church councils strongly condemned them as the 'Manichaean Heresy'. Among other places, the Manichaeans were active in southern Gaul.

Always present in the Byzantine Empire, Manichaean ideas hit the Balkans in the 9th century; the 'Bogomil' or 'Bulgar' dualists reached a wide following, leaving hundreds of oddly carved crosses as monuments. From there, the idea spread rapidly throughout Europe. The new sect appears in chronicles of the 11th century, variously called Bulgars or Patarenes, Albigensians or Cathars (from a Greek word meaning 'pure'). The Church was not slow to respond. In Italy and northern France the heretics were massacred and burned; in England, apparently, they were only branded with hot irons. In worldly and open Occitania, however, they gained a foothold and kept it. The new faith was popular among peasants, townspeople and even many nobles. Occitan Catharism was organized into a church at a council at St-Félix-de-Caraman in 1167, presided over by a prelate named Nicetas, or Nikita, from Dragovici in the Balkans.

The Cathars probably believed that their faith was a return to the virtue and simplicity of the early Church. Their teaching encouraged complete separation from the Devil's world; feudal oaths, for example, were forbidden, and believers solved differences between themselves by arbitration rather than going to law. Some features were quite modern: Cathars promoted vegetarianism and non-violence, and marriage was by simple agreement, not a sacrament, enhancing the freedom and status of women by doing away with the old Roman paternalist tradition and laws. Two other points made Catharism especially attractive to an increasingly modern society. It had a much more mature attitude towards money and capitalism than the Roman church – no condemnation of loans as usury, and no church tithes. This earned it support in the growing cities; like the later Protestants, many Cathars were involved in the textile trades. Cathar simplicity and its lack of a big church organization made a very favourable contrast with the bloated, bullying and thoroughly corrupt machinery of the Church of Rome.

Best of all, Catharism had a very forgiving attitude towards sinners. If creation itself was the Devil's work, how could we not err? Cathars were divided into two levels: the mass of simple believers, upon whom the religion was a light yoke indeed – no Mass and few ceremonies, no money-grubbing, easy absolution – and the few *perfecti*, those who had received the sacrament called the *consolament*, and were thenceforth required to lead a totally ascetic life devoted to faith and prayer. Most Cathars conveniently took the *consolament* on their deathbeds.

Catharism was a strong and growing force when the Albigensian Crusade began in 1209; the papacy, the behaviour of which had always been a strong argument for the basic tenet of dualism, saw enough of a threat to its power to require a policy of eradication by death. The terror, enforced by French arms and overseen by the Dominicans and Cistercians, was vicious and successful. Its climax came in 1244, with the fall of the Cathar holy-of-holies, the temple-fortress at Montségur in the Pyrenees (*département* of Ariège). Cathars who survived the mass exterminations were hunted down ruthlessly by the new Inquisition; Guillaume Bélibaste, the last of the *perfecti*, was burned at Villerouge-Termenès in the Aude in 1321. Nevertheless, doctrines are always more difficult to kill than human beings, and Catharism survived its persecutors in a number of forms, especially in its influence on the later southern Protestants and on the Catholic Jansenists of the 17th century.

There are practising Cathars today; if you want to seek them out, the village of Arques, in the Aude, might be a good place to start, or else consult the worthy books (in French) of a modern-day sympathizer named René Nelli. There are probably fewer actual Cathars than books about them. Catharism did have a strong esoteric tinge to it, reserved for the *perfecti*. In the past few decades, this angle has been explored in every sort of work, from the serious to the inane, speculating on various 'treasures', real or metaphysical, that the last *perfecti* may have hidden, or connecting the sect with other favourite occult themes: the Templars (who in fact were their enemies), the Holy Grail (said to have been kept at Montségur), the Illuminati and Rosicrucians of the 15th century and onwards, and the body and possible descendants of Jesus Christ (*see* 'Rennes-le-Château', pp.212–14).

Nelli and other authors have some provocative things to say about the greatest and most mysterious of all the Arthurian epics, Wolfram von Eschenbach's *Parzifal* – they see the poem as a sweeping Cathar allegory, confirming Montségur as the Grail castle and identifying Parzifal with the Cathars' protector, Raymond Trencavel of Carcassonne. Trencavel's chroniclers also have an uncanny habit of comparing the viscount to Christ, especially after his betrayal and death at the hands of Simon de Montfort; his dynasty, like that of the counts of Toulouse, was quite a vortex for this sort of weirdness. The weirdest of all modern Europe's occultist sects, the Nazis, were obsessed with the Cathars and the legends that have grown up around them. After their occupation of the south in 1942, they sealed off all the important Cathar sites and cave refuges in the Pyrenees, and Nazi high-priest Alfred Rosenberg sent teams of archaeologists to dig them up amidst the utmost secrecy. In 1944, not long before liberation, a group of local Cathars sneaked up to Montségur for an observance to commemorate the 700th anniversary of their forebears' last stand. A small German plane, with a pilot and one passenger, appeared and circled the castle. The Cathars, expecting the police, watched in amazement as the plane, by means of skywriting equipment, traced a strange, eight-branched cross over their heads, and then disappeared beyond the horizon.

Troubadours

Lyric poetry in the modern Western world was born around the year 1095 with the rhymes of Count William (1071–1127), grandfather of Eleanor of Aquitaine. William wrote in the courtly language of Old Provençal (or Occitan), although his subject matter was hardly courtly ('Do you know how many times I screwed them? / One hundred and eighty-eight to be precise; / So much so that I almost broke my girth and harness...'). A descendant of the royal house of Aragon, William had Spanish-Arab blood in his lusty veins and had battled against the Moors in Spain on several occasions, but at the same time he found inspiration (for his form, if not his content) in a civilization that was centuries ahead of Christian Europe in culture.

The word *troubadour* may be derived from the Arabic root for lutenist (*trb*), and the ideal of courtly love makes its first appearance in the writings of the spiritual Islamic Sufis. The Sufis believed that true understanding could not be expressed in doctrines, but could be suggested obliquely in poetry and fables. Much of what they wrote was love poetry addressed to an ideal if unkind and irrational muse, whom the poet hopes will reward his devotion with enlightenment and inspiration. Christians who encountered this poetry in the Crusades converted this ideal muse into the Virgin, giving birth to the great 12th-century cult of Mary. But in Occitania this mystic strain was reinterpreted in a more worldly fashion by troubadours, whose muses became flesh and blood women, although these darlings were equally unattainable in the literary conventions of courtly love. The lady in question could only be addressed by a pseudonym. She had to be married to someone else. The poet's hopeless suit to her hinged not on his rank, but on his virtue and worthiness. The greatest novelty of all was that this love had to go unrequited.

Art songs of courtly love were known as *cansos*, and rarely translate well, as their merit was in the poet's skill in inventing new forms in his rhyming schemes, metres, melodies and images. The troubadours wrote other songs as well, called *sirventes*, which followed established forms but took for their subjects politics, war, miserly patrons and even satires on courtly love itself. The golden age of the troubadours began in the 1150s, when the feudal lords of Occitania warred among each other with so little success that behind the sound and fury the land enjoyed a rare political stability. Courts indulged in new luxuries and the arts flourished, and troubadours found ready audiences, travelling from castle to castle.

One of their great patrons was En Barral, Viscount of Marseille, who was especially fond of the reputedly mad but charming Peire Vidal. Vidal not only wrote of his love for En Barral's beautiful wife, but in a famous incident even went beyond the bounds of convention by stealing a kiss from her while she slept (her husband, who thought it was funny, had to plead with her to forgive him). Vidal travelled widely, especially after the death of En Barral in 1192, and wrote a rare nostalgic poem for the homeland of his lady fair:

With each breath I draw in the air / I feel coming from Provence; / I so love everything from there / that when people speak well of it, / I listen smiling, and with each word ask for a hundred more, / so much does the hearing please me.

(trans. by Anthony Bonner in *Songs of the Troubadours*)

A Man, a Plan, a Canal

Languedoc owns its share of the great works of man, enough to delight any engineer on holiday. There's the great Pont du Gard, of course (and another sturdy Roman aqueduct that no one ever sees at the region's opposite end, at Ansignan). In between is something the French, back in the days of Louis XIV, trumpeted as the 'Eighth Wonder of the World'. Today, the Canal du Midi seems more of a decoration than a practical economic asset. Avenues of plane and poplar trees still shade much of its extent, just as they once did along all the great highways of France. Cyclists cruise the old towpaths in summer, stopping to admire the graceful stone bridges and the hand-operated locks of the pre-industrial age. You can hire a boat for a lazy canal tour, and stop for a memorable lunch of *confits de canard* at any of the sweet and drowsy villages that grew up along its landings. There are few better places to be in all of France; time spent on the canal charms the soul. For our enjoyment today, it required only that 12,000 men work for 15 years, and remove 12 million cubic feet of earth and cart it away by hand. And develop a technique for ordering the flow of waters, uphill and down, that no one had ever dreamed possible.

Pierre Paul Riquet, a man of infinite stubbornness, was born in Béziers in 1604. Well connected and wealthy from the start, he managed to land one of the jammiest jobs *ancien régime* France had to offer – tax farmer for Languedoc's salt pans. Taxation in those days was privatized; a tax farmer guaranteed the government an agreed amount of revenue, and was allowed to keep whatever else he could wring out of people and businesses. Forty years of this allowed Riquet to build up quite a fortune, and we can imagine he had plenty of time on his hands. Apparently, he spent much of it dreaming about canals. A presentation he had seen at court as a child left a lasting impression. People had dreamt of cutting through the 'French Isthmus' since Roman times, but no one had ever figured out a way to do it. Gated locks (a medieval contribution, invented independently by the Chinese and the Dutch) would help, but the problem would be keeping the entire system filled with water. Riquet liked to go on long walks up in the wild Montagne Noire, an unusual pastime for a Frenchman of that era. He was probably thinking about his canal all the while. Eventually the idea came to him – build a huge reservoir up here in the mountains, near the watershed, and dig down channels east and west from it to keep the entire waterway full.

Riquet took his plan to Versailles, where it was warmly received by Jean-Baptiste Colbert, Louis XIV's mercantile-minded chief minister. The king was interested too. Connecting the Atlantic and the Mediterranean would save French traders the perils of sailing around hostile Spain, not to mention the Barbary pirates and the pesky English. Even so, it took four years of navigating the treacherous, intrigue-filled waters of the court at Versailles before the king finally gave his assent. The argument was about money. The canal was going to gobble up a lot of it, and Riquet could only seal the bargain by putting up his own great fortune, even his daughters' dowries, for the works. Riquet wasn't entirely mad; in return for his two million *livres* his family would have the right to collect canal tolls in perpetuity.

Work began on the 'Canal Royal des Deux Mers' in 1667. Riquet oversaw the works himself, and his men rewrote the engineering textbooks along the way. The great reservoir, in its day the largest ever built, came first, along with its supply channels. You can visit it today; the Bassin de St-Ferréol now also serves as a popular recreation area, north of Castelnaudary near the town of Revel. That worked fine, but digging the actual canal provided some novel problems too. Beside the little matter of building 130 bridges, 64 locks and an entire town, the canal's Mediterranean terminus of Sète, they had to find a way of keeping the water level on a constant slope over 240km. When it became apparent that the canal would cause flooding in its surrounding villages after heavy rains, just as a river does, they had to design a system of channels to carry off excess water.

That was only one of their firsts. Riquet couldn't find a way around the great hill at Ensérune, near Béziers, so he dug 173m through it, creating the world's first canal tunnel. A canal of any length has to cross streams and even rivers. Usually, the problem could be solved by turning it into the natural waterway by means of a lock, following its course for a while, and then using another lock to get it out again. One little river, near the village of Paraza, could not be crossed in this way, and here Riquet produced his greatest trick, the first canal bridge, the Pont-canal de Répudre. Running one waterway over another one so astonished the French that, for some years after the opening of the canal, passenger boats would stop and let everyone off to admire it. Riquet's children installed a plaque over the central arch, weathered though still readable today, to remind people that it was their father's invention.

Riquet was equally ahead of his time in the way he treated his labourers. Like Henry Ford, he startled his contemporaries by paying them twice the going wage – 20 *livres* a month. Furious protests from the region's landowners reached the ear of King Louis, claiming that now their men wanted higher wages too, and Riquet was soon forced to cut his down to 12 *livres*. Still, he didn't deduct for holidays or rainy days. He also provided subsidized housing and other benefits. French historians sometimes give him credit for inventing the welfare state, 200 years ahead of its time.

But social welfare and engineering advances were only the means to an end. All Riquet cared about was building his canal. He didn't live to see it, dying in October 1680, with slightly over a mile left to go. The part he almost completed was in truth only half of the original plan, between Toulouse and the Mediterranean. But it gave a big economic boost to that city, which erected a statue in his honour, and later on it made possible the textile and other industries in the Haut-Languedoc. His family didn't fare so well. Riquet ran up such enormous personal debts to speed along the construction that his descendants didn't get to keep a penny of the tolls for themselves until 1724.

Without Riquet to push things through, the rest of the original plan, the Canal latéral de la Garonne that linked Toulouse to the Atlantic, wasn't completed until 1830. For a while, the canal would be the great highway of the southwest, the centre of its economic life. The landings that Riquet placed along its length for rest stops grew into villages. 1856 proved to be its record year, when it carried 110 million tons of goods and 100,000 passengers. But it would soon suffer the fate that awaited all the old canals. The very next year, the railroad men completed the Chemin de Fer du Midi from Bordeaux to Sète. When the Riquets lowered the tolls to compete, the railroad simply bought the canal from them to avoid the threat. Some commercial traffic continued to use the canal, though it had become a relic – motor transport didn't replace mule teams until the 1930s. The last commercial boat finally retired in 1979.

Paul Riquet never dreamed his great work would end up as nothing more than a tourist attraction. But his canal survives also to remind us of a truth about real building. Almost everything along its length is both functional and beautiful, built on a human scale. Utility and aesthetics combine in endless ways – the 45,000 trees that line the canal were planted not for decoration, but to hold the soil along its banks. A modern engineer would probably just line them with concrete. Behind it all is a way of thinking we have lost, a natural instinct for fitness and rightness. Imagine if we could bring back Riquet and his men today to design a motorway, with all its interchanges, overpasses and rest stops.

Beyond that, while you are lazing down the canal on your *péniche*, you might also reflect that something rather important happened here. Paul Riquet, this provincial contemporary of Newton and Descartes, pulled off an impressive job. The very scale of it, along with the technical precision and capacity for innovation, the can-do spirit and the vast mobilization of men and machines, were all something new in his day. Like the first printing presses, or the voyages of discovery to distant lands, or the beginnings of the Industrial Revolution, Paul Riquet's canal was a major step towards a new world, the world we know today.

The Best Political Show in France

He's an enormous man, both in height and girth, a man full of life. You wouldn't miss him in a crowd, with his owlish glasses and electrified shock of hair, and crowds are exactly where Georges Frêche likes to be. The socialist mayor of Montpellier from 1977 to 2004, Frêche presided over its remarkable transformation into one of the most vibrant and fastest-growing cities in France, while still finding time to teach a full schedule of courses on the history of law at the university. No mayor in France ever presided over such a gargantuan building programme: shopping malls, convention halls and cultural institutions, governmental palaces and a middle-income housing project called 'Antigone' that looks like Versailles on steroids.

To accompany it, Frêche created an equally gargantuan public relations machine that embarrasses many of the French. In truth, it would have embarrassed P.T. Barnum. New slogans were churned out on an annual basis, most memorably *Montpellier le surdoué* (the 'specially gifted'). Frêche is big on mascots, too. All his projects seem to have one; the new tramway's was a sort of pink panther. Meanwhile the government painted giant blue Ms all over town to remind citizens of their imperial destiny.

Amidst all the hoopla, it's understandable that a fellow like Frêche might arouse some controversy. And that's the best part; Montpellier's flamboyant, controversial former mayor has become so public that nothing he does is a bigger issue than the man himself. Frêche often compared himself to the Medici of Florence or (with an eye to the local Muslim vote) the Caliphs of Córdoba. Opponents called him

'Ramses II', among other things; one of them likens him to a 'tyrannosaurus' who has gobbled up Montpellier, and now turns his appetites on the entire region.

Frêche is a former Maoist, and anyone who's ever crossed him will tell you he has carried over some old totalitarian attitudes into his new persona. Anyone who disagrees with him, whether intellectuals or associations of cyclists, gets covered in vituperation and then methodically squashed. Unlike most high-profile French mayors, Frêche has never had a seat in the cabinet. He's too outspoken for that, and perhaps too contemptuous of what he calls the 'Caviar Left'. François Mitterrand himself put the kibosh on his national aspirations. He once publicly called the former mayor a traitor to his party – it isn't clear whether the old scoundrel couldn't tolerate an uncorrupted politician, or just couldn't stand Georges Frêche.

While the fur flies, all is not necessarily rosy in the Specially Gifted City. Crime and taxes are high (according to Le Figaro, in 2005 Montpellier had a crime level of 124.31 per 1,000 inhabitants, and 126 in 2006; the national average is 83 per 1,000). The economy has attracted some big firms, such as IBM, though unemployment remains significantly higher than the national average. Montpellier has made a big gamble on its incubator for new technology businesses, the Centre Européen d'Entreprises et d'Innovation. Scores of small start-up firms have already appeared from its research, but it's still too early to tell whether many will really grow. In the long run, though, the worst of the city's problems may be Ramses' monumental works. France, to put it charitably, is not a country where urban design flourishes; other ambitious cities such as Toulouse and Grenoble have already built futuristic grand developments they now heartily regret. We may not be around to collect, but we'll wager a big sum that the city's centrepiece Antigone project (see p.131) will decline to a slum and have to be demolished within 30 years (some of the works of the architect who built it are already falling down by themselves). In a time when planners around the world have finally come to realize that mixing land uses is the right way to create lively, successful neighbourhoods, Montpellier planners still file everything into separate pigeonholes: one zone for residences, another for government offices, another for green space, another for shopping and entertain-ment. If they have a vision at all, it would be for somewhere like Milton Keynes.

There's a strange American streak in the works of the former Maoist. One of Frêche's projects is France's answer to Minnesota's Mall of America: 'Odysseum', a giant suburban shopping mall and retail power centre with cinemas, a skating rink, planetarium, bowling alley and spa, surrounded by a sea of car parks. Many people in Montpellier worry it will suck all the life out of the rest of the city, and they've been fighting it for over a decade.

Georges Frêche, in the woozy twilight of his career, has moved on to bigger things. In 2004 he led the socialists in capturing the Languedoc-Roussillon regional council, for the first time in 18 years; he is now president of the Regional Council of Languedoc-Roussillon and the Community of the Agglomeration of Montpellier. He immediately proposed raising taxes by 52 per cent, and the then interior minister Nicolas Sarkozy acerbically awarded him the 'National Grand Prize for Taxation'. Frêche's presence in the grandiose new Hôtel de Région in Montpellier has made the regional political circus more fun than ever. He called the Harkis, Algerians who fought to support French rule in the 1950s, 'sub-humans', and earned a big fine in court for it. Most recently, in 2007 he was booted out of his own Socialist Party for complaining that the national soccer team had too many black players. (On the other hand, he once mystified reporters by lecturing them on how the Senegalese were 'more French' than the Bretons.)

Frêche isn't the only bad cat in the ring. His conservative nemesis, who ran the region all those years with the help of the Front National, is the Union pour un Mouvement Populaire (UMP)'s MP's Jacques Blanc, a neuropsychologist who enjoys psychoanalyzing Frêche before the cameras. He finds him the most difficult pathological case history he has ever encountered. Blanc claims he only played footsie with the FN for so long because he 'couldn't let such a brute have so much power'.

Another political enemy is Jean-Paul Fournier, the mayor of Montpellier's arch-rival Nîmes. In 2001 Fournier took over the city from Jean Bousquet, CEO of Cacharel, who had run the city deep into debt trying to keep up with Frêche. In 1950, Nîmes was bigger than Montpellier; now it has slipped far behind. Fournier credits the problem to its not being the regional capital, to the lack of an important university, and to the city's old habit of electing Communist mayors. Nîmes realizes now that it doesn't need to build megaprojects. Montpellier can have the temporary fizz, and the debt; Nîmes has charm and a sense of place. In truth, the cities' destinies are too close together to fight; underneath the gaudy headlines, they have to work closely together on such issues as economic strategy, a common airport and a common TGV terminal. About Frêche, Fournier only says 'lui c'est lui, et moi c'est moi'.

Frêche may have met his match in the Catalans – specifically in the nationalist party in Roussillon, the Convergència Démocràtica de Catalunya (formerly called Bloc Català). What riled the Catalans most was Frêche's ill-fated plan to change the name of the region to 'Septimanie', thus erasing Roussillon's identity. They put up posters screaming 'No to Septicemia!', and referred to Frêche and his allies as 'Septimaniacs'. To make it worse, Frêche made the unforgivable gaffe of suggesting that the Catalan language was only a *patois*. The then Bloc Català's activists cornered him soon after, at the opening of a new school in Perpignan, and forced him to admit Catalan was really a language after all. 'Now can you say a few words in Catalan for us?' they asked politely. Frêche replied 'Bon dia!', and went home to Montpellier. His 'Septimanie' plans foundered in October 2005.

Since April 2004 the mayor of Montpellier has been Hélène Mandroux, a former GP. She was groomed for the job by Frêche and although she has to some extent followed in his footsteps, Dr Mandroux has also initiated her own projects. One such example is the regeneration of the run-down neighbourhood Petit Bard, over which she and Frêche were at loggerheads. The media centre here is called William Shakespeare.

Food and Drink

05

Some of the most celebrated restaurants in the world grace the south of France, but no matter where you go, eating is a pleasure. The Mediterranean climate translates into seafood, herbs, fruit and vegetables, often within plucking distance of the table. The exceptional quality of the ingredients demands minimal preparation – southern cooking is perhaps the least fussy of any regional French cuisine.

When the dramatist Jean Racine stayed at Uzès in the 1670s, he noted that 'twenty cooks could make a living here, but a bookseller would starve to death'. If the last few centuries found Languedoc one of the poorer parts of France, it doesn't mean the Languedociens don't know how to eat. Languedoc-Roussillon is not one of the French regions best-known for its food, but its reputation is rising. Caught between Provence, the Southwest and the Catalans, the region shows influences from all three.

Restaurant Basics

Restaurants generally serve between 12 noon and 2pm and in the evening from 7 to 10pm, with later summer hours; *brasseries* in the cities generally stay open continuously. Most post menus outside the door so you know what to expect, and offer a choice of set-price menus; if prices aren't listed, you can bet it's not because they're a bargain. If you summon up the appetite to eat the biggest meal of the day at noon, you'll spend a lot less money, as many restaurants offer special lunch menus – an economical way to experience some of the finer gourmet temples. Some of these offer a set-price gourmet *menu dégustation* – a selection of chef's specialities, which can be a great treat. At the humbler end of the scale, bars and brasseries often serve a simple *plat du jour* (daily special) and the no-choice *formule*, which is more often than not steak and *frites*. Eating *à la carte* anywhere will always be more expensive, in many cases twice as much.

Menus sometimes include the house wine (*vin compris*). If you choose a better wine anywhere, expect a scandalous mark-up; the French wouldn't dream of a meal without wine, and the arrangement is a simple device to make food prices seem lower. If service is included it will say *service compris* or *s.c.*, if not *service non compris* or *s.n.c.*

French restaurants, especially the cheaper ones, presume everyone has the appetite of Gargantua. A full meal consists of: an *apéritif*, *hors-d'œuvre* or a starter (typically, soup, pâté or *charcuterie*), an *entrée* (usually fish, or an omelette), a main course (usually meat, poultry, game or offal, *garni* with vegetables, rice or potatoes), often followed by a green salad (to 'lighten' the stomach), then cheese, dessert, coffee, chocolates and *mignardises* (or *petits fours*) and perhaps a *digestif* to round things off. Most people only devour the whole whack on Sunday afternoons, and at other times condense this feast to a starter, *entrée* or main course, and cheese or dessert. Vegetarians usually have a hard time in France, especially if they don't eat fish or eggs, but most establishments will try to accommodate them. When looking for a restaurant, homing in on the one place crowded with locals is as sound a policy in France as anywhere. Don't overlook hotel restaurants, some of which are absolutely top notch even if a certain red book refuses on some obscure principle to give them more than two stars. To avoid disappointment, call ahead in the morning to reserve a table, especially at the smarter restaurants, and in the summer.

You'll soon notice that the big cities have a wide choice of regional and ethnic restaurants: Breton *crêperies* or *galetteries*, restaurants from Alsace serving *choucroute* (sauerkraut) and sausage, Périgord restaurants featuring *foie gras* and truffles, Lyonnaise *haute cuisine*, and *les fast foods* offering *basse cuisine* of chips, hot dogs and cheese sandwiches. North African restaurants are a favourite for their economical couscous – spicy meat and vegetables served on a bed of steamed semolina with a side dish of *harissa*, a hot red pepper sauce; Asian (usually Vietnamese, sometimes Chinese, Cambodian or Thai) and Italian are popular as well, the latter often combined with a pizzeria. On the whole, though, regional *cuisine de terroir*, modern Mediterranean and fusion are the rule.

Markets, Picnic Food and Snacks

The markets in the south of France are justly celebrated for the colour and perfumes of their produce and flowers. They are fun to visit, and become even more interesting if you're cooking or gathering the ingredients for a picnic. In the larger cities food markets take place every day, while smaller towns and villages have markets on one day a week (we've listed all the ones we know in the text), which double as social occasions for the locals. Most markets finish around noon.

Other good sources for picnic food are the *charcuteries* or *traiteurs*, both of which sell prepared dishes sold by weight in cartons or tubs. You can also find deli counters at larger supermarkets. Cities are snack-food wonderlands, with outdoor counters selling pastries, crêpes, pizza slices, *frites*, *croque-monsieur* (toasted ham and cheese sandwiches) and a wide variety of sandwiches made from baguettes.

The Cuisine of Languedoc and Roussillon

They have an expression here, *manjar fòrça estofat* (to eat lots of stew), which describes a masochist or someone who suffers martyrdom without complaint. Only 15 years ago, a food critic could refer to this region as France's 'culinary desert'. It was unkind at the time, though not *entirely* unkind; we remember that stew all too well. They used to say the same things about Spain. But, as in Spain, increasing prosperity and tourism, and a renewed pride in the country and its traditions, has brought about a little revolution here. The cooking's lots better, with a new, stylish treatment of Languedocien and Catalan classics.

There have always been two gustatory divides ambling irregularly through this region. Close to the Rhône, you'll find cooking much like that of neighbouring Provence. From upper Languedoc up towards Toulouse, it's the good hearty food of the southwest: duck and beans, roast and grilled meats, *foie gras*, *cèpes*, occasionally truffles, and everything else that makes one walk away from the table slowly. In Roussillon, it's Catalan, another world altogether. There's a trend towards the mashing together of all styles of Mediterranean cooking these days, and in restaurants you'll often be treated to something that seems a *mélange* of all three.

Stay away from the older, dreary-looking places in the towns; a few of these still offer cuisine on the level of the average London sandwich bar. But out in the villages, in a growing number of new hotel-restaurants with younger owners and in scores of *fermes-auberges*, you'll find something more to your liking, an honest, earthy cuisine entirely based on traditional local ingredients.

On the Provençal side, fish soups like *bouillabaisse* are popular, although here they may call it a *bourride*, and you may find tomatoes, ham and leeks involved. Along with it goes the familiar Provençal *aïoli* (or *aïllade*), garlic mayonnaise. Here, it may be flavoured with cayenne pepper, to make what's called a *rouille* – which is even better. There's also *bourboulhade*, a kind of poor man's *bouillabaisse* made of salt cod and garlic, or yet another 'B' soup, *boullinade*, a thicker fish soup made with Banyuls wine. Sète, France's biggest Mediterranean fishing port, is famous for its seafood; the area also specializes in *seiches farcies*, cuttlefish stuffed with the meat of its tentacles mixed with sausage, and *langouste à la Sètoise*, crayfish with cognac, tomatoes and garlic, not to mention the *tielle Sètoise*, the little seafood pie that has become a favourite around the Midi. Ever since the Middle Ages, Nîmes has been known for its *brandade de morue*, salt cod puréed with garlic, olive oil and milk. Other seafood is always good along the coast; there are plenty of excellent mussels and oysters raised in the coastal lagoons, one of the best treats the region can offer.

Land dishes you may encounter include beef from the Camargue, often in a rich stew called a *gardiane de taureau* with olives, garlic, red wine and vegetables. Lamb is one of the most popular staples, especially in the mountains, and there'll always be plenty of *cèpes* and other wild mushrooms. Escargots, or snails, come at you in all directions, with anchovies, as in Nîmes, or grilled (*cargolade*), or even in a fish soup. Some special dishes to look out for are *mourtayrol*, a delicious chicken *pot-au-feu* flavoured with saffron, and *rouzoles*, crêpes filled with ham and bacon. When the cheese platter comes around, it may have *pelardons*, the favourite goat's cheese from the Cévennes. There's a fondness for such exotic aromas as saffron, cinnamon and almond paste, which may well date back to the long-ago times when the Arabs ruled here (they also introduced oranges and lemons, and many other good things). In Pézenas, the special dish is called *petits pâtés de Pézenas*, little spool-shaped pies stuffed with lamb and raisins. This speciality comes from India, courtesy of Lord Clive, a former royal governor who settled here in the 18th century with his cook.

Throughout this rustic region, there's also a rich tradition of what the Italians call *cucina povera*: up in the mountains, this includes *soupe de châtaignes* (chestnut soup) or a *potée cévenole* with pork, bacon and cabbage, or *aligot*, a big hot, fragrant mess of cheese, cream, garlic and mashed potatoes. A *rousole* is the traditional omelette of the Aude, an area that also makes cornbread (*millas*).

The closer you get to Toulouse, that eternal baked bean dish *cassoulet* (*see* p.227), with sausage, garlic and duck or goose, is still the king of the Languedocien table, along with regional variations like the *fricassée* of Limoux. In western Languedoc there's plenty of duck – fatted duck, the ones from which *foie gras* is made. Usually it comes in the form of a *confit* (cooked and preserved in its own fat – much better than it sounds), or a *maigret*, a grilled duck breast which can be better than a steak.

In Catalan Roussillon, the totem fish is the little anchovy of Collioure, which hardy souls from Spain to Marseille pulverize with garlic, onion, basil and oil to make *anchoïade*, a favourite *apéritif* spread on raw celery or toast. You'll also find them served with strips of red pepper. A popular starter is *gambas à la planxa*, prawns grilled and served on a 'plank'. Main courses include *roussillonnade*, a dish of *bolet* mushrooms and sausages grilled over a pine-cone fire, and *boles de Picolat*, Catalan meatballs with mushrooms cooked in sauce. The classic dessert is *crème catalane*, a caramel-covered baked cream flavoured with anise and cinnamon.

Drink

You can order any kind of drink at any bar or café – except cocktails, unless it has a certain cosmopolitan *savoir-faire* or stays open into the night. Cafés are also a home from home, places to read the papers, meet friends and watch the world go by. You can spend hours over a coffee and no one will hurry you. Prices are listed on the *tarif des consommations*: note they are more expensive depending on whether you're served at the bar (*comptoir*), at a table (*la salle*) or outside (*la terrasse*).

French **coffee** is strong and black, but lacklustre next to the aromatic brews of Italy or Spain. If you order *un café* you'll get a small black *express* (espresso); if you want milk, order *un crème*. If you want more than a few drops of caffeine, ask them to make it *grand*. For decaffeinated, the word is *déca*. Some bars offer cappuccinos, but again they're only really good near the Italian border; in the summer try a *frappé* (iced coffee). The French only order *café au lait* (a small coffee topped off with lots of hot milk) when they stop in for breakfast, and if what your hotel offers is expensive or boring, consider joining them. There are baskets of croissants and pastries, and some bars will make you a baguette with butter, jam or honey. *Chocolat chaud* (**hot chocolate**) is usually good; if you order *thé* (**tea**), you'll get an ordinary bag and the water will be hot rather than boiling. An *infusion* is a **herbal tea** – *camomille*, *menthe* (mint), *tilleul* (linden blossom), or *verveine* (verbena). These are kind to the all-precious *foie*, or liver, after you've over-indulged at the table.

Mineral water (*eau minérale*) can be addictive, and comes either sparkling (*gazeuse* or *pétillante*) or still (*non-gazeuse*). If you feel run-down, Badoit has lots of peppy magnesium in it. The usual international corporate **soft drinks** are available, and all kinds of bottled fruit juices (*jus de fruits*) including delicious apricot (*abricot*). Some bars also do fresh lemon and orange juices (*citron pressé* or *orange pressée*, served with a separate *carafe d'eau* to dilute to taste). The French are also fond of fruit syrups – red *grenadine* and ghastly green *menthe*, which are mixed with lemonade to form a *diabolo* (e.g. *diabolo menthe*). If you like mint but not so sweet, try a refreshing clear sparkling Riqlès.

Beer (*bière*) in most bars and cafés is run-of-the-mill big brands from Alsace, Germany and Belgium. Draft (*à la pression*) is cheaper than bottled beer. Nearly all resorts have bars or pubs offering wider selections of drafts and bottles.

The strong spirit of the Midi comes in a liquid form called ***pastis***, first made popular in Marseille as a plague remedy; its name comes from the Latin *passe-sitis*, or thirst-quencher. A pale yellow 90 per cent nectar flavoured with anise, vanilla and cinnamon, *pastis* is drunk as an *apéritif* before lunch and in rounds after work. The three major brands, Ricard, Pernod and Pastis 51, all taste slightly different; most people drink their '*pastaga*' with lots of water and ice (*glaçons*), which makes it almost palatable. A thimble-sized *pastis* is a *momie*; mixed with grenadine it becomes a *tomate*; with *orgeat* (almond and orange flower syrup) it's a *mauresque*, and a *perroquet* is mint. Other popular **apéritifs** come from Languedoc-Roussillon, including Byrrh 'from the world's largest barrel', a sweet wine mixed with quinine and orange peel, similar to Dubonnet. **Spirits** include the familiar cognac and armagnac brandies, liqueurs and digestifs made from walnuts, cherries, pears and herbs (these are a speciality of the Alps), and fiery *marc*, the grape spirit that is the same as Italian *grappa* (but usually better).

Wine

One of the pleasures of travelling in France is drinking great wines for a fraction of what you pay at home, and discovering new ones you've never seen. The south holds a special place in the saga of French wines, with a tradition dating back to the Greeks, who are said to have introduced an essential Côtes-du-Rhône grape variety called syrah, originally grown in Shiraz, Persia. Nurtured in the Dark and Middle Ages by popes and kings, the vineyards of Provence and Languedoc-Roussillon still produce most of France's wine – some graded only by its alcohol content.

If a wine is labelled AOC (*Appellation d'Origine Contrôlée*) it means that the wine comes from a certain defined area and is made from certain varieties of grapes, guaranteeing a standard of quality. *Cru* on the label means vintage; a *grand cru* is a great, noble vintage. Down the list in the vinous hierarchy are those labelled VDQS (*Vin de Qualité Supérieure*), followed by *Vin de Pays* (guaranteed at least to originate in a certain region), with *Vin Ordinaire* (or *Vin de Table*) at the bottom, which is usually drinkable and cheap. In a restaurant if you order a *rouge* (red), *blanc* (white) or *rosé* (pink), this is what you'll get, either by the glass (*un verre*), by the quarter-litre (*un pichet*) or bottle (*une bouteille*). *Brut* is very dry, *sec* dry, *demi-sec* and *moelleux* are sweetish, *doux* sweet, and *méthode champenoise* sparkling.

Long the most productive wine region in France, mostly for reds, Languedoc-Roussillon lately has also become one of the most interesting for wine-lovers. Traditionally, the region concentrated on quantity rather than quality. Wine-makers believed that it hadn't quite the right soil and climate to compete with Bordeaux and Burgundy, and the region's ancient poverty left small growers unable to keep up with advancing techniques. So Languedoc got to be France's land of plonk, the biggest contributor to the European wine lake. It is also the place where wine first started a political movement. The phylloxera epidemic of 1875 left small growers destitute, and after that competition from cheaper products led to the revolt of 1907 (*see* p.30). Languedoc's farmers fought the government through most of the century, and they pooled their interests in village co-operatives that still make most of the wine today.

All that has been changing rapidly over the last 20 years. Wine-makers have made great strides in boosting quality in the past 30 years, recognized in a number of

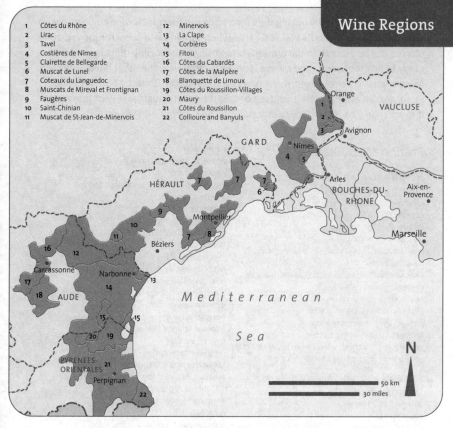

1	Côtes du Rhône	12	Minervois
2	Lirac	13	La Clape
3	Tavel	14	Corbières
4	Costières de Nîmes	15	Fitou
5	Clairette de Bellegarde	16	Côtes du Cabardès
6	Muscat de Lunel	17	Côtes de la Malpère
7	Coteaux du Languedoc	18	Blanquette de Limoux
8	Muscats de Mireval et Frontignan	19	Côtes du Roussillon-Villages
9	Faugères	20	Maury
10	Saint-Chinian	21	Côtes du Roussillon
11	Muscat de St-Jean-de-Minervois	22	Collioure and Banyuls

new AOC districts. Plenty of new faces have appeared on the scene, convinced that the region can make great wines after all; they've backed up that belief by producing countless new, distinctive estate-bottled wines. The critics are impressed; some have called Languedoc the 'most exciting new wine district in France'. More recently, vintners in Roussillon have been getting in on the act, too.

Information on the different wines can be found in boxes throughout this book, but here's a brief summary to see what you have to look forward to. **Côtes du Rhône** is probably the region's best-known variety, made on both sides of the river, here and in Provence. The Gard department produces some others, including **Costières de Nîmes**. The Hérault still makes more wine than any other department in France, much of it **Coteaux du Languedoc** from the plains around Montpellier and Pézenas, and this is one of the places where new ideas and new producers are making the wine revolution happen. The same is true for the smaller varieties up in the hills. Among these are **Faugères** and **St-Chinian**, **Minervois** and **Cabardès**, not to mention **Fitou**, from a tiny coastal area, the oldest AOC wine in the region. The Aude makes **Corbières**, with a wide variety of tastes. Roussillon has always been known for its sweet dessert wines, popular throughout France; the most familiar are **Maury** and **Banyuls**. But the Catalans have some good varieties too, such as **Côtes du Roussillon-Villages**.

You can save money by buying direct from the producer (or a wine co-operative, or *syndicat*, a group of producers). Note that when you go tasting, each wine you are offered will be older than the previous one until you are feeling quite jolly and ready to buy the oldest (and most expensive) vintage. On the other hand, some sell loose wine *à la* petrol pump; many *caves* even sell the little plastic barrels to put it in, so you can either bottle it yourself or take it home to quaff as is (just don't leave it more than a couple of weeks, especially in the summer, or it will go off).

French Menu Reader

Hors-d'œuvre et Soupes (Starters and Soups)

amuse-gueule appetizers
assiette assortie mixed cold *hors-d'œuvre*
bisque shellfish soup
bouchées mini *vol-au-vents*
bouillabaisse famous fish soup of Marseille
bouillon broth
charcuterie mixed cold meats, salami, ham, etc.
consommé clear soup
coulis thick sieved sauce
crudités raw vegetable platter
potage thick vegetable soup
tourrain garlic and bread soup
velouté thick smooth soup, often fish or chicken
vol-au-vent puff-pastry case with savoury filling

Poissons et Coquillages (Crustacés) (Fish and Shellfish)

aiglefin little haddock
alose shad
anchois anchovies
anguille eel
bar sea bass
barbue brill
baudroie angler fish
belons flat oysters
bigorneau winkle
blanchailles whitebait
brème bream
brochet pike
bulot whelk
cabillaud cod
calmar squid
carrelet plaice
colin hake
congre conger eel
coques cockles
coquillages shellfish
coquilles St-Jacques scallops
crabe crab
crevettes grises shrimps
crevettes roses prawns
cuisses de grenouilles frogs' legs
darne slice or steak of fish

daurade sea bream
écrevisse freshwater crayfish
éperlan smelt
escabèche fish fried, marinated and served cold
escargots snails
espadon swordfish
esturgeon sturgeon
flétan halibut
friture deep-fried fish
fruits de mer seafood
gambas giant prawns
gigot de mer a large fish cooked whole
grondin red gurnard
hareng herring
homard Atlantic (Norway) lobster
huîtres oysters
lamproie lamprey
langouste spiny Mediterranean lobster
langoustines Norway lobster (often called Dublin Bay prawns)
limande lemon sole
lotte monkfish
loup (de mer) sea bass
louvine sea bass (in Aquitaine)
maquereau mackerel
merlan whiting
morue salt cod
moules mussels
oursin sea urchin
pagel sea bream
palourdes clams
poulpe octopus
praires small clams
raie skate
rascasse scorpion fish
rouget red mullet
St-Pierre John Dory
saumon salmon
sole (meunière) sole (with butter, lemon and parsley)
stockfisch stockfish (wind-dried cod)
telline tiny clam
thon tuna
truite trout
truite saumonée salmon trout

Viandes et Volailles
(Meat and Poultry)

agneau (de pré-salé) lamb (grazed in fields by the sea)
ailerons chicken wings
aloyau sirloin
andouillette chitterling (tripe) sausage
autruche ostrich
biftek beefsteak
blanc breast or white meat
blanquette stew of white meat, thickened with egg yolk
bœuf beef
boudin blanc sausage of white meat
boudin noir black pudding
brochette meat (or fish) on a skewer
caille quail
canard, caneton duck, duckling
carré crown roast
cassoulet haricot bean stew with sausage, duck, goose, etc.
cervelle brains
chair flesh, meat
chapon capon
châteaubriand porterhouse steak
cheval horsemeat
chevreau kid
chorizo spicy Spanish sausage
civet meat (usually game) stew, in wine and blood sauce
cœur heart
confit meat cooked and preserved in its own fat
côte, côtelette chop, cutlet
cou d'oie farci goose neck stuffed with pork, foie gras and truffles
crépinette small sausage
cuisse thigh or leg
dinde, dindon turkey
entrecôte ribsteak
épaule shoulder
estouffade a meat stew marinated, fried and then braised
faisan pheasant
faux-filet sirloin
foie liver
frais de veau veal testicles
fricadelle meatball
gésier gizzard
gibier game
gigot leg of lamb
graisse, gras fat
grillade grilled meat, often a mixed grill
grive thrush
jambon ham
jarret knuckle
langue tongue

lapereau young rabbit
lapin rabbit
lard, lardons bacon, diced bacon
lièvre hare
maigret, magret de canard breast of duck
manchons duck or goose wings
marcassin young wild boar
merguez spicy red sausage
moelle bone marrow
mouton mutton
museau muzzle
navarin lamb stew with root vegetables
noix de veau topside of veal
oie goose
os bone
perdreau, perdrix partridge
petit salé salt pork
pieds trotters
pintade guinea fowl
plat-de-côtes short ribs or rib chops
porc pork
pot au feu meat and vegetables cooked in stock
poulet chicken
poussin baby chicken
quenelle poached dumplings made of fish, fowl or meat
queue de bœuf oxtail
ris (de veau) sweetbreads (veal)
rognons kidneys
rosbif roast beef
rôti roast
sanglier wild boar
saucisses sausages
saucisson dry sausage, like salami
selle (d'agneau) saddle (of lamb)
steak tartare raw minced beef, often topped with a raw egg yolk
suprême de volaille fillet of chicken breast and wing
taureau bull meat
tête (de veau) calf's head, fatty and usually served with a mustardy vinaigrette
tortue turtle
tournedos thick round slices of beef fillet
travers de porc spare ribs
tripes tripe
veau veal
venaison venison

Légumes, Herbes, etc.
(Vegetables, Herbs, etc.)

ail garlic
aïoli garlic mayonnaise
algue seaweed
aneth dill
anis anis
artichaut artichoke
asperges asparagus

aubergine aubergine (US eggplant)
avocat avocado
basilic basil
betterave beetroot (US red beet)
blette Swiss chard
bouquet garni mixed herbs in a little bag
cannelle cinnamon
céleri celery
céleri-rave celeriac
cèpes ceps, wild boletus mushrooms
champignons mushrooms
chanterelles wild yellow mushrooms
chicorée curly endive (US chicory)
chou cabbage
choucroute sauerkraut
chou-fleur cauliflower
choux de bruxelles Brussels sprouts
ciboulette chives
citrouille pumpkin
clou de girofle clove
cœur de palmier heart of palm
concombre cucumber
cornichons gherkins
courgettes courgettes (zucchini)
cresson watercress
échalote shallot
endive chicory (endive)
épinards spinach
épis de maïs sweetcorn (on the cob)
estragon tarragon
fenouil fennel
fèves broad (fava) beans
flageolets white beans
fleurs de courgette courgette blossoms
frites chips (French fries)
genièvre juniper
gingembre ginger
haricots blancs white beans
haricots rouges kidney beans
haricots verts green (French) beans
jardinière with diced garden vegetables
laitue lettuce
laurier bay leaf
lavande lavender
lentilles lentils
marjolaine marjoram
menthe mint
mesclun salad of various leaves
morilles morel mushrooms
moutarde mustard
navet turnip
oignons onions
oseille sorrel
panais parsnip
persil parsley
petits pois peas
piment pimento
pissenlits dandelion greens

poireaux leeks
pois chiches chickpeas (US garbanzo beans)
pois mange-tout sugar peas or mangetout
poivron sweet pepper (US capsicum)
pomme de terre potato
potiron pumpkin
primeurs young vegetables
radis radishes
raifort horseradish
riz rice
romarin rosemary
roquette rocket
safran saffron
salade verte green salad
salsifis salsify
sarrasin buckwheat
sarriette savory
sauge sage
seigle rye
serpolet wild thyme
thym thyme
truffes truffles

Fruits et Noix (Fruit and Nuts)

abricot apricot
amandes almonds
ananas pineapple
banane banana
bigarreaux black cherries
brugnon nectarine
cacahouètes peanuts
cassis blackcurrant
cerise cherry
citron lemon
citron vert lime
coing quince
dattes dates
figues (de Barbarie) figs (prickly pear)
fraises (des bois) strawberries (wild)
framboises raspberries
fruit de la passion passion fruit
grenade pomegranate
groseilles redcurrants
mandarine tangerine
mangue mango
marrons chestnuts
mirabelles mirabelle plums
mûre (sauvage) mulberry, blackberry
myrtilles bilberries
noisette hazelnut
noix walnuts
noix de cajou cashews
noix de coco coconut
pamplemousse grapefruit
pastèque watermelon
pêche, pêche blanche peach, white peach
pignons pine nuts
pistache pistachio
poire pear

pomme apple
prune plum
pruneau prune
raisins, raisins secs grapes, raisins
reine-claude greengage plums

Desserts

Bavarois mousse or custard in a mould
biscuit biscuit, cracker, cake
bombe ice-cream dessert in a round mould
bonbons sweets (US candy)
brioche light sweet yeast bread
charlotte sponge fingers and custard cream
    dessert
chausson turnover
clafoutis baked batter pudding with fruit
compote stewed fruit
corbeille de fruits basket of fruit
coulis thick fruit sauce
coupe ice cream: a scoop or in cup
crème anglaise egg custard
crème caramel vanilla custard with
    caramel sauce
crème Chantilly sweet whipped cream
crème fraîche slightly sour cream
crème pâtissière thick pastry cream filling made
    with eggs
gâteau cake
gaufre waffle
génoise rich sponge cake
glace ice cream
macarons macaroons
madeleine small sponge cake
miel honey
mignardise same as petits fours
mousse 'foam': frothy dessert
œufs à la neige floating islands/meringues on a
    bed of custard
pain d'épice gingerbread
parfait frozen mousse
petits fours sweetmeats; tiny cakes and
    pastries
profiteroles choux pastry balls, often filled with
    chocolate or ice cream
sablé shortbread
savarin a filled cake, shaped like a ring
tarte, tartelette tart, little tart
tarte tropézienne sponge cake filled with
    custard and topped with nuts
truffes chocolate truffles
yaourt yoghurt

Fromage (Cheese)

cabécou sharp local goat's cheese
chèvre goat's cheese
doux/fort mild/strong
fromage blanc yoghurty cream cheese
fromage de brebis sheep's cheese
fromage frais a bit like sour cream

fromage sec general name for solid cheeses
plateau de fromage cheese (board)

Cooking Terms and Sauces

bien cuit well-done steak
à point medium steak
saignant rare steak
bleu very rare steak
aigre-doux sweet and sour
aiguillette thin slice
à l'anglaise boiled
à la bordelaise cooked in wine and
    diced vegetables
à la châtelaine with chestnut purée and
    artichoke hearts
à la diable in spicy mustard sauce
à la grecque cooked in olive oil and lemon
à la jardinière with garden vegetables
à la périgourdine in a truffle and foie gras sauce
à la provençale cooked with tomatoes, garlic
    and olive oil
allumettes strips of puff pastry
au feu de bois cooked over a wood fire
au four baked
auvergnat with sausage, bacon and cabbage
barquette pastry boat
béarnaise sauce of egg yolks, shallots and
    white wine
beignets fritters
broche roasted on a spit
chasseur mushrooms and shallots in white
    wine
chaud hot
cru raw
diable spicy mustard or green pepper
    sauce
émincé thinly sliced
en croûte cooked in a pastry crust
en papillote baked in buttered paper
épices spices
farci stuffed
feuilleté flaky pastry
flambé set aflame with alcohol
forestière with bacon and mushrooms
fourré stuffed
frais, fraîche fresh
frappé with crushed ice
frit fried
froid cold
fumé smoked
galantine cooked food served in cold jelly
galette puff pastry case or pancake
garni with vegetables
(au) gratin topped with cheese and
    breadcrumbs and browned
grillé grilled
haché minced (US ground)
hollandaise a sauce of egg yolks, butter
    and vinegar

marmite casserole
médaillon round piece
mijoté simmered
mornay cheese sauce
pané breaded
parmentier with potatoes
pâte pastry, pasta
pâte brisée shortcrust pastry
pâte à chou choux pastry
pâte feuilletée puff pastry
paupiette thin slices of fish or meat, filled and rolled
pavé slab
piquant spicy hot
poché poached
pommes allumettes thin chips (fries)
raclette melted cheese with potatoes, onions and pickles
salé salted, spicy
sucré sweet
timbale pie cooked in a dome-shaped mould
tranche slice
vapeur steamed
véronique grape, wine and cream sauce
vinaigrette oil and vinegar dressing

Miscellaneous
addition bill (check)
baguette long loaf of bread
beurre butter
carte non-set menu
confiture jam
couteau knife
crème cream
cuillère spoon
formule set menu
fourchette fork
fromage cheese
huile (d'olive) (olive) oil
menu set menu
nouilles noodles
pain bread
œufs eggs
poivre pepper
sel salt
service compris/non compris service included/not included
sucre sugar
vinaigre vinegar

Snacks
chips crisps (US potato chips)
crêpe thin pancake

croque-madame toasted ham and cheese sandwich with fried egg
croque-monsieur toasted ham and cheese sandwich
croustade small savoury pastry
frites chips (US French fries)
gaufre waffle
pissaladière a kind of pizza with onions, anchovies, etc.
sandwich canapé open sandwich

Boissons (Drinks)
bière (pression) (draught) beer
bouteille (demi) half-bottle
brut very dry
café coffee
café au lait white coffee
café express espresso coffee
café filtre filter coffee
café turc Turkish coffee
chocolat chaud hot chocolate
citron pressé fresh lemon juice
demi a third of a litre
doux sweet (wine)
eau (minérale, non-gazeuse ou gazeuse) water (mineral, still or sparkling)
eau-de-vie brandy
eau potable drinking water
gazeuse sparkling
glaçons ice cubes
infusion or *tisane (camomille, verveine, tilleul, menthe)* herbal tea (camomile, verbena, lime flower, mint)
jus juice
lait milk
menthe à l'eau peppermint cordial
moelleux semi-dry
mousseux sparkling (wine)
orange pressée fresh orange juice
pastis anis liqueur
pichet carafe
pression draught
ratafia home-made liqueur made by steeping fruit or green walnuts in alcohol or wine
sec dry
sirop d'orange/de citron orange/lemon squash
thé tea
verre glass
vin blanc/rosé/rouge white/rosé/red wine

Planning
Your Trip

06

When to Go

Climate

Languedoc has a basically Mediterranean climate, one wafted by **winds** that give it a special character. The most notorious is the *mistral* (from the Provençal *mistrau*, or master – supposedly sent by northerners jealous of the south's climate), rushing down the Rhône and gusting west as far as Narbonne. On average the *mistral* blows 100–150 days a year, nearly always in multiples of three, except when it begins at night. It is responsible for the dryness in the air and soil (hence its nickname, *mangio fango*, or mud-eater). Besides the Master, there are 22 other winds, most importantly: the *levant*, the east or southeasterly 'Greek' wind, which brings the much desired rain; the *pounent*, or west wind; and the suffocatingly hot *sirocco* from Africa. The region from the Spanish border to Montpellier is occasionally bulldozed by the *tramontane*, the 'Catalan wind' from the northwest; heading west towards Toulouse it's the *autan* wind that sweeps across the Lauragais.

Rainfall varies widely. The higher Pyrenees get more rain than most places on this planet – over 2m a year (Prats de Mollo once got 838mm in 16 hours, the European record). Other upland regions, Haut-Languedoc and the Montagne Noire, also get their share. On the other hand, the coasts are one of the driest and sunniest regions in France.

Each season has its pros and cons. In **January** and **February** all the tourists are in the Alps or Pyrenees. **April** and **May** bring lots of flowers, capricious weather, and an agreeable lack of crowds. By **June**, the *mistral* is slowing down and the resorts begin to fill; walking is safe in the highest mountains. **July** and **August** are bad months, when everything is crowded, temperatures and prices soar (Perpignan has the highest average summer temperatures in France), and tempers flare, but it's also the season of concerts and festivals. Once French school holidays end in early **September**, prices and crowds decrease with the temperature. In **October** the weather is traditionally mild on the coast, although torrential downpours and floods are not unknown; the first snows fall in the Pyrenees. **November** is another bad month; it rains and many museums, hotels and restaurants close down. **December** brings Christmas tourists and the first skiers.

Festivals

Languedoc-Roussillon offers everything from international culture festivals in Montpellier to the village fête. The latter may come with a pilgrimage or religious procession, bumper cars, a *pétanque* tournament, a feast (anything from sardines to *cassoulet* to paella) and an all-night dance. Bullfights, either traditional ones or the non-lethal Languedocien version (*see* p.81) play a part in many fêtes. To complete the Spanish influence, fêtes may be called *férias*, in which much of the merriment is carried on in tents furnished by groups or families, called *bodegas*. A *corso* is a parade with carts or floats. The Hérault has the peculiarity of many towns and villages possessing a kind of totem animal (a donkey in Gignac, a camel in Béziers), often associated with the patron saint. A representation of these will always be the centrepiece of the procession.

Another Hérault speciality, at least around the coast, is the *joutes nautiques* – real jousting, but carried on from boats rowed by eight men; the jouster stands high on a platform and tries to knock his opponent into the water. Like the bullfights, these may coincide with local festivals or they may not.

St John's Day (24 June) is a big favourite and often features bonfires and fireworks, especially in Catalan areas. The midsummer bonfires around the Catalan holy mountain, Canigou, have been part of the culture since ancient times. At Catalan *festas* you're bound to see the national dance, the *sardana*,

Average Temperatures in °C (°F)

	Jan	Feb	Mar	April	May	June	July	Aug	Sept	Oct	Nov	Dec
Nîmes	7 (44)	7 (44)	11 (52)	15 (59)	17 (62)	21 (70)	23 (73)	25 (77)	23 (73)	16 (61)	10 (50)	8 (45)
Perpignan	12 (54)	12 (54)	13 (55)	17 (62)	20 (69)	23 (73)	28 (82)	28 (82)	26 (79)	20 (69)	16 (61)	14 (56)

a complex, circular dance that alternates 16 long steps with eight short ones, properly accompanied by a *cobla*, a band of a dozen instruments, some unique to Catalunya. In the southern Rhône valley, people still like to celebrate with a *farandole*, a dance in 6/8 time with held hands or a handkerchief, which may be as old as the ancient Greeks. One-man musical accompaniment is provided by a little three-holed flute called a *galoubet*, played with the left hand, and a *tambourin*, a drum played with the right.

Calendar of Events

Towns and villages here lay on over 1,400 events each year; here is a select list. Note that dates may change from year to year; for complete listings and precise dates, pick up a copy of the annual lists in most tourist offices, or consult local tourist office websites. For cultural events, see *www.francefestivals.com*, *www.whatsonwhen.com* and *www.culture.fr*.

February

Mid-Feb *Fête de Jean de l'Ours*: men dressed as bears and covered with soot and grease are chased through the village, and finally vanquished by the good 'white bears', Prats-de-Mollo, Arles-sur-Tech and nearby villages.

Carnival Limoux has traditional celebrations at weekends from mid-Jan throughout Feb and into March. Other towns and villages celebrate in different ways, with big doings in Nîmes and Perpignan.

April

Maundy Thurs *Procession de La Sanch*, Perpignan, Collioure and Arles-sur-Tech.

April *Fête de St-Aphrodise*, with procession of the 'camel', Béziers.

May

Ascension weekend *L'âne Martin*: fête in honour of the donkey who saved Gignac from the Arabs.

5 days at Pentecost *Féria de Pentecôte*, the biggest of the city's *férias*, with *corridas* and everything else, Nîmes.

June

First/second week *Festival Ida y Vuelta*, music from around the world, Perpignan; music festival, early/Baroque, Maguelone.

21 *Fête de la musique*, with outdoor concerts, celebrated all over France.

23–24 *Fête de la St-Jean*, big Catalan holiday with bonfires in villages all around sacred Mt Canigou in the Cerdagne, also dancing, and fireworks in Perpignan, Céret and Villefranche-de-Conflent.

25 *St-Eloi*, procession and blessing of the mules, Amélie-les-Bains.

Last weekend *Fête des pêcheurs*, Gruissan.

Late June–early July *Festival international de danse*, Montpellier.

Late June Wine festival, Perpignan.

July

July–Aug *Festival de la cité*, dancing, music and theatre, including medieval spectacles in early Aug, Carcassonne; *Saison Musicale*, Baroque and other sacred music, St-Guilhem-le-Désert.

All month *Fugue en Aude Romane*, classical music in churches and abbeys of the Aude.

Mid-July to mid-Aug *Festival d'opérettes*, an international festival of operettas and operas in Lamalou-les-Bains.

14 Fireworks and celebrations in many places for Bastille Day, superb in Carcassonne; *Fête du volo biou*, folklore festival dedicated to the 'flying cow', St-Ambroix (Roussillon).

15 *Féria*, music, *corridas*, wine in Béziers.

Mid–late July *Festival de Radio France*, two weeks of classical music, Montpellier.

Last weekend *Fêtes votives*, Vergèze and Marsillargues.

Late July Folklore festivals in Quillan; *Les Estivales*, Beaucaire.

Late July–early Aug *Montpellier danse*.

Late July Poetry and art festival, Lodève.

August

Late July–early Aug *Festival Pablo Casals*, chamber music in the medieval abbeys, Prades.

Second week International Folklore Festival, an important event since 1936, Amélie-les-Bains.

Mid-Aug *Féria*, with *corridas*, dancing and fireworks, Collioure; *joutes nautiques*, Balaruc-les-Bains, Sète; *Féria d'Août*, Béziers.

Late Aug *Fête de Saint-Louis*, with historical re-enactment, Aigues-Mortes; *joutes nautiques*, Sète; Carnival, La Grande Motte.

Last weekend *Fête votive*, St-Gilles.

September

Mid-Sept *Féria des vendanges*, wine harvest festival, Spanish-style, with *corridas*, Nîmes; *Danseurs catalans*, Amélie-les-Bains; *Festa Major de Sant-Ferriol*, dancing, folklore, sports, dinners, Ceret.

Third weekend *Journées du patrimoine*, special events across France to showcase national treasures (some normally locked up); free entry to museums.

October

Early Oct *Fête des vendanges* to celebrate grape harvest, various locations.
Mid-Oct *Fête votive*, with bullfights, Aigues-Mortes.
Late Oct–early Nov Mediterranean Film Festival (new talent), Montpellier.

Last week *Festival de la marionnette*, Jonquières-St-Vincent (Gard).

November
Mid-Nov *Festival Rockabilly*, Vergèze.

December
Mid-Dec Christmas market, Carcassonne and Perpignan.
24 Midnight Mass in the Arènes, Nîmes.

Tourist Information

Every city and town, and most villages, have a tourist information office, usually called an *Office de/du Tourisme* (sometimes a *Maison de/du Tourisme*). In smaller villages this service is provided by the town hall (*mairie*). Most offices, even in the small villages, have a website. If you plan to stay in one area, look on the websites of the local tourist offices listed in the text or write to them for lists of self-catering accommodation, hotels and camp sites, or else contact one of the companies in the UK or USA.

For more general information and a complete list of tour operators, get in touch with a French Government Tourist Office, or check the **Maison de la France** website (*www.franceguide.com*).

Useful Web Addresses

www.france.com
www.aito.co.uk
www.angloinfo.com
www.francekeys.com
www.frenchconnections.co.uk
www.holidayfrance.org.uk

French Tourist Offices Abroad

UK: 178 Piccadilly, London W1J 9AL, **t** 09068 244123 (calls charged at 60p/min), *http://uk.franceguide.com*.

Ireland: 30 Merrion St, Dublin 4, **t** (01) 672 6172, *http://ie.franceguide.com*.

USA: New York: 825 Third Avenue, 29th floor (entrance on 50th Street), New York, NY 10022, **t** (514) 288 1904. Other Maison de la France offices can be found in Los Angeles: 9454 Wilshire Bd, Suite 210, 90212 Beverly Hills, California, **t** (514) 288 1904; and Chicago:

Consulate General of France, 205 N. Michigan Ave, Suite 3770, 60601 Chicago, Illinois, **t** (514) 288 1904; *http://us.franceguide.com*.

Canada: 1800 Avenue McGill College, Suite 1010, Montréal, Québec H3A 3J6, **t** (514) 288 2026, *http://ca.franceguide.com*.

Consulates and Embassies

Foreign Embassies, etc. in France

UK: British Consulate-General, 24 Avenue de Prado, 13006 Marseille, **t** 04 91 15 72 10, *www.fco.gov.uk*. Honorary consul in Toulouse, **t** 05 61 30 37 91. Honorary consul in Montpellier, **t** 04 67 15 52 07.

Ireland: 4 Rue Rude, Paris, **t** 01 44 17 67 00, *http://foreignaffairs.gov.ie/irishembassy/France.htm*.

USA: Consulate-General, 12 Place Varian Fry, 13286 Marseille, **t** 04 91 54 92 00, *www.amb-usa.fr/marseille*; also Toulouse (American Presence Post), 25 Allées Jean Jaurès, 31000 Toulouse, **t** 05 34 41 36 50, *www.amb-usa.fr/toulouse*.

Canada: Canadian Embassy in France, 35 Ave Montaigne, 75008 Paris, **t** 01 44 43 29 00, *www.amb-canada.fr*.

French Embassies, etc. Abroad

UK: 58 Knightsbridge, London SW1X 7JT, **t** (020) 7073 1000, *www.ambafrance-uk.org*; 21 Cromwell Rd, London SW7 2EN, **t** (020) 7073 1200, *www.consulfrance-londres.org* (*for visas*); 11 Randolph Crescent, Edinburgh EH3 7TT, **t** (0131) 225 7954, *www.consulfrance-edimbourg.org*.

Ireland: 36 Ailesbury Rd, Ballsbridge, Dublin 4, **t** (01) 277 5000, *www.ambafrance.ie*.

USA: 4101 Reservoir Rd NW, Washington, DC 20007-2185, **t** (202) 944 6195, *www.ambafrance-us.org*; 205 North Michigan Avenue, Suite 3700, Chicago, IL 60601, **t** (312) 327 5200, *www.consulfrance-chicago.org*; 10990 Wilshire Bd, Suite 300, Los Angeles, CA 90024, **t** (310) 235 3200, *www.consulfrance-losangeles.org*; 934 Fifth Av, New York, NY 10021, **t** (212) 606 3600, *www.consulfrance-newyork.org*. There are also French consulates in Atlanta, Boston, Houston, Miami, New Orleans and San Francisco.

Entry Formalities

Passports and Visas

Holders of EU, US, Canadian, Australian, New Zealand and Israeli passports do not need a visa to enter France for stays of up to three months; most other nationals do (see *www.diplomatie.gouv.fr*). Apply at your nearest French consulate before leaving home.

Customs

Those over the age of 17 arriving from another **EU country** do not have to declare goods imported into France for personal use if they have paid duty on them in the country of origin. In theory, you can buy as much as you like, provided you can prove the purchase is for your own use and not for other purposes (e.g. selling on to friends). In practice, customs will be more likely to ask questions if you buy in bulk, e.g. more than 3,200 cigarettes or 400 cigarillos, 200 cigars or 3kg of tobacco; plus 10 litres of spirits, 90 litres of wine and 110 litres of beer. Travellers caught importing any of the above for resale will have the goods seized along with the vehicle they travelled in, and could face imprisonment for up to seven years.

Travellers from **outside the EU** must pay duty on goods worth more than €175 that they import into France.

Travellers from the USA are allowed to bring home, duty-free, goods to the value of $400, including 200 cigarettes or 100 cigars; plus one litre of alcohol. For more information, call the US Customs Service. You're not allowed to bring back absinthe or Cuban cigars. Canadians can bring home $300 worth of goods in a year, plus their tobacco and alcohol allowances.

French Customs, *www.douane.gouv.fr*.
UK Customs, **t** 0845 010 9000, *www.hmce.gov.uk*.
US Customs, **t** (202) 354 1000, *www.customs.gov*.

Disabled Travellers

When it comes to providing access for all, France isn't exactly in the vanguard, but things are beginning to change. All SNCF TGVs are fully equipped to transport disabled people; alternatively you can ask for an assistant to accompany you on your journey (although you will have to pay for them). For more information contact the French Railways office in your country, or write to **Mission Voyageurs Handicapés SNCF**, 12 Rue Traversière, 75571 Paris, or in France call **t** 08 00 15 47 53, or **t** 08 92 35 35 39 (information in English).

The Channel Tunnel is a good way to travel by car; on Eurotunnel trains passengers stay

Specialist Organizations

In France

Association des Paralysés de France, Siège National, 17 Bd Auguste Blanqui, 75013 Paris, **t** 01 40 78 69 00, *www.apf.asso.fr*. A national organization with offices in all *départements*.

Comité National Français de Liaison pour la Réadaptation des Handicapés, 236B Rue de Tolbiac, 75013 Paris, **t** 01 53 8066 66. Provides info on access, and produces useful guides.

In the UK

RADAR, 12 City Forum, 250 City Rd, London EC1V 8AF, **t** (020) 7250 3222, *www.radar.org.uk*.

Holiday Care Service, The Hawkins Suite, Enham Palace, Enham Alamein, Andover SP11 6JS, **t** 0845 124 9971, *www.holidaycare.org.uk*.

Can be Done, **t** (020) 8907 2400, *www.canbedone.co.uk*. Specialist holidays.

In the USA

Mobility International USA, 132 E. Broadway, Suite 343, Eugene, Oregon 97401, **t/TTY** (541) 343 1284, *www.miusa.org*.

SATH, 347 5th Avenue, Suite 605, New York NY 10016, **t** (212) 447 7284, *www.sath.org*.

Emerging Horizons, *www.emerginghorizons.com*. An international subscription-based online (or mailed) quarterly travel newsletter for people with disabilities.

in their vehicles, while Eurostar has a special area reserved for wheelchair-users and their assistants (who can travel at reduced rates; t 08705 186 186, www.eurostar.com).

Ferry companies offer special assistance if contacted beforehand. Vehicles modified for disabled people are charged reduced tolls on autoroutes. For more information contact the **Ministère des Transports**, Grande Arche, Paroi Sud, 92055 La Défense Cedex, Paris, t 01 40 81 21 22, www.transports.equipement.gouv.fr.

Gîtes accessibles aux personnes handi-capées, by Gîtes de France (www.gites-de-france.fr), lists self-catering accommodation. Hotels with facilities for the disabled are listed in Michelin's *Red Guide to France*.

Insurance and EHIC Cards

Citizens of the EU who bring along their **European Health Insurance Card** (EHIC – apply online at www.ehic.org.uk, or pick up a form from a post office) are entitled to the same health services as French citizens. This means paying upfront for medical care and prescriptions, of which 75–80 per cent of the costs are reimbursed later – a complex proce-dure for the non-French (*see* p.79).

Like the old E111 form, the card is available for UK residents for free. Unlike the forms, however, you'll need to apply for a card for every member of the family (you'll need passports and national insurance numbers). The EHIC must be stamped and signed to be valid, and the card must be renewed annually.

As an alternative, consider a **travel insur-ance** policy, covering theft and losses and offering 100 per cent medical refund; check to see if it covers extra expenses if you get bogged down in airport or train strikes. Beware that accidents resulting from sports are rarely covered by ordinary insurance.

Canadians are usually covered in France by their provincial health coverage; Americans and others should check their policies.

Money and Banks

Euros come in denominations of €500, €200, €100, €50, €20, €10 and €5 (banknotes) and €2, €1, 50 cents, 20 cents, 10 cents, 5 cents, 2 cents and 1 cent (coins). For the latest **exchange rates**, see www.xe.com/ucc.

Under the Cirrus system, withdrawals in euros can be made from bank and post office automatic cash machines (**ATMs**; *distribu-teurs de billets*) using your usual debit or credit card and PIN number. The specific cards accepted are marked on each machine, and most give instructions in English. The wide acceptance of **credit cards** in ATM machines for withdrawing cash make them by far the most convenient way of carrying cash for the traveller, although there are a few things to note. Although it is always wise to have some euros in cash on hand, you'll often come out better by using your card to pay when you can rather than taking out loads of cash from the machine and paying the fee for cash advances. On the other hand, some British credit cards lack the microchip required to work automatic machines such as petrol station pumps.

Visa (Carte Bleue) is by far the most widely recognized credit card, followed by **MasterCard** and **American Express**. It must also be said that smaller establishments (especially *chambres d'hôtes* and *fermes-auberges*) tend to accept only cash, and that there are few ATMs outside the main towns.

If your card is lost or stolen in France, ring the **Interbank service** (for Visa, t 0800 90 11 79; for Mastercard, t 0800 90 1387; for American Express, t 0800 832 820; for Diners' Club, t 0810 314 159) and they will block it. The police will provide you with a certificate called the *Récépissé de déclaration de vol* to give to your bank or insurance company.

Banks are generally open 8.30am–12.30pm and 1.30–4pm; they close on Sunday, and most close either on Saturday or Monday as well. Exchange rates vary, and nearly all take a commission of varying proportions. *Bureaux de change* that do nothing but exchange money usually have the worst rates or take the heftiest commissions.

Getting There

By Air

The main **airports** in the region are at Montpellier, Nîmes, Carcassonne, Perpignan and Toulouse; in addition, some travellers might find it convenient going through Marseille. Thanks to no-frills airlines such as easyJet and Ryanair in the UK, plus deregulation and the disintegration of state monopolies, prices are competitive. Budget flights are usually cheaper if booked early and online – last-minute bookings don't tend to be much less expensive than flights on major carriers. Shop around and book ahead, especially in summer and at Easter.

Fares on low-cost carriers are highly competitive, changing frequently and at short notice. Shop around and try to book ahead; bear in mind that quoted prices usually exclude airport taxes and, for example with Ryanair, baggage fees.

There are a number of flights from London to Marseille and a good selection of both scheduled and low-cost flights from UK regional airports, but from most other points of departure – North America, Australia, etc. – it's often cheaper to fly to Paris, and from there catch a cheap flight or train. London, with the most cheap flights by far, is an option too, though getting across town from one airport to another can take up to 3hrs.

Domestic flights on Air France from Paris-Orly fly to Toulouse and, less frequently, Montpellier, Perpignan and Nîmes. Services may be less frequent in winter.

Students with the relevant ID cards are eligible for considerable reductions, not only on flights but also on trains and admission fees to museums, concerts and more. Agencies (see box, p.68) specializing in student and youth travel can supply ISICs (International Student Identity Cards).

Airline Carriers

UK and Ireland

Aer Lingus, t 0818 365 000, UK **t** 0870 876 5000, www.aerlingus.com. Dublin to Marseille and Toulouse.

Air France, t 0870 142 4343, www.airfrance. co.uk. Via Paris to Toulouse, Marseille and Montpellier; from London City (with City Jet) to Toulouse, Montpellier or Marseille via Paris.

bmiBaby, t 0871 224 0224 (10p/min), www.bmibaby.com. Manchester to Perpignan and Birmingham to Marseille.

British Airways (BA), t 0870 850 9850, www.ba. com. To Marseille and Toulouse from London Gatwick; plus Montpellier from Gatwick.

British Midland (BMI), t 0870 607 0555, www. flybmi.com. Aberdeen, Edinburgh, Glasgow and Manchester to Toulouse.

easyJet, t 0905 821 0905 (65p/min), www. easyjet.com. London Gatwick to Marseille and Toulouse, and Bristol to Toulouse.

Flybe, (UK) **t** 0871 522 6100 (10p/min), (Ireland) **t** 0044 1392 268529, www.flybe.com. Birmingham to Toulouse, and Southampton to Perpignan.

Jet2, t 0871 226 1737 (10p/min), www.jet2.com. Belfast, Leeds and Manchester to Toulouse and Edinburgh to Avignon.

Ryanair, (UK) **t** 0871 246 0000 (10p/min), (Ireland) **t** 0818 30 30 30, www.ryanair.com. To Nîmes from London Luton, East Midlands and Liverpool. To Montpellier and Perpignan from London Stansted. To Carcassonne from Stansted, Dublin, East Midlands, Liverpool and Shannon. To Marseille from Bournemouth, Dublin, Glasgow and London Stansted.

USA and Canada

Air Canada, (Canada and USA) **t** 1-888 247 2262 (USA), www.aircanada.ca. To Paris from Toronto. To London (Heathrow) from Montreal, Ottawa, Toronto and Vancouver.

Air France, (USA) **t** 800 237 2747, (Canada) **t** 800 667 2747, www.airfrance.us. Regular services to Paris from numerous cities.

American Airlines, t 800 433 7300, **t** 800 543 1586 (TDD), www.aa.com. To Paris from Boston, Chicago, Dallas, New York JFK, Miami, San Diego and San Francisco. To London Heathrow from Boston, Chicago, LA, Miami and New York JFK. To Paris from JFK.

British Airways, t 800 AIRWAYS, www.ba.com. Up to seven flights a day from New York to Paris via London. Up to two flights a day from San Francisco to Paris via London.

Continental, (USA and Canada) **t** 800 231 0856, **t** 800 343 9195 (hearing-impaired), www. continental.com. Flights to Paris and London from Houston and Newark.

Delta, (USA and Canada) **t** 800 241 4141, **t** 800 831 4488 (TDD), www.delta.com. Co-share flights (with Air France and Continental) to Paris from Atlanta, Boston, Cincinnati, Chicago, Los Angeles, New York, Philadelphia and San Francisco.

Northwest Airlines, t 800 225 2525, **t** 800 328 2298 (hearing impaired), www.nwa.com. To Paris and London from Detroit.

United Airlines, t 800 538 2929, **t** 800 323 0170 (TDD), www.united.com. To Paris from Chicago, Los Angeles, Philadelphia, San Francisco and Washington.

Charters, Discounts, Students and Special Deals

UK and Ireland

Budget Travel, 134 Lower Baggot St, Dublin 2, t (01) 631 1111, *www.budgettravel.ie*.

Club Travel, 30 Lower Abbey St, Dublin 1, t (01) 500 5555, within Eire, *www.clubtravel.ie*.

Europe Student Travel, 6 Campden St, London W8, t (020) 7727 7647. A small travel agent catering to non-students too.

STA, 52 Grosvenor Gardens, London SW1W, *www.statravel.co.uk*, t 0871 2300 040, with 51 branches throughout the UK.

Trailfinders, 194 Kensington High St, London W8, t 0845 050 5945, *www.trailfinders.com*.

United Travel, 2 Old Dublin Rd, Stillorgan, County Dublin, t (01) 215 9300, *www. unitedtravel.ie*.

Websites (UK and Ireland)

www.aboutflights.co.uk (t 0870 330 7311)
www.cheapflights.co.uk
www.expedia.co.uk
www.flyaow.com
www.lastminute.com
www.majortravel.co.uk
www.opodo.co.uk
www.orbitz.com
www.sky-tours.co.uk
www.traveljungle.co.uk
www.travellersweb.com
www.travelocity.com
www.travelselect.com

USA and Canada

If you're resilient, flexible and/or youthful and prepared to shop around for budget deals on stand-bys or even courier flights (you can usually only take hand luggage on the latter), you should be able to get yourself some rock-bottom prices. Check the *Yellow Pages* for courier companies. For discounted flights, try the small ads in newspaper travel pages (for example, *New York Times*, *Chicago Tribune*, and *Toronto Globe and Mail*). Numerous travel clubs and agencies also specialize in discount fares, but they may require you to pay an annual membership fee. See *www.traveldiscounts.com* and *www.smartertravel.com*.

Airhitch, *www.airhitch.org*. Last-minute discount tickets to Europe.

Last Minute Travel Club, (USA/Canada) t 800 442 0568, *www.lastminutetravel.com*. Annual membership entitles you to cheap stand-by deals, special car rental rates in Europe and deals on train passes.

STA, *www.statravel.com*, with branches at most universities and at 2871 Broadway, New York, NY, t (212) 865 2700, and ASUC Building, 1st Floor, Berkeley, CA 94720, t (510) 642 3000.

Travel Cuts, 187 College St, Toronto, Ontario ON M5T 1P7, t (888) FLY CUTS (toll free) or t (416) 979 2406 from the USA, *www.travelcuts.com*. Canada's largest student travel specialists, with six offices plus one in New York.

Websites (USA and Canada)

www.eurovacations.com
www.expedia.com
www.flights.com
www.priceline.com (bid for tickets)
www.smartertravel.com
www.traveldiscounts.com
www.travelocity.com

By Train

Airport awfulness makes France's high-speed **TGVs** (*trains à grande vitesse*) an attractive (but not necessarily cheaper) alternative. **Eurostar** trains leave from London St Pancras, Ashford and a new station in north Kent, Ebbsfleet International (near Dartford). There are direct connections to Paris Gare du Nord (2hrs 15mins), Lille (1hr 20mins) and Avignon (6hrs 10mins). You can also book Eurostar-ticketed connections to Nîmes, Montpellier, Perpignan and Toulouse.

Fares are non-refundable and non-changeable; be sure to book ahead. As a general rule of thumb, fares on the Eurostar are cheaper if booked at least 7 or 14 days in advance, and best of all at 21 days' notice or if you include a Saturday night away. Check in at least 30mins before departure or you will not be allowed on the train.

In Paris, go to the Gare de Lyon for a TGV to the south, or Gare Montparnasse or Gare d'Austerlitz for Toulouse (check when you book). France's TGVs shoot along at an average of 180mph when they're not breaking world records, and the journey from Paris to Montpellier takes only 3½hrs, 3hrs to Toulouse. A new TGV line cuts right through the region, connecting Toulouse with Marseille. Costs are only minimally higher on a TGV, and there are plenty of discounts.

Another pleasant, if slower, way of getting south is by overnight sleeper after dinner in Paris. Some weekday departures require a very small supplement; all require a seat reservation, which you make when you buy your ticket or at the station before departure. People under 26 are eligible for a 25 per cent discount on fares if they have an ISIC or other student ID card, and there are also discounts if you're 60 or over, available from major travel agents.

If you plan to take some long train trips, it may be worth investing in a **rail pass** for international travellers (see *www.raileurope.co.uk/inter-rail*). The Eurodomino pass, now part of **InterRail**, entitles **European citizens** to unlimited rail travel through France for 3–8 days in a month for £189–299 for adult second class, or £125–194 for students.

Passes for **North Americans** include the **France Railpass**, giving 3 days' unlimited travel throughout the country in any one month for $237–278 including special rates on Eurostar and an option to purchase 6 extra days if required. The equivalent **France Youthpass** entitles under-26s to 3 days' unlimited travel through France over a one-month period including reduced rates on Eurostar, for $175–206. There's also the 6-day **France Rail 'n' Drive** pass, giving 2 days' unlimited first-class rail travel through France and 2 days' car rental for $356–576.

Also for non-Europeans, the **Eurailpass** allows unlimited 1st-class travel through 18 European countries for 15, 21, 30, 60 or 90 days; it saves the hassle of buying numerous tickets but will only pay for itself if you use it a lot; a 15-day (second-class) Eurailpass Youth costs $440; 26-year-olds and over can get a 15-day Eurailpass for $675, a 21-day pass for $877, 30 days for $1,088, or 3 months for $1,895; all fares include discounted fares on Eurostar plus free or discounted travel on selected ferries, lake steamers, boats and buses. Passes are not valid in the UK. There are other combinations of passes available, such as for couples travelling together.

See the **Rail Europe** websites for full details. Rail Europe handles bookings for all services, including Eurostar and Motorail, sells passes and acts for other continental rail companies.

Note that the German railways website *www.deutsche-bahn.co.uk* has a useful English-language journey planner and ticket-booking service for all of Europe. You can book tickets online on the French railways website *www.sncf.com*, available in French and English, and have them sent to addresses outside France.

Rail Europe (UK), 178 Piccadilly, London W1, t 08708 371 371, *www.raileurope.co.uk*.

Rail Europe (USA and Canada), t 877 257 2887 (US), or t 800 361 RAIL (Canada), *www.raileurope.com*.

Eurostar, t 08705 186 186, *www.eurostar.com*.

www.seat61.com. An incredibly informative, reliable independent train travel website.

By Coach

National Express Eurolines offers services from London to Marseille, Toulouse and Perpignan (all about 20 hours, travel times vary). There are up to four services a week and tickets start at around £69 (book 30 days ahead), £80 (book 15 days ahead) or £99 (standard flexible return).

Eurolines: t 08705 80 80 80 (7.91p/min), *www.eurolines.co.uk*.

By Car

A car entering France must have its **registration and insurance papers**. **Green cards** are no longer compulsory but are worth getting, as they give fully comprehensive cover – your home insurance may only provide minimum cover. Drivers with a valid licence from an EU country, Canada, the USA or Australia don't need an **international licence**. If you're coming from the UK or Ireland, the dip of the car **headlights** must be adjusted to the right. Carrying a **warning triangle** is not mandatory (unless you don't have hazard warning lights) but is advisable; it should be placed 50m behind the car if you have a breakdown.

Drivers' Clubs

For more information on driving in France, contact the AA, RAC or, in the USA, the AAA:

AA, general enquiries, t 0870 600 0371, *www.theaa.com*.

RAC, general enquiries, t 0870 572 2722, *www.rac.co.uk*.

AAA (USA), t 800 222 4357, *www.aaa.com*.

If you're **driving down from the UK**, you can either go through or around Paris, or take the A26 via Reims and Troyes. The *autoroutes* will get you south the fastest, but be prepared to pay some €50–100 in **tolls**; the N7 south of Paris takes longer, but costs nothing. For **toll charges** and route information, see *www. autoroutes.fr*. For information on driving in France, *see* 'Getting Around', pp.71–2.

By Car and Train

A fairly comfortable option is to put your car on the train. It can be costly, but there is a sleeper service that is well priced if bought in advance and in conjunction with Eurotunnel.

Taking your car on a **Eurotunnel train** is a convenient (if fairly costly) way of crossing the Channel between the UK and France. It takes only 35mins to get through the tunnel from Folkestone to Calais; you remain in the car, although you can get up to stretch your legs. Fares start from around £125 for a standard return in low season, rising substantially in summer and high seasons. The price for all tickets is per car less than 6.5m in length and 1.85m high, plus the driver and all passengers.

In mid-April–mid-Oct **Motorail** offers up to six departures a week from Calais to Toulouse and Narbonne, or Avignon. Accommodation is compulsory, in a 4-berth (1st class) or 6-berth (2nd class) carriage. Linen is provided, along with washing facilities. Compartments are not segregated by sex.

Eurotunnel, t 08705 35 35 35, *www.eurotunnel.com*.

Motorail, contact Rail Europe on **t** 08702 415 415, *www.raileurope.co.uk/frenchmotorail*.

By Car and Sea

If you prefer a dose of bracing sea air, you've plenty of choice, although changes and mergers are always on the horizon and crossing may cost significantly more than travelling by air or rail. The shortest ferry/catamaran crossing from the UK is currently **Dover–Calais** with P&O Ferries or SeaFrance.

Speed Ferries operates a Dover–Bologne crossing, **Norfolkline** travels Dover–Dunkirk, **Transmanche** Newhaven–Dieppe, Newhaven–Le Havre and Portsmouth–Le Havre, and **Brittany Ferries** operates between Cork and Plymouth to Roscoff in Brittany, Portsmouth to Caen, to Cherbourg and to St-Malo, and

Ferry Operators

Brittany Ferries, t 08709 076 103, *www.brittanyferries.com*.

Condor Ferries, t 0845 243 5140, *www.condorferries.co.uk*.

Irish Ferries, (UK) **t** 08705 17 17 17, (Ireland) **t** 0818 300 400, *www.irishferries.com*.

Norfolkline, t 08708 70 10 20, *www.norfolklineferries.co.uk*.

P&O Ferries, t 08705 980 333, *www.poferries.com*.

Sea France, t 08705 711 711, *www.seafrance.com*.

Speed Ferries, t 08702 200 570, *www.speedferries.com*.

Transmanche, t 0800 917 1201, *www.transmancheferries.com*.

See also ***www.ferrybooker.com*** for both ferry and Eurotunnel bookings.

Poole to Cherbourg. **Condor Ferries** sail between Poole and St-Malo, via Jersey or Guernsey, mid-May–Sept, and between Weymouth and St-Malo year-round, with a change of ferry in the Channel Islands. **Irish Ferries** sails from Rosslare to Cherbourg and Roscoff. **Prices** vary considerably according to season and demand so shop around for the best deal.

Getting Around

By Train

SNCF nationwide information number, t 08 92 35 35 35 (€0.50/min), *www.sncf.com*.

The SNCF runs a decent and efficient network of trains through the major cities of the south, with an added service called the **Petit Train Jaune** from Villefranche-de-Conflent to Latour-de-Carol in the Pyrenees, with bus connections at either end to Perpignan and Andorra.

If you plan on making only a few long hauls, **international rail passes** (*see* p.69) may save you money. Other possible discounts can be obtained once in France and hinge on the exact time of your departure. The SNCF has divided the year into **blue** (off-peak; *bleue*) and **white** (peak; *blanche*) **periods**, based on demand; white periods run from Friday noon to midnight Saturday, and from Sunday 3pm to Monday 10am and during holidays (all stations give out little calendars). There is then a complicated system of discounts aimed mainly at French residents but which may just fit your circumstances – *découverte* discounts, which are free but only available on tickets booked in advance, and annual *cartes*, which must be paid for. There are *découverte* discounts for children under 12, young people aged 12–25, over-60s, and for return trips departing in a blue period, travelling at least 200km and staying a Saturday night away (*Découverte Séjour*). Log on to *www.voyages-sncf.com* to check them out, or ask at a station for *Le Guide du Voyageur*.

Tickets must be stamped in the little orange machines by the entrance to the lines that say *Compostez votre billet* (this puts the date on the ticket). Any time you interrupt a journey until another day, you have to revalidate your ticket. Long-distance trains (*trains Corail*) have snack trolleys and bar/cafeteria cars; some have play areas.

Nearly every station has large computerized **lockers** (*consigne automatique*) which take a while to puzzle out the first time; note that any threat of terrorist activity in France tends to close them down across the board.

By Bus

Do not count on seeing much of rural France by public transport. The bus network is barely adequate between major cities and towns (places often already well served by rail) and rotten in rural areas, where the one bus a day fits the school schedule, leaving at the crack of dawn and returning in the afternoon; more remote villages are linked to civilization only once a week or not at all.

Buses are run either by the **SNCF** (replacing discontinued rail routes) or **private firms**. Rail passes are valid on SNCF lines, which generally coincide with trains. Private bus firms, especially when they have a monopoly, tend to be a bit more expensive than trains.

Some towns have a *gare routière* (coach station), usually near the train station, though many lines start from any place that catches their fancy.

By Car

Unless you plan to stick to the major cities, a car is unfortunately the only way to see

most of Languedoc. This has its drawbacks: relatively high car rental rates and petrol prices, and an accident rate double that of the UK (and much higher than the USA).

Though **roads** are generally excellently maintained, anything of lesser status than a departmental route (D-road) may be uncomfortably narrow. Mountain roads, though, are reasonable, even in the Pyrenees.

Petrol (*essence*) is relatively expensive in France. The cheapest place to buy petrol is at the big supermarkets; the most expensive is on motorways. Petrol stations keep shop hours (*most close Sun and/or Mon, plus lunchtimes*) and are rare in rural areas, so replenish your fuel supply before making any forays into the mountains. Unleaded is *sans plomb*; diesel is *gazole* or *gasoil*. Automated machines functioning outside these hours don't currently accept foreign debit/credit cards. If you come across a garage with attendants, they will expect a tip for oil, windscreen-cleaning and air. In recent years young chaps have appeared at traffic lights in cities waiting to ambush you into letting them clean your windscreen for payment; you will need to be very firm in refusing.

Speed limits are 130km/80mph on the *autoroutes* (toll motorways); 110km/69mph on dual carriageways (divided highways); 90km/55mph on other roads; 50km/30mph in an 'urbanized area' – as soon as you pass a white sign with a town's name on it and until you pass another sign with the town's name barred. **Fines** for speeding, payable on the spot, are high (from €200), and can be astronomical (up to €4,500) if you fail a breathalyser test.

If you wind up in an **accident**, the procedure is to fill out and sign a *constat amiable*. If your French isn't sufficient to deal with this, hold off until you find someone to translate for you so you don't accidentally incriminate yourself. If you have a **breakdown**, it is best to telephone the police (**t** 17). In some places you still need to give **priority to the right** at unmarked intersections. Watch out for the *cédez le passage* (give way) signs, and wherever there aren't any, be very careful.

When you (inevitably) get lost in a town or city, the *toutes directions* or *autres directions* signs are like Get Out of Jail Free cards. Blue 'P' signs will infallibly direct you to a village or town's already full car park. Watch out for the tiny signs that indicate which streets are meant for pedestrians only (with complicated schedules in even tinier print); and for Byzantine street parking rules (which would take pages to explain – do as the natives do, and be especially careful about village centres on market days).

Europ Assistance, t 0870 737 5720, *www.europ-assistance.co.uk.* Help with car insurance for abroad.

Useful Websites

Route planners: *www.mappy.com,* *www.rac.co.uk, www.theaa.com.*

Autoroute information: *www.route. equipement.gouv.fr* (includes information in English).

Road and traffic information: *www.asf.fr,* *www.autoroutes.fr.*

Car Hire

The minimum age for hiring a car in France is often 25 (though younger drivers with a year's experience can sometimes get a car with the payment of an insurance supplement), and the maximum around 70. For an instant online price comparison, log on to *www.autosabroad. com.*

Car Hire Companies

Local car hire firms are also listed for the larger towns in this book.

UK

Avis, t 0844 581 0147, *www.avis.co.uk.*
Budget, t 08701 56 56 56, *www.budget.com.*
easyCar, t 08710 500 444, *www.easycar.com.*
Europcar, t 0870 607 5000, *www.europcar.com.*
Hertz, t 08708 44 88 44, *www.hertz.co.uk.*
Thrifty, t 01494 751500, *www.thrifty.co.uk.*

USA and Canada

Auto Europe, t 1 888 223 5555, *www.autoeurope.com.*
Avis Rent a Car, t 800 331 1212 or **t** 800 331 2323 (hearing-impaired), *www.avis.com.*
Budget, t 800 527 0700, *www.budget.com.*
Europcar, t 877 940 6900, *www.europcar.com.*
Europe by Car, t 800 223 1516, *www.europebycar.com.*
Hertz, t 800 654 3131, *www.hertz.com.*

By Boat

Yacht, motorboat and sailing-boat charters are available at some of the resorts, such as Cap d'Agde or Argelès-sur-Mer. In Languedoc, though, the real attraction is messing about in boats on the Canal du Midi, through some of the region's loveliest countryside. Between March and November, when the canal is open to navigation, there is a wide choice of boat rentals available: anything from little boats for two or three people that you can rent by the day, to fully fitted barges with crew.

Houseboats are increasingly popular. Some companies charge by the week for the boat, some per person; on average, count on €400–650 a week depending on season. *See* the 'Getting Around' sections for Narbonne (p.191) and the Canal du Midi (p.176) for information on cruises and boat rentals on the canal and the lagoons.

By Bicycle

One of the hazards of driving in the Pyrenees is suddenly coming upon bands of cyclists pumping up the kinds of inclines that most people require escalators for. If you mean to cycle in the summer, start and stop early to avoid heatstroke.

French drivers, not always courteous to fellow motorists, usually give cyclists a wide berth; and yet on any summer day, half the patients in hospital are from accidents on two-wheeled transport. Consider a helmet, and beware: bike thefts are fairly common. Avoid the busy N roads as far as possible.

Getting your own bike to France is fairly easy: Air France and British Airways carry them free from Britain, for example. From the USA or Australia, most airlines will carry them as long as they're boxed and are included in your total baggage weight. In all cases, telephone ahead to the relevant airline to check on terms and conditions. On Eurostar cross-Channel trains, passengers (in summer only) may take a bike with them provided it can be folded and carried on board in a bicycle bag (front wheel removed, etc.). The bike will count as one item of your baggage allowance; for further information see *www.eurostar.com.*

Certain French trains (*autotrains*, with a bicycle symbol in the timetable) carry bikes for free; otherwise you have to send them as registered luggage and pay a fee of around €50, for delivery within 48hrs (though delays are common). For cycling holidays, *see* the list of special-interest companies, p.76.

Fédération Française de Cyclotourisme, 12 Rue Louis Bertrand, 94207 Ivry-sur-Seine, **t** 01 56 20 88 88, *www.ffct.org*. Maps and cycling information in France.

Cyclists' Touring Club, Parklands, Railton Road, Guildford, Surrey GU2 9JX, **t** 0870 873 0060, *www.ctc.org.uk*. Information in Britain.

Bike Hire

The French are keen cyclists and, if you haven't brought a bike, main towns and holiday centres always seem to have at least one shop that hires them out – local tourist offices have lists. A *vélo tout terrain* (abbreviated to VTT) is a mountain bike. You may want to enquire about theft insurance.

You can also hire bikes from most SNCF train stations in major towns; they vary in quality, so check them. The advantage of hiring from a station is that you can drop the bike back off at another, as long as you specify where when you hire it. Rates should be around €9 a day, with a deposit of up to €80 or the yielding of a credit card number.

On Foot

A network of long-distance paths or *Grandes Randonnées* (**GRs**; marked by red and white signs, or splodges of red and white paint; at path junctions, an 'X' denotes this is not the right one to take) take in some of the most beautiful scenery in the south of France. Each GR is described in a *Topoguide*, with maps and details about camping sites, *refuges* and so on, available in local bookshops or the **Fédération Française de la Randonnée Pédestre**, 14 Rue Riquet, 75019 Paris, **t** 01 44 89 93 93, *www.ffrandonnee.fr*. Most tourist information centres have maps and leaflets on walks in the area.

The Pyrenees are magnificent walking country, and the ideal way to take in the beauties of the Corbières and famous citadels of the Cathars from Padern, Peyrepertuse and Puilaurens to Montségur is by way of the *Sentier Cathare*, well marked and endowed with places to eat and stay

en route. The Geocentre map of Southern France is a good guide to walks in the region. Other walks in the mountains are covered in the excellent book *Randonnées pyrénéennes* by J. L. Sarret.

Where to Stay

Hotels

As in most of Europe, the tourist authorities grade hotels by their facilities (not by charm or location) with **stars** from four (or four with an L for luxury – a bit confusing, so in the text luxury places are given five stars) to one, and there are cheap but adequate places undignified by any stars at all.

We would have liked to put the exact prices in the text, but almost every establishment has a wide range of rooms and prices – a very useful and logical way of doing things, once you're used to it. In some hotels, every single room has its own personality, and the difference in quality and price can be enormous: a large room with antique furniture, a television or a balcony over the sea and a complete bathroom will cost much more than a poky back room in the same hotel, with a window overlooking a car park, no antiques and the WC down the hall. Some proprietors will drag out a sort of room menu for you to choose the level of price and facilities you would like. Most two-star hotel rooms have their own showers and WCs; most one stars offer rooms with or without. The coastal resorts are much pricier than the rest of the region, but even here you might find deals in the off-season. Hotels with no stars are not necessarily dives; the owners probably never bothered filling out a form for the tourist authorities. Prices are usually the same as one-star places.

Standards vary so widely that it's impossible to be more precise, but we can add a

Hotel Price Categories

Note that prices listed here and elsewhere in this book are for a double room in high season.

luxury	€€€€€	€230+
very expensive	€€€€	€150–230
expensive	€€€	€100–150
moderate	€€	€60–100
inexpensive	€	€60

few more generalizations. **Single rooms** are relatively rare, and usually two-thirds the price of a double; rarely will a hotelier give you a discount if only doubles are available (again, because each room has its own price). On the other hand, if there are three or four of you, triples or quads or adding extra beds to a double room is usually cheaper than staying in two rooms.

Breakfast (usually coffee, a croissant, bread and jam for €6 or €7) is nearly always optional: you'll do as well for less in a bar. As usual, rates rise in the busy season, when many hotels with restaurants will require that you take **half-board** (demi-pension – breakfast and a set lunch or dinner). Many hotel restaurants are superb and non-residents are welcome. At worst the food will be boring. In the off-season, board requirements vanish into thin air.

Your holiday will be much sweeter if you **book ahead**, especially from May to October. July and August are the only really impossible months; otherwise it usually isn't too difficult to find something. Phoning a day or two ahead is always a good policy, although beware that hotels will only confirm a room with the receipt of a cheque or credit card number to cover the first night. Tourist offices have lists of accommodation in their given areas or even *département*, which come in handy during the peak season; many will even call around and book a room for you on the spot for free or a nominal fee.

There are **chain hotels** (Sofitel, Formula One, etc.) in most cities, but these are always dreary and geared to the business traveller more than the tourist. Don't confuse chains with the various umbrella organizations like Logis et Auberges de France (*www.logis-de-france.fr*), Relais du Silence (*www.silencehotel.com*) or the prestigious Relais et Châteaux (*www.relaischateaux.fr*), which promote and guarantee the quality of independently owned hotels and their restaurants. Many are recommended in the text. Larger tourist offices usually stock their booklets.

If you plan to do a lot of driving, you may want to pick up the French truckers' bible *Les Routiers*, an annual guide with maps listing reasonably priced lodgings and food along the highways and byways of France, *www.routiers.com*.

Bed and Breakfast

In rural areas, there are plenty of opportunities for a stay in a private home or farm. *Chambres d'hôtes* are listed separately from hotels in the tourist office brochures, along with the various *gîtes* (*see* opposite). Some are connected to restaurants, others to wine estates or a château; prices tend to be moderate to inexpensive.

Association Française BAB France, 23 Centre Commercial Les Vergers, 95350 St Brice Sous Forêt, t 01 34 19 90 00, *www.babfrance.fr*.

B&B France, PO Box 47085, London SW18 9AB, *www.bedbreak.com*.

Fleurs de Soleil, *www.fleurs-soleil.tm.fr*. Offers *maisons d'hôtes* and B&Bs throughout southern France.

Youth Hostels

Most cities and resort areas have youth hostels (*auberges de jeunesse*) that offer simple dormitory accommodation and breakfast to people of any age for around €14–25 a night. Most offer kitchen facilities as well, or inexpensive meals. They are the best deal going for people travelling on their own; for people travelling together, a one-star hotel can work out just as cheap. Another downside is that many are in the most ungodly locations – in the suburbs where the last bus goes by at 7pm, or miles from any transport at all in the country.

For further information on youth hostels in France, contact the **Fédération Unie des Auberges de Jeunesse**, 27 Rue Pajol, 75018 Paris, t 01 44 89 87 27, *www.fuaj.org*.

In summer the only way to be sure of getting a room is to arrive early in the day. Most require a **Hostelling International** (**HI**; *www.hihostels.com*) membership card, which you can usually purchase on the spot, although regulations say you should buy them in your home country.

UK: HI International Youth Hostel Federation, 2nd Floor, Gate House, Fretherne Road, Welwyn Garden City, Herts AL8 6RD, t (01707) 324 170, *www.hihostels.com*. Also contact **YHA**, Trevelyan House, Dimple Rd, Matlock, Derbyshire DE4 3YH, t 0870 770 8868, *www.yha.org.uk*.

USA: **Hostelling International USA**, 8401 Colesville Rd, Suite 600, Silver Spring, MD 20910, t (301) 495 1240, *www.hiayh.org*.

Canada: Hostelling International Canada, 75 Nicholas St, Ottawa, ON K1N 7B9, t (613) 235 2595, *www.hihostels.ca*.

Another option in cities is single-sex dormitories for young workers (*foyers de jeunes travailleurs et de jeunes travailleuses*), which rent out individual rooms if available, for slightly more than a youth hostel.

Gîtes d'Etape, Refuges and Fermes Auberges

A *gîte d'étape* (*www.gite-etape.com*) is a simple shelter with bunk beds and a rudimentary kitchen set up by a village along GR walking paths (*see* p.73) or scenic bike routes. Again, lists are available for each *département*; the detailed maps listed under 'Getting Around' (*see* p.73) mark them as well. In the mountains, similar rough shelters along the GR paths are called *refuges*, most of them open in summer only. Both charge around €15 a night.

Fermes auberges, which combine rural living with B&B comforts, are becoming a popular option. Check with the regional tourist offices for lists.

Gîtes de France and Other Self-catering Accommodation

The south of France offers a vast range of self-catering: inexpensive farm cottages, history-laden châteaux with gourmet frills, sprawling coastal villas, flats in modern beach resorts, even canal boats.

The **Fédération Nationale des Gîtes de France** is a French government service offering inexpensive accommodation by the week in rural areas. Lists with photos arranged by *département* are available from the **Maison des Gîtes de France et du Tourisme Vert**, 59 Rue St-Lazare, 75009 Paris Cedex 09, t 01 49 70 75 75, *www.gites-de-france.fr*, or in the UK from the Gîtes de France representative, **Maison de la France**, 178 Piccadilly, London W1J 9AL, t 09068 244 123. If you want to stay in a château, request the *Chambres d'hôtes et gîtes de prestige* list. Prices range from €250 to €1,000 a week,

depending very much on the time of year as well as facilities; nearly always you'll be expected to begin your stay on a Saturday. Many *départements* also have a second (and usually less expensive) listing of *gîtes* in the guide *Clévacances* (*www.clevacances.com*). Or try getting back to nature (but with a villa included), with a Panda Gîte, one of a network of about 250 rural *gîtes* and B&Bs in collaboration with Gîtes de France, WWF France and the Federation of French Nature Reserves, *www.wwf.fr*.

Other options are advertised in the Sunday papers, or contact one of the firms listed overleaf. The accommodation they offer will nearly always be more comfortable and costly than a *gîte*, but the discounts that holiday firms can offer on the ferries, aeroplane tickets or car rental can make up for the price difference. For private *gîte* rentals booked directly with the owners, try *www.frenchconnections.co.uk*, which also offers ferry discounts, and *www.abritel.fr*.

Camping

Camping is very popular, especially among the French, and there's at least one campsite in every town, often an inexpensive, no-frills place run by the town itself (*camping municipal*). Other campsites are graded with stars like hotels from four to one: at the top of the line you can expect lots of trees and grass, hot showers, a pool or beach, sports facilities, and a grocer's, bar and/or restaurant; on the coast, prices are rather similar to one-star hotels (although these, of course, never have all the extras). Beware that July and August are terrible months to camp, when sites become overcrowded. You'll find more *Lebensraum* off the coast. If you want to camp outside official sites, ask permission from the landowner first, or risk a furious farmer and perhaps police. Tourist offices have complete lists of campsites in their regions, or if you plan to move around a lot pick up a *Guide officiel camping/caravaning*, available in French bookshops. A number of UK holiday firms book camping holidays; try:

Eurocamp Travel, t 08709 019 410, *www.eurocamp.co.uk*.

Keycamp Holidays, t 0870 7000 740, *www.keycamp.co.uk*.

Special-interest Holidays

In France

Vinetude, Domaine du Brousson, Av du Château, 34260 La Tour sur Orb, (France) **t** 04 67 23 76 89, (UK mobile) **t** 07710 217902, *www.vinetude.com*. Locally run wine tours, with accommodation in a gracious bed-and-breakfast and meals.

From the UK

Belle France, t (0870) 405 4056, *www.bellefrance.co.uk*. Walking, cycling, activity, motoring and cruising tours, including tours on the Canal du Mldi.

Connoisseur Holidays Afloat, t 0870 160 5648, *www.connoisseurafloat.com*. Cruises in the Camargue and along the Canal du Midi, Canal de la Robine and other canals.

French Country Cruises, Andrew Brock Travel Ltd, 29A Main Street, Lyddington, Oakham, Rutland LE15 9LR, **t** (01572) 821 330, *www.frenchcountrycruises.com*. Rent a *penichette* for holidays on the Canal du Midi or the coast.

French Cycling Holidays Ltd, 73 High Road, Leavesden, Watford, Hertfordshire WD25 7AL, **t** (020) 8861 5888, *www.frenchcycling holidays.com*. For serious cyclists.

Golf Par Excellence, 2 Birkheads Road, Reigate, Surrey RH2 0AR, **t** (01737) 211 818, *www.golfparexcellence.com*. Golf holidays to the best Languedoc courses.

Sherpa Expeditions, 131a Heston Rd, Hounslow, Middlesex TW5 0RF, **t** (020) 8577 2717, *www.sherpa-walking-holidays.co.uk*. 'Inn-to-inn' walking tours in Roussillon.

Waymark Holidays, Grange Mills, Weir Road, Balham, London SW12 0NE, **t** 0870 950 9800, *www.waymarkholidays.com*. Walking and cross-country skiing in the Roussillon Pyrenees.

From the USA

Abercrombie & Kent, 1520 Kensington Rd, Oak Brook, Illinois 60523, **t** 800 554 7016, *www.abercrombiekent.com*. Quality canal and river cruises, city and countryside short and long breaks.

Active Gourmet Holidays, 1 Gaidosz Way, Derby, Connecticut 06418, **t** (203) 732 0771, *www.activegourmetholidays.com*. Cooking in the Minervois, and other activities besides.

Discover France, t 1-800 960 2221, *www.discoverfrance.com*. Self-guided walking, hiking, bicycle and food tours in Roussillon and Languedoc.

Self-catering Operators

In the UK and France

A.I.P.L.V., *www.pour-les-vacances.com*. French site that matches you with villa owners.

Bowhills, Unit 3, Furze Court, 114 Wickham Rd, Fareham PO16 7SH, **t** 0870 235 2727, *www.bowhills.co.uk*. Luxury villas and farmhouses, mostly with pools.

Chez Nous, Spring Mill, Earby, Barnoldswick, Lancashire BB94 0AA, **t** 0870 197 1000, *www.cheznous.com*. Over 3,000 privately owned holiday cottages and B&Bs.

Dominique's Villas, The Plough Brewery, 516 Wandsworth Rd, London SW8 3JX, **t** (020) 7738 8772, *www.dominiquesvillas.co.uk*. Large villas and châteaux with pools.

French Country, *www.frenchcountry.co.uk*. Small selection of listings placed by owners.

Holiday Lettings, *www.holidaylettings.co.uk*. Extensive listings.

Individual Traveller Co., address as Chez Nous above, **t** 0845 604 3829, *www.indiv-travellers.com*. Villas, cottages and farmhouses.

Mldi Hideaways, *www.midihideaways.com*. Properties in and around St-Chinian in the Hérault.

Pézenas Properties, *www.pezenasproperties.com*. Villas in the Hérault.

VFB Holidays, t (01452) 716 830, *www.vfb holidays.co.uk*. A. few rustic *gîtes*, luxurious farmhouses and hotels.

Villa Renters, *www.villarenters.com*. A selection of mostly moderately priced accommodation around the region.

VRBO, *www.vrbo.com*. Stands for 'vacation rentals by owner', a website where owners list their properties, including a wide range of cottages, villas, châteaux, lodges and apartments.

In the USA

At Home in France, PO Box 643, Ashland, OR 97520, **t** (541) 488 9467, *www.athomeinfrance.com*. Apartments, cottages, farmhouses, manor houses and villas; moderate to de luxe.

Doorways Ltd., 900 County Line Rd, Bryn Mawr, PA 19010, **t** (610) 520 0806, *www.villavacations.com*. Villas and apartments all over France.

France by Heart, PO Box 614, Mill Valley, CA 94942, **t** (415) 388 3075, *www.francebyheart.com*. Hundreds of properties.

Vacances Provençales, 247 Davenport Rd, Suite 200, Toronto, Ontario M5R 1JT, **t** 800 263 7152, *www.europeanhomerentals.com*. Luxury villas, country homes, châlets and apartments.

Practical A–Z

07

Conversions: Imperial–Metric

Length (multiply by)
Inches to centimetres: 2.54
Centimetres to inches: 0.39
Feet to metres: 0.3
Metres to feet: 3.28
Yards to metres: 0.91
Metres to yards: 1.1
Miles to kilometres: 1.61
Kilometres to miles: 0.62

Area (multiply by)
Inches square to centimetres square: 6.45
Centimetres square to inches square: 0.15
Feet square to metres square: 0.09
Metres square to feet square: 10.76
Miles square to kilometres square: 2.59
Kilometres square to miles square: 0.39
Acres to hectares: 0.40
Hectares to acres: 2.47

Weight (multiply by)
Ounces to grams: 28.35
Grammes to ounces: 0.035
Pounds to kilograms: 0.45
Kilograms to pounds: 2.2
Stones to kilograms: 6.35
Kilograms to stones: 0.16
Tons (UK) to kilograms: 1,016
Kilograms to tons (UK): 0.0009
1 UK ton (2,240lbs) = 1.12 US tonnes (2,000lbs)

Volume (multiply by)
Pints (UK) to litres: 0.57
Litres to pints (UK): 1.76
Quarts (UK) to litres: 1.13
Litres to quarts (UK): 0.88
Gallons (UK) to litres: 4.55
Litres to gallons (UK): 0.22
1 UK pint/quart/gallon = 1.2 US pints/quarts/gallons

Temperature
Celsius to Fahrenheit: multiply by 1.8 then add 32

Fahrenheit to Celsius: subtract 32 then multiply by 0.55

France Information

Time Differences
Country: + 1hr GMT; + 6hrs EST
Daylight saving from last weekend in March to end of October

Dialling Codes
Note: omit first zero of area code
France country code 33
To France from: UK, Ireland, New Zealand 00 / USA, Canada 011 / Australia 0011 then dial 33 and then the number without the initial zero
From France to: UK 00 44; Ireland 00 353; USA, Canada 001; Australia 00 61; New Zealand 00 64 then the number without the initial zero
Directory enquiries: 118 712
International directory enquiries: 32 12

Emergency Numbers
Police: 17
Ambulance: 15
Fire: 18

Embassy Numbers in France
UK: 04 91 15 72 10; **Ireland** 01 44 17 67 00;
USA: 04 91 54 92 00; **Canada** 01 44 43 29 00
Australia 01 40 59 33 00; **NZ** 01 45 01 43 43

Shoe Sizes

Europe	UK	USA
35	2½ / 3	4
36	3 / 3½	4½ / 5
37	4	5½ / 6
38	5	6½
39	5½ / 6	7 / 7½
40	6 / 6½	8 / 8½
41	7	9 / 9½
42	8	9½ / 10
43	9	10½
44	9½ / 10	11
45	10½	12
46	11	12½ / 13

Women's Clothing

Europe	UK	USA
34	6	2
36	8	4
38	10	6
40	12	8
42	14	10
44	16	12

°C	°F
40	104
35	95
30	86
25	77
20	68
15	59
10	50
5	41
-0	32
-5	23
-10	14
-15	5

Crime and the Police

Police t 17

Though it isn't widely publicized, right now Montpellier, Perpignan and Nîmes rank among the very highest crime cities of France – Montpellier is third in the nation. Béziers, Toulouse and Carcassonne also rank in the top third. In recent years, most crimes have been dropping a bit (car theft, especially), though violent crimes have risen sharply.

Don't be too alarmed, though. Violent crime rates are still considerably lower than in British or American cities, and you're probably safer here than you would be at home. Take the usual precautions concerning your valuables and your car. Leave anything you'd really miss at home and insure your property, especially if you're driving.

Report **thefts** to the nearest *gendarmerie*, not a pleasant task but the reward is the bit of paper you need for an insurance claim.

If your **passport** is stolen, contact the police and your nearest consulate for emergency travel documents. Carry photocopies of your passport, driver's licence, etc.; it makes it easier when reporting a loss.

By law, the police in France can stop anyone anywhere and demand to see ID; in practice, they only tend to do it to harass minorities, the homeless and scruffy hippy types. If they really don't like the look of you they can salt you away for a long time ('*garde à vue*') without any reason.

The **drug** situation is the same in France as anywhere in the West: soft and hard drugs are widely available and the police only make an issue of victimless crime when it suits them. Smuggling any amount of marijuana into the country can mean a prison term.

Eating Out

In this guide, price ranges have been used based on the set menu for one person that almost every restaurant offers in addition to its *à la carte* menu, or for an average two-course meal for one without wine (*see* box). *A la carte* is usually more expensive.

For more information about food and local specialities, *see* **Food and Drink**, pp.49–60.

Restaurant Price Categories

For full meal, per person, but not including wine, based on set menus.

very expensive	€€€€	over €60
expensive	€€€	€30–60
moderate	€€	€15–30
inexpensive	€	below €15

Electricity

French electricity is all 220V. British and Irish appliances need an adapter with two round prongs; North American 110V appliances usually need a transformer as well.

Health and Emergencies

Ambulance (SAMU) **t** 15; **Fire t** 18

Local **hospitals** are the place to go in an emergency (*urgence*). **Doctors** take turns on duty at night and on holidays, even in rural areas: ring one to listen to the recorded message to find out what to do. To be on the safe side, always carry a phonecard.

If it's not an emergency, **pharmacists** are trained to administer first aid and dispense free advice for minor problems. In rural areas there is always someone on duty if you ring the bell; in cities pharmacies are open on a rotating basis on Sundays and holidays, and addresses are posted in their windows and in the local newspaper.

For information on **EHIC cards** and health and travel **insurance**, *see* p.66. In France, you must pay upfront for any treatment or prescription, then apply for a refund of part of the costs (around 70 per cent of standard doctors' and dentists' fees, between 35 per cent and 65 per cent of the cost of most, but not all, prescribed medicines, and around 75 per cent of in-patient hospital treatment). Ensure that the doctor or dentist you consult is *conventionné* (within the French health system). Take with you the booklet you get with the EHIC card; this will tell you what to do if you need to claim. The refund process normally takes around two months.

The Internet

Most cities and towns now have **cybercafés**, and you can often e-mail from the tourist office or your hotel, and from some post offices. Most French hotels happily give out their e-mail addresses (we've included them in the text if you can't e-mail via the website), but don't rely on this as your only means of communication with them.

National Holidays

On national holidays, banks, shops and businesses close; some museums do too, but most restaurants stay open. The French have a healthy approach to holidays: if there is a holiday near a weekend, they often 'make a bridge' (*faire le pont*) to the weekend, and take the extra day in between off too.

1 January New Year's Day
Easter Sunday and Monday (Mar or April)
1 May *Fête du Travail* (Labour Day)
8 May VE Day, Victory 1945
Ascension Day (usually end of May)
Pentecost (Whitsun) and following Monday (early June)
14 July Bastille Day
15 August Assumption of the Virgin Mary
1 November All Saints' Day
11 November Remembrance Day (First World War Armistice)
25 December Christmas Day

Opening Hours

Shops: While many shops and supermarkets in large cities now open Mon–Sat 9–7 or later, businesses in smaller towns still close for lunch from 12 or 12.30pm to 2pm (3pm in summer). There are local exceptions, but nearly everything shuts on Monday, except grocers and *supermarchés*. **Markets** (daily in cities, weekly in villages, often on a Sunday) usually run mornings only, except clothes, flea and antiques markets.

Banks: Banks generally open 8.30– 12.30 and 1.30–4. They close on Sun, and most either on Sat or Mon as well.

Post offices: Open in cities Mon–Fri 8am–7pm and Sat 8–noon. In villages, offices may not open until 9am, then break for lunch and close at 4.30 or 5pm.

Museums: Most museums close for lunch, and often all day Mon or Tues, and some-times for all of Nov or the entire winter. Hours change with the season: longer

summer hours begin in May or June and last until the end of Sept – usually. Most museums close on national holidays. We've done our best to include opening hours in the text, but some change their hours every month, so call in advance if you're making a special trip. Most museums give **discounts** on admission (which ranges from €2–10) if you have a student ID card. National museums are free if you're under 18. The third weekend of Sept is usually the *Journées du Patrimoine*, when state-owned museums throw open their doors to the public for free (or at least reduced) entry to give everyone a taste of France's national heritage. Though queues can spiral around the museums and the hordes have to shuffle past the national treasures, everyone is very cheerful at the thought of a freebie.

Churches: Churches are either open all day, or closed all day and only open for Mass. Sometimes notes on the door direct you to the *mairie* or priest's house (*presbytère*) to pick up the key. There are often admission fees for cloisters, crypts and special chapels.

Post Offices

Known as **La Poste**, post offices (for opening times, *see* left) are discernible by their sign of a blue bird on a yellow back-ground. Larger offices are equipped with special machines for you to weigh and stamp your package, letter or postcard without having to even see a real person. They are surprisingly easy to use, with an English-language option. You can receive letters *poste restante* at any post office; the postal codes in this book should help your mail get there in a timely fashion. To collect it, take some ID.

You can purchase **stamps** in tobacconists (*tabacs*) as well as post offices.

Racism

Unfortunately, in the south of France the forces of bigotry and reaction are strong enough to make racism a serious concern. The rise of the National Front in France has created a particularly febrile atmosphere of late. We've heard some horror stories, espe-cially about Roussillon, where campsites and restaurants suddenly have no places if the colour of your skin doesn't suit the proprietor; the bouncers at clubs will inevitably say it's really the cut of your hair or trousers they find offensive. If any place recommended in this book is guilty of such behaviour, please write and let us know.

Sports and Activities

Bullfights

The Roman amphitheatre at Nîmes had hardly been restored in the early 1800s when it once again became a venue for *tauromachie*; if anything, bullfights are now more popular than they ever were.

However, the most traditional bullfights in Languedoc are not bloody. The *courses*, as they are called, can be traced back to the bull games described by Heliodorus in ancient Thessaly. Played by daring young men dressed in white called *razeteurs*, the sport demands grace, daring and dexterity, especially in leaping over the barriers before a charging bull. The object is to remove a round cockade from between the horns of the bull (or cow) by cutting its ribbons with a blunt razor comb – a sport far more dangerous to the human players than the animals. The animals used for the *courses* are the small, lithe, high-horned breed from the Camargue; good sporty ones retire with fat pensions.

You will see three other types of bullfight advertised. *Corrida* is the traditional Spanish bullfight, where the bull is put to death; it spread to France only in the 1850s. The bullfighters are usually Spanish as well, and the major festivals, or *férias*, bring some of the top *toreros* to France. A *novillada*, pitting younger bulls against apprentice *toreros* (*novilleros*), is less expensive, but much more likely to be a butchery void of *arte*. In a *corrida portugaise* the bullfighter (*rejoneador*) fights from horseback, but doesn't kill the bull.

Canoeing and Kayaking

This is popular in Haut-Languedoc above all.

Fédération Française de Canoë-Kayak, 87 Quai de la Marne, 94344 Joinville-le-Pont t 01 45 11 08 50, *www.ffck.org*.

Fishing

You can fish in the sea without a permit as long as your catch is for local consumption. Freshwater fishing requires an easily obtained permit from a local club; tourist offices can tell you where to find them.

Horse-riding

Every tourist office has a list of *centres hippiques* or *centres équestres* that offer group excursions, though if you prove yourself an experienced rider you can usually head down the trails on your own. The Camargue, with its many ranches, cowboy traditions and open spaces, is the most popular place to ride in the region.

Most of the posher country inns can also find you a horse.

Pétanque

Like *pastis* and olive oil, *pétanque* is one of the essential ingredients of the Midi; even the smallest village has a rough, hard court under the plane trees for its practitioners – nearly all male, although women are welcome to join in. Similar to *boules*, the rules of *pétanque* were, according to tradition, developed in La Ciotat, near Marseille. The object is to get your metal ball closest to the marker (*bouchon* or *cochonnet*).

Rugby Union

Rugby is the national sport of Languedoc and the southwest, cradle of most of the players on the national team (although movements to change one of the Five Nations from France to Occitania have so far fallen flat). The best team lately has been Stade Toulousain, the 2005 European champions, and you can see fiery matches in Perpignan, Narbonne, Béziers (the town has three rugby schools), and Carcassonne. In some places they play heretical 'Cathar rugby' – 13 a side instead of 15.

Sailing

Most resorts along the southern coast have sailing schools and boats to hire.

Fédération Française de Voile, 17 Rue Henri Bocquillon, 75015 Paris Cedex, t 01 40 60 37 00, *www.ffvoile.org*. For a complete list.

Skiing

On the Mediterranean end of the Pyrenees, there's Font-Romeu and Les Angles. Snowfall has been unreliable there in recent years, but Font Romeu is one of the biggest stations in the Pyrenees and has created its own snow with its 500 snow cannons. Font-Romeu is not known as particularly challenging; the area is, however, good for cross-country skiing. Package deals going from abroad are practically non-existent.

Fédération Française de Ski, 50 Rue des Marquisats, B.P. 2451, 74011 Annecy Cedex, t 04 50 51 40 34, *www.ffs.fr*.

Association Nationale des Maires de Stations de Montagne, 9 Rue de Madrid, 75008 Paris, t 01 47 42 23 32, *www.skifrance.fr*.

Water Sports and Beaches

Languedoc-Roussillon may be less glamorous than Provence or the Costa Brava, but it has more miles of free sandy beaches than anywhere in the western Mediterranean, stretching into the horizon on either side of its scores of small resorts – until you reach the rocky Côte Vermeille, at any rate. Areas are always set aside for *les naturistes*, or nudists: Cap d'Agde is Europe's biggest naturist resort.

Every town on the coast hires out equipment for water sports, often for hefty prices.

Fédération Française d'Etudes et de Sports Sous-Marins, 24 Quai de Rive Neuve, 13284 Marseille, t 04 91 33 99 31, *www.ffessm.fr*. Can supply a list of diving clubs.

Telephones

Nearly all public telephones have switched from coins to *télécartes* (phonecards) which you can buy at any post office or news-stand. You can also purchase the US-style phonecards which use a PIN-number system. Even more common is to use your **credit card** like a phonecard.

The French have eliminated area codes, giving everyone a 10-digit number.

If **ringing France from abroad**, the international dialling code is 33, and drop the first 'o' of the number. For **international calls from**

France, dial oo then the country code (UK 44; Ireland 353; US and Canada 1; Australia 61; New Zealand 64), and then the local code (minus the o for UK numbers) and number.

The easiest way to **reverse charges** is to spend a couple of euros ringing the number and giving your number in France, which is always posted by public phones.

For **directory enquiries**, dial t 118 712, or see *www.pagesjaunes.fr* (the *Yellow Pages*). For **international enquiries** call t 32 12.

While all three French **mobile phone** providers – Orange (partially owned by France Telecom), SFR and Bouygues Telecom – are represented in the region, your mobile may well not work in more remote areas; US cell phones won't be compatible unless they have tri-band technology. The downside of taking your mobile to France can be the huge roaming charges you used to pay to receive and make calls, at up to 10 times the price you paid at home. However, following a recent EU regulation, operators have been forced to cap charges for calls made abroad. Before leaving home, contact your provider to see what international services they offer. Some phones can make use of local providers by changing the SIM cards, which requires 'unlocking' your phone (some UK phones are locked to a UK network), do-able in shops in France (check first to see if it's necessary by trying someone else's card in your phone). Alternatively, check offers on line at *www.0044.co.uk*, *www.SIM4travel.com*, *www.textbay.net* and *www.uk2abroad.com*.

Time

France is 1 hour ahead of GMT, 6 hours ahead of US Eastern Standard Time, 9 hours ahead of Pacific Coast Time. French summertime (daylight-saving), as in the UK, runs from the last Sunday in March to the last Sunday in October.

Tipping

Many people leave a tip if they're happy with their meal and service; if you eat *à la carte*, you might add a gratuity of around 10% (service is included in the price of set menus).

Nîmes, the Gard and Montpellier

Like most French départements, the Gard is named after a river – a river made famous by a feat of Roman engineering that symbolizes the Midi as boldly as the Eiffel Tower does Paris. Its spirit, or at least something intangibly Classical, lingers in the Gard's luminous, sun-blond landscapes and clear air; note how often a solitary windswept pine or cypress dominates the view, as if lifted straight from a painting by Claude Lorrain.

o8

Don't miss

⭐ City of the crocodile and palm tree
Nîmes p.85

⭐ A legendary Roman aqueduct
Pont du Gard p.97

⭐ Saint Louis' walled city
Aigues-Mortes p.120

⭐ Lawrence Durrell's old haunts
Sommières p.123

⭐ Urbane energy
Montpellier p.127

See map overleaf

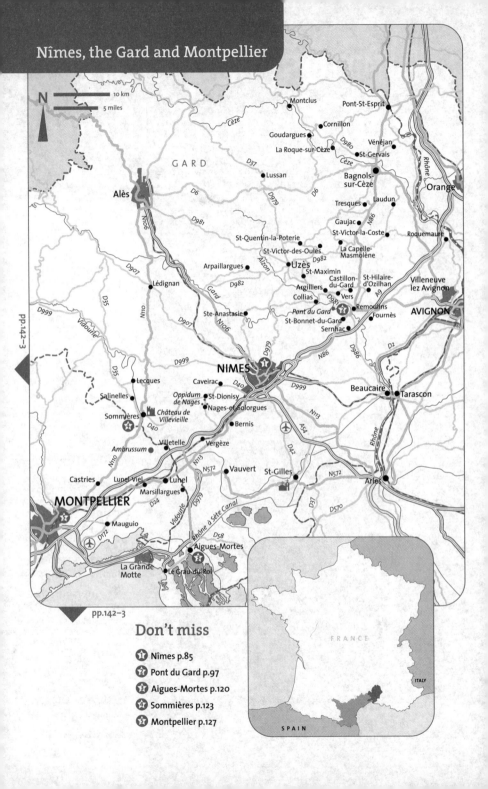

N

10 km

5 miles

Montclus

Pont-St-Esprit

Cèze

Cornillon

Goudargues

Vénéjan

La Roque-sur-Cèze

St-Gervais

D980

GARD

D37

Cèze

Lussan

Bagnols-sur-Cèze

Orange

Alès

D6

D6

Tresques

Laudun

D981

Gaujac

St-Victor-la-Coste

N86

Roquemaure

St-Quentin-la-Poterie

La Capelle-Masmolène

St-Victor-des-Oules

D982

D907

Arpaillargues

Uzès

Alzon

St-Maximin

St-Hilaire-d'Ozilhan

Villeneuve lez Avignon

Lédignan

D982

Castillon-du-Gard

Argilliers

Vers

A9

Gard

Collias

Remoulins

AVIGNON

D35

Ste-Anastasie

Pont du Gard

Fournès

Vidourle

N106

D907

St-Bonnet-du-Gard

D986

Sernhac

D2

N110

D979

D386

D999

N86

Lecques

Caveirac

NÎMES

Beaucaire

Tarascon

Salinelles

D40

Oppidum de Nages

St-Dionisy

Rhône

D999

D35

Sommières

Château de Villevieille

Nages-et-Solorgues

N113

D40

Bernis

A54

Villetelle

Ambrussum

Vergèze

D42

Castries

N110

N113

Vauvert

St-Gilles

Arles

Lunel-Viel

Lunel

N572

N572

MONTPELLIER

Marsillargues

D24

D979

D37

D570

Mauguio

Vidourle

Rhône à Sète Canal

D172

D58

Aigues-Mortes

La Grande Motte

Le Grau-du-Roi

pp.142–3

pp.142–3

Don't miss

1 Nîmes p.85

2 Pont du Gard p.97

3 Aigues-Mortes p.120

4 Sommières p.123

5 Montpellier p.127

FRANCE

ITALY

SPAIN

The Gard's capital, Nîmes, was especially coddled by Rome and still has a full share of grand monuments; Sommières, one of the *département*'s most charming (and most flooded) towns, stands by its Roman bridge. The Gard is also home to Uzès, *ville d'art* and the 'First Duchy of France', Bagnols-sur-Cèze, with its exceptional little museum of modern art, and the natural charms and vineyards of the lower valley of the Cèze. The *département* also owns a slice of the Camargue, the romantically swampy delta of the Rhône that includes the once-great medieval towns of St-Gilles and Aigues-Mortes.

Note that this chapter also includes Montpellier, Nîmes' fierce rival in the Hérault. The competition between these two cities, usually expressed in new building projects and cultural exertions, provides much of the fizz in Languedoc today, and a look at the two of them together makes for some interesting comparisons.

Nîmes

⭐ Nîmes

The approach along the *autoroute* from Montpellier is hardly flattering; however, inside, built of stone the colour of old piano keys, Nîmes disputes with Arles the honour of being the 'Rome of France' – the Rome of the Caesars, of course, not of the popes: neither the Church (nor, for that matter, bossy old Paris) have ever gone down well in this mercantile, Protestant town. But after the passions of the Wars of Religion, Nîmes fell into a doze that lasted for centuries. Travellers in the 19th century found it the quintessential dusty southern city; they came to marvel at the city's famous Maison Carrée, the best-preserved Roman temple in the world, and wrote that it was so neglected that it looked as if it was dedicated to the goddess of sewage.

The city saw some spectacular changes under dynamic Jean Bousquet, elected mayor in 1983. He was former head of Cacharel, Nîmes' fashionable *prêt-à-porter* firm, and he not only wakened Nîmes from its daydreams but also, by devoting nearly 14 per cent of its budget to culture, urged it to echo the ambitious efforts of upstart Montpellier, its chief rival in Languedoc. The opening of the new Carré d'Art, designed by Sir Norman Foster, threw down the gauntlet to the former mayor of Montpellier, Georges Frêche. Bousquet then signed up Sir Norman to redevelop Nîmes' old centre, with plans for a '*Grand Axe*' running from the Jardin de la Fontaine to surrounding smaller villages. In addition, a university has been built, specializing in law, literature and medicine. Just like the one in Montpellier. The current mayor, Jean-Paul Fournier, was elected in 2001, and he isn't resting on his laurels either. Fournier declared 2005 'protection of our architectural heritage' year, which

Getting to and around Nîmes

By Air

You can fly direct from the UK to Nîmes, *see* **Planning Your Trip**. Nîmes-Garons **airport**, *www.nimes-aeroport.fr*, is 8km from Nîmes along Rte de St-Gilles (A54). Call **t** 04 66 70 49 49 for flight information. *Navettes* (shuttle buses) run between the airport and Nîmes (train station and other parts of town; call **t** 04 66 29 27 29).

By Train

Nîmes' **train station**, at the south end of Av Feuchères on Bd Sgt Triaire, is a kind of arcaded train-aduct that perfectly suits *la Rome française*. There are direct trains (**t** 36 35) to Carcassonne, Montpellier, Arles and Marseille; and TGVs to Paris (4hrs) and Lille (5hrs).

By Bus

The *gare routière* is just behind the train station in Rue Ste-Félicité, **t** 04 66 29 52 00; there are services to the Pont du Gard, Uzès, St-Gilles, Aigues-Mortes, Le Grau-du-Roi, La Grande Motte, Avignon and Montpellier.

Car and Bike Hire

Avis is at Avenue du Maréchal Juin, **t** 04 66 29 05 33, and at the airport along with a selection of other companies.

The baggage area at the train station has bicycle hire, as does **Cycles Passieu**, 2 Place Montcalm, **t** 04 66 21 09 16.

included the restoration of the Maison Carrée (*see* p.90) on its 2,000th birthday. He was decorated as an *Officier* of the *Légion d'Honneur* in July 2007.

Most Nîmois view the battle for avant-garde supremacy in this corner of France with detached amusement, for what really makes the juices flow here is not modern architecture but bulls. Nîmes is passionate about its *ferias*, featuring top matadors from France, Spain and Portugal and a beautiful blonde *torera*, a native of Nîmes who learned her art at the city's Ecole Française de Tauromachie.

History

Geography dealt Nîmes a pair of trump cards: first, a mighty spring, the **Fontaine**, whose god, Nemausus, was worshipped by the first known residents, the Celtic Volcae-Arecomici, and second, a position on the main route from Italy to Spain, a trail blazed by Hercules himself during his Tenth Labour, as he herded Geryon's cattle back to Greece from the Pillars that bear his name. The Romans paved his route and called it the **Via Domitia**, and made Celtic Nîmes into their 'Colonia Nemausensis'. The Volcae-Arecomici Celts, unlike Astérix and Obélix, thought the Romans were just swell, and Augustus reciprocated by endowing Nîmes with the Maison Carrée, a sanctuary for the Fontaine, an aqueduct (the Pont du Gard) to augment the spring, and four miles of walls. The Nîmois celebrated Augustus' conquest of Egypt, and the arrival of a colony of veterans from the Battle of Actium, by minting a coin with a crocodile chained to a palm, a striking image which François Ier adopted as the city's coat of arms in 1535.

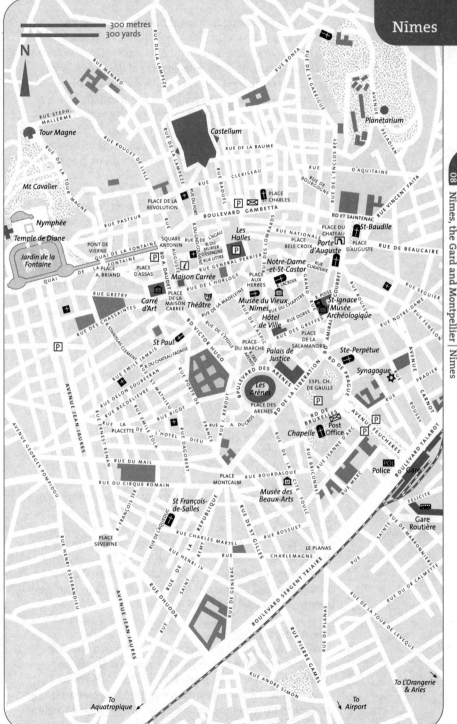

300 metres
300 yards

N

Tour Magne

Mt Cavalier

Nymphée

Temple de Diane

Jardin de la
Fontaine

RUE STEPH.
MALLERME

RUE MENARD

RUE DE LA LAMPEZE

RUE DE LA LAMPEZE

RUE ROUGET DE LISLE

RUE DE LA TOUR MAGNE

RUE PASTEUR

PONT DE
VIERNE

QUAI DE LA FONTAINE
DE LA PLACE
A. BRIAND
FONTAINE

QUAI

RUE GRETRY

RUE DES CHASSAINTES

RUE STANISLAS CLEMENT

Castellum

RUE DE LA BAUME

RUE BADUEL

CLERISEAU

PLACE DE LA
REVOLUTION

BOULEVARD GAMBETTA

SQUARE
ANTONIN

R. DU
MURIER
D'ESPAGNE

RUE DE L'AGAU

BD A. DAUDET

RUE LITTRE

RUE GENERAL PERRIER

Maison Carrée

PLACE
D'ASSAS

RUE DE L'HORLOGE

PLACE DE LA
MAISON
CARREE

Carré
d'Art

Théâtre

RUE DE LA MADELEINE

RUE EMILE JAMAIS

CR. DU CHATEAU FADAISE

St Paul

BD VICTOR HUGO

RUE DE L'ETOILE

RUE DE L'ASPIC

PLACE
AUX
HERBES

Les
Halles

RUE NATIONAL

RUE DES LOMBARDS

PLACE
BELE CROIX

Notre-Dame
-et-St-Castor

R. LACROIX

Musée du Vieux
Nîmes

RUE DU CHAPITRE

Hôtel
de Ville

RUE DOREE

PLACE DU CHATEAU

Porte
d'Auguste

RUE CURATERIE

GRAND RUE

R. POISE

St-Ignace
Musée
Archéologique

PLACE
ST CHARLES

PLACE
D'AUGUSTE

St-Baudile

BD ET SAINTENAC

RUE VINCENT FAITA

RUE DE BEAUCAIRE

RUE SEGUIER

RUE AMIRAL COURBET

RUE DES GREFFES

RUE NOTRE-DAME

RUE FENELON

PLACE
DE LA
SALAMANDRE

Ste-Perpétue

Synagogue

BD DE PRAGUE

PRADIER

AVENUE CARNOT

RUE ROUSSY

RUE DE L'ENCLOS REY

RUE DE LA GARIGUE

RUE BONFA

AVENUE PELADIAN

Planétarium

D'AQUITAINE

RUE
DE
BOURGOGNE

PLACE
DU
CHATEAU

St Paul

BD VICTOR HUGO

RUE PORTE DE FRANCE

RUE DELON SOUBEYRAN

RUE MATHIEU LACROIX

RUE BECDELIEVRE

RUE BIGOT

RUE J. REBOUL

Palais de
Justice

PLACE
DU MARCHE

BD DES ARENES

Les
Arènes

PLACE DES
ARENES

BD DE LA LIBERATION

ESPL. CH.
DE GAULLE

BD DE
BRUXELLES

Chapelle

Post
Office

AVENUE FEUCHERES

POL
Police

Gare

BOULEVARD TALABOT

FELICITE

Gare
Routière

RUE SAINTE DE MARRONNIERS

AVENUE JEAN JAURES

AVENUE GEORGES POMPIDOU

RUE LA
PLACETTE DE L'HOTEL DIEU

RUE EMILE ZOLA

RUE ERNEST RENAN

RUE A. DUCROS

RUE DAGOBERT

PLACE
MONTCALM

RUE DE LA CITE FOULC

RUE JEANNE D'ARC

RUE BRICONNET

RUE MARC

RUE DU MAIL

RUE DU CIRQUE ROMAIN

RUE BOURDALOUE

Musée des
Beaux-Arts

RUE FRANÇOIS 1ER

PLACE
SEVERINE

R. HENRI ESPERANDIEU

St François-
de-Salles

RUE DE L'AQUEDUC

RUE DHUODA

RUE SAINT REMY

RUE HENRI IV

RUE CHARLES MARTEL

RUE DE LA REPUBLIQUE

RUE DE ST GILLES

RUE BOSSUET

LE PLANAS

CHARLEMAGNE

RUE GENERAC

BOULEVARD SERGENT TRIAIRE

RUE PLANAS

RUE PIERRE GAMEL

RUE ANDRE SIMON

RUE DE LA TOUR DE LEVEQUE

RUE DU DR CALMETTE

To
Aquatropique

To
Airport

To L'Orangerie
& Arles

Nîmes declined along with Rome; the city contracted and became a mere frontier post for the Visigothic kings of Toledo. After a brief Arab occupation in the 8th century, Nîmes was ruled by Frankish viscounts, who restored some of the town's former prestige in the 11th century by dominating Narbonne and Carcassonne; the Roman amphitheatre was transformed into a fort, the *castrum arenae*, whose knights played a major role in urban affairs. Nîmes, like much of Languedoc, got into trouble with the Church in the early 13th century by taking up the Cathar heresy, although at the approach of the terrible Simon de Montfort the city surrendered without a fight.

Catholicism never went down well in Nîmes, and, when the Protestant alternative presented itself in the 16th century, three-quarters of the population took to the new religion immediately and attacked the other quarter's churches and prelates. The terror reached a peak with the 1567 massacre of 200 priests, monks and nuns, known as the **Michelade**, but continued off and on until the Edict of Nantes (1598); this brought Nîmes enough peace for its Protestants to set up a prosperous textile industry, and the city seemed happy to settle down as the Huguenot capital of the south.

Louis XIV spoiled everything by revoking the Edict in 1685; troops were quartered in the Huguenots' homes, forcing them to abjure their faith or face exile or slavery aboard the king's galleys. Nîmes and the Cévennes, the wild hilly region to the north, responded with the desperate war of the **Camisards**, tying up an important part of the French army by inventing, or reinventing, many of the techniques used in modern guerrilla warfare.

After the troubles, Nîmes went back to its second concern after religion: textiles. Its heavy-duty blue *serge de Nîmes* was reduced to the more familiar 'denim' in 1695, in London – where many of the Protestants went in exile – and it was exported widely. Some of it found its way to California, where in 1848 a certain Levi Strauss discovered it to be perfect for outfitting goldrushers.

More recently, Nîmes made the headlines on 3 October 1988, when violent storms in the rocky hills of the *garrigues* brought down a torrent that engulfed the city in eight feet of mud. The victory of the French Davis Cup tennis team at Nîmes' Roman arena in 1991 and the opening in May 1993 of the Carré d'Art have done much to dispel this muddy memory.

Arènes
www.arenes-nimes.com; open summer 9–7 (tickets until 6.30); winter 9.30–5 (tickets until 4.15); closed public holidays and events; adm

The Arènes

Twentieth in size, but the best preserved of the 70 surviving amphitheatres of the Roman world, the arena at Nîmes (late 1st century AD) is just a bit smaller than its twin at Arles in Provence. Like the Maison Carrée, it escaped being cannibalized for its stone by being put to constant use: as a castle for the Visigoths and the knightly militia of the Frankish viscounts, who bricked up the arches facing the Palais de Justice and made them their headquarters; then, after union with France, as a slum, where some 2,000 people lived in shanties jammed into the arches, seats and *vomitoria*. When restorers came in 1809 to clear it out, they had to shovel 20ft of rubbish to reach the floor where the sands (*arènes*) were spread to soak up the blood of the men and animals who died here to amuse the crowd.

When new, the arena could accommodate 24,000 people, who were able to reach or leave their seats in only a few minutes thanks to an ingenious system of five concentric galleries and 126 stairways. Near the top of the arena are holes pierced in the stone for the supports of the canvas awning (*velum*) that sheltered the spectators from sun and rain – an idea that Mayor Bousquet revived in 1988, with a mobile plexiglass and aluminium roof that from the air looks like a giant toilet seat, but which allows the amphitheatre to host events all year round. The event that has packed the crowds in since 1853 is the *corrida*, a sport always close to the hearts of the Nîmois – even in ancient times, judging by the two bulls carved over the main gate.

Wandering around the outside, note the curious Siamese-twin figure embedded in the wall of the Palais de Justice, known as the '**Four-Legged Man**', made of ancient sculptural fragments pieced together wrongly long ago. You may also notice Rue Bigot, named after a 19th-century fable writer from Nîmes. The name is particularly pertinent to local attitudes in the Wars of Religion. 'Bigot', after all, comes from the Old French and refers to the first religious intolerance to shake Nîmes – the conflict between the Catholicism of the Franks and the Arianism of the Visigoths, or *Bigothi*.

Crocodiles Galore, the Maison Carrée and the Carré d'Art

The *hôtels particuliers* in the historic centre – the area between the Arènes, the Maison Carrée and the cathedral – date mostly from the 17th and 18th centuries, when Nîmes' textile magnates and financiers enjoyed their greatest prosperity. Beginning at the Four-Legged Man, **Rue de l'Aspic** (which in French evokes vipers as well as jelly) is one of the candidates for the *cardo*, the shorter of the two main streets of a Roman town. **Place du Marché** opens up to the left, the city's most charming square and site of a fine new **crocodile fountain** designed by Martial Raysse. Four more examples of the city's saurian emblem (donated by well-wishers to the city between 1597 and 1703) can be seen stuffed and dangling over the stair in the high-tech designer interior of the 18th-century **Hôtel de Ville**, to the right of Rue de l'Aspic.

Around the corner, at 16 Rue Dorée, Nîmes' very own Académie meets behind the elaborate portal of the 17th-century **Hôtel de l'Académie**. This body was granted the same privileges as the Académie Française in 1682 by Louis XIV, and even today the Académiciens of Nîmes may sit with their fellows in Paris.

To the south, the amphibian community is represented in **Place de la Salamandre**, named after François Ier's totem animal. Many Renaissance rulers had similar emblems, and used to represent them in works of art; François chose the salamander for the belief that it could survive in fire – the first fabrics woven of asbestos were called 'salamander skins'. The salamander sculpture that once adorned this square now stands in the courtyard of the Archaeology Museum, but note the square's 17th-century **Hôtel de Chazelles**, another fine example of civic architecture.

To the north stands Nîmes' **Cathédrale Notre-Dame-et-St-Castor**, which was consecrated in 1096 but almost completely flattened by rampaging Huguenots in 1597 and 1622, who spared only the campanile to use as a watchtower. Across the façade runs a vigorous frieze of the Old Testament. Lower down, and sadly damaged, are reliefs of Samson and the lion, and Alexander the Great being pulled up to heaven by a pair of griffons, coaxed by a piece of liver dangled over their heads – a favourite medieval fancy. There's a Romanesque frieze nearby, on the corner of Place aux Herbes and Rue de la Madeleine, adorning a rare 12th-century house (the **Maison Romane**).

Of course, more remarkable still is the state of that graceful little 1st-century BC temple known as the **Maison Carrée**, just off the Via Domitia in Place de la Maison Carrée. The best-preserved Roman temple anywhere, it was built by the great General Agrippa (who also built the Pantheon in Rome) and was dedicated to the Imperial cult of Augustus' grandsons, Caius and Lucius, known as the 'Princes of Youth' – their 'deification' a form of flattery to the emperor. Called *carrée*, or square, because of its right angles and 'long' square shape (85ft by 50ft), it has a *cella* (or cult sanctuary) that is perfectly intact, as are the Corinthian columns of the porch. Nîmes always found it useful for something, most notably as the meeting hall of the consuls and least notably as a stable. The temple was originally surrounded by a colonnaded forum, similar to the Imperial Fora of Rome.

In his 1787 *Travels*, Englishman Arthur Young couldn't get enough of the Maison Carrée: 'What an infatuation in modern architects, that can overlook the chaste and elegant simplicity of taste manifest in such a work, and yet rear such piles of laboured foppery and heaviness as are to be met with in France.' One modern architect (and another Englishman), Sir Norman Foster, was given the chance to respond to Mr Young's gripe, on a site next to the

Maison Carrée
open summer 10–7.30; winter 10–1 and 2–5; adm

Maison Carrée, now unimaginatively known as the **Carré d'Art**. Inaugurated in May 1993, this palace of glass and steel houses a modern art museum, audiovisual centre and extensive library, and cost 400 million francs to build. While many of ex-Mayor Bousquet's critics condemned the project as further evidence of his advanced megalomania, the mayor cheerfully pointed out that his own *'petits projets'* in Nîmes were merely a response to President Mitterrand's *'Grands Projets'* in Paris. The ancient columns of the Maison Carrée are reflected in Sir Norman's own slender columns of steel; the walls and even the stairways are of glass to let light stream through the building. Inside, the **Musée d'Art Contemporain** on the first floor contains over 250 post-1960 works, plus temporary exhibitions. The library has over 360,000 volumes and is especially strong in two local obsessions – Protestantism and bullfighting. The smaller library, part of the Musée d'Art, has 12,000 works dedicated to art post 1950.

Musée d'Art Contemporain
t 04 66 76 35 70; open Tues–Sun 10–6; closed Mon; adm; library open Tues and Thurs 10.30–7, Wed, Fri and Sat 10.30–6; museum library open mid-Aug–mid-July Tues–Sat pm only plus Sat am; adm; guided tours Tues–Sun 4.30 during hols, otherwise Sat and Sun only

Water and Other Mysteries

A block north of the Carré d'Art is another recent project, the **Place d'Assas**, designed by Martial Raysse as a kind of expiatory gesture, one imagines, to the two religions that went down in Nîmes without a fight: that of the Celts (the two figures in the central fountain represent the indigenous gods, 'Nemausa' and 'Nemausus') and the Cathars (the mysterious seven-pointed stars, the magic square *Rotas Sator*, and inscription *'Les Nuages Sont Sans Age'*). It's all a bit silly, and no one seems to pay much attention to it any more. The statue at the west end, on the other hand, is of Ernest Denis of Nîmes, whose writing championed the founding of Czechoslovakia in 1918. Just north, in the irregular polygonal **Square Antonin**, is a 19th-century statue of Emperor Antoninus Pius (whose family was from Nîmes), holding his hand out, as the Nîmois say, to see if it's raining.

A short stroll to the west down Quai de la Fontaine is Nemausus' first abode, the great spring that originates in the karst caverns of the *garrigue*, to gush out at the foot of Mont Cavalier. It was domesticated as the **Jardin de la Fontaine** in the 18th century, and the waters were marshalled to flow in a neo-Roman *nymphaeum* below a maze of balustrades and urns. Narrow, stone-walled canals surround the gardens and extend down the centre of the Quai de la Fontaine into the surrounding neighbourhoods; altogether, the ensemble is one of the loveliest city parks in France. In ancient times a complex of temples and sanctuaries stood here, of which only the so-called **Temple de Diane** remains.

Paths wind up among the flowerbeds and leafy arbours of Mont Cavalier to the oldest Roman monument in Gaul, the octagonal

Wine: Costières-de-Nîmes

Covering 24 *communes* between Estézargues and Vauvert, the AOC Région des Costières de Nîmes rides the high terraces and hills of the Rhône, where the vineyards are planted amid round pebbles (*les grès*). Near Nîmes, the rough landscape is tempered by the sea, and although the district is best known for rosés, the reds (similar to Côtes du Rhône) and whites (made from clairette, grenache blanc, maccabéo and marsanne) are good, inexpensive, fresh young wines; the reds are only aged two or three years at the most.

The easiest place to get acquainted with them is near Nîmes' airport at the prize-winning **Château de la Tuilerie**, Rte de St-Gilles, **t** 04 66 70 07 52, *www.chateautuilerie.com*, which also sells rum from Martinique. Or try the medal-winning reds and rosés from the **Domaine des Goubins** just outside Nîmes (*not open to the public*). For an inexpensive bottle of sunshine, look out for rosé Marcellus from **Les Caves Saint-Ronain**.

In Nîmes itself, try the **Syndicat Vignerons des Costières de Nîmes**, 19 Place Aristide Briand, Quai de la Fontaine (near the Impérator Hotel), **t** 04 66 36 96 20, for tastings, information on local wines and, as an added bonus, a *bodega* at *feria* time. The Syndicat des Costières does not sell to the public, but will direct you to local producers and *caves* in town.

Tour Magne
*viewing platform
open summer daily
9.30–7; winter daily
9.30–1 and 2–4.30; adm*

Tour Magne. No record of its origin or purpose has survived, though some speculate that it may have been a trophy dedicated to the opening of the Via Domitia, or a signal tower, or simply the mightiest of the 30 towers in the city wall – a sort of 'homage tower' like those of Aigues-Mortes and other medieval cities. Although 106ft high today, the tower was once half as big again; stairs spiral up to the viewing platform. The Tour Magne made news in 1601, when a gardener named François Traucat read Nostradamus' prediction that a gardener would uncover an immense buried treasure. As it was commonly believed that the Romans, like leprechauns, hid pots of gold in their ruins, Traucat decided the treasure must be buried under the Tour Magne. Henri IV gave him permission to dig (at his own expense, and with two-thirds of the loot going to the crown), but instead of finding gold he found another pre-Roman tower around which the even larger Tour Magne had been built. No one could identify the rubble at the time, and the Consul of Nîmes, fearing that any more digging would undermine the Tour Magne, ordered the now bankrupt Traucat back to his garden.

Two hundred years later there was another discovery of something very rare, though not of gold, down below in Rue Lampèze: a round basin 18ft in diameter called the **Castellum**, where the water rushing in from the Pont du Gard was distributed to the city through 10 pipes of lead. The only other one to survive is at Pompeii. Like so many things in Nîmes it was built under Augustus, and to him was dedicated the city's east gate on the Via Domitia (Rue Nationale), the **Porte d'Auguste**. Built in 15 BC, it had two large entrances for vehicles, and two smaller ones for pedestrians.

Nîmes' Caesar from 1983 to 1995, Mayor Bousquet, hired Jean Nouvel (architect of Paris' Institut du Monde Arabe) to design a subsidized housing project known as **Nemausus I**. It's south of the station, off Avenue du Général Leclerc, and looks like a pair of beached ocean liners from the future. It isn't really a nice place to visit, and you wouldn't want to live there.

Museum-crawling

The former Jesuit college at 13 bis Boulevard Amiral Courbet was, after the Edict of Nantes, diplomatically divided into a Protestant half and a Catholic half. Nowadays, the division is between pot-shards and possums, the first half devoted to archaeology and the second to natural history. The **Musée Archéologique** is filled with odds and ends for the expert, such as France's largest collection of ancient inscriptions, but there are some crowd-pleasers as well: the 4th- to 3rd-century BC figure of the *Guerrier de Grézen*, in his curved hood-helmet and belt, and nearby a rare Celtic lintel, the *Linteau de Nages*, found near the *oppidum*'s spring (*see* 'Nages', p.122). The lintel has a frieze of galloping horses and human heads – favourite Celtic motifs, but rarely carved with such pizzazz. Upstairs is a fine collection of ancient glass and everyday Roman items, Greek vases, bronze figurines and miniature altars, some bearing the mallet of the Celtic god Sucellus, whom the Romans adapted to become their Silvanus. The medieval collection is displayed in temporary exhibitions.

The other half of the college is the charmingly old-fashioned **Musée d'Histoire Naturelle**, home to a collection of those mysterious menhirs-with-personality, the statue-steles. Carved with stylized faces, and sometimes with arms, a knife and a belt (*c.* 2000 BC), they are similar to those found in the Hérault, and also in Tuscany and Corsica. Large glass cases of scary masks and spears and turn-of-the-20th-century photographs fill the ethnographic hall, and beyond, a brave little natural history collection that may be the highlight of your trip to Nîmes. It features a 9ft stuffed moose, a beaver foetus, a wide selection of faded bats, two-headed lambs and deformed kittens, pine-cone-shaped animals called pangolins, stuffed *corrida* bulls from the 1890s, two baby rabbits in formaldehyde retrieved from the belly of a snake, and an armadillo 'captured near the Pont du Gard'.

Adjacent is the Jesuit church **St-Ignace** (1678), a fine piece of Baroque architecture with an unusual pattern of vaults and openings, now used for exhibitions.

For the **Musée du Vieux Nîmes** in Place aux Herbes, follow Grand-Rue behind the museums, north to Rue Lacroix. It has an exceptional collection of 19th-century textiles and 500 print designs from Nîmes' wool and silk industries – a real eye-opener for anyone who thought the paisley design was invented in the 1960s. There are 17th-century carved *armoires*, painted ones from

---

Musée Archéologique
t 04 66 76 74 80; open Tues–Sun 10–6; closed Mon; programme of specialist guided tours

Musée d'Histoire Naturelle
t 04 66 76 73 45; open Tues–Sun 10–6; closed Mon

Musée du Vieux Nîmes
t 04 66 76 73 70; open Tues–Sun 10–6; closed Mon

Uzès, a Charles X billiard table, thousands of socks, a 19th-century bed supported by weightlifters, and ceramics and an abundance of curios.

Musée des Beaux-Arts
t 04 66 67 38 21; open Tues–Sun 10–6; closed Mon

The **Musée des Beaux-Arts** is on the other side of the Arènes, 440 yards along on Rue de la Cité-Foulc, in a charming 1907 building by a local architect, who chiselled the façade with the names of Nîmes' painters and sculptors, and optimistically left plenty of room for future geniuses. It was opulently restored by architect Jean-Michel Wilmotte in 1986–7. In the centre of the ground floor is an enormous Roman mosaic, *The Betrothal of Admetus*, surrounded by a frieze of scenes. Upstairs, look out for two Venetian paintings: an example of 15th-century retro in Michele Giambono's *Mystic Marriage of St Catherine*, and one of Jacopo Bassano's finest works, *Susanna and the Elders* (1585), with a serene bunny rabbit in the corner. As usual, it's the Dutch paintings, with their buxom wenches and oyster-slurping sessions, that one would most like to be in. Of the French offerings, the outstanding painting is Paul Delaroche's *Cromwell Looking into the Coffin of Charles I*, an 18th-century painting as memorable as its subject is odd.

Planétarium
t 04 66 67 60 94; public shows Wed, Sat and Sun 3pm, Fri 8.30pm; adm

If you are tired of terrestrial culture, Nîmes' small **Planétarium** off Avenue du Mont Duplan takes you to the stars with glittering displays of the universe.

Musée des Cultures Taurines
t 04 66 36 83 77; open mid-May–early Nov Tues–Sun 10–6; closed Mon; adm

Appropriately located near to the Arena, the **Musée des Cultures Taurines** at 6 Rue Alexandre Ducros is one of only a few museums dedicated to bullfighting in France. Over 8,000 exhibits illustrate the different forms of the fight, the history of the *tauromachie*, the famous *toreros*, and the culture of the *corridas*.

Tourist Information in Nîmes

ⓘ **Nîmes >**
6 Rue Auguste, near the Maison Carrée, t 04 66 58 38 00, www.ot-nimes.fr; open daily all year

A tourist **mini-train** does the sites April–Oct, non-stop 10–7.30 in July and Aug, leaving from the Esplanade, opposite the Palais de Justice, next to the roundabout.

Market Days in Nîmes

Mon: Parking du Stade des Costières, flowers.
Mon am: Av Jean Jaurès, flea market.
Tues am: Av de Lattre de Tassigny.
Fri am: Bd Jean Jaurès Sud, organic and farmers' market.

Festivals in Nîmes

To find out what's going on, call the tourist office on t 04 66 58 38 00.

There are usually a couple of bullfights each month in the summer, but, to see the best *toreros* come for the *ferias* at Carnival time in February/early March or the third week of September, and especially the six-day *Feria de Pentecôte* (Whitsun), which draws even bigger crowds than Munich's *Oktoberfest*. As in Seville, people open up their homes as *bodegas* to take the overflow of aficionados from the cafés, and the drinking and music go on until dawn. The Arènes come to life during July, with contemporary and popular music at the *Festival de Nîmes*, *www.festivaldenimes.com*.

Where to Stay in Nîmes

Nîmes ✉ 30000

Reservations are essential during the *ferias*, and prices may also be higher.

Very Expensive (€€€€)

****Hôtel Impérator Concorde, Quai de la Fontaine, t 04 66 21 90 30, *www. hotel-imperator.com*. A 19th-century dowager with a facelift, a lovely garden, TVs, air-conditioning, and Nîmes' top restaurant to boot (*see* 'Eating Out'). *Open all year*.

***L'Hacienda, Le Mas de Brignon, Marguerittes ✉ 30320 (8km northeast on N86), t 04 66 75 02 25, *www.hotel-hacienda-nimes.com*. A large farm-house in the *garrigue*, converted into a hotel with a spacious swimming pool, terraces and an excellent restaurant (€€€; dinner only), part of the Relais du Silence group. *Book out of season*.

Expensive (€€€)

***New Hôtel La Baume, 21 Rue Nationale, t 04 66 76 28 42, *www. new-hotel.com*. Stylish modern rooms in a 17th-century mansion with a garden terrace. More expensive during *ferias*.

Expensive–Moderate (€€€–€€)

***L'Orangerie, 755 Rue de la Tour de l'Evêque, t 04 66 84 50 57, *www. orangerie.fr*. Best Western hotel just outside the centre with a garden, small pool and restaurant (€€). *Open all year*.

Moderate (€€)

***Royal, 3 Bd Alphonse Daudet, t 04 66 58 28 27, *www.royalhotel-nimes.com*. A delightful Art Deco hotel with artistic rooms and a palm-fronded lobby and restaurant serving Spanish specialities (€€€). Reserve early in the summer because it fills up fast. Parking under the hotel. *Restaurant closed lunch and Sun*.

**Kyriad, 10 Rue Roussy, t 04 66 76 16 20, *www.hotel-kyriad-nimes.com*. An old house (with a private garage) converted into an air-conditioned hotel with attractive retro furnishings.

**Hôtel de l'Amphithéâtre, 4 Rue des Arènes, t 04 66 67 28 51, *http:// perso.orange.fr/hotel-amphitheatre*. Sweetly restored 18th-century building in the old town, with antique furniture and nice big bathrooms. *Closed Nov and Feb school hols, and weekends in Jan*.

Inexpensive (€)

**Hôtel Central, 2 Place du Château, t 04 66 67 27 75, *www.hotel-central. org*. A small, simple, unpretentious hotel, with several rooms looking out over the roofs of the old city. Private garage, and rooms for up to 4 people.

**Hôtel de la Mairie, 11 Rue des Greffes, t 04 66 67 65 91. Rugged, simple and in the historic centre.

*Hôtel Brasserie des Arènes, 4 Bd des Arènes, t 04 66 67 23 05, *www. brasserie-arenes.com*. Not very quiet, but the brasserie within the hotel serves Provençal cuisine (€€).

Auberge de Jeunesse, 257 Chemin de l'Auberge de Jeunesse, t 04 66 68 03 20, *www.fuaj.org*. On a hill 2km from the centre (bus I from the station, direction Alès or Villeverte, get off at stop '*Stade*' and follow signs).

Eating Out in Nîmes

Nîmes isn't exactly famous for its restaurants, but it has some delicious specialities: *brandade de morue* (pounded cod mixed with fine olive oil), a recipe said to date back to Roman times, and *tapenade d'olives*, an appetizer made of olives, anchovies and herbs. Its *pélardons*, the little goat's cheeses from the *garrigues*, are among the best anywhere. In the sweet category, the city is proudest of its *croquants Villaret*, almond biscuits cooked by the same family in the same oven since 1775, available at **Maison Villaret**, 13 Rue de la Madeleine, t 04 66 67 41 79.

L'Enclos de la Fontaine, Hôtel Impérator (*see* above), t 04 66 21 90 30 (€€€). *Brandade* is often on the menu at one of Nîmes' top restaurants, and alongside the classics (*escalope de foie gras*, *rouget*) the chef cooks up imaginative, subtle dishes that melt in your mouth, served outside in the courtyard.

Magister, 5 Rue Nationale, t 04 66 76 11 00 (€€€). A smart Nîmes restaurant with good service and highly professional cooking (*brandade* and *taureau* – bull's meat – *au pistou* especially recommended), as well as a good local wine list. *Closed Mon, Sat lunch and Sun*.

Le Lisita, 2 Bd des Arènes, t 04 66 67 29 15, *www.lelisita.com* (€€€). Next to the amphitheatre, a restaurant decorated with bullfighting memorabilia, serving regional and gastronomic cuisine. *Closed Sun and Mon.*

(★) Le Jardin d'Hadrien >

Le Jardin d'Hadrien, 11 Rue de l'Enclos Rey, t 04 66 21 86 65 (€€€–€€). A favourite, with its beamed dining room and veranda; try the cod with olive oil, or courgette flowers stuffed with *brandade*. *Closed Nov and Feb school hols and end of Aug; July–Sept closed Sun, and Mon lunch; Oct–June closed Wed.*

Aux Plaisirs des Halles, 4 Rue Littré, t 04 66 36 01 02 (€€€–€€). Cosy little bistro near the market. Ask the chef for aïoli with vegetables or *brandade* with truffles and black olives. *Closed Sun, Mon, early Nov and most of Feb.*

Nicolas, Rue Poise (off Bd Amiral Courbet), t 04 66 67 50 47 (€€€–€€). One of the more affordable fine restaurants in town, and always busy. *Closed Sat lunch, Mon, plus Sun eve in April–Oct, plus most of July.*

Le Petit Bec, 87 bis Rue de la République, t 04 66 38 05 83 (€€€–€€). A tempting selection of seasonal dishes; eat in the garden. *Closed Sun eve, Mon, most of Aug and of Feb.*

La Fontaine du Temple, 22 Rue de la Curaterie, t 04 66 21 21 13 (€€). Friendly bar and restaurant; a good place to try *taureau* or lamb with thyme. *Closed Sun.*

Le Chapon Fin, 3 Place du Château-Fadaise (behind St Paul's church), t 04 66 67 34 73 (€€). Serves local, filling dishes. *Closed Wed lunch, Sat lunch and Sun.*

Au Flan Coco, 31 Rue du Mûrier d'Espagne, t 04 66 21 84 81 (€€). A delightful tiny restaurant run by two *traiteurs* alongside their shop; the food comes fresh from the market

and is whipped up before your eyes. *Closed Sun, 3 wks Aug and 3 wks Feb.*

Entertainment and Nightlife in Nîmes

Clubs and Bars

O'Flaherty's, 21 Bd Amiral Courbet, t 04 66 67 22 63. Nîmes' Irish pub. *Closed until 5pm at weekends.*

Café Napoléon, **Bar de la Bourse** and several other bars are on Bd V. Hugo.

La Bodeguita, 3 Bd Alphonse Daudet, t 04 66 58 28 29. A *tapas* and music bar (jazz, tango, flamenco and salsa) in the Royal Hôtel, especially popular during *feria* time.

Les Trois Maures, 10 Bd des Arènes, t 04 66 36 23 23. A big traditional brasserie hung with tributes to bullfighting and rugby. *Closed Sun in July and Aug.*

Haddock Café, 13 Rue de l'Agau, t 04 66 67 86 57, *www.haddock-cafe.com*. Popular local club and café with food served late, music concerts and art exhibitions. *Closed Sat lunch and Sun except July and Aug.*

Classical Music and Theatre

Opera, dance and concerts take place in July, Aug and Sept. For events at Les Arènes, ask the tourist office.

Cinema

Le Sémaphore, 25 Rue Porte de France, t 04 66 67 83 11, *www.semaphore. free.fr*. Sometimes shows films in their original language (*v.o.*).

Leisure

Aquatropic, 39 Chemin de l'Hostellerie, near the *autoroute* exit Nîmes-Ouest, t 04 66 38 31 00, *www. vert-marine.com/nimes*. Indoor/outdoor water park, with sauna, tennis and keep-fit centre.

The Northern Gard

The Pont du Gard and Around

By 19 BC the fountain of Nemausus could no longer slake Nîmes' thirst, and the search was on for a new source. The Romans were obsessed with the quality of their water, and when they found a

Getting to and around the Northern Gard

STDG-Cévennes Cars buses (t 04 66 29 17 27) from Nîmes, Uzès and Avignon pass frequently within a kilometre of the Pont du Gard. Note that you can no longer **drive** over the Pont du Gard, but will have to leave your car in one of the pay car parks (€5) on either side.

Canoe and **kayak hire** is available upstream at Collias: contact **Kayak Vert**, t 04 66 22 80 76, www.canoe-france.com/riviere-gardon-canoe-france.html.

crystal-clear spring called the Eure near Uzès, the fact that it was 48km away hardly posed an obstacle to antiquity's star engineers. The resulting aqueduct, built under Augustus' son-in-law Agrippa, was like a giant needle hemming the landscape, piercing tunnels through hills and looping its arches over the open spaces of the garrigues, and all measured precisely to allow a slope of 0.07 centimetres per metre. Where the water had to cross the gorge of the unpredictable River Gard (or Gardon, as it's usually called), the Roman engineers knuckled down, ordered a goodly supply of neatly dressed stone from the nearby quarries at Vers and built the Pont du Gard, at 157ft the highest of all Roman aqueducts and, along with the span in Segovia, the best preserved in the world.

The Pont du Gard

② Pont du Gard
www.pontdugard.fr

No matter how many photos you've seen before, the aqueduct's three tiers of arches of golden stone without mortar makes a brave and lovely sight; since the 1920s the natural setting and river have been maintained as intact as possible. What the photos never show are the two million people who come to pay it homage every year – the Pont du Gard is the second most visited site in France outside Paris – and you may well find it more evocative if you arrive very early in the morning or about an hour before sunset, when the site regains some of its ancient dignity. As you walk over it, note how it's slightly curved (the better to stand up to floods) and how the Roman engineers left cavities and protruding stones to support future scaffolding. In the 18th century, the bottom tier was expanded to take a road. This is now limited to pedestrians, due to the damaging vibrations caused by cars. A major renovation project has been completed, with new visitors' centres on either side of the bridge, an auditorium in the former quarry, a pedestrianized promenade and restaurants and shops. **La Grande Expo du Pont du Gard** presents archaeological and engineering projects for children, films and permanent exhibitions. In summer the site is lit up at night. For the restoration, the ancient quarries were reopened in Vers (see p.99), so the patches should blend right in. Some of the original blocks weigh six tonnes; many have inscriptions, a few left by the Roman builders, but most left by the compagnons, French journeyman masons who, as part of their training, travelled about France studying its most important

La Grande Expo du Pont du Gard

t 08 20 90 33 30; open May–Sept Tues–Sun 9.30–7, Mon 2.30–7.30; Oct–April Tues–Sun 9.30–5.30, Mon 2.30–5.30; adm; museum, cinema and discovery centre free first Sun of month in Nov–Mar

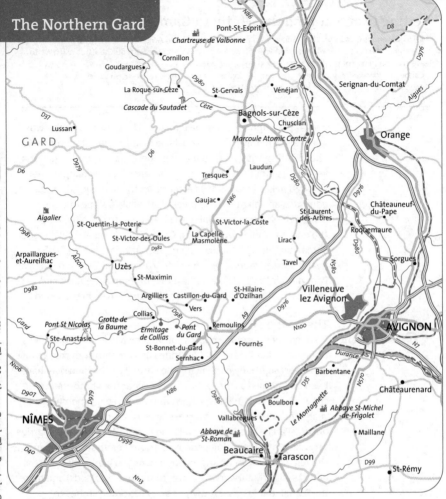

monuments. On the Remoulins side, a palaeolithic shelter, the **Abri Préhistorique de la Salpêtrière**, is being excavated (*no visitors*).

Paddling down the gorge and under the Pont du Gard in a kayak (*see p.97*) can be great fun, but avoid rush hour!

Wine Villages Around the Aqueduct

Just north, hilltop **Castillon-du-Gard** exudes medieval atmosphere, even if it was mostly rebuilt in the 16th century. Other attractions include views down to the Pont du Gard and a Romanesque chapel, St-Caprais, a setting for summer concerts and art exhibitions. East of Castillon, 11th-century **St-Hilaire-d'Ozilhan** is another charming village with an even older chapel, the Clastre, standing on its own just to the south. If it's *supermarchés* or bustling sprawl you're after, there's **Remoulins**, the area's market town and gateway to the **Fosses de Fournès**, a weirdly eroded lunar landscape to the east.

Southwest of Remoulins, you can explore traces of the aqueduct in the hills around **Sernhac** (the local IGN map may come in handy here). Here the Romans dug two impressive tunnels, one for the water and one for maintenance, still bearing the grooves left by the hammers that excavated them, stroke by stroke. The extraordinarily hard calcium deposits that accumulated in the water channels were chiselled out as a prized building material in the Middle Ages: some went into the walls of the fortified Romanesque church of **St-Bonnet-du-Gard**, near Sernhac.

Columns, Columns, Columns and a Bridge

The Roman (and later) stone quarries that produced the Pont du Gard are just off the Uzès road in **Vers**, another pleasant little village with another Romanesque church. Here, by the level crossing on the D227 and down the white road a couple of hundred yards to the south, stand a few aqueduct arches in a state of romantic abandon; other vestiges may be seen between Vers and Argilliers, just off the D3B, taking the side road that veers sharply to the left. At **Argilliers**, a Romanesque chapel and a neoclassical colonnaded funeral chapel dedicated to Saint Louis (Louis IX) on the D981 mark the entrance to one of Languedoc's most curious follies, the **Château de Castille**, the private mania of Froment Fromentès, Baron de Castille (1747–1829). One of the great travellers of his day, the baron was afflicted by a serious case of columnitis in Rome, and on his return to his estates in the Gard he erected over 200 pillars and columns, of which only some 50 survive, incorporated into garden follies, porticoes and hemicycles inspired by Bernini. Unfortunately, the estate isn't open.

South of Argilliers, down on the banks of the river, **Collias** has a popular beach, kayak rental and paths going up and down the river from the Pont du Gard to Pont St-Nicolas. The dramatic, wild beauty of the sheer-walled Gardon gorge around Collias inspired an awe of religious proportions in the past, and there are several old hermitages in caves, one near the **Grotte de la Baume**, with an 11th-century chapel (an hour's walk), and another, the **Ermitage de Collias**, in a place so beautiful that it has been classed like a historic monument. People have worshipped here since prehistoric times – there's a little chapel by the cave, a Roman bridge and fountain dedicated to Minerva. Further west, the D112 will take you to **Pont St-Nicolas**, where an impressive 13th-century bridge takes the scenic old Nîmes–Uzès road over the Gardon gorge. Just above it to the west, the 12th-century church of **Ste-Anastasie** is all that survives of the Priory of St-Nicolas de Campagnac; built with exquisite care, the church is unusually large, sober, pure and empty.

(i) **Pont du Gard**
200 yards from the aqueduct on the Remoulins side of the Pont du Gard

(i) **Remoulins >**
Place des Grands Jours (by the eastern roundabout), t 04 66 37 22 34, www.ot-pontdugard.com; open July and Aug daily; June and Sept Mon–Fri and Sat am; Oct–May Mon–Fri

Where to Stay and Eat near the Pont du Gard

Castillon-du-Gard ✉ 30210

****Le Vieux Castillon**, Rue Turion Sabatier, **t** 04 66 37 61 61, *www.vieux castillon.com* (€€€€€–€€€€). A Relais & Châteaux hotel in the heart of the village. The rooms are in several houses connected by patios; there are tennis courts, a stunning swimming pool, and an excellent restaurant (€€€€) featuring dishes with truffles (the Gard produces 15% of France's crop), *langoustines* and various Côtes du Rhône wines. *Closed Jan–mid-Feb; restaurant closed Mon, and Tues lunch. Musical eves in spring and autumn.*

Remoulins ✉ 30210

***Le Colombier**, Rte du Pont du Gard, **t** 04 66 37 05 28 (€). With 18

comfortable rooms behind its broad awnings, and a restaurant (€€).

Pouzilhac ✉ 30210

****La Closeraie, t** 04 66 37 12 66, *www.lacloseraie.com* (€). North of Castillon, off the N 86. Comfortable rooms, some with balcony or private garden, and a friendly welcome. Ample grounds, parking and a pool. Restaurant (€€) with a terrace.

Collias ✉ 30210

*****Le Castellas**, Grand-Rue, **t** 04 66 22 88 88, *www.lecastellas.fr* (€€€). A friendly, Art Deco hotel spread out in two large houses, with a good and stylish restaurant (€€€€–€€€), plus a very pretty garden and deep enclosed pool. Cookery lessons are available. *Closed Jan, Feb and one week Dec; restaurant closed Wed except in July and Aug.*

Uzès, the First Duchy of France

Few towns of 8,000 souls have so bold a skyline of towers, or so little truck with the modern industrial world. Uzès seems to have been vacuum-packed when its wealthy, Protestant merchants of cloth and silk stockings picked up their bags and left at the Revocation of the Edict of Nantes. 'O little town of Uzès,' wrote André Gide (whose father was a Uzétien), 'were you in Umbria, the Parisians would flock to visit you!' Now they do, more or less, ever since 1962, when Uzès was selected as one of France's 50 *villes d'art*, entitling it to dig into the historical preservation funds set aside by De Gaulle's culture minister, André Malraux. Houses tumbling into ruin have been repaired, creating the perfect stage for films like *Cyrano de Bergerac*.

The Duché and Around

Duché
t 04 66 22 18 96, www.duche-uzes.fr; daily guided tours July–mid-Sept 10–1 and 2–6.30; mid-Sept–June 10–12 and 2–6; English translation available; adm exp

Café life in Uzès engulfs most of the available space in and around Place Albert Ier, just under the residence of the dukes, the Duché. The de Crussols of Uzès, claiming a family tree that sent out its first shoots under Charlemagne, became the first dukes and peers of the realm when the Duc de Montmorency forfeited the title (along with his head) in 1632. The current title-holders, a handsome young couple (he can often be spotted messing about with his car collection, she shopping with the kids in the local Carrefour supermarket), open their grand fortified home to visitors. The oldest section, the rectangular *donjon* called the **Tour Bermonde**, was built over a Roman tower in the 10th or 11th

Getting to and around Uzès

Uzès is linked by frequent **buses** to Nîmes, Avignon, Alès and the Pont du Gard, run by **STD Gard, t** 04 66 29 27 29, *www.stdgard.com*. For **bike** hire, try **Ets Payan**, 16 Av Général Vincent, **t** 04 66 22 13 94, or **Village Vélo** at St-Quentin-la-Poterie, **t** 04 66 37 27 33, *www.villagevelo.org*.

century; its crenellations were designed by the inevitable Viollet-le-Duc to replace the originals destroyed in the Revolution. The **Renaissance façade** in the central courtyard, a three-layered classical cake of Doric, Ionic and Corinthian orders, was constructed in 1550 and bears the motto of the dukes: *Ferro non auro* ('iron, not gold' – i.e. they were warriors, not financiers). This didn't keep the women of the family from sometimes donning the trousers: in 1565 the Duchess of Uzès became the first woman to be sent abroad as an ambassador, and then there's the amazing Duchess Anne, heiress to the Veuve Clicquot fortune, talented sculptress, enthusiastic huntress who rode until the age of 86, feminist, friend of anarchist Louise Michel (of Paris Commune fame) but still an ardent monarchist (she personally financed General Boulanger's attempt to overthrow the Republic to the tune of three million gold *écus*); the first woman in France to get a driving licence – and the first to get a speeding ticket. The tour of the Duché includes several furnished rooms.

Across Place du Duché is the attractive 18th-century **Hôtel de Ville**, while to the left of the Duché is a rock-cut **crypt** that lost its church (the Jesuits discovered it under their monastery); it is believed to date from the 4th century and has some primitive bas-reliefs of St John the Baptist and a convert. Uzès is a lot smaller than it seems, and a short wander will soon bring you to the irregular, arcaded, perfectly delightful **Place aux Herbes**, with its old plane trees, for centuries the centre of public life. The nearby church of **St-Etienne**, with an attractive Baroque façade, was rebuilt in the 18th century after destruction in the Wars of Religion two centuries earlier, and contains a handful of good paintings.

The Cathedral and Tour Fenestrelle

Set apart from the rest of the old town on a terrace, the 1671 **Ancien Palais Episcopal** was the seat of the powerful bishops of Uzès (64 bishops reigned here between the 5th century and the Revolution). A restoration attempt in the 1970s caused the interior to cave in behind the façade, although the right wing is in good enough nick to hold the eclectic collections of the **Musée Municipal**, with its fossils, paintings, and memorabilia of the Gide family.

Musée Municipal
t 04 66 22 40 23; open July and Aug Tues–Sun 10–12 and 3–6; Mar–June and Sept–Oct Tues–Sun 3–6; Nov and Feb Tues–Sun 2–5; closed Jan

Behind it stretches the pleasant **Promenade des Marronniers**, while, adjacent, the **Cathédrale St-Théodorit** was built in 1663, the third to occupy the site after its predecessors were destroyed in the Albigensian Crusade and the Wars of Religion. The quaint

08

Nîmes, the Gard and Montpellier | The Northern Gard: Uzès, the First Duchy of France neo-Romanesque façade was tacked on in 1875, with the idea of making a better partner to the stunning 12th-century **Tour Fenestrelle**, spared by the Protestants only because they found it useful as a watchtower. Unique in France, the 137ft tower is encircled by six storeys of double-lit windows, inspired by the Romanesque campaniles of Ravenna and Lombardy.

The cathedral's interior was severely damaged during the Revolution, when it was converted into a Temple of Reason, leaving only the peculiar upper gallery with its wrought iron railing (erected right after the revocation of the Edict of Nantes, to make room for the former Protestants) and the cathedral's pride and joy: a splendid **organ** of 1670, the only one in France to have retained its original painted shutters. Restored, it is the centrepiece of the mid-July/beginning-of-August festival, *Nuits Musicales d'Uzès*.

The odd building just below the terrace is the **Hôtel du Baron de Castille**, its façade adorned with columns; tall slender ones that don't conform to any classical order but which have a charm all their own. There is also a lovely herb garden in the Impasse Port Royal, the

Jardin Médiéval
t 04 66 22 38 21; open July and Aug daily 10.30–12.30 and 2–6; April–June and Sept Mon–Fri 2–6, Sat and Sun 10.30–12.30 and 2–6; Oct daily 2–5; closed Nov–Mar; adm

Jardin Médiéval, with a collection of carefully labelled local plants, and medicinal and culinary herbs used since the Middle Ages.

The funny little domed building abutting the belvedere-cum-*pétanque* courts on the far side of the cathedral is the so-called **Pavillon Racine**, named after the playwright and poet who, in spite of popular belief, never sat there, because it was built a quarter of a century too late. In 1661, at the age of 22, Racine spent a year with his uncle, the Vicar-General of Uzès, during which time his family hoped he would forget his foolish love of poetry and turn to the priesthood. Just the opposite happened. The climate, the friendly welcome, the charming girls, the food and the inscrutable *patois* made a great impression on the young man.

Around Uzès: The Uzège

Musée du Bonbon
t 04 66 22 74 39; open July–Aug daily 10–7; Sept–June Tues–Sun 10–1 and 2–6; closed most of Jan

Haras Nationaux d'Uzès
t 04 66 22 68 88, www.haras-nationaux. fr; open mid-Mar–June Mon–Sat 2–5; June–mid-Sept Tues and Thurs guided visits only; contact tourist office

Close enough to walk to from Uzès (from Parc du Duché, follow the Chemin André Gide; the Uzès tourist office sells a map), the **Vallée de l'Alzon** is the arcadian setting of the **Fontaine d'Eure**, the spring where the Roman aqueduct to Nîmes began; you can see the large basin that regulated the flow down the canal, excavated in 1993.

If you have kids, note that the Haribo candy company runs a **Musée du Bonbon** south of town at Pont des Charrettes, where you can watch them make little jelly crocodiles and more. Horse-lovers can meet the 65 stallions at the national stud farm, the **Haras Nationaux d'Uzès** at the Mas des Tailles, Route d'Alès.

The countryside around Uzès – where fields of asparagus, cherry orchards, forests of truffle oaks and vineyards alternate with

Musée 1900/ Musée du Train et du Jouet
t 04 66 22 58 64; open July and Aug daily 10–7; Mar–June Tues–Sun 10–12 and 2–7; Sept and Oct plus school hols in Feb, Nov and Dec Tues–Sun 10–12 and 2–6; rest of Nov and Dec Wed, Sat and Sun 10–12 and 2–6; closed Jan, and Feb outside hols; adm

Maison de la Terre
t 04 66 22 74 38; open July–Sept daily 10–1 and 3–6; April–June and Oct–Dec Wed–Sun 2–6; closed Jan–Mar

Musée de la Poterie Méditerranéenne
t 04 66 03 65 86

Jardin de la Noria
t 04 66 22 90 40, www.jardin-de-la-noria.com; open late June–late Sept Thurs–Sun 10–12 and 4–6.30; adm

garrigues – is dotted with delightful old villages. **Arpaillargues**, 4km west on the D982, has the added attraction of the **Musée 1900** at Moulin de Charlier, one man's amazing 30-year accumulation of period cars, motorcycles, gramophones, movie posters, locomotives and more; there is also a **Musée du Train et du Jouet**, with model trains and toys. Just west of Arpaillargues, the walled hilltop hamlet of **Aureilhac** has a superb view of Uzès' skyline. Nine kilometres northwest of Uzès, off the road to Alès, **Aigalier**, with its medieval lanes, dungeons, Saracen wall and Romanesque church all piled under a ruined castle, has long been a favourite subject of local painters.

The clay-rich soil north of Uzès has provided **St-Quentin-la-Poterie** with its vocation since the cows came home, and in some strange tangential way inspired its most famous son, Joseph Monier (1823–1906), to invent reinforced concrete. After producing thousands of amphorae, roof tiles, bricks, ceramic pipes and all the glazed tiles for the floors of the Popes' Palace in Avignon, the last ceramic factory closed in 1974; but in 1983 the kilns were fired up again as the village made a concerted effort to bring the potters back. Fifteen now live in the village year-round; you can visit their workshops or get an overview of their work at the **Maison de la Terre**, 5 Rue de la Fontaine. The adjoining **Musée de la Poterie Méditerranéenne** has a wonderful selection of examples of pottery from all over the Mediterranean, in a beautiful variety of glazes.

The **Jardin de la Noria** at the **Mas de Licorne**, on Chemin de Montaren, is a modernistic garden with contemporary sculptures, the name of which is inspired by an old *noria* (a wheel for lifting water into an aqueduct) on the site. You might catch one of the demonstrations of the *noria* in action.

Lovely **Lussan** is 18km north of Uzès, but well worth the detour: a nearly perfect, unspoiled medieval *village perché* below a 13th-century château. Near Lussan, the sheer gorge of the river Aiguillon, **Les Concluses**, makes a magnificent and easy walk in the summer when the river is dry, with potholes (*marmites*) formed by the river, eagle's nests and a remarkable steep and narrow **Portail** that closes in on top. Leave your car in one of the car parks along the D643; the walk takes about 30 minutes.

Northeast of Uzès, towards Bagnols-sur-Cèze, strange sandstone formations and quarzite quarries mark the environs of **St-Victor-des-Oules**, 'of the pots', another pottery village, this one specializing in stoneware (*grès*). Paths lead up **Mont Aigu**, for scant ruins of a 5th-century BC *oppidum* and superb views of the Cévennes to the west. Further east, the 12th-century château in **La Capelle-Masmolène** was the summer palace of the bishops of Uzès.

Market Days in Uzès

Uzès: Wed, and a massive general one on Sat. Also a *marché aux truffes*, Sat in Dec–Mar, Av de la Libération.

Where to Stay and Eat in and around Uzès

Uzès ✉ 30700

Uzès ›
Chapelle des Capucins, Place Albert 1er, t 04 66 22 68 88, www.uzes-tourisme.com; open June–Sept daily; Oct–May Mon–Fri and Sat am; guided tours include one at night in summer

***Hôtel d'Entraigues**, 8 Rue de la Calade, t 04 66 22 32 68 (€€€–€€). A fine old hotel fit for a duke in a 15th-century building opposite the cathedral, with a pool suspended over the dining room; try to get a room near the top. The restaurant, **Les Jardins de Castille** (€€€–€€), is elegant, with a classy lunch menu.

**Le St-Geniès, Route de St-Ambroix, t 04 66 222 999, www.hotel-saint genies.com (€€). An oasis of tranquility half a mile from the centre, with a charming pool and three-star rooms. You can hire bikes here, too. *Closed mid-Nov–Feb.*

**La Taverne, 7 Rue Sigalon (just off Place Albert 1er), t 04 66 22 13 10, www.lataverne-uzes.com (€€). Renovated rooms in the centre of town; you can dine on a pretty garden terrace (€€). *Closed Jan.*

Hôtel de l'Ancienne Gare ›

Hôtel de l'Ancienne Gare, outside Uzès on the Remoulins road, t 04 66 03 19 15, www.anciennegare.eu (€€). In a former train station; delicious, refined cooking. The menus change

frequently, and specialities include *tête de veau*.

La Boulangerie Uzétienne, 9 Place des Herbes. The best bakery in town, famous for the local speciality, *fougasse*, a savoury flat bread made with bits of bacon.

Around Uzès ✉ 30700

***Château d'Arpaillargues**, 4km west of Uzès at Arpaillargues et Aureillac, t 04 66 22 14 48, www.chateau darpaillargues.com (€€€€–€€€). Sleep in an antique bed (or just dine) at this 18th-century hotel. Marie d'Agoult was Liszt's muse and Wagner's mother-in-law, and a frequent guest. There's a pool and tennis courts, and courtyard restaurant (€€€) serving truffles in season. *Closed mid-Oct–mid-April.*

***Le Clos de Pradines**, Place du Pigeonnier, St-Quentin-la-Poterie, t 04 66 20 04 89, www.clos-de-pradines.com (€€). Elegant hotel at the top of the village with a pool and gastronomic restaurant (€€€–€€) with terrace. Part of Relais du Silence group. *Closed 2nd half Nov and mid-Jan–mid Feb.*

La Ferme de Cruviers, Montée de Larnac, Route de St-Ambroix, t 04 66 22 10 89, www.mas-cruviers.com (€). Orchards and views surround this B&B 5km north of Uzès. There's also a *table d'hôte* (€€) for guests only, serving dishes based on asparagus, chicken and duck.

Bagnols-sur-Cèze and the Cèze Valley

North of Uzès, where the river Cèze meets the Rhône, **Bagnols-sur-Cèze** is the traditional gateway – or exit – of Languedoc. The Romans named it for its sulphur baths, but these days Bagnols is more famous for its green beans (*les bagnolais*), and the nearby nuclear power plant at Marcoule, the construction of which saw Bagnols' population quadruple. In spite of all the new building, the narrow lanes of the old town have changed little; every now and then you'll see the city's quaint emblem of three golden pots.

Musée Albert André
t 04 66 50 50 56, www.gard-provencal.com/musees/aandre.htm; open Tues–Sun 10–12 and 2–6; closed Mon and Feb; adm

The prettiest square in Bagnols, central, arcaded **Place Mallet**, has a tower, the **Tour de l'Horloge**, erected by Philippe le Bel, and an 18th-century Hôtel de Ville housing the only real reason for visiting Bagnols: the **Musée Albert André**. In 1854, Léon Alègre, a local

Getting to and around Bagnols-sur-Cèze

The nearest passenger **train stations** are in Orange, Avignon and Nîmes. **Buses** link Bagnols with Uzès, Orange, Avignon and Nîmes.

humanist and Sunday painter, set up a museum to instruct his fellow citizens, with everything from Roman pots to paintings to stuffed animals. In 1918, Albert André, a painter friend of Renoir's, became volunteer curator and gave the museum the first provincial collection of contemporary art in France – only to have the whole thing go up in smoke in 1924, when the local firemen set it alight during their annual ball. It proved to be a blessing in disguise when Albert André sent out a message to France's artists: 'I am the curator of a museum of naked walls. Help me fill them!' They did. The eight rooms blaze with colour: Fauvist Albert Marquet's famous *14 Juillet au Havre* (1906); Pierre Bonnard's *Bouquet des fleurs des champs*; Matisse's *La Fenêtre ouverte à Nice* (1919); and other works by Renoir, Van Dongen, Paul Signac, Gauguin, Jongkind and Picasso, as well as a room of Albert André's own works.

Musée Léon Alègre

www.gard-provencal. com/musees/alegre. htm; open Tues, Thurs and Fri 10–12 and 2–6; closed Feb; adm

Bagnols also has the **Musée Léon Alègre** at 24 Av Paul Langevin, with archaeological finds from the Iron Age to the Romans.

Many of the items in Bagnols' archaeology museum were found at the lofty *oppidum* of **St-Vincent de Gaujac**, 13km south of Bagnols and then a 2km walk up from the car park. Dating from the 5th century BC to the 6th century AD, it became a holy site in Gallo-Roman times, and has the foundations of temples and a bath complex from the 3rd century AD. If you're in the vicinity, don't miss medieval **St-Victor-la-Coste**, a picturesque village gathered around its ruined castle, with a pair of 11th-century chapels.

Laudun, between St-Victor-la-Coste and Bagnols, is another handsome medieval village, with a 14th-century church, Renaissance château and above, on a high plateau with superb views, the **Camp de César**, a 40-acre archaeological site. After its start as a Celtic *oppidum* in the 5th century BC, it grew into a Roman city and was abandoned in the 7th century: Cyclopean walls, towers, a Forum, a basilica, some houses and a few other buildings have so far been excavated. Some of the items found on the site are on permanent exhibition in Laudun's **town hall**.

Camp de César

t 04 66 50 55 50, www.ville-laudun.fr; call for guided tours

The Romans later built villas in the area: around **Tresques**, just southwest, many were converted into Romanesque chapels. One, **St-Martin de Jussan**, on the north end of Tresques, is Lombard in inspiration – companies of builders from the banks of Lake Como roved far and wide in the Middle Ages – and has a carved portal. Another church, **St-Pierre de Castres**, 4km northeast, is one of the oldest, with archaic chapels.

Wine: Côtes du Rhône Gardoise

Bagnols is the centre of Languedoc's Côtes du Rhône production, while three villages, Chusclan, Laudun and St-Gervais, take pride in bottling their own Côtes du Rhône-Villages, as well as good red table wines. Try the **Cave des Vignerons de Chusclan**, at Chusclan, t 04 66 90 11 03, *www. vigneronsdechusclan.com (open 9–12 and 2–6.30)*, for bottled or by-the-litre wines (Côtes du Rhône, Côtes du Rhône Villages, Côtes du Rhône Village Chusclan); and the exceptional wines of **Domaine Ste-Anne**, at Les Celettes in St-Gervais, t 04 66 82 77 41 *(open 9–11 and 2–6; closed Sun and bank holidays)*, especially the Cuvée Notre-Dame and their pure syrah Côtes du Rhône. One of the finest white Côtes du Rhône is made by **Luc Pelaquie**, at Laudun, *www.domaine-pelaquie.com (open Mon–Sat 9–12 and 2–6, Sun by appt)* Pelaquie's wine has a natural freshness that is unusual for such a hot area. It has great depth and will age well for several years. The *domaine* produces a good range of other wines, too, including Tavel, Lirac red and rosé, and Côtes du Rhône red; the **Vignerons d'Estézargues** produce a delightful, fresh, fruity red under the Terra Vitis label (try the 2005). Producers signing up to Terra Vitis undertake to produce wine in an environmentally friendly way (see *www.terravitis.com* for further information). If you are near Bagnols in mid-July, ask the tourist office about the *Festival des Vins et Saveurs du Gard*, an opportunity to taste many local wines and delicacies.

Five kilometres north of Bagnols, there are more views over the Rhône valley from **Vénéjan**; and 2km northeast from there the charming 11th-century **Chapelle de St-Pierre** is decorated with Lombard-style bands of stone and a little square bell-tower. If you're lucky and find it open, you'll see the interior has curious, primitive sculptural decoration: six-pointed stars, concentric circles, solar discs, birds, animals and two praying figures.

Further north, **Pont-St-Esprit** was named for its famous bridge over the Rhône, erected between 1265 and 1309 by a confraternity of builders called the Brothers of the Holy Ghost. Nineteen of the 25 arches are original, but the mighty towers that once controlled access from either bank are long gone. There are fine views of the bridge from the terrace by the 15th-century parish church, once part of the influential Cluniac abbey of St-Saturnin-du-Port. Pilgrims to Santiago de Compostela would cross the bridge, stop at the church and head down Rue St-Jacques, a street that has preserved many of its medieval houses. Appropriately enough for a town named Holy Ghost Bridge, one of these (No.2) now has a museum of religious art, the Musée d'Art Sacré du Gard. The house itself, the Maison des Chevaliers, was built in the 12th century by a family of merchants, who kept right on enlarging and improving their home until the 18th century. The museum displays a wide range of works from the 15th to the 19th centuries, from paintings to *santons*. Just up the street in Place de l'Ancienne Mairie, the Musée Paul-Raymond has a collection of prehistoric finds, ceramics, a reconstruction of an 18th-century pharmacy and more religious and other art.

Bagnols is also a good base for exploring the scenic lower valley of the Cèze, beginning with **St-Gervais**, a wine village set under steep cliffs. Further upstream, **La Roque-sur-Cèze** is piled on a hill opposite a 13th-century bridge, with streets so narrow that cars are forbidden. La Roque overlooks the **Cascade du Sautadet**, where the

Musée d'Art Sacré du Gard
t 04 66 39 17 61; open July and Aug Tues–Sun 10–7; Sept–Jan and Mar–June Tues–Sun 10–12 and 2–6; closed Mon and Feb; adm

Musée Paul-Raymond
t 04 66 39 09 98, www.gard-provencal. com/musees/ praymond.htm; open June–Sept Tues–Sun 10–12 and 3–7; Oct–May Wed, Thurs and Sun 10–12 and 2–6

Cèze flows through a mini-canyon that looks as if it was clawed out of the rock by a giant bear.

Chartreuse de Valbonne
t 04 66 90 41 03,
www.chartreusede
valbonne.com

In an oak forest to the north, the **Chartreuse de Valbonne** dates from 1203, and was rebuilt in a grand Baroque style with a beautiful tile roof after the Wars of Religion, only to be abandoned again in 1901. In the 1920s it became a hospital for tropical diseases: you can visit the church, with its stuccos and stone vaults, and the huge cloister. It has now been converted into a hotel complex; 13 of the monks' cells are now bedrooms. There is also a 16-hectare vineyard.

At the beginning of the 9th century, St Guilhem of Toulouse founded an abbey in **Goudargues**, which Louis the Pious gave to the abbey of Aniane: the ruins of St Guilhem's original Chapelle St-Michelet still stand over the village, while the later abbey church, built in the 12th century and remodelled in the 18th and 19th centuries, is particularly grand. The Benedictines drained the marsh that once surrounded Goudargues into a canal, to water their crops and make Goudargues, with no little exaggeration, 'the Venice of the Gard'; in high summer it often has more water in it than the Cèze. Across the Cèze, **Cornillon** is a 17th-century village with a ruined château and a grand view. Little **Montclus**, further up, is prettily set in a tight loop of the Cèze, with a ruined castle keep.

ⓘ **Bagnols-sur-Cèze >**
Espace St-Gilles, Av Léon Blum, t 04 66 89 54 61, www. tourisme-bagnols surceze.com; open Mon–Sat and Sun am

ⓘ **Pont-St-Esprit >>**
1 Av Kennedy, t 04 66 39 44 45, www.ot-pont-saint-esprit.fr; open July and Aug Mon–Sat and Sun am; Sept–June Mon–Fri and Sat am

ⓘ **Goudargues >>**
4 Rte de Pont-St-Esprit, t 04 66 82 30 02, www. tourisme-ceze-ardeche. com; open July–Aug Mon–Fri and Sat/Sun am; Sept–June Mon–Fri and Sat am

Market Days in the Cèze Valley

Bagnols: Wed and Thurs.
Laudun: Mon.
Pont-St-Esprit: Sat.
Goudargues: Wed.

Where to Stay and Eat in the Cèze Valley

Bagnols-sur-Cèze ✉ 30200

****Château de Montcaud, Route d'Alès, in Sabran, **t** 04 66 89 60 60, *www.chateau-de-montcaud.com* (€€€€€). Part of the Relais & Châteaux group, in a park, with comfortable, air-conditioned rooms, a gym and Turkish bath, a pool, and an equally exquisite restaurant (€€€€) and cheaper *bistrot*. *Closed mid-Oct–early April; restaurant closed lunch, bistrot closed Sat and Sun.*

***Château du Val de Cèze, 69 Route d'Avignon, **t** 04 66 89 61 26, *www.sud-provence.com* (€€€). Bagnols' most luxurious hotel, with individual bungalows around a 13th-century château. In a park, with tennis and a pool. No restaurant. *Closed Nov–Mar.*

Le St-Georges, 210 Av Roger Salengro, **t 04 66 89 53 65, *www. restaurantlesaintgeorges.com* (€). A small, typical place; all rooms have bath. The restaurant (€€) is the best in town, with local specialities served on a terrace. *Restaurant closed Sat lunch and Sun.*

Pont-St-Esprit

L'Auberge Provençale, Av Général de Gaulle, **t 04 66 39 08 79 (€). Simple Logis de France hotel with a restaurant serving local cuisine.

Goudargues/Cornillon ✉ 30630

Mas Rodières, 7km north (take the D980 to the D141 towards Salazac), **t** 04 66 82 29 25, *www.masrodieres.ch* (€€€€€). A 17th-century building, beautifully restored to house four elegant suites (from €580 for a week).

***La Vieille Fontaine, Cornillon, **t** 04 66 82 20 56, *www.lavieillefontaine.net* (€€€). In the walls of the castle, with eight rooms, each furnished with antiques. Garden terraces descend to a pool. The restaurant (€€€) is delightful. *Closed Nov–early Mar; restaurant closed lunch exc Sun.*

The Left Bank of the Rhône

The eastern edge of the Gard, across the river from Orange and Avignon in Provence, is an austere land, its knobby limestone hills and cliffs softened by crowns of silver olives and the green pinstripes of vines, especially in the river-bend north of Villeneuve lez Avignon along the D976. The landmark here is **Roquemaure**, where Pope Clement V died from eating a plate of ground emeralds (prescribed by his doctor for stomach ache) in its now-ruined castle, although it's not his ghost who haunts it, but that of a lovely but leprous queen who was quarantined in the tower. After she died, Rhône boatmen would see her on summer nights, flitting along the bank, dressed in white and sparkling with jewels. Roquemaure's church of **St-Jean-Baptiste**, opened by Clement V in 1329, has sheltered since 1868 the relics of a certain St Valentine, whom it celebrates with a Festival of Lovers, involving locals in 19th-century costume (Terni, in Umbria, which enshrines the relics of its first bishop San Valentino in a basilica and celebrates his feast day on 14 February, would be surprised to learn this). The church also houses a superb organ of 1680, built for the *Cordeliers* in Avignon and transferred here in 1800, which still has all of its original pipes.

From here, the D976 continues southwest past the charming little village of **Tavel**, a place that is equally haunted – in this instance by wine fiends come to slake their thirst on the pale ruby

Wine: Tavel and Lirac

The sun-soaked, pebbly limestone hills on the left bank of the Rhône are as celebrated for their rosés as Châteauneuf-du-Pape is for its reds and whites. Tavel, which has the longest pedigree, has been beloved of kings since the 13th century, when Philippe le Bel declared: 'It isn't good wine unless it's Tavel.' By the 1930s, the vine stocks – grenache, cinsault, bourboulenc, carignan and red clairette – were so old that Tavel nearly went the way of the dodo. Since revived to the tune of 825 healthy hectares, it has once again been crowned by the French as king of the rosé, the universal, harmonious summer wine that goes with everything from red meat to seafood. Be warned, however, that Tavel may be a little strong to less acclimatized, non-French constitutions.

Some growers add syrah and mourvèdre to give their Tavels extra body and colour, including the two best-known producers in the village, whom you can visit by ringing ahead: the de Bez family at the **Château d'Aquéria, t** 04 66 50 04 56, and the prize-winning **Domaine de la Mordorée, t** 04 66 50 00 75, *www.domaine-mordoree.com*, where the talented Christophe Delorme also bottles a potent red Côtes du Rhône, Lirac and Châteauneuf-du-Pape.

The Lirac district begins 3km to the north of Tavel and encompasses four *communes* – Roquemaure, Lirac, St-Laurent-des-Arbres and St-Geniès-de-Comolas. Its pebbly hills are similar to those of Tavel, and the *appellation* differs in the addition of two grape varieties – white ugni and maccabeo – and the fact that everything doesn't come up rosé: Lirac is making a name for its fruity whites, with a fragrance reminiscent of the wildflowers of the nearby *garrigue*, and for its well-structured reds. Both 1998 and 1999 were fine years and the wine can be sampled weekdays by appointment at **Domaine Duseigneur**, St-Laurent-des-Arbres, **t** 04 66 50 02 57, *www.domaineduseigneur.com*, and at **Château St-Roch**, Roquemaure, **t** 04 66 82 82 59, *www.chateau-saint-roch.com*.

Where to Stay and Eat on the Left Bank of the Rhône

Roquemaure ✉ 30150

★Château de Varenne >

***Château de Varenne**, Sauveterre, 4km from town, **t** 04 66 82 59 45, *www.chateaudevarenne.com* (€€€€). An 18th-century building set in a beautiful park with a pool. *Closed Jan–mid-Feb.*

****Le Clément V**, Rue Pierre Sémard (Route de Nîmes), **t** 04 66 82 67 58, *http://hotel-clementv.com* (€€). An excellent, moderately priced hotel complete with a swimming pool. *Closed Jan; restaurant closed lunch.*

Tavel ✉ 30126

***Auberge de Tavel**, Voie Romaine, **t** 04 66 50 03 41, *www.auberge-de-tavel.com* (€€). Charming, quiet, well-equipped rooms and a good restaurant (€€€). *Closed May–Oct; restaurant closed Wed and sometimes also Tues and Thurs.*

La Louisia, north of town near St-Laurent-des-Arbres, at crossroads on N580, **t** 04 66 50 20 60 (€€). A good place to try *gâteau de rascasse à l'américaine* (scorpion fish). *Closed Tues.*

blood of the earth. **Lirac**, situated 2km to the north, is even smaller; a pretty kilometre's walk westwards from the village leads to the **Sainte-Baume**, a cave holy since time immemorial, and in which a statue of the Virgin was discovered in 1647; a hermitage was built on the outside of the cave-chapel. To the north, little **St-Laurent-des-Arbres** used to be owned by the medieval bishops of Avignon, and has a fortified Romanesque church that was built in 1150, a tower and a castle keep.

If you're crossing over to Provence from this corner of the Gard, you'll be in the famous (but tiny) wine region of **Châteauneuf-du-Pape**. Just beyond it lies **Orange**, a drab town with a long history and some remarkable relics, including a triumphal arch and the best-preserved Roman theatre anywhere.

Villeneuve lez Avignon

Just across the Rhône, you can see **Avignon**, the great city of the popes with its famous half-bridge and its wealth of medieval and Renaissance art and architecture. It's in Provence and there's no room to include it here, but if you cross over, don't miss the main attraction, the Palais des Papes, as well as the great collections of the Musée du Petit Palais and Musée Calvet.

Here on the Languedoc side, a wealthy abbey grew into the King of France's bastion on the Rhône, a place where he could keep an eye on the popes. In 586, on Puy Andaon, the rock that dominates Villeneuve lez Avignon, a Visigoth princess-hermit named Casarie died in the odour of sanctity (holiness smells like crushed violets, apparently). In the 10th century, Benedictines built the abbey of St-André to shelter her bones and lodge pilgrims on the route to Compostela. St-André grew to become one of the mightiest monasteries in the south of France, and in 1226, when Louis VIII besieged pro-Albigensian Avignon, the abbot offered the king co-sovereignty of the abbey in exchange for royal privileges. And so what was once an abbey town became a frontier-fortress of the king of France, a new town (*ville neuve*), heavily fortified in case the pope over the river should start feeling frisky. But Villeneuve was soon invaded in another way; wanton, squalid Avignon didn't suit all tastes, and the pope gave permission to his cardinals who preferred it not-so-hot to retreat across the Rhône into princely *livrées cardinalices* (palaces 'freed' from their original owners by the Curia).

Though a dormitory suburb these days, Villeneuve still maintains a separate peace, with well-fed cats snoozing in the sun, leisurely afternoons at the *pétanque* court and some amazing works of art.

Around Town

In 1307, when Philip the Fair ratified the deal that made Villeneuve royal property, he ordered that a citadel be built on the approach to Pont St-Bénezet, named after guess who. As times grew more perilous, this bright white **Tour Philippe-le-Bel** was made higher to keep out the riff-raff, and from its terrace, reached by a superb winding stair, it offers splendid views of Avignon, Mont Ventoux and, on a clear day, the Alpilles.

From here, Montée de la Tour leads up to the 14th-century **Collégiale Notre-Dame**, once the chapel of a *livrée* and now Villeneuve's parish church. From Villeneuve's Chartreuse (charterhouse) it has inherited an elaborate marble altar of 1745, and it contains a copy of Enguerrand Quarton's famous *Pietà de Villeneuve lez Avignon* (the original is in the Louvre).

The church's most famous work, a beaming, swivel-hipped, polychrome ivory statue of the Virgin, carved in Paris out of an elephant's tusk c. 1320, has been removed to safer quarters in the nearby **Musée Pierre-de-Luxembourg**, which is housed in yet another *livrée*. The museum's other prize is the masterpiece of the Avignon school: Enguerrand Quarton's 1454 *Couronnement de la Vierge*, one of the greatest works of 15th-century French painting, commissioned for the Chartreuse (*see* opposite). Unusually, it portrays God the Father and God the Son as twins, clothed in sumptuous crimson and gold, like the Virgin herself, whose fine sculptural features were perhaps inspired by the ivory Virgin. Around these central figures the painting evokes the spiritual route travelled by the Carthusians through vigilant prayer, to purify the world and reconcile it to God. St Bruno, founder of the Order, saints, kings and commoners are present, hierarchically arranged, while the landscape encompasses heaven, hell, Rome and Jerusalem, and local touches such as the Montagne Ste-Victoire and the cliffs of L'Estaque.

Tour Philippe-le-Bel
t 04 32 70 08 57; open April–Sept daily 10–12.30 and 2–6.30; Oct–Nov and Mar Tues–Sun 10–12 and 2–5; closed Dec–Feb

Collégiale Notre-Dame
t 04 90 27 49 28; open April–Sept daily 10–12.30 and 2–6.30; Oct–Nov and Mar Tues–Sun 10–12 and 2–5; closed Dec–Feb

Musée Pierre-de-Luxembourg
t 04 90 27 49 66; open April–Sept daily 10–12.30 and 2–6.30; Oct–Nov and Mar Tues–Sun 10–12 and 2–5; closed Dec–Feb; adm

Other notable works in the museum include a curious 14th-century double-faced Virgin, the 'Eve' face evoking original sin and the 'Mary' face human redemption; Simon de Châlon's 1552 *Entombment*; and, amid the uninspired 17th-century fluff, Philippe de Champaigne's *Visitation*.

La Chartreuse and Fort St-André

From the museum, take Rue de la République up as far as No.53, the **Livrée de la Thurroye**, the best-preserved in Villeneuve; a cardinal would maintain a household of 100 or so people here. Further up the street and up the scale rises what used to be the largest and wealthiest charterhouse in France, the **Chartreuse du Val de Bénédiction**. This began life as the *livrée* of Etienne Aubert who, upon his election to the papacy in 1352 as Innocent VI, deeded his palace to the Carthusians for a monastery. For 450 years it was expanded and rebuilt, acquired immense estates on either side of the Rhône from kings and popes, accumulated a precious library, two more cloisters and various works of art, and in general lived high on the hog by the usual Carthusian standards. In 1792, the Revolution forced the monks out, and the Chartreuse was sold in 17 lots; squatters took over the cells and outsiders feared to enter after dark. Now repurchased and beautifully restored, the buildings house the **CNES** (Centre National des Ecritures du Spectacle), where playwrights and others are given grants to work in peace in some of the former cells; it hosts seminars, exhibitions and performances, especially during the Avignon Festival.

Still, the sensation that lingers in the charterhouse is one of vast silences and austerity, the hallmark of an order where conversation was limited (at least at the outset) to one hour a week; monks who disobeyed the rule of prayer, work and silence ended up in one of the seven prison cells that are set around the laundry in the Great Cloister, each with a cleverly arranged window on the prison chapel altar. Explanations (in English) throughout offer an in-depth view of Carthusian life: one cell has been furnished as it originally was. Pierre Boulez discovered that the dining hall, or *tinel*, has some of the finest acoustics in the whole of France, designed so that everyone could hear the monk who read aloud during mealtimes. In the *tinel*'s **chapel** are some ruined 14th-century frescoes by Matteo Giovannetti and his school: originally their work covered the walls of the huge **church**, now bare except for their masons' marks and minus its apse, which collapsed. The star attraction here is **Innocent VI's tomb**, which boasts an alabaster effigy under a fine Gothic baldachin. Innocent was solemnly reburied here in 1960: a century ago the tomb was being used as a rabbit hutch. Popes who took the name Innocent have tended to suffer similar posthumous indignities: the great Innocent III was

Chartreuse du Val de Bénédiction
t 04 90 15 24 24;
www.chartreuse.org;
open April–Sept daily 9–6.30; Oct–Mar daily 9.30–5.30; adm

found stark naked in Perugia cathedral, a victim of poisoned slippers, while the corpse of Innocent X – the last of the series – was dumped in a toolshed in St Peter's.

Gazing down into the charterhouse from the summit of Puy Andaon are the bleached walls of **Fort St-André**, built by the French kings around the old abbey in the 1360s, not only to stare down the pope over the river but to defend French turf during the heyday of the *Grandes Compagnies* (bands of unemployed mercenaries who pillaged the countryside and held towns to ransom). The two round towers afford a famous vantage point over Avignon; the southwestern tower is called the **Tour des Masques** (or Tour des Sorcières, or Tour des Fées); no one remembers why. Jumbly ruins are all that remain of the once splendid **Abbaye St-André** amid beautiful Italian gardens – sumptuous in springtime – restored and presided over by Roseline Bacou, former curator at the Louvre.

Fort St-André
t 04 90 25 45 35; open mid-May–mid-Sept daily 10–1 and 2–6; April–mid-May and mid–end Sept daily 10–1 and 2–5.30; Oct–Mar daily 10–1 and 2–5

Abbaye St-André
t 04 90 25 55 95; open April–Sept Tues–Sat 10–12.30 and 2–6; Oct–Mar Tues–Sat 10–12.30 and 2–5

(i) **Villeneuve lez Avignon >**
1 Place Charles David, t 04 90 25 61 33, www.villeneuvelez avignon.fr/tourisme; open daily all year

(★) **Le Prieuré >**

Market Days in Villeneuve lez Avignon

Thurs: Place Charles David.
Sat am: Place Jean Jaurès.
Sat am: flea market.

Where to Stay in Villeneuve lez Avignon

Villeneuve lez Avignon
✉ 30400

Villeneuve makes an attractive alternative to Avignon, and has some fine places to stay.

****Le Prieuré, 7 Place du Chapitre, t 04 90 15 90 15, *www.leprieure.fr* (€€€€€–€€€€). An exquisite, centrally located hotel that gives you the option of sleeping in a 14th-century *livrée*, where the rooms are furnished with antiques, or in the more comfortable annexe by the large swimming pool. Further attractions are its gardens, tennis court and splendid restaurant. *Closed Nov–mid-Mar.*

****Hostellerie La Magnaneraie, 37 Rue Camp-de-Bataille, t 04 90 25 11 11, *www.hostellerie-la-magnaneraie.com* (€€€€€–€€€€). A Best Western hotel with old-fashioned rooms in a former silkworm nursery, and a modern annexe, plus a swimming pool, gardens and Le Prieuré's rival for the best restaurant in town. *Closed Jan; restaurant closed Wed, Sat lunch and Sun eve.*

Aux Ecuries des Chartreux, 66 Rue de la République, t 04 90 25 79 93, *www.ecuries-des-chartreux.com* (€€€–€€). Nicely decorated 17th-century B&B with studios next to the Chartreuse.

**L'Atelier, 5 Rue de la Foire, t 04 90 25 01 84, *www.hoteldelatelier.com* (€€). A charming, beautifully restored 16th-century building with stylishly furnished rooms and a walled garden, in the centre. *Closed 3 weeks Jan.*

**Les Cèdres, 39 Av Pasteur Bellevue, t 04 90 25 43 92, *www.logis-de-france.fr* (€€). A 17th-century building with a swimming pool, restaurant and bungalows. *Closed Nov–Mar; restaurant closed Mon lunch except in July.*

UCJG Centre YMCA, 7 bis Chemin de la Justice, t 04 90 25 46 20, *www.ymca-avignon.com* (€). A hostel with superb views of the Rhône and a pool.

Eating Out in Villeneuve lez Avignon

Aubertin, 1 Rue de l'Hôpital, t 04 90 25 94 84 (€€€). An intimate, popular *restaurant gastronomique* under the porticoes. *Book ahead. Closed Sun, Mon eve, and last 2 weeks Aug.*

La Maison, 1 Rue Montée-du-Fort, t 04 90 25 20 81 (€€). A friendly old favourite with traditional Provençal food. *Closed Tues, Wed and Aug.*

Beaucaire

South of Avignon, twin towns glower at each other across the Rhône, each with its castle, and each with its particular monster. In **Tarascon** on the Provençal side, it's the Tarasque, a sort of mustachioed armadillo that gobbled locals before St Martha put an end to it in the 9th century. Languedocien Beaucaire's is a river monster, called the **Drac** – a dragon in some versions, or a handsome young man who liked to stroll invisibly through Beaucaire, before luring his victims into the Rhône by holding a bright jewel just below the surface. When the Drac became a father, he kidnapped a washerwoman to nurse his baby for seven years, during which time the woman learned how to see him when he was invisible. Years later, during one of his town prowls, she saw him and greeted him loudly. He was so mortified that he was never seen again, although like the Tarasque he makes an annual reappearance by proxy, on the first weekend in June. Beaucaire was also the setting of one of the most charming medieval romances: of **Aucassin**, son of the count of Beaucaire, and his 'sweet sister friend' Nicolette, daughter of the king of Carthage, whom Aucassin loved so dizzily that he fell off his horse and dislocated his shoulder, among other adventures.

But in those days Beaucaire was on everyone's lips. It was here, in 1208, that a local squire assassinated Pope Innocent III's legate, who had come to demand stricter measures against the Cathars. It gave Innocent the excuse he needed to launch the **Albigensian Crusade** against Beaucaire's overlords in Toulouse, and all their lands in Languedoc. In 1216, when the war was in full swing, Raymond VII, the son of the count of Toulouse, recaptured the town from its French occupiers, who took refuge in the castle. As soon as word reached Simon de Montfort, he set off in person to succour his stranded men and to teach Beaucaire a lesson, besieging the town walls, while his troops took up the fight from inside the castle, so that Beaucaire was sandwiched in a double attack. The siege lasted 13 weeks before the troops in the castle ran out of food and surrendered and Simon de Montfort had to admit to one of his very few defeats. In gratitude, Raymond VI granted Beaucaire the right to hold a duty-free fair. But five years later the town was gobbled up by France along with the rest of Languedoc.

In 1464, Louis XI restored its freedoms and fair franchise; before long its *Foire de la Ste-Madeleine* became one of the biggest in western Europe. For 10 days in July, merchants from all over the Mediterranean, Germany and England would wheel and deal in the *pré*, a vast meadow on the banks of the Rhône; by the 18th century, when the fair was at its height, Beaucaire (with a population of 8,000) attracted some 300,000 traders, as well as acrobats, thieves and sweethearts, who came to buy each other rings of spun glass as a symbol of love's fragile beauty. So much money changed hands that Beaucaire earned as much in a week as Marseille did in a year.

The loss of Beaucaire's duty-free privileges just after Napoleon lost at Waterloo put an end to the fair, and since then Beaucaire has had to make do with traffic on the Rhône and the Rhône–Sète Canal, its quarries and its wine, ranging from good plonk to the more illustrious AOC Costière du Gard. But in the spring you can try one last legacy of the great fair in Beaucaire: the *pastissoun*, a patty filled with preserved fruits, introduced by merchants from the Levant. Nowadays roadworks often occupy the main streets and driving and walking are not a pleasure.

The Château and Historic Centre

Les Aigles de Beaucaire
t 04 66 59 26 72, www. aigles-de-beaucaire. com; open mid–end Mar, Sept and Oct Thurs–Tues 2.30–4.30; April, May and June Thurs–Tues 2–4.30; July and Aug Thurs–Tues 3–5; closed Wed and Nov–mid-Mar; adm

Musée Municipal Auguste Jacquet
t 04 66 59 47 61; open July–Aug Wed–Mon 10–12 and 2–7.15; April–June Wed–Mon 10–12 and 2.15–6.15; Sept–Oct Wed–Mon 10–12 and 2–6; Nov–Mar Wed–Mon 10–12 and 2–5.15; closed Tues; adm

Louis XI's restoration of Beaucaire's rights paid off for a later Louis (XIII); in 1632, when the **château** was besieged by the troops of the king's rebellious brother, Gaston d'Orléans, the loyal citizens forced them out. To prevent further mishaps, Richelieu ordered that Beaucaire's castle be razed to the ground. But after the south wall had been demolished, the shell was left to fall into ruins romantic enough for an illustration to *Aucassin et Nicolette*. It's a fitting background to **Les Aigles de Beaucaire**, displays of the falconer's art in Roman costume. There are sweeping views of the Rhône and the old fairgrounds, the Champ de Foire, from the 80ft **Tour Polygonale**.

In the castle gardens below, the **Musée Municipal Auguste Jacquet** has finds from Roman Beaucaire (then clumsily called Ugernum), including a fine statue of Jupiter on his throne, and another of the lusty Priapus found in a villa. There's a geological collection, popular arts, and advertising posters and mementoes from the fair, when thousands of brightly coloured cloths swung over the streets, each bearing a merchant's name, his home address and his address in Beaucaire; it was the only way in the vast, polyglot throng to find anyone.

From the château, arrows point the way to the venerable **Place de la République**, shaded by giant plane trees, and the grand, elegant Baroque church of **Notre-Dame-des-Pommiers** (1744), which perhaps more than anything proves how many annual visitors this town once expected. It replaced a much smaller Romanesque church but conserves, on its exterior transept wall (facing Rue Charlier), a superb 12th-century frieze depicting Passion scenes in the same strong, lively relief as at St-Gilles (*see* pp.118–19).

The stately French classical **Hôtel de Ville** (1683), situated in Place Georges Clemenceau, was designed by Jacques Cubizol and

ⓘ **Beaucaire >>**

24 Cours Gambetta,
t 04 66 59 26 57,
www.ot-beaucaire.fr;
open July Mon–Sat and
Sun am; Easter–June
and Aug–Sept Mon–Sat;
Oct–Easter Mon–Fri;
guided tours in English

★ **Les**
Doctrinaires >>

Market Days in Beaucaire

Beaucaire: Thurs am and Sun am, Place de la Mairie and Cours Gambetta; Fri eves in July and Aug there's a market along the canal, with local produce, crafts and entertainment.

Where to Stay and Eat in Beaucaire

For a real escape from the hustle and bustle, why not hire a houseboat and make the leisurely loop down the Rhône–Sète canal to the Camargue, west to Aigues-Mortes and up the Languedoc canal past St-Gilles to Beaucaire? To book, contact **Connoisseur Cruisers**, 14 Quai de la Paix, **t** 04 66 59 46 08, UK **t** 0870 160 5648, *www.connoisseurafloat.com*.

The tourist office can also provide lists of *chambres d'hôtes*.

Beaucaire ✉ 30300

★★★Les Doctrinaires, 6 Quai du Général de Gaulle, **t** 04 66 59 23 70, *www.hoteldoctrinaires.com* (€€€). A rather old-fashioned hostelry set in the former home of the Doctrinaire fathers of Avignon before the Revolution. The restaurant (€€€–€€), which in summer is set in the hotel's pretty courtyard, is a very pleasant place in which to have a meal. *Closed Sat lunch, and mid-Dec–mid-Jan.*

★★★**Robinson**, 2km north of town on Route de Remoulins (D986), **t** 04 66 59 21 32, *www.hotel-robinson.fr* (€€). Thirty rooms set in acres of countryside, with a swimming pool, tennis court, playground and restaurant (€€). *Closed Feb.*

bestowed on Beaucaire by Louis XIV, who wanted to give the town a monument worthy of its importance: note Louis' sun symbols on the façade, the town's coat of arms set in the Collar of St Michael (the French equivalent of the Order of the Garter – Beaucaire was the only town in France awarded the honour), and Beaucaire's motto: 'Renowned for its Fair, Illustrious for its Fidelity'.

If it's a holiday, there's likely to be some dramatic bull follies in the **Arènes**: 100 bulls are brought in for the *Estivales*, a week-long re-creation of the medieval market and other celebrations in late July. Beaucaire's *razeteurs* have a reputation as the most daring of them all; statues of Clairon and Goya, the bulls that gave them the best sport, greet visitors respectively by the Rhône bridge and in Place Jean Jaurès.

Le Vieux Mas
t 04 66 59 60 13; open July and Aug daily 10–7; April–June and Sept daily 10–6; Oct–Mar Wed, Sat, Sun and hols 1.30–6; adm

Mas Gallo Romain des Tourelles
t 04 66 59 19 72; www.tourelles.com; open July and Aug Mon–Sat 10–12 and 2–7, Sun 2–7; April–June and Sept–Oct daily 2–6; Nov–Mar Sat 2–6, other days by appt

Around Beaucaire

The outskirts of Beaucaire are home to two attractions. **Le Vieux Mas**, 8km south on the road to Fourques, is a living evocation of a Provençal farmhouse at the turn of the 19th century, complete with a working blacksmith and other artisans to view at their labour, plus farm animals dotted around, and regional products to buy and take home.

The **Mas Gallo Romain des Tourelles**, 4km southwest at 4294 Route de Bellegarde, is more original: since 1983 archaeologists have been working on the 210-acre vineyard of the Château des

Tourelles (which has been owned by the Durands for 250 years), excavating a huge 1st-century AD agricultural estate that produced olives, wheat and wine, complete with a vast and efficient pottery factory capable of producing 4,000 amphorae a day.

The current Durand in charge, Hervé, became so fascinated with the digs that, together with the Centre National de la Recherche Scientifique, he has re-created a Gallo-Roman winery – during the harvest you can watch the grapes as they are gathered and pressed in the old Roman way and later see the wine bottled, or rather amphora-ed, in jars ranging in size from five to 1,000 litres, wrapped in straw to keep them from breaking in transit. You can taste and buy the result, although there's really no way of knowing how close it comes to the stuff quaffed by Nero and company – the Romans added lime, egg whites, plaster, clay, mushroom ashes and pig blood to 'improve' their wines, and Durand, thankfully, does not.

Beaucaire's Roman incarnation made its living transferring goods (including its wine) along the Roman 'superhighway', the **Via Domitia** that linked Rome to Spain. An 8km stretch of this ancient roadway has come through in remarkably good nick, especially in a place known as **Les Bornes Milliaires** (take the D999 1km northwest past the train tracks, turn left and continue for 800m, following the Enclos d'Argent lane). Nowhere else along the route have the milestones survived so well: these three, on the 13th mile between Nîmes and Ugernum, were erected by Augustus, Tiberius and Antoninus Pius.

Abbaye Troglodytique Saint-Roman de l'Aiguille
t 04 66 59 19 72; www.abbaye-saint-roman.com; open July and Aug daily 10–6.30; April–June and Sept daily 10–6; Oct–Mar Sat and Sun 2–5; adm

In the same area, the unique and vaguely spooky **Abbaye Troglodytique Saint-Roman de l'Aiguille**, 4km up the D999, was founded in a cave during the perilous 5th century and was laboriously carved out of the living rock. It was mentioned in the chronicles in 1363, when Pope Urban V made it a *studium*, a school open even to the poorest children; but by 1537 it had lost its importance and was engulfed in the construction of a fortress. When the fortress in turn lost its importance in the 19th century and was destroyed, the abbey was rediscovered: you can see the chapel, with its remarkable abbot's chair; the subterranean cells; the water cisterns and wine press; and 150 rock-cut tombs in the necropolis on the upper terrace, from where the dead monks had better views than the live ones down below.

Musée de la Vannerie et de l'Artisanat
t 04 66 59 48 14; open Easter–Oct daily 3–7; Nov–Easter by appt only; adm

Northeast of Beaucaire, **Vallabrègues**, 'the most Provençal town of Languedoc', was cut off from the rest of the Gard when the Rhône changed its bed. Surrounded by clumps of osier, it makes its living from wicker and basketry: learn all about the long-standing local craft in the interesting **Musée de la Vannerie et de l'Artisanat**.

South of Nîmes: The Petite Camargue

The Rhône finishes its long journey south in the Camargue, the delta swampland that is France's salt cellar, home to its greatest concentration of waterfowl and some of its most exotic land-scapes. Here too, most of the choice bits are on the Provençal side: it's there that you'll find the white Camargue horses, the flamingo-filled lagoons and the herds of very special cows looked after by the Provençal cowboys, the gardiens. There too is **Arles**, the ancient city at the head of the delta, with its Roman ruins, medieval sculpture and memories of Van Gogh.

The Gard's section, the 'Petite Camargue', is indeed small, part of the delta of a distributary called the Petit-Rhône. It's doing its best to get bigger. The two attractions on its edge, St-Gilles and Aigues-Mortes, were in the Middle Ages among the most flourishing towns in the south; both have long since been marooned by the advancing delta.

St-Gilles

In medieval times and earlier, much nearer the sea, St-Gilles was a port. Remains have been found of a Phoenician merchant colony, and the Greek-Celtic *oppidum* that replaced it, but the place did not really blossom until the 11th century. The popes and the monks of Cluny, who owned it, conspired to make the resting place of Gilles, an obscure 8th-century Greek hermit, a major stop along the great pilgrim road to Compostela. The powerful counts of Toulouse helped too – the family originally came from St-Gilles. Soon pilgrims were pouring in from as far away as Germany and Poland, the port boomed with the onset of the Crusades, and both the Templars and Knights Hospitallers (who owned large tracts in the Camargue) built important *commanderies*. In 1116 the abbey church of St-Gilles was begun, one of the most ambitious projects ever undertaken in medieval Provence.

Destiny, however, soon began making it clear that this was not the place. As the delta gradually expanded, the canals silted up and St-Gilles could no longer function as a port (a major reason for the building of Aigues-Mortes; *see* pp.120–21). The real disaster came with the Wars of Religion, when the town became a Protestant stronghold; the leaders of the Protestant army thought the church, that obsolete relic from the Age of Faith that took 200 years to build, would look much better as a fortress, and they demolished nearly all of it to that end. It was rebuilt, in a much smaller version, after 1650. What was left suffered more indignities during the Revolution – the loss of many of the figures' faces is nothing short of tragic – but it is a miracle that otherwise one of the greatest ensembles of medieval sculpture has survived more or less intact.

The Abbey of St-Gilles

Abbey of St-Gilles
*open Mon, Tues and
Thurs–Sat; guided visits
by arrangement; call
the tourist office on
t 04 66 87 33 75*

This is the masterpiece of the Provençal school of 12th-century sculptors, the famous work that was copied, life-size, in the Cloisters Museum in New York. Created roughly at the same time as the façade of St-Trophime in Arles, it is likewise inspired by the ancient Roman triumphal arches.

Instead of Roman worthies and battle scenes, the 12 Apostles hold place of honour between the Corinthian columns. This is a bold, confident sculpture, taking delight in naturalistic detail and elaborately folded draperies, with little of the conscious stylization that characterizes contemporary work in other parts of France. In this, too, the Romans were their masters. The scheme is complex, and worth describing in detail.

The Church Façade (*see diagram, below*)

Left portal: tympanum of the Adoration of the Magi (1); beneath it, Jesus' entry into Jerusalem (2); flanking the door, a beautiful St Michael slaying the dragon (3); and on the right the first four Apostles, SS Matthew and Bartholomew, Thomas and James the Lesser (4–7).

Central portal: tympanum of Christ in Majesty (8), with symbols of the Evangelists; underneath, a long frieze that runs from one side portal across to the other: from left to right, Judas with his silver (9); Jesus expelling the money-changers from the temple (10);

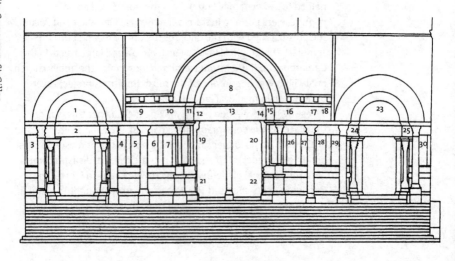

the resurrection of Lazarus (11); Jesus prophesying the denial of
Peter and the washing of the Apostles' feet (12); the Last Supper
(13); the Kiss of Judas, a superb, intact work (14); the Arrest of
Christ (15); Christ before Pilate (16); the Flagellation (17); Christ
carrying the Cross (18). Left of the door, saints John and Peter (19);
right of the door, saints James the Greater and Paul, with the
soul-devouring Tarasque under his feet (20). Beneath these, at
ground level, are small panels representing the sacrifices of Cain
and Abel and the murder of Abel (21); a deer hunt and Balaam
and his ass, and Samson and the Lion (22).

Right portal: tympanum of the Crucifixion (23), and, beneath it, two
unusual scenes: the three Marys purchasing spices to anoint
the body of Jesus, and the three Marys at the tomb. To the left
of this, the Magdalen and Jesus (24); to the right, Jesus appearing
to his disciples (25). Left of the door, four more unidentifiable
Apostles (26–29; note how the 12 represented here are not the
canonical list – better-known figures such as John the Evangelist
and Paul were commonly substituted for the more obscure of
the original Apostles). To the right of the door, Archangels
combat Satan (30).

The Vis de St-Gilles

The 17th-century interior of the rebuilt church holds little of
interest, but beneath it the original, wide-vaulted **crypt** or lower
church (*adm*) survives (so many pilgrims came to St-Gilles that
upper and lower churches were built to hold them). Behind the
church, you can see the ruins of the **choir** and **apse** of the original,
which was much longer than the present structure.

Here is the *vis* or 'screw' of St-Gilles, a spiral staircase of 50 steps
that once led up one of the bell-towers. Built about 1142, it is a
tour de force. The stones are cut with amazing precision to make a
self-supporting spiral vault; medieval masons always tried to make
the St-Gilles pilgrimage just to see it. Its author, Master Mateo of
Cluny, also worked on the church of Santiago de Compostela,
where he is buried.

The Maison Romane

The rest of the town shows few traces of its former greatness.
The medieval centre is unusually large, if a bit forlorn. Near the
façade of the church, on Place de la République, is a fine 13th-
century mansion, claimed to be the birthplace of Guy Folques,
who became Pope Clement IV. Today this 'Maison Romane' houses
St-Gilles' **Musée Lapidaire**, with a number of sculptures and
architectural fragments from the church, and collections
displaying the folk life and nature of the Camargue.

Musée Lapidaire
*t 04 66 87 40 42; open
July and Aug Mon–Sat
9–12 and 3–7; June and
Sept Mon–Sat 9–12 and
2–6; Feb–May and Oct–
Dec Mon–Sat 9–12 and
2–5; closed Jan; adm*

Market Days in St-Gilles

St-Gilles: Thurs and Sun am.

Where to Stay and Eat in St-Gilles

St-Gilles ✉ 30800

During the Middle Ages scores of pilgrims (sometimes thousands of them), would stay over at St-Gilles every night; if you tried it today, even the innkeepers would wonder what you were thinking of.

**Le Cours, 10 Allée François Griffeuille, t 04 66 87 31 93, *www. hotel-le-cours.com* (€€–€). A typically traditional Logis de France residence (you pay extra for air-conditioning), with a shady restaurant terrace (€€) where you can try the likes of Camargue *pilaf* and frogs' legs. *Closed mid-Dec–Feb.*

***L'Héraclée, 30 Quai du Canal, t 04 66 87 44 10, *www.hotel-heraclee. com* (€). Unexciting but well run.

ⓘ St-Gilles ›
Place Frédéric Mistral, t 04 66 87 33 75, www.ot-saint-gilles.fr; open Mon–Fri; on Sat go to Point Annexe, Place de l'Eglise

Aigues-Mortes

Aigues-Mortes: History, Salt and Walls

Every French history or geography textbook has a photo of Aigues-Mortes in it, and every French person, most likely, carries in their mind the haunting picture of the great walls of the port from which Saint Louis sailed off to the Crusades, now marooned in the muck of the advancing Rhône delta. It is as compelling a symbol of time and fate as any Roman ruin, and as evocative of medieval France as any Gothic cathedral.

In 1241 the Camargue was the only stretch of Mediterranean coast held by France. To solidify this precarious strip, Louis IX (Saint Louis) began construction of a new port and a town, laid out in an irregular grid to stop the wind from racing up the streets. In 1248 the port was complete enough to hold the 1,500 ships that carried Louis and his knights to the Holy Land on the Seventh Crusade, which was to bring Louis disasters both at home and abroad (the town was the last he saw of France – he died in Tunis of the plague in 1270). His successor, Philippe III, finished Aigues-Mortes and built its great walls. Being the only French Mediterranean port, by the late 13th century it was booming, with perhaps four times as many inhabitants as its present 4,800, its harbour filled with ships from as far away as Constantinople and Antioch.

Aigues-Mortes means 'dead waters', and it proved to be a prophetic name. The sea deserted Aigues and, despite efforts to keep the harbour dredged, the port went into decline after 1350. Attempts to revive it in the 1830s failed, ensuring Aigues' demise, but allowing the works of Louis and Philippe to survive undisturbed. Forgotten and nearly empty a century ago, Aigues now makes its living from tourists, and from salt; half of France's supply is collected here, at the 10,000-hectare **Salins-du-Midi** pans south of town in the Petite Camargue. Now the sea wants to return, and attempts to keep the tides from draining the lucrative saltpans could be futile, or at least very expensive.

Salins-du-Midi
t 04 66 73 40 00, www.salins.com; open April–Sept, call for times

Getting to and around Aigues-Mortes

For **trains** from Nîmes, contact t 08 92 35 35 35; the station is on the Route de Nîmes.
For **buses** to and from Montpellier and Nîmes, call t 08 25 34 01 34 and t 04 66 29 27 29 respectively.
There are signs around all the entrances to the town forbidding **cars**; ignore them (everyone else does).
There is no problem driving around Aigues-Mortes or finding parking, except in July and August.

Tour de Constance
*t 04 66 53 61 55; open
May–Aug daily 10–7;
Sept–April daily
10–5.30; adm*

Aigues-Mortes' **walls** are more than 1.5km in length, streamlined and almost perfectly rectangular. The highly impressive **Tour de Constance** (entry inside the walls on Rue Zola) is an enormous cylindrical defence tower used to guard the northeastern land approach to the town. After the Crusades, the tower was turned into a prison, first for Templars and later for Protestants. One of them, Marie Durand, spent 38 years here in unspeakable conditions. On her release in 1768, she left her credo, *register* ('resist' in Provençal) chiselled into the wall, where it can still be seen.

The tower to the south was used as a temporary mortuary in 1431, during the Hundred Years' War, when the Bourguignons, who held the city, were suddenly attacked and decimated by their arch-enemies, the Armagnacs. There were so many gruesome bodies lying around that the Armagnacs simply stacked them up in the tower, covering each of them with a layer of salt: hence the rather eloquent name – the **Tower of the Salted Bourguignons**.

Eight kilometres southwest of Aigues-Mortes, **Le Grau-du-Roi** with its 18th-century lighthouse doubles as France's most important fishing port and has a charmless if hyperactive beach resort (*see* p.160).

Market Days in Aigues-Mortes

Aigues-Mortes: Av Frédéric Mistral: Wed and Sun am.

Activities in Aigues-Mortes

Aigues-Mortes offers many guided tours of local flora and fauna.
Pescalune, t 04 66 53 79 47, *www.pescalune-aiguesmortes.com*, and **L'Isles de Stel, t** 06 09 47 52 59, offer barge tours of the Petite Camargue.

Four-wheel-drive safari tours are efficiently run out of Le Grau-du-Roi by **Le Gitan, t** 06 08 60 97 56, and **Pierrot le Camarguais, t** 04 66 51 90 90.

Where to Stay and Eat in Aigues-Mortes

Aigues-Mortes ✉ 30220
***Le Saint-Louis, 10 Rue de l'Amiral Courbet, t 04 66 53 72 68, *www. lesaintlouis.fr* (€€). A distinguished and beautifully furnished 18th-century building just off Place Saint-Louis, with gracious staff and a restaurant. *Closed mid-Nov–April.*

Hermitage de St-Antoine, 9 Bd Intérieur Nord, t 06 03 04 34 05, *www.hermitagesa.com* (€€). *Chambres d'hôtes* just inside the Porte St-Antoine in the medieval walls; all three rooms have en suite bathrooms. Added bonuses are a tranquil patio area and fantastic breakfasts.

La Camargue, 19 Rue de la République, t 04 66 53 86 88, *www.restaurantla*

ⓘ **Aigues-Mortes** >>
*Place Saint-Louis,
t 04 66 53 73 00, www.
ot-aiguesmortes.fr;
open daily all year;
offers historical tours of
the town, year-round*

camargue.fr (€€). The place where the Gypsy Kings got their musical start, and still the liveliest and most popular place in town, with flamenco guitars strumming in the background. Eat in the garden in summer.

Between Nîmes and Montpellier

There are three routes between the two cities: the *autoroute*; its southern parallel, the N113; or the longest, prettiest and most interesting route, along the back roads through Sommières – the D40 from Nîmes to Sommières, then the N110 to Montpellier.

Via Nages and Sommières

Nages: A Celtic *Oppidum*

The D40 from Nîmes is a winding, pretty route that passes through lush, hilly country and slumberous villages like **Caveirac** and **St-Dionisy**. Above the latter, off the D737, is the 3rd-century BC *oppidum* of **Nages**, one of the outstanding pre-Roman sites in the south (easy access on foot, signposted from the village of **Nages-et-Solorgues**). Like Nîmes, Nages was built around a spring, entirely of dry stone, with a temple, and walls punctuated by round towers; on top of the tallest, the **Tour Monumentale**, a cache of stones for slings was discovered. The streets, with their rectangular houses, were laid out in a tidy grid – long before the Romans introduced their waffle-shaped city plans. The first floor of Nages-et-Solorgues' *mairie* has been converted into a small **archaeology museum**.

Archaeology museum
t 04 66 35 05 26; open Mon 8.30–11.45 and 2–6, Tues 8.30–11.45, Wed 8.30–11.45 and 2–6, Thurs 8.30–11.45 and 5–7, Fri 8.30–11.45

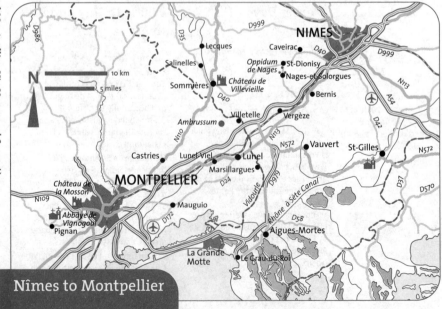

Nîmes to Montpellier

Sommières

⭐ Sommières

Hidden under the cliffs of the river Vidourle, Sommières suffers only moderately from the usual plagues besetting picturesque southern villages: the Parisians, the English, the trinket shops – it has even had to do without a famous writer since long-time resident Lawrence Durrell died in October 1990. Its streets and squares could be paintings by Maurice Utrillo: soft and pastel, well worn and well lived-in, with faded shop signs of a century ago and flowers under every window. Huge plane trees, a little bullring and an enormous *boulodrome* (for *pétanque*) line the river, and swans and mallards float calmly by, except, one imagines, during the *vidourlades*, the local name for the Vidourle's seasonal floods, when it pours down hell-for-leather from the Cevennes: recent measures have dampened some of its impetuosity, but the town is still badly flooded from time to time.

Before Sommières, there was Sommières' **bridge**, built by Tiberius between AD 19 and 31. Its 17 arches have withstood centuries of *vidourlades*; they carry road traffic to this day and still look in mint condition. The top was restored in 1715. Oddly, almost half of the bridge is now hidden inside the town; medieval Sommières expanded into the dry parts of the riverbed and eventually an embankment was built. The **Tour de l'Horloge**, the entrance to the town, was built over the bridge's fifth arch in 1659.

The other arches of the bridge lie under Rue Marx Dormoy, the street leading from the bridge to **Place des Docteurs Dax** (natives of Sommières who discovered the exact spot in the brain in charge of language), a lovely 12th-century market square that everyone still calls by its old name, the **Marché-Bas**. It preserves the Pierre d'Inquant, where slaves were once made to stand when they were being sold. The houses are all built on stone arcades: in the old days, the square would be underwater every spring, forcing the market up two streets to the **Marché-Haut** (now Place Jean Jaurès). The web of lanes radiating from these squares has its share of handsome *hôtels particuliers*. Sommières was an enthusiastically Protestant town and was destroyed during the Wars of Religion after two terrible sieges, in 1573 and 1575, then again in 1622, so most of what you see is from the 17th-century rebuilding.

Rue de la Taillade, cut into the cliffs by the Romans for the Nîmes–Lodève road, is one of the most attractive streets, with well-preserved old shops; the former Ursuline convent here, now the **Espace Lawrence Durrell**, is used for temporary exhibitions. From here, the Montée des Régordanes leads up to the half-ruined **Château de Sommières** and the **Tour Bermond**, worth the climb for its views up and down the valley of the Vidourle, as far as Pic St-Loup and Aigues-Mortes.

Tour Bermond
open July–Aug Sun– Fri 4–7; closed Sat; adm

08

Nîmes, the Gard and Montpellier | Between Nîmes and Montpellier: Via Nages and Sommières

Around Sommières

Château de Villevieille
t 04 66 80 01 62; open July–Sept daily 2–6; April–June Sat and Sun 2–6; adm

A mile away, on a hill above Sommières, the **Château de Villevieille** was first built in the 11th century by the lords of Sommières, the Bermond de Sauve, whose most famous scion was a Cathar and brother-in-law of Raymond VII of Toulouse – excuse enough for Saint Louis to confiscate their estate in 1243. He divided the vast property in two, leaving a bit for the family's daughter and trading the remainder to the monks of Psalmody in exchange for Aigues-Mortes – which Louis built into France's first Mediterranean port. In 1527 the château was ceded to the Pavée family, who have owned it since. It escaped being sold off in the Revolution, thanks to the Marquis de Villevieille's friendship with Mirabeau and Voltaire. You can count on one hand the châteaux in France that have preserved their original family furnishings – this is one.

St-Julien-de-Montredon
ring the keyholder, René Peyrolle, t 04 66 80 01 95, before setting out and he will accompany you

Four kilometres northwest of Sommières, along a Roman road, you can visit a pretty country chapel, **St-Julien-de-Montredon**, at **Salinelles**, in a lovely setting among the vines, with an ancient cemetery. First mentioned in 813, it was rebuilt by the monks of Psalmody in the 11th century and decorated with archaic carvings of animals and birds. Salinelles also has a **beach** along the Vidourle; others are nearby at Lecques and Villetelle.

Maison du Boutis
www.la-maison-du-boutis.com, t 04 66 01 63 75; open Thurs–Sun 2.30–6.30

At **Calvisson**, 10km east of Sommières, is the **Maison du Boutis**, a museum and shop dedicated to local embroidery.

Castries

Continuing towards Montpellier, Castries has a Renaissance-era **château** belonging to one of the 19 barons of Languedoc. Though it was wrecked in the Revolution, this castle came back into the possession of its original owners, the de Castries family, who restored it. It was once open to the public for visits, but now belongs to the Académie Française, which meets here once a year. It is also undergoing further restoration.

ⓘ **Sommières >>**
5 Quai Frédéric Gaussorgues, t 04 66 80 99 30, www.ot-sommieres.fr; open July–Aug daily; Sept–June Mon–Fri and Sat am

★ **Hôtel de l'Orange >>**

★ **Auberge du Pont Romain >**

Market Days around Sommières

Sommières: Sat.
Calvisson: Sun.
Castries: Tues and Fri.

Where to Stay and Eat around Sommières

Sommières ✉ 30250

***Auberge du Pont Romain**, 2 Rue E. Jamais, t 04 66 80 00 58, *www.aubergedupontromain.com* (€€). Lovely, spacious rooms in a 19th-century herbal distillery close to the river, with a pool and a gourmet restaurant (€€€) serving the house *foie gras* and other delights on a peaceful garden terrace. *Closed Nov and mid-Jan–mid-Mar.*

Hôtel de l'Orange, 7 Rue des Beaumes, t 04 66 77 79 94, *http://hotel.delorange.free.fr* (€€). A 17th-century building, lovingly converted into a guesthouse, with a pool and a garage but only five rooms, so book early in the summer; ask to see the *baume* (cave). There's also a bungalow for weekly self-catering rental.

L'Olivette, 11 Rue Abbé Fabre, t 04 66 80 97 71 (€€). This restaurant in the centre is a local favourite, serving regional cuisine with an original twist, such as snails *à la sommiéroise*. *Closed Tues summer, Tues eve and Wed winter.*

L'Evasion, 6 Rue Paulin Capmal, t 04 66 77 74 64 (€). At lunchtime, watch the life of the Marché-Bas pass by from an outdoor table; the menu includes pizza and mussels. *Closed Thurs, Sun eve and Mon in winter.*

Castries ✉ 34160

L'Art du Feu, 13 Av du 8 Mai 1945, t 04 67 70 05 97 (€€). Offers refined cooking on bargain menus; the house speciality is *filet de taureau* in a red wine sauce. *Closed Sun eve and Wed, plus 3 wks July, 1 wk Jan and 1 wk Sept.*

Nîmes to Montpellier by Way of Perrier and Lunel

This faster, southern route along the N113 isn't as scenic as the Sommières route but has its own rewards, especially if you combine it with a detour to historic Aigues-Mortes in the Camargue (*see* pp.120–21).

Fizzy Water and a Statue of Liberty

Bernis, 7km southwest of Nîmes, offers the first potential stop, for the sake of its 12th-century church, once a possession of the abbey of St-Gilles. Though mostly rebuilt after the Wars of Religion, its façade is intact, carved in a style archaic back in the 12th century, especially the Carolingian-inspired decorations by the door. The capitals are carved with people, birds, animals, a dragon and a mermaid.

Source Perrier
t 04 66 87 61 01
for the tour

Just off the the N113 at **Vergèze**, trendies may make a pilgrimage to the **Source Perrier**. Surprisingly, the vast water-producing complex was established by an Englishman in 1903, and looks less like a natural spring than an obsessively tidy aeroplane factory; the green bottles come whizzing off the line in their billions, all guaranteed benzene-free.

The big town along this route is **Lunel**, and a peculiar place it is. Legend has it that Lunel was founded by Jews from Jericho under the reign of Vespasian – a story now dismissed as a play on words (Jericho was the city of the moon, the *ville de la lune*). Historians now say the first Jews probably settled in the 11th century and, until their expulsion in 1306, Lunel was their educational centre in France, with well-known schools of everything from medicine (predating even Montpellier's) to the Kabbala.

Today, the town raises steers for bloodless *course libre* bullfights. Its landmark is a copy of the Statue of Liberty (erected in 1989 to commemorate the bicentenary of the French Revolution), its cops wear star-and-crescent badges just like those of New Orleans, and one of its biggest businesses is dog food research and development. Little remains of medieval Lunel: some bits of the Jewish schools on Rue Ménard, and a vaulted alley called the Passage des Caladons that once was part of a Templar commandery. In the 19th century the Lunel area was the holiday retreat of a man who hardly seemed the type to take a vacation in the south of France – Karl Marx. Marx suffered from asthma, and whenever he had a bad bout his wife Jenny sent him down to the Château de la Tour de Fages, owned by the husband of her best friend, opera diva Caroline Ungher.

South of Lunel, the sweet and shady village of **Marsillargues** has an elegant Renaissance château. The rooms, with their marble and plaster relief decoration of the 1570s and later, are lovely, but empty; it's sad that this château, one of the few undamaged in the Revolution, should have lost most of its furnishings in a fire in 1936. Recently, four of the rooms have been filled up with the contents of the villagers' attics as the **Musée Pastre**. There are various events and theatre performances at the château.

The **Château de Teillan**, at **Aimargues**, on an unpaved road across the river Vidourle from Marsillargues, has a large park with fragmentary Roman ruins, milestones, the largest *noria* in Languedoc and a gigantic *pigeonnier*, once part of a 7th-century military depot.

By the *autoroute* north of Lunel in **Villetelle**, a single arch of a Roman bridge stands in the middle of the Vidourle at **Ambrussum**, a Celtic *oppidum* from the same period as Nages (*see* p.122) and later way-station on the Via Domitia. Archaeologists have uncovered 200 metres of paved Roman road (the deep grooves near the bridge mark the spot where the wagons and chariots stopped to pay their toll), as well as villas and public buildings.

Musée Pastre
t 04 67 83 52 10; open Wed 2–6

Château de Teillan
open by appt only, call the Hôtel de Ville on t 04 66 73 12 12

Ambrussum bridge
tourist office organizes guided visits July and Aug Tues and Fri 10am, with a tour of the excavations of the lower quarter Tues eve; also open Wed in Sept

ⓘ **Lunel >>**
16 Cours Gabriel Péri, t 04 67 71 01 37, www. ot-paysdelunel.com; open Mon–Sat, and Sun am

⭐ **La Passiflore >**

Market Days around Lunel

Lunel: Tues–Sun food, Halles, Cour G. Péri; Thurs and Sun, mixed market; Sat am, flea market.
Marsillargues: Tues, Thurs and Sat.

Where to Stay and Eat around Lunel

Vergèze ✉ 30310
La Passiflore, 1 Rue Neuve, t 04 66 35 00 00 (€€–€). Well placed for the *autoroute* and the Camargue, this gorgeous little hotel with enclosed courtyard in a small village is run by an English couple. It's beautifully decorated, the service is friendly, and they like kids.

Lunel ✉ 34400
**Les Mimosas, Av du Vidourle, t 04 67 71 25 40, www.hotelmimosas.fr (€). Just outside the centre. *Open daily, year round.*
Mas St-Félix, St-Séries, 7km north of Lunel, t 04 67 86 05 83 (€). A B&B in an old posthouse of the Knights Hospitallers (with use of the kitchen). *Closed Oct–mid-June.*
Didier Chodoreille, 140 Rue Lakanal, t 04 67 71 55 77, www.chodoreille.fr (€€€–€€). Dine well on French classics; it's by the station and has a pretty garden terrace that makes Lunel's traffic seem far away. *Closed Mon eve and Sun plus part of Aug.*

Montpellier

⚙ Montpellier

*If that town
could suck as
hard as it can
blow, it could
bring the ocean
to it and
become a
seaport.*

Although an old saying (*see* left) originally referred to the brash, booming, braggart Atlanta of the 1880s, it applies just as fairly to France's eighth city. The public relations geniuses in Montpellier have managed to outdo even Atlanta: their beloved city has been cockadoodled as the '*Technopole*', the *Surdoué* (the Specially Gifted), the 'Synergetic Euro-cité', the 'Capital of Southern Europe', rightful 'heir to the Florence of the Medicis', the 'French California', and indeed nothing less than 'the Rome of Tomorrow'. Unlike Atlanta, Montpellier has actually sucked hard enough to get a port of its own (for sailing boats at least) by widening a puny river called the Lez, a feat that gave it a new horn to toot: *Montpellier la Méditerranée!* Today it is merely '*Montpellier, la ville où le soleil ne se couche jamais*' ('the town where the sun never sets') or '*Montpellier mille et une vies*', a reference to its dynamic growth.

Until 1977 and the election of the irrepressible socialist Mayor Georges Frêche (*see* pp.46–8), Montpellier was a pleasant, sleepy university backwater of fawn-coloured stone with a population of 100,000, one that could put forth the modest claim that Stendhal found it the 'only French city of the interior that doesn't look stupid'. The population of the agglomeration now approaches 400,000, making it the eighth biggest city in France, including the large staff of IBM and more than 60,000 students from around the world who come to study where Rabelais and Nostradamus learned medicine. With his huge development projects, notably the monumental modern quarter of Antigone, Frêche made Montpellier a European model for innovative and effective city government. He stayed in charge for 27 years. The current mayor, Hélène Mandroux, was elected in April 2004; she was groomed for the job by Frêche, but is coming out from under his giant shadow.

History

Compared with its venerable Roman neighbours, Narbonne, Béziers and Nîmes, Montpellier is a relative newcomer, tracing its roots back a mere thousand years, to 985, when the count of Mauguio bestowed a large farm at Monspestelarius on a certain Master Guilhem. It was a fortunate site, near the old Via Domitia and the newer *Cami Salinié* (salt route) and *Cami Roumieu* (the pilgrimage route between St-Gilles and Compostela), and it had access to the sea through the river Lez.

Guilhem's farm soon grew into a village of merchants, who made their fortunes by importing spices from the Levant, especially spices with medicinal uses taught to the merchants by their Arab and Jewish trading partners and by graduates of the medical school of Salerno; by the year 1000 they were training pupils in

Getting to and around Montpellier

By Air

The **airport**, Montpellier-Méditerranée, is 8km southeast of the centre on the D21 (**t** 04 67 20 85 00, *www.montpellier.aeroport.fr*). There are flights from the UK, and via Paris. The airport **shuttle bus** travels to and from Place de l'Europe, in Antigone quarter, at roughly one-hour intervals, **t** 04 67 92 01 43, or see the airport website.

By Train

The **train station** is in Place Auguste Gibert, just south of the Ecusson, **t** 04 99 74 15 10. You can race there from Paris in 4hrs 40mins on the TGV, or catch direct trains to Avignon, Nîmes, Marseille, Nice, Perpignan, Béziers, Narbonne, Agde, Lunel, Sète and Carcassonne.

By Bus

The train station is linked by an escalator to the *gare routière* in nearby Rue du Grand St-Jean (**t** 04 67 92 01 43), which has buses to Nîmes, La Grande Motte, Béziers, Aigues-Mortes, etc. For Palavas, take bus 131 (run by Hérault Transport), from the Port Marianne quarter (*www.cg34.fr/herault-transport*).

By Tram

In summer 2000, Montpellier launched its new tram project. The first line crosses the city centre from northwest to southeast; the second line goes northeast to southwest. Information from **TAM**, **t** 04 67 22 87 87, *www.montpellier-agglo.com/tam*, or the tourist office.

Car and Bike Hire

Big-name car hire firms are at the airport, or try **Avis** at 900 Av des Prés d'Arènes (south of the centre), **t** 08 20 61 16 44, or **Hertz France**, Place Auguste Gibert, **t** 04 67 06 87 90 (outside the station). You can also hire a less expensive used car from **A.D.A.**, 58 bis Av G. Clemenceau, **t** 04 67 58 34 35. Hire a **bike** at 27 Rue Maguelone (off Pl de la Comédie), **t** 04 67 22 87 82 – the entire historic centre is a pedestrian zone.

Montpellier. By the late 12th century, the town was big enough to need a wall with 25 towers, shaped like an escutcheon, or *écusson* (as the old town is still known). It lost its independence when Guilhem VIII failed to produce a son and gave his only daughter, Marie, to Pedro II of Aragon. Montpellier was her dowry, just in time to spare the town from the Albigensian Crusade. When Marie and Pedro's son, Jaime the Conqueror, divided Aragon between his two sons, Montpellier joined the Kingdom of Majorca.

In 1220 the teachers of medicine formed a *Universitas Medicorum*, and began to attract students from all over Europe; in 1250 it was supplemented by a *studium* of law, both of which were given Pope Nicholas IV's seal of approval in 1289. Another impetus behind Montpellier's huge growth in the 13th and 14th centuries was dead bugs – dark red cochineal insects found on oaks in the nearby *garrigues*, believed at the time to be grains and used for dyeing cloth scarlet. The spice and gold-working trades thrived, particularly after those mega-consumers, the popes, moved to Avignon.

In 1349 the Kings of Majorca sold Montpellier to France for 120,000 golden *écus*. A period of relative peace and prosperity continued until the 1560s, when the university academics and tradesmen embraced the Reformation. For the next 70 years much of what Montpellier had achieved was wiped out; churches and suburbs were destroyed, building and art came to a halt. In 1622,

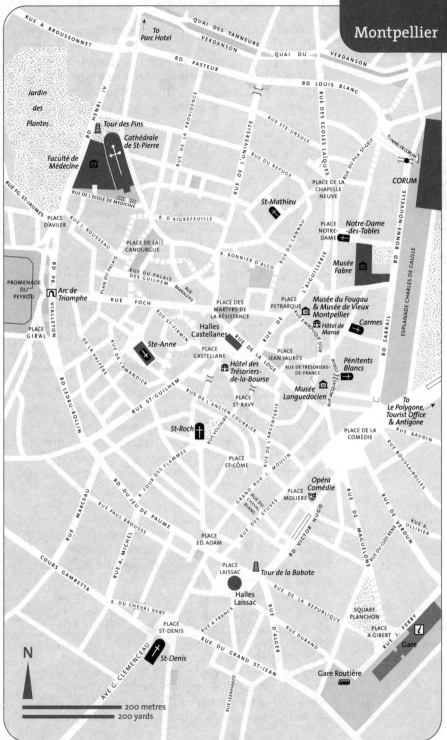

RUE A. BROUSSONNET

QUAI DES TANNEURS

To
Parc Hotel

VERDANSON

QUAI DU VERDANSON

BD PASTEUR

BD LOUIS BLANC

Jardin
des
Plantes

BD HENRI IV

Tour des Pins

Cathédrale
de St-Pierre

RUE DE LA PROVIDENCE

RUE STE-URSULE

RUE DES ECOLES LAIQUES

RUE DU PILA ST-GÉLY

TUNNEL DE CORUM

CORUM

Faculté de
Médecine

RUE DE L'UNIVERSITE

RUE DU REFUGE

PLACE DE LA
CHAPELLE
NEUVE

BD BONNE-NOUVELLE

RUE DE L'ECOLE DE MEDECINE

St-Mathieu

PLACE
NOTRE-
DAME

Notre-Dame
-des-Tables

RUE FG. ST-JAUMES

RUE J. ROUSSEAU

PLACE
D'AVILER

R. D'AIGREFEUILLE

RUE DU CANNAU

ESPLANADE CHARLES DE GAULLE

Musée
Fabre

PLACE DE LA
CANOURGUE

R. BONNIER D'ALCO

L'AIGUILLERIE

PROMENADE
DU
PEYROU

BD PR. VIALLETON

Arc de
Triomphe

PLAN DU PALAIS

RUE DU PALAIS
DES GUILHEM

RUE BARRALERIE

RUE FOCH

PLACE DES
MARTYRS DE
LA RÉSISTANCE

PLACE
PETRARQUE

RUE DE L'AIGUILLERIE

RUE EMBOUQUE D'OR

Musée du Fougau
& Musée de Vieux
Montpellier

Hôtel de
Manse

Carmes

BD SARRAIL

PLACE
GIRAL

Halles
Castellanes

RUE DE LA LOGE

Ste-Anne

RUE ST-FIRMIN

DE LA VALFÈRE

RUE DE L'AMANDIER

PLACE
CASTELLANE

Hôtel des
Trésoriers-
de-la-Bourse

PLACE
JEAN JAURÈS

RUE DE TRÉSORIERS-
DE-FRANCE

Pénitents
Blancs

RUE JACQUES CŒUR

BD LEDRU-ROLLIN

RUE ST-GUILHEM

RUE DE L'ANCIEN COURRIER

PLACE
ST-RAVY

Musée
Languedocien

To
Le Polygone,
Tourist Office
& Antigone

St-Roch

RUE VOLTAIRE COURRIER

RUE DE L'ARGENTERIE

RUE DU MOULIN

PLACE DE LA
COMÉDIE

RUE BAUDIN

PLACE
ST-CÔME

RUE BOUSSAIROLLES

BD DU JEU DE PAUME

R. FOUR DES FLAMMES

GRAND RUE
RUE DU
CHEVAL
BLANC

Opéra
Comédie

PLACE
MOLIÈRE

RUE DE MAGUELONE

RUE DE
L'OLLIVIER

RUE A.
OLLIVIER

RUE MARCEAU

RUE PAUL BROUSSE

RUE A. MICHEL

RUE DES ETUVES

BD VICTOR HUGO

RUE DU CLOS RENÉ VERDUN

COURS GAMBETTA

PLACE
ED. ADAM

R. DU CHEVAL VERT

PLACE
LAISSAC

Tour de la Babote

RUE DE LA REPUBLIQUE

SQUARE
PLANCHON

Halles
Laissac

PLACE
A GIBERT

PLACE
ST-DENIS

RUE A FRANCE

RUE DURAND

RUE ST-FERRY

Gare

AVE. G. CLEMENCEAU

St-Denis

RUE DU GRAND ST-JEAN

RUE D'AIGER

Gare Routière

RUE LEENHARDT

N

200 metres
200 yards

Louis XIII came in person to besiege the rebellious city and reassert royal authority; he built a citadel to watch the Montpellerains, then transferred here from Pézenas the Estates-General of Languedoc, with all its nobles, prelates and deputies, who built themselves the patrician *hôtels particuliers* that still dominate the old city.

Putting its merchant republic days behind it, Montpellier settled down to the life of a university town and regional capital. The Revolution passed without kicking up much dust; a far bigger crisis for Montpellier occurred in the 1890s, when phylloxera knocked out the wine-making industry the city had come to depend on – an economic blow from which it only began to recover in the 1950s.

With the French mania for categorizing, Montpellier now pigeonholes its economy into five 'poles': *Euromédecine* (including its numerous labs and pharmaceutical industries), *Héliopolis* (tourism), *Informatique* (IBM has been here since 1965), *Agropolis* (it boasts the first European research centre of agronomy in hot climates, among other institutes) and *Pole Antenna*, for its role as the telecommunications centre of Languedoc. Meanwhile, the city used to teasingly threaten to tax the balconies of its residents to pay for the ambitious 'follies' of Mayor Frêche, follies that are the envy of nearly every other city in France. One of the last was a high-tech, ultramodern tramway, like those of Strasbourg and Nantes; even the stops are decorated with artworks and nicely landscaped.

A Place Named Comédie

The various personalities of Montpellier all come together in the lively, café-lined **Place de la Comédie**, locally known as *l'Œuf*, or the Egg, owing to the shape it had in the 18th century. Now flattened into an omelette, its centre is watered by the fountain of the *Three Graces* (1796), while along one side stretches the waist-level trough of a modern fountain, where three bronze stooges gesticulate frantically, presumably because they forgot their trousers. Other ornaments of the square include a *doppelgänger* of the Paris Opera, and various 19th-century larded bourgeois buildings with domes reminiscent of bathyspheres, while opposite the square looms a modern glass-and-steel semi-ziggurat, the **Polygone**, a shopping mall and town hall complex.

To the north of Place de la Comédie extends the **Esplanade Charles de Gaulle**, replacing the city walls demolished by Louis XIII after the siege of 1622, the better to keep Montpellier at the mercy of the cannons of his new citadel. In the 18th century the Esplanade was planted with rows of trees and became Montpellier's chief *promenade*; among its monuments is a rare survival of 1908, the **Cinématographe Pathé**, a little cockerel-emblazoned palace from the magical early days of cinema (now renamed the **Rabelais Cultural Centre**, it often shows foreign films). The north end of the Esplanade is flanked by the mastodontic **CORUM**, 'the House of Innovation' designed by Claude Vasconi, one of Georges Frêche's Euro-Cité showcases, which encompasses the Opéra Berlioz and two smaller congress halls.

Antigone

East of the Comédie lies another of the jewels in the Euro-Cité's crown: Antigone, a mostly moderate-income quarter with housing for 10,000 people, and shops and restaurants, all designed by Barcelona architect Ricardo Bofill in 1979 and spread along a huge formal axis down to the river Lez. Bofill understood just what a Rome of Tomorrow needs: 'a parody of neo-Classicism', as Robert Hughes wrote – Mannerist neo-Roman arches, cornices, pilasters, and columns as big as California redwoods, built around the **Place du Nombre d'Or** and the **Place du Millénaire**, the squares of the 'Golden Number' and the 'Millennium' that link Montpellier to its newly dredged-out Tiber, the Lez. Does Antigone work? Even though it stretches nearly to the centre of the city, there was no attempt to relate the project to the rest of town – as you'll discover when you try to find it (from Comédie, the only way to reach Antigone is to pass through the Polygone shopping mall and walk out the back door of the Galeries Lafayette department store). On a bad day, Antigone looks like the surreal background to a De Chirico painting, as troubling as the Antigone of myth; on a good day, it seems like a delightful place to live, especially for kids, who can play football in the monumental Place du Millénaire and still hear their parents call them in for lunch. The newest parts of the project lie along the Lez: a gargantuan semicircle of apartments with a vaguely Stalinist air called the **Esplanade d'Europe**, decorated with a huge blue 'M' for Montpellier on the pavement. This part of the river has been blocked off by two bridges that hug the waterline, forming a space for paddling canoes; opposite Antigone across the river, and closing the long axis, stands a sharp glass and stone castle housing the Hérault regional council, the **Hôtel de Région**.

Musée Fabre

Musée Fabre
t 04 67 14 83 00; open Tues, Thurs, Fri and Sun 10–6, Wed 1–9, Sat 11–6; closed Mon and hols; adm

At 39 Bd Bonne Nouvelle, between the Cinématographe and CORUM, in the fastness of a former Jesuit College, the Musée Fabre has long been the main reason for visiting Montpellier, with one of the most important collections of art in provincial France, now even bigger since reopening in 2007 after four years of renovation.

This museum was founded on a Florentine romance. François Xavier Fabre (1766–1837), a pupil of David, was in Florence at the outbreak of the French Revolution, where he became a close friend of the countess of Albany, the merry widow of Bonnie Prince Charlie, and her lover, the Italian dramatist Vittore Alfieri. When

Alfieri died in 1805, he left the countess his library and paintings. Fabre in turn inherited the countess's affections, and when she died in 1824, she left everything to her young man from Montpellier. A year later, Fabre donated the lot to his native city; the valuable Alfieri and Albany libraries are now in the **Médiathèque Centrale Emile Zola**.

The museum has been entirely renovated and today has a total area of 9,200 square metres and contains 900 works of art from the 15th to the 21st centuries, including paintings, sculptures and drawings. The collection spreads across three buildings including the Jesuit College, the Hôtel Massillian and 19th-century annexes. A new wing has been added containing over 30 pieces dating from 1951–2005 by artist Pierre Soulages, who was born in Rodez, in the *département* of Aveyron.

The entrance to the museum is through a marble and granite work of art in itself: *La Portée*, conceived by artist Daniel Buren. A chronological visit starts downstairs with Dutch and Flemish painters including a good Rubens portrait and works by Ruysdael, Jan Steen and David Teniers. Then it's up to the first floor for European paintings and sculpture from the mid-15th to the mid-18th centuries including some gems such as the lush *Mystic Marriage of St Catherine* by Veronese, which explains why 'Veronese green' is such a popular colour in France. There is also a self-portrait by Bernini and, from Spain, a Ribera and a pair of Zurbarans, including *St Agatha* carrying her breasts on a plate and the *Angel Gabriel*, who looks as if he can't find the right address. Also included are works by Montpellier-born artists including Sébastien Bourdon (including his best known work *Homme aux Rubans Noirs*, painted while he was in the city in 1657–8), Jean Ranc and Jean Raoux.

The neoclassical section includes works by Fabre himself, who proves to be as romantic in art as in his life (*St Sébastian* and *The Death of Narcissus*), and, more influential, Jean-Baptiste Greuze, who seems to have invented the simpering genre of big-eyed kid pictures sold in supermarkets. There is also Joshua Reynolds' famous *Infant Samuel in Prayer*.

The section 'Romanticism and Classicism' is largely composed of works donated by the museum's other great benefactor, Alfred Bruyas (1821–77). Born into a Montpellier banking family, Bruyas resolved the frustration of not being able to paint himself by befriending many of the artists of his day and asking them to paint him instead – as a result there are 24 portraits of the red-bearded patron in this museum alone, including examples by Delacroix and Alexandre Cabanel of Montpellier (1823–89). The latter studied in Rome but left his best work in Montpellier including the pre-Raphaelesque *Albaydé*, *La Chiarruccia* and *Self-Portrait at Age 29*.

Four of Bruyas' portraits are by Gustave Courbet (1819–77), who became the great man's friend and whose works are the highlight of the museum. Two paintings were pivotal in Courbet's proto-impressionist discovery of light; the *Baigneuses*, which caused such a scandal in the Paris Salon of 1853 that Napoléon III ordered it to be removed, and the delightful, sun-drenched *Bonjour, Monsieur Courbet* (1854) in which the jaunty Courbet, strutting down a country lane with easel and paints strapped to his back, meets who else but Alfred Bruyas?

Other paintings in this section cover the artistic movements on either side of Courbet; the later cold classicism of Ingres' *Stratonice* (1866) and David's clean, unbloodied *Dead Hector*, which stand as the antithesis of the warm, exotic romanticism of Delacroix's *Mulatress and Algerian Odalisques* (1849) or the melting landscapes of Corot. From southern painters of the period there are big historical and exotic scenes and landscapes. The gloomy young romantic artist Théodore Gericault (1791–1824) is represented by an idealized *Portrait of Lord Byron* and a surreal *Study of Arms and Legs*, cannibal leftovers painted in a medical school while students dissected the corpses. There is a landscape by English painter Richard Parkes Bonington.

On the second floor, in the modern section '1850–Abstractionism', there is a room dedicated to the early impressionist Frédéric Bazille, who died at war aged only 28. He was a friend of Renoir and Monet (some of whose paintings are also present). His best works glow with the strong sun of Languedoc: *Les Remparts d'Aigues-Mortes* and *La Vue du Village* (Castelnau, now engulfed by Montpellier). Eugène Castelneau (1827–94) painted bright landscapes around Languedoc like the *Vue du Pic Saint-Loup* (1859). There are also works by Berthe Morisot, Robert Delaunay, Kees Van Dongen and Nicolas de Stael's painting of Ménerbes, which if it really looked like that wouldn't attract so many tourists or disciples of Peter Mayle. The Soulages collection is also on the second floor, of interest if you are into the artistic possibilities of the colour black. Other modern artists are represented back on the first floor, including Claude Viallat, Vincent Bioulès and other followers of the movement '*Supports-Surfaces*'.

Prestigious temporary exhibitions are also organized at the museum and a programme is in place up to two years ahead. Other new additions to the museum include a resource centre, shop, auditorium and restaurant.

The museum's collection of furniture, decorative pieces, ceramics and *objets d'art* will be exhibited at the **Hôtel Sabatier d'Espeyran** (6 bis Rue Montpelliéret), which is currently being renovated and is due to open at the end of 2008.

Into the Ecusson

There is nothing else as compelling as the Musée Fabre in Montpellier's historic centre; much was lost in the Wars of Religion, and even the many 17th- and 18th-century *hôtels particuliers*, stuccoed and ornate though many of them are inside, show mostly blank walls to the street. But few cities in the south of France manage to be as pleasant and lively. Instead of gaggles of tourists, Montpellier has students to keep the city on its toes; this is the second-biggest university town in the south after Toulouse. Mayor Frêche made the entire Ecusson a pedestrian zone, and a delightful place for walking.

One of the major crossroads of the Ecusson is Place Notre-Dame, under the cool gaze of the neoclassical **Notre-Dame-des-Tables** (1748), originally the chapel connected to the Jesuit college that is now the Musée Fabre. In front passes the old pilgrims' route, the Cami Romieu, now Rue de l'Aiguillerie, where St Roch was arrested as a spy (see the plaque by Rue du Pila-St-Gély), and where Montpellier merchants and innkeepers cashed in on passing pilgrims. In the crypt is the **Musée de l'Histoire de Montpellier**, with audiovisuals and other techniques telling the city's history.

Residential *hôtels particuliers* went up later; nearby **Rue du Cannau** has some of the flashiest 17th-century models, while, in Place Pétrarque, the **Hôtel de Varennes**' façade (1758) conceals a pair of Gothic halls, one a depository for architectural fragments salvaged from medieval Montpellier. Upstairs, there's a pair of small museums devoted to the good old days. The **Musée du Fougau** ('the Foyer') was founded to preserve the arts and traditions of old Montpellier by the local Félibres, the artificially contrived literary movement founded by the 24-year-old Frédéric Mistral and five other poets in 1854 to safeguard the seven 'grand dialects' of Occitan, including Provençal and Languedocien. The **Musée du Vieux Montpellier** exhibits portraits of notables, and plans and views of the city from the 16th century on, along with some peculiar relics, such as the model of the Bastille carved from one of the fortress's stones soon after it was demolished in 1789.

Around the corner, at 4 Rue Embouque-d'Or, the 1670 **Hôtel de Manse** is famous for its richly decorated openwork staircase, designed by Italian architects – a stair that became the prototype for a score of others in Montpellier, including the one in the gorgeous Renaissance courtyard of the nearby **Hôtel de Lunaret**, at 5 Rue des Trésoriers-de-France. This, combined with the adjoining **Hôtel des Trésoriers de France**, around the block at 7 Rue Jacques Cœur, was the residence of the famous merchant and financier Jacques Cœur, whose motto was 'flies can't enter a closed mouth'. In 1441 he was appointed a treasurer of Charles VII, and charged with obtaining royal subsidies from Languedoc. Reasoning that the

Musée de l'Histoire de Montpellier
open Tues–Sat 10.30–12.30 and 1.30–6; last entry 11.50 and 5.20

Musée du Fougau
open Wed and Thurs 3–6

Musée du Vieux Montpellier
open Tues–Sat 9.30–12 and 1.30–5; adm

wealthier the land, the easier it is to tax, Cœur became one of Montpellier's greatest benefactors, among other things building a merchants' exchange and dredging the outlets of the Lez to make them navigable; this town house originally had a tower so high that he could scan the sea and its traffic. His career ended abruptly in 1451, when he was accused of poisoning the king's mistress, Agnès Sorel; he escaped prison in 1454 and died on the Greek island of Chios, fighting the Ottomans for the pope.

Although much renovated since Jacques Cœur's day, most of the contents of the *hôtel particulier* predate him, as it's now the **Musée Languedocien**. Although you may have to arrange your schedule to fit theirs (*see* opening times, left), it has its rewards – Greek vases, dolmens, funeral steles and other prehistoric finds from the Hérault; an excellent collection of Romanesque sculpture salvaged from the 11th-century version of Notre-Dame-des-Tables and from surrounding abbeys; the rock-crystal seal of King Sancho of Aragon; and three 12th-century Islamic funeral steles discovered in Montpellier, a rare relic of the city's cosmopolitan spice-trading days. From Jacques Cœur's day there are two fine paintings, an anonymous Catalan *SS. Apolline and Guilhem* and, from the Clouets' workshop, *Gabrielle d'Estrées and her Sister in their Bath*. A major collection of 16th–18th-century faïence made in Montpellier rounds things off, together with a grand ceiling painting of 1660, *Justice Discovering Truth with the Help of Time* by Jean de Troy, the city's top interior decorator of the age. A plaque nearby in Rue des Trésoriers-de-France recalls that another of the city's colourful cast of characters lived here: that great wanderer Rabelais, who enrolled at Montpellier's medical school in 1530, at the age of 40, and became a doctor as well as a priest, although he later wrote that 'physicians always smelled of enemas, like old devils' (*Pantagruel*, 1532).

To the south, Rue Jacques Cœur becomes **Grand-Rue Jean Moulin**, one of the city's most elegant streets. On guided visits organized by the tourist office you can see the **Amphithéâtre Anatomique St-Côme**, built in 1757 with funds left by Louis XV's surgeon, François Gigot de Lapeyronie. Turn left at the foot of Grand Rue Jean Moulin for the **Tour de la Babote**, a recently restored medieval tower topped by an astronomical observatory in 1741.

Musée Languedocien
open mid-June–mid-Sept Mon–Sat 3–6; mid-Sept–mid-June Mon–Sat 2.30–5.30; adm

Western Quarters: Rue Foch and the Promenade du Peyrou

Despite its Protestant leanings, Montpellier's fame in heaven's circle hinges on Roch, the pious son of a wealthy merchant, who was born around 1350 and abandoned all of his worldly goods to make the pilgrimage to Rome in 1367. On his way home, he came to an Italian village decimated by plague; after curing a number of victims with the sign of the Cross, Roch went down with the disease himself, and retreated to the country where no one could hear his groans. Nourished by a friendly dog who stole food for him from its master's table, Roch recovered and returned to Montpellier, so ravaged and changed by his illness that he wasn't recognized and was thrown into prison as a spy, where he died in 1379. Only then did his grandmother recognize him by a birthmark in the shape of a cross. News of Roch's reputation as an inter-mediary against the Black Death reached plague-torn Venice, and even though he had yet to be canonized, Venetians disguised as pilgrims stole his bones and built the magnificent Confraternity of San Rocco in his honour – one of the wonders of the lagoon city. As patron saint of Montpellier, St Roch came through for his home town in the cholera epidemics of 1832 and 1849, and finally a church of **St-Roch** was built, in Viollet-le-Duc's Ideal Gothic, in the medieval quarter of the Ecusson.

Rue Voltaire leads up to the socializing centre of the neighbour-hood, Rue de l'Ancien Courrier and Place St-Ravy. Here, too, is one of the most handsome residences in old Montpellier, **Hôtel des Trésoriers-de-la-Bourse** (1631–93), on the street of the same name.

From the centre of the Ecusson, **Rue Foch** was sliced out in the 18th century as a grand formal boulevard, just missing a rare Jewish ritual bath, or Mikveh, at 1 Rue Barralerie. Dating from c. 1200, it was part of the synagogue in the midst of what was then a large, active Jewish quarter. Since the late 17th century, however, this loftiest edge of Montpellier has been devoted to tons of mouldy fol-de-rol glorifying Louis XIV, beginning with an **Arc de Triomphe** (the triumphs referred to include digging a canal, wrestling the English lion to the ground and conquering heresy – with the Revocation of the Edict of Nantes, a nasty piece of bigotry that went down like a lead balloon in Montpellier). You can climb its 103 steps on a guided visit from the tourist office. Beyond stretches the **Promenade du Peyrou**, a nice park spoiled by an equestrian statue of his megalomaniac majesty as big as the Trojan horse. It was brought down laboriously from Paris in 1718, fell into the Garonne en route, whence it was rescued and brought here, only to be smashed to bits in the Revolution – a fact that didn't prevent the erection of the present copy in 1838. At the edge of the promontory stands the far more elegant **Château d'Eau**, one of Montpellier's landmarks, a neoclassical temple designed by Jean Giral to disguise the reservoir of the **Aqueduc St-Clément** (1771) snaking below in curious perspec-tive, a triple-tiered work inspired by the Pont du Gard that brings in water from the river Lez. The promenade has recently undergone an upheaval: American architect Richard Meier was charged with adding the **Espace Pitot** to the area, a complex including a swim-ming pool and car park. The huge **cross** you can see looking south of the Promenade was erected by a Catholic society in the 1820s.

Mikveh
to visit, contact the tourist office

The Cathedral and the Jardin des Plantes

The waters of the aqueduct feed the unicorn fountain in the nearby **Place de la Canourgue**, a charming 17th-century square shaded by nettle trees (*micocouliers*). It looks down on the medieval monastery college of St-Benoît, on Rue de l'Ecole de Médecine, built by papal architects from Avignon, currently (since 1795) the **Faculté de Médecine**, housing an enormous medical library. Adjacent, the former monastic chapel has been Montpellier's **Cathédrale St-Pierre** ever since the see was transferred here from Maguelone in 1563, although its status didn't spare it the usual depredations in the Wars of Religion and the Revolution. The cathedral's greatest distinction is its unusual porch, supported by two conical turrets.

Boulevard Henri IV, running alongside the Faculté, descends to the tree-topped **Tour des Pins**, a last vestige of the medieval walls. Beyond lies the lovely **Jardin des Plantes**, France's oldest botanical garden, founded by a decree of Henri IV in 1593 to instruct students on native and exotic plants used for healing. It has several magnificent 400-year-old trees, exotic succulents, *garrigue* plants, and an *orangerie*; near the latter, in a spot celebrated for its exquisite melancholy, there's a plaque with the inscription *Placandis Narcissae Manibus*. The Narcissa is said to be the consumptive 18-year-old daughter of the poet Edward Young (best known for his *Night Thoughts*, illustrated by Blake). In 1734 he brought Narcissa to France, hoping the warm climate would cure her; instead the exertion of travelling killed her, and she was buried either in Lyon or here 'in the garden she loved' – a story that made this a favourite rendezvous for romantic students like Paul Valéry and André Gide. At the highest point of the garden is the Tree of Secrets, its trunk pitted with niches where lovers would leave *billets d'amour*.

The Montpellier Follies

Montpellier, one of the fastest-growing cities in France, is spreading its tentacles to suck in all that surrounds it, and has already gobbled up a number of 18th-century châteaux and gardens that were the country retreats of its élite.

One of the oldest is 3km east of Antigone on the D24: the **Château de Flaugergues**. Begun in the 1690s, the place is impressively filled with 17th- and 18th-century furnishings and tapestries, and a collection of optical instruments. It also produces wine. A bit further east (take the D172), **Château de la Mogère** is a refined *folie* of 1716, with period furnishings, family portraits and, in the garden, a delightful Baroque *buffet d'eau*, a fountain built into a wall.

North of Montpellier, on the road to Mende, the **Parc Zoologique de Lunaret** has exotic and regional fauna, where you can wander amid woodlands and *garrigues*. They are proud of their brand new

---

Faculté de Médecine
can be visited on a tourist office tour

Jardin des Plantes
www.jardindesplantes. univ-montp1.fr, **t** *04 67 63 43 22; open June– Sept Tues–Sun 12–8; Oct–May Tues–Sun 12–6*

Les Folies
Before setting out, check hours at the tourist office; some places can only be visited on the office's 'Les Folies' tour

Château de Flaugergues
t *04 99 52 66 37, www.flaugergues.com; guided tours June, July and Sept Tues–Sun 2.30– 6.30, otherwise phone; gardens open June, July and Sept Mon–Sat 9–12.30 and 2.30–7, Sun 2.30–7; winter by appt only; closed Sun; adm*

Château de la Mogère
t *04 67 65 72 01, www. lamogere.com; guided tours June–Sept Sun–Fri 2.30–6.30; Oct–May Sat, Sun and hols only, by appt; adm*

Parc Zoologique de Lunaret
www.zoo.montpellier.fr; open summer Mon–Sat 9–7; winter till dusk; adm

---

Amazonia greenhouse encompassing the main eco-systems and fauna of the region. The 1750 **Château d'O** (northwest, on the road to Grabels), now used for receptions, art exhibitions and theatrical performances, is famous for its park, decorated with statues taken from the gardens of the **Château de la Mosson** (1729), which lies to the south, just off the N109. La Mosson was the most opulent of all the follies until the Revolution and its conversion into a soap factory; after decades of neglect the city of Montpellier acquired it in 1982 and is still restoring it. It has a lovely oval, Venetian-style music chamber and a poignant seashell-and-pebble *buffet d'eau* in the garden, now stripped of all its ornaments.

From Mosson, take the D27E/D5E and turn towards Pignan for the remarkable 1250 church of the Cistercian **Abbaye St-Martin-du-Vignogoul**. Believed to be the first attempt at Gothic in Languedoc, the church is small in size but grand in vision, a lofty, single-naved, pint-sized cathedral decorated with a trefoil arch, finely sculpted capitals (still more Romanesque than Gothic), and a unique polygonal choir, lit by a row of bull's-eye windows.

Abbaye St-Martin-du-Vignogoul
t 04 67 42 76 68;
open Mon–Fri 10–12
and 2–6

Tourist Information in Montpellier

ⓘ **Montpellier >**
Town centre: Allée Jean de Lattre de Tassigny, Esplanade de la Comédie,
t 04 67 60 60 60,
www.ot-montpellier.fr;
open daily

Airport, *Arrivals hall, between doors A and B*

The **tourist offices** have a hotel reservation service in season and offer tours of the city centre in English, every Sat at 5.30 in season. Ask about the **City Card**, which can be bought for between one and three days and gives free transport plus free entrance to certain sights plus reductions on concerts and activities.

Market Days in Montpellier

At Espace Mosson (La Paillade), there is a **flower** market on Tues and a **flea** market on Sun am. Daily **food** markets take place in Halles Castellanes (Rue de la Loge) and Halles Laissac (Place A. Laissac); Tues–Sat there's a market at Bd des Arceaux, by Rue Marioge; and at Antigone a market of **farmers' produce** every Wed, Place du Nombre d'Or. Ask at the tourist office for others.

Festivals in Montpellier

The city hosts many festivals: among them are theatre in June and early July, during the ***Printemps des***

Comédiens at Château d'O, **t** 04 67 63 66 67, *www.printempsdescomediens. com;* dance performances of all kinds, including whirling dervishes, films and workshops at the ***Festival International Montpellier Danse***, **t** 04 67 60 83 60, *www.montpellierdanse.com*, also June and July; and all-star music from opera to jazz at the ***Festival de Radio France et Montpellier***, **t** 04 67 61 66 81, *www.festivalradiofrance montpellier.com*, in the last three weeks of July. The end of October sees the ***Festival International du Cinéma Méditerranéen***, **t** 04 99 13 73 73, *www.cinemed.tm.fr.*

Shopping in Montpellier

The tourist office has a display of wine, *confits* and other regional products; antiques shops cluster around Place de la Canourgue and the district of Ste-Anne.

The Bookshop, 6 Rue de l'Université, **t** 04 67 66 09 08, *www.bookshop-montpellier.com*. A good selection of English books and videos, and the latest lowdown on Montpellier. *Open Mon–Sat 9.30–1 and 2.30–7.*

Caves Notre-Dame, 1,348 Av de la Mer, on the other side of the river, **t** 04 67

64 48 00, *www.cavesnotredame.com*. An excellent source of local wines and information, including tastings. *Open Mon–Fri 9–12 and 3–7.30.*

Maison Régionale des Vins et des Produits du Terroir, 34 Rue St-Guilhem, **t** 04 67 60 40 41, *www.maison regionaledesvins.com*. A good range of local wines and food products from olive oil to caviar. *Open Mon–Sat 9.30–8.*

Where to Stay in Montpellier

Montpellier ✉ 30400

Montpellier is well endowed with hotels, especially two-star hotels for small business travellers that double well enough for pleasure travellers. You'll find a choice of inexpensive places on the side streets around Place de la Comédie.

******Le Jardin des Sens**, 11 Av St-Lazare (off the N113 towards Nîmes; bus 4), **t** 04 99 58 38 38, *www.jardindessens. com* (€€€€€–€€€€). Modern rooms, and with a pool and restaurant. *See* 'Eating Out'.

⭐ Le Jardin de Sens ≫

******Holiday Inn Métropole**, 3 Rue du Clos-René, **t** 04 67 12 32 32, *www. holidayinn-montpellier.com* (€€€€). Top of the line: antique-furnished, with a quiet garden courtyard and restaurant (€€), between the train station and Place de la Comédie.

⭐ Demeure des Brousses ≯

*****Demeure des Brousses**, Rte des Vauguières (4km east of town on the D24 and D172E), **t** 04 67 65 77 66, *www.demeure-des-brousses.fr* (€€€–€€€). If you have a car, note that the most charming place to stay is this 18th-century ivy-covered *mas* in a vast park, a few minutes from the city or the sea. No restaurant, but next door is the gastronomic haven of **Le Mas des Brousses**, **t** 04 67 64 18 91 (€€€€–€€). *Restaurant closed Sat lunch, Sun eve and Mon.*

*****La Maison Blanche**, 1796 Av de la Pompignane (off the route to Carnon), **t** 04 99 58 20 70, *www.hotelmaison blanche.fr* (€€). Another gem requiring your own transport: a big, balconied house that looks as if it has escaped from the French quarter of New

Orleans, surrounded by a park. *Restaurant closed Sat lunch and Sun.*

****Parc**, 8 Rue Achille Bégé, **t** 04 67 41 16 49, *www.hotelduparc-montpellier. com* (€€). An 18th-century *hôtel particulier* fitted out with air-conditioning, TV, etc.

****Palais**, 3 Rue Palais des Guilhem (just off Rue Foch), **t** 04 67 60 47 38 (€€). Comfortable rooms in a recently restored building.

****Arceaux**, 33–5 Bd Arceaux, **t** 04 67 92 03 03, *www.hoteldesarceaux.com* (€€). Attractive, clean and comfortable, with a small garden and terrace.

Majestic, 4 Rue du Cheval Blanc, **t** 04 67 66 26 85, *hotelmajestic34@ yahoo.fr* (€€–€). Around the corner from the Etuves.

***Les Fauvettes**, 8 Rue Bonnard, **t** 04 67 63 17 60 (€). Good value for money near the Jardin des Plantes, with quiet rooms overlooking interior courtyards.

Etuves, 24 Rue des Etuves, **t** 04 67 60 78 19, *www.hoteldesetuves.fr* (€). Cheap and comfortable.

Eating Out in Montpellier

Le Jardin des Sens, 11 Av St-Lazare (off the N113 towards Nîmes), **t** 04 99 58 38 38, *www.jardin-des-sens.com* (€€€€). Montpellier, not formerly celebrated for its cuisine, is now home to one of the most celebrated restaurants in the southwest. It is run by local twins Jacques and Laurent Pourcel, who are devoted to the *cuisine* of Languedoc and the Med. Try the squid stuffed with ratatouille and crayfish tails, *bourride* soup, fish soup and traditional *oreillette* pastries. Fifteen rooms are also available (*see* 'Where to Stay'). *Closed Sun, Mon lunch and Wed lunch in July and Aug, Sept–June Sun, Mon, Tues lunch, and Wed lunch; also 2 weeks Jan.*

Cellier Morel, 27 Rue de l'Aiguillerie, **t** 04 67 66 46 36, *www.celliermorel. com* (€€€). Serves local produce in a 13th-century vaulted dining room, and sells it in the adjoining shop. *Closed Sun all day, Mon lunch, Wed lunch and Sat lunch.*

Le Petit Jardin >

Le Petit Jardin, 20 Rue J-J Rousseau, t 04 67 60 78 78, *www.petit-jardin.com* (€€€–€€). Remarkably quiet restaurant in the centre of town, with a delightful large shady garden with a view of the cathedral. Good local fish, salads and fresh pasta with vegetables. *Closed Mon.*

L'Olivier, 12 Rue Aristide Olivier, t 04 67 92 86 28 (€€). A popular family restaurant bang on the new tramway; smooth service, classic cuisine specialising in fish, and the best local wine. *Closed Sun and Mon.*

Lively Rue des Ecoles Laïques and Place de la Chapelle Neuve make up Montpellier's **Latin Quarter**, where the colours and smells from the assorted Turkish, Greek, Spanish and Tunisian restaurants collide in gleeful culinary discord.

Tripti-Kulai, 20 Rue Jacques Cœur, t 04 67 66 30 51, *www.triptikulai.com* (€). A vegetarian restaurant and tea room near the Musée Languedocien that offers some exotic dishes. *Closed Sun.*

Pizzéria du Palais, 22 Rue Palais des Guilhem, t 04 67 60 67 97 (€). Here you may safely break the Languedoc-Roussillon pizza rule (never order a pizza in Languedoc-Roussillon): it's Italian-run, with a wide choice of toppings to put together.

Entertainment and Nightlife in Montpellier

Montpellier is a great town for cinema, both recent releases and classics; complete listings for these, as well as clubs, theatre and music, can be found in the city weekly *La Gazette*. FNAC, in the Polygone, sells tickets for events.

CORUM, t 04 67 61 67 61, *www.corum-montpellier.fr*. Home of the Orchestre National de Montpellier and the Opéra Berlioz.

Opéra Comédie, 11 Bd Victor Hugo, t 04 67 60 19 80, *www.opera-montpellier.com*. Opera and theatrical performances.

Most **bars** and **clubs** do not heat up until after 11pm.

Rockstore Odéon, down from Place de la Comédie at 20 Rue de Verdun, t 04 67 06 80 00, *www.rockstore.fr*. Still the place to be. A café, five bars, concert hall and disco. *Open Mon–Sat till 4am.*

La Villa Rouge, at Lattes, t 04 67 06 50 54. Buzzy place on the beachfront – disco, concerts and themed evenings. *Closed Mon and Tues.*

At weekends and often weekdays there's live **jazz**, **blues** or **world music:**

Le Fil, 16 Rue du Pila St-Gély, t 04 67 66 20 67. A philosophy café, with French music and jazz. *Closed Sat and Sun.*

The Hérault

*For devotees of rural France, this
seemingly innocuous area may be
the ultimate find. Just enough
tourists come for there to be plenty
of country inns and fermes-
auberges, though in some villages
foreigners are still a novelty. The
food is good, and there's enough
wine to make anyone happy. That's
an understatement – the Hérault is
the most prolific wine-producing
region in France. It can be a perfect
alternative to overcrowded and
overpraised Provence: just as
beautiful, more real and relaxed,
full of things to see – and
considerably less expensive.*

*In this region, some 150km across
at most, the diversity is tremendous:
a microcosm of France, from
mountain forests of oak and pine,
and limestone cirques and causses,
to the endless beaches of the coast
and the rolling hills around the
Canal du Midi.*

09

Don't miss

⭐ **A town scarcely
changed since
Molière's day**
Pézenas p.170

⭐ **A stately canal
for boating down**
The Canal du Midi p.175

⭐ **A fishing port
with a sardine
museum**
Sète p.163

⭐ **A seven-sided
church**
Rieux-Minervois p.182

⭐ **The ruins of a
decadent abbey**
Abbaye de Valmagne
p.166

See map overleaf

The Hérault

pp.268–9

pp.188–9

pp.188–9

France isn't the sort of country that allows itself to be neatly
dissected for the benefit of geographers and travel writers. So it
is only for convenience's sake that the rugged *garrigue* of the
upper Hérault, the green hills of the Espinouse and the flat
expanses of the Béziers coast are combined together in one
chapter (along with an adjacent corner of the Aude *département*,
the Minervois).

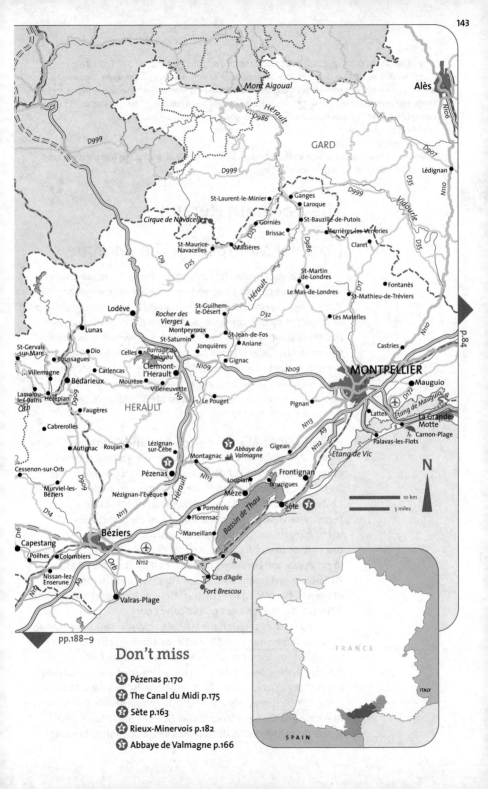

Don't miss

⭐ Pézenas p.170

⭐ The Canal du Midi p.175

⭐ Sète p.163

⭐ Rieux-Minervois p.182

⭐ Abbaye de Valmagne p.166

Beaches

The sands of the Camargue continue around the elbow of the French coast. The Golfe d'Aigues-Mortes washes against immense swaths of sand, much of which is being eaten up by concrete development, such as the resort of **La Grande Motte**. **Palavas** is Montpellier's summer cruising zone – trendy and overpopulated. For more space and fewer frills, head south past Sète, or stop at the tranquil **Plage des Aresquiers**, accessible only by a dead-end road from Frontignan.

The **best beaches** are:

Palavas: wide sand, quite lively.

Espiguette: this lovely beach, signposted from Le Grau-de-Roi, is wild, with dunes and plenty of sand grass. Try a picnic at dusk for a breathtaking sunset.

The Northern Hérault

North of Montpellier: The *Garrigue*

On a map, you'll notice lots of blank space in this region, a *pays* without a name. It is a geographer's textbook example of *garrigue*, a dry limestone plateau with sparse vegetation, where even sheep only just get by. *Garrigue* is an old Occitan word for the holly oak, and these scrubby would-be trees grow everywhere, along with thyme and lavender-scented *maquis* and, increasingly, vines, which not only thrive but also are quickly changing the local economy. The windblown landscapes are as romantic as anything in Provence, although a shade more sombre. The few villages seem huddled, closed into themselves.

Pic St-Loup, St-Martin-de-Londres and Cambous

From Montpellier, the best approach to the *garrigue* is by way of the D17 to **St-Mathieu-de-Tréviers**, where you can pick up the D1/D122 west, a scenic high road that passes below the ruined **Château de Montferrand**, a long climb but one that offers a memorable view. Montferrand was one of the first castles to fall to the Albigensian Crusade, but the real damage was done by Louis XIV, as part of his general royal policy of cleaning up unnecessary and possibly dangerous castles. The view takes in **Pic St-Loup**, just up the road, a striking 2,110ft exclamation point of the *garrigue*. Along with the cliff-rimmed lump of the **Montagne d'Hortus**, it is the remnant of a volcanic crater.

The D122 passes through the typical *garrigue* village of **Le Mas de Londres** before arriving at **St-Martin-de-Londres** (25km direct on the D986 from Montpellier). St-Martin is a surprise package. Passing the tiny, densely built village on the road, you would never guess that it conceals one of the most exquisite medieval squares anywhere, picturesquely asymmetrical and surrounded by houses that have not changed for centuries. The ensemble has a church to match, an architecturally sophisticated 11th-century building

Getting around the Hérault

Except along the coast, public transport is rudimentary at best; the coastal **SNCF line** runs from Montpellier through Frontignan, Sète, Agde and Béziers on its way to Narbonne and Perpignan, with around six **trains** a day. For the interior there is a service from Béziers to Bédarieux, and trains from Béziers to Castres in the Tarn go via Toulouse.

Olargues is connected by **bus** to Bédarieux, St-Pons and Montpellier. From the *gare routière* in Montpellier there are regular bus services to Gignac, Clermont l'Hérault and Lodève, less frequently to other villages; there are buses to tourist attractions (like St-Guilhem-le-Désert) in summer.

---

with a rare elliptical cupola. A recent restoration, clearing out the dross of a brutal 19th-century remodelling, has uncovered some charming fragments of the original decoration: St Martin on horseback, carved Celtic spirals, and neo-Byzantine capitals. 'Londres' is a local place name, and has nothing to do with the big town on the island over the Channel.

Cambous
visits April–Oct for groups only; call the Société Languedocienne de Préhistoire, t 04 67 86 34 37, www.archeologue.org for further information

South of St-Martin, in a military zone just off the D32, a 5,000-year-old settlement was discovered at Cambous in 1967. With considerable intelligence and dedication, the archaeologists have made the site into a veritable re-creation of ancient life. They have reconstructed a communal house of this 'Fontbouisse civilization' and gathered together enough artefacts to make you feel entirely at home among the Fontbouissians. These peaceful folk knew both farming and husbandry, and were just learning about copper tools. They also had a well-developed cultural life, as evidenced by their geometrically decorated pottery and stone statue steles.

Verrerie de Couloubrines
call Claret tourist office on t 04 67 59 06 39; open-air site, guided visits for groups by appt

In the 13th–18th centuries, the country north of the **Causse d'Hortus** was famous for its 'Gentlemen Glassblowers', who passed their secrets down through the generations. North of St-Martin, on the D107E, learn about their art at the Renaissance Verrerie de Couloubrines in **Ferrières-les-Verreries**, restored in 1989. The *verrerie* in **Claret** has been closed until spring 2008, when it will be replaced by a museum on the history of glass and glass-blowing; there is still a glass-blower in action opposite the site. The tourist office in Claret has information on the **Chemin des Verriers**, a route set up to explore the tiny villages once attached in some way to the trade. In Claret you can also visit Europe's only family-run cade oil mill, the **Distillerie des Cévennes**; cade oil has been used for embalming since antiquity, and the mill offers a range of modern products made from the stuff.

Distillerie des Cévennes
t 04 67 59 02 50, www.cc-orthus.fr; call first

Ganges, Caves and the Cirque de Navacelles

Grotte des Demoiselles
t 04 67 73 70 02, www.demoiselles.com; open for tours July and Aug hourly 10–6; April–June and Sept hourly 10–12 and 1.45–5.30; Mar and Oct at 10, 11 and 2–4.30; Nov–Feb Mon–Fri hourly 2–4, plus Sun 10 and 11; adm

From St-Martin, the main D986 leads northwards towards the Cévennes. From the village of **St-Bauzille-de-Putois** (a *putois* is a polecat) there is a steep side road to the Grotte des Demoiselles, an important Protestant hideout during the war of the Camisards (1702–1704) which also has one of France's most spectacular displays of pipe-organ stalactites and stalagmites in the

The *Garrigue* and the Hérault Valley

St-Laurent-le-Minier • Ganges • Montoulieu
Laroque • Grotte de Laroque
Grotte des Demoiselles
Cirque de Navacelles St-Bauzille-de-Putois
Gorniès • Ferrières-les-Verreries
Gorges de la Vis Brissac
St-Maurice-Navacelles • Madières Claret •

5 km
2.5 miles
N

D9
D25

St-Martin de-Londres
Château de Montferrand
Le Mas-de-Londres
St-Mathieu-de-Tréviers •
Cambous

Lodève • † Prieuré St-Michel-de-Grandmont St-Guilhem-le-Désert Gorges de l'Hérault D32
Rocher des Vierges ▲ Grotte de Clamouse Les Matelles •
Pont du Diable HERAULT
St-Saturnin • St-Jean-de-Fos
Montpeyroux • Aniane
Jonquières

Celles •
Barrage du Salagou N109 MONTPELLIER
Clermont-l'Hérault Gignac •
Cirque de Mourèze N109
Mourèze • Villeneuvette
N9 Le Pouget •
Château d'Aumelas
Pignan •

staggeringly enormous 'Cathedral of the Abysses'. Visits take an hour by subterranean funicular; bring a sweater.

Geologically, this is folded country; along the Hérault you can clearly see the lines of stratification of limestone and schist in the cliffs. See them from river level by floating down the Hérault in a canoe (hire one at Canoë Le Moulin) to **Brissac**, which is guarded by a ruined castle perched on a pinnacle of rock.

Canoë Le Moulin
t 04 67 73 30 73,
www.canoe-france.
com/herault

Ganges is the only real town around, and quite a pleasant one, closed in between the river Hérault and *maquis*-carpeted hills. In the 18th century it was France's capital of silk stockings. Like most of the Cévennes, Ganges was and remains a mostly Protestant area; the old part of town is crisscrossed by *chemins de traverse*, labyrinthine passes laid out to confuse Catholic troops, and it has an imposing, peculiar seven-sided Protestant 'temple', built in 1850.

Ganges makes a good base for exploring this pretty region, between the *garrigue* and the Causse du Larzac. The **Gorges de la Vis** can be followed on the D25 west of town, passing a waterfall and a 17th-century château (at **St-Laurent-le-Minier**). The route through the gorges is 34km long (one-way only); the best parts, after **Madières**, can only be reached on foot. If you go the whole route, there's a real curiosity to be seen at the end: the famous **Cirque de Navacelles**. A cirque looks like a deep lunar crater, though it is in fact a loop dug deep into the limestone of the *garrigue* by

Wine: Coteaux du Languedoc

By the time Caesar conquered Gaul, the vineyards in the hills and the great plain of Languedoc (north and west of modern Montpellier) were already well established, thanks to the Greeks. Amphorae full of wine sent back to Rome met with such fervent demands for more that the winemakers back in Italy went to court to curtail the competition – history's first round of the great French–Italian wine battle. The Gauls won this one, perhaps because they hired the oratory of Cicero.

Zoom ahead to the 18th century, when the Canal du Midi made it easy to ship wine to northern Europe and the New World through Bordeaux. The region boomed, but boom turned to bust in the phylloxera epidemics of the 1880s. In the subsequent depression, recovery was hastened by grafting, and vintners, in response to the increased demand of the new industrial society, set their sights on the mass production of a soulless wine dubbed *bibine du Midi*, competing with tankers of high-octane plonk from Algeria and graded, as if it were crude oil, by its alcohol content – as French rotgut is to this day. All of this is only worth mentioning to help the newcomer better savour the revelation that now awaits in the bottles of Coteaux du Languedoc (AOC since 1985, *www.coteaux-languedoc.com*). The post-war return to Gallo-Roman techniques and craftsmanship have so improved matters that Coteaux du Languedoc has become one of the brightest stars in the French wine firmament. A huge, confusing region that takes in pockets from Lunel to Narbonne-Plage, it has been divided into 13 specialized micro-areas but the hierarchical arrangements and categories are mutable: as of 2007, AOC Coteaux du Languedoc encompasses 168 *communes*, 20 of which produce AOC St-Chinian, seven produce AOC Faugères, 102 produce AOC Coteaux du Languedoc followed by a geographical precision and 39 produce AOC Coteaux du Languedoc without any geographical zone being mentioned.

Dramatic *garrigue* landscapes characterize one of the top areas, Pic St-Loup. The hills and valleys create varying microclimates able to grow such diverse varietals as mourvèdre, syrah and grenache, producing earthy, meaty wines. There's a co-op there and three dozen or so producers, all tuned into new styles and producing excellent meaty red wines that can take considerable ageing. Recommended estates include **Mas Bruguière**, at Valflaunès, t 04 67 55 20 97; and the **Château La Roque**, at Fontanès, t 04 67 55 34 47, *www.chateau-laroque.eu* (*open Mon–Fri 9–12 and 3–7; Sept–June Mon, Wed and Sat 9–12 and 2–6*). Part of AOC Coteaux du Languedoc Terrasses du Larzac is the prize-winning **Domaine de la Devèze**, at Montoulieu, 6km northeast of St-Bauzille-de-Putois towards La Cadière, t 04 67 73 70 21, *www.deveze.com*.

Just west of Montpellier, at Lavérune, **Château de l'Engarran**, t 04 67 27 60 89, *www.chateau-engarran.com* (*open all year 9–7*), part of the *terroir* St-Georges d'Orques (AOC Coteaux du Languedoc Grès de Montpellier), produces fine red wines with a scent of dried herbs. The 2000 is highly recommended. In Jonquières, west of Gignac, the Julliens, father and son, have a fine array of wines at the **Mas Jullien**, t 04 67 96 60 04 (*open April–end Dec*).

At the far end of the region, southeast of Narbonne, AOC Coteaux du Languedoc-La Clape (*www.laclape.com*; *see* pp.199–201) is becoming an increasingly exciting area for wine lovers. The top-rated **Château de la Negly**, Fleury d'Aude, t 04 68 32 36 28, produces excellent whites as well as reds; the top of their line is named the 'Door to Heaven', **Porte du Ciel**. Other estates to look out for are **Château de Pech Redon**, t 04 68 90 41 22, where one of the first Languedoc pioneers, the late Jean Demolombe, produced his superb L'Epervier wines (*see* p.201), and **Château l'Hospitalet**, t 04 68 45 36 00 (*see* p.201).

The **Château de la Vernède** at Nissan-lez-Ensérune (*see* p.176), t 04 67 37 00 30, *www.chateaula vernede.com*, falls into AOC Coteaux du Languedoc Terrasses de Béziers, and produces among its offerings the ruby-red, intense and quite lively Château Ribet-Calet.

Observatoire Météo du Mont Aigoual
t 04 67 82 60 01,
www.aigoual.asso.fr;
open July and Aug 10–7;
May–June and Sept 10–1 and 2–7

the meandering river Vis long ago. There are many in the *garrigue*s of the Midi, and this is the most striking, with steep walls and a rocky 'island' in the centre. You can spend a day walking through it by picking up the GR7 at **St-Maurice-de-Navacelles**.

A second popular excursion from Ganges is the 30km drive north to the **Observatoire Météo du Mont Aigoual** (5,141ft), in the

Silk museum
t 04 66 77 66 47,
www.museedelasoie-
cevennes.com; open July
and Aug daily 10–12.30
and 2–6; April–June and
Sept–Nov Tues–Sun 10–
12.30 and 2–6; call for
hours of guided visits

(i) Ganges >>
Plan de l'Ormeau,
t 04 67 73 00 56,
www.ot-cevennes.com;
open Mon–Sat

(i) St-Martin-
de-Londres >
Place de la Mairie,
t 04 67 55 09 59,
www.tourismed.com;
open July and Aug daily;
Sept–June Sat am

(★) Ferme-
Auberge Domaine
de Blancardy >>

northern Gard. Set on the summit of the Cévennes, this has been the training ground for France's weather forecasters since 1887, and you can see why: on a clear day the view encompasses all the territory covered in this book, from Mont Blanc and the Alps to Canigou in the Pyrenees, down to the Mediterranean. Inside, a museum has photos, information on the work of the observatory, and old and high-tech new weather instruments. East of Ganges at St-Hippolyte du Fort there is a museum on the local silk industry, once so important to the Cévennes.

Market Days North of Montpellier

Ganges: Tues and especially Fri am, when the lively market takes over half the town.

Where to Stay and Eat North of Montpellier

St-Martin-de-Londres ✉ 34380

**Hostellerie Le Vieux Chêne, Causse de la Selle, west of Frouzet, t 04 67 73 11 00 (€€–€). Three double rooms and a good restaurant (€€€–€€) serving French classics on a pretty terrace. Closed early Jan–early Feb and 2 weeks Oct–Nov; restaurant closed Wed and Sun eve out of season.

Auberge de Saugras, Argelliers, south of St-Martin-de-Londres, t 04 67 55 08 71 (€€–€). A stone mas with several rooms and gourmet menus (€€€–€€). Book ahead, and ask for directions! Closed mid-Dec–mid-Jan; also Tues and Wed except July and Aug; restaurant closed Mon lunch, Tues lunch and Wed.

Bergerie du Bayle, in the garrigue just west of Frouzet, t 04 67 55 72 16, www.bergeriedubayle.com (€1,075 for 2 nights; 1 week minimum stay in summer, €2,550). Gîte accommodation for groups of up to 29. You do your own cooking.

Les Muscardins, 19 Route des Cévennes, t 04 67 55 75 90, www.les-muscardins.fr (€€€€–€€€). Gourmets from Montpellier drive up especially to feast on the fancy terrines and pâté, game dishes, formidable desserts and a selection of the best regional wines on a choice of four menus. Closed mid-Feb–mid-Mar, plus Mon and Tues.

Ganges ✉ 34190

***Les Norias, 254 Av des 2 Ponts, to the east of Ganges on the D25, t 04 67 73 55 90, www.les-norias.fr (€€–€). The dining room and terrace overlook the Hérault river and the restaurant (€€€–€€) features Mediterranean cooking. Closed mid-Nov–early Dec and part of Feb; restaurant closed Mon, and Tues lunch, except July and Aug.

Le Parc aux Cèdres, Laroques, south of Ganges, t 04 67 73 82 63 (€€–€). With a garden, pool and restaurant (€€). Closed Oct–Easter.

**Hôtel de la Poste, 8 Plan de l'Ormeau, t 04 67 73 85 88, www.hoteldelaposteganges.com (€). A prettily restored hotel.

Ferme-Auberge Domaine de Blancardy, Moules et Baucels, 7km east of Ganges on the D999, t 04 67 73 94 94, www.blancardy.com (€). With 14 rooms in a distinctive old mas from the 12th century, where home-made confits and pâté accompany fine wine (€€€–€€). Also has a gîte.

Maurice, Pont d'Hérault, 11km north of Ganges, t 04 67 82 40 02 (€€€€). The best cuisine du terroir around. Book early on the day you wish to eat; the number of non-residents allowed to dine depends on number of guests in the rooms (€). Closed Dec and Jan.

Gorniès ✉ 34190

****Château de Madières, 7km west of Gorniès, t 04 67 73 84 03, http://chateau-madieres.com (€€€€). If you want to combine the austerity of the garrigue with style and creature comforts, this hotel has 12 super-luxurious rooms in a 14th-century fort. Park, pool, fitness centre/gym and beautiful vaulted dining room (€€€). Closed Nov–Easter.

The Valley of the Hérault:
The Haut Pays d'Oc

The Hérault river slices dramatically through the *garrigue*, and the atmosphere is clear, luminous, otherworldly – the perfect landscape for saints and pilgrims, and for wine.

St-Guilhem-le-Désert

'Desert' might seem a little unfair to this rosemary-scented jumble of *garrigue* around St-Guilhem northwest of Montpellier; there are plenty of green, shady spots for a picnic, and even forests of pines. But *desert*, in French or English, originally meant deserted or uninhabited, as in 'desert island', and this is still as lonely a region as it was when the hermit St Guilhem came here, in the reign of Charlemagne. Besides being a delightful place to visit, St-Guilhem is a living history lesson, evoking the time when the 'desert' was a troubled frontier between Frank and Saracen, and later, when it became a key cultural outpost in the process of making the Midi Christian and French.

The little village of St-Guilhem is stretched on the edge of a ravine. Its one street being too narrow for traffic, a parallel road and car park has been built on the other side; from here you'll have a good view of its rugged stone houses, their gardens and tiny bridges, little changed since medieval times. On the village's main street, some modest Romanesque palaces survive from the 13th century, an especially picturesque one housing the *mairie*; at the opposite end, facing the D4 at the entrance to the village, the church of **St-Laurent** (now the tourist office) has a fine apse like that of the abbey church of St-Guilhem.

The Abbaye de Gellone

Abbaye de Gellone
*open July and Aug
Mon–Sat 8–6.10, Sun
and hols 8.30–10.45 and
12–6.10; Sept–June
Mon–Sat 7.45–5.40, Sun
and hols 8.30–10.45 and
12–5.45; abbey church
open same hours*

Guilhem Court-Nez, the powerful Frankish count of Toulouse, Aquitaine and Orange, was a grandson of Charles Martel and a cousin, liegeman and friend to Charlemagne. For over 30 years he campaigned from the Atlantic to the Alps, mostly against the Arabs, whose wave of 8th-century expansion through Spain had washed up as far north as Narbonne. Another of Guilhem's friends was Benedict, the monastic reformer from Aniane; Benedict, too, had once been a warrior, and he convinced Guilhem to follow his example and renounce the world. Guilhem spent the last six years of his life in a humble cell here, at a place near the gorges of the Hérault, originally called Gellone, and was canonized soon after his death in 812.

And soon after that, pilgrims began to visit. St-Guilhem was a popular saint with the Spaniards, and with northerners on their way to Compostela. The original community of hermit cells grew

Abbaye de Gellone

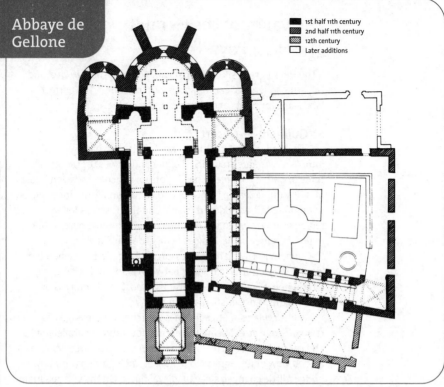

Legend:
- 1st half 11th century
- 2nd half 11th century
- 12th century
- Later additions

into a wealthy monastery; construction of the great abbey church began about 1050. Already in decline during the Wars of Religion, it was sacked by the Protestants in 1569 – its celebrated library was burnt in the process. The final indignity came not during the Revolution, surprisingly, but a decade before, when clerics from Lodève and other towns succeeded in having the monastery suppressed, apportioning its treasures and holy relics among themselves.

The **abbey church** is a remarkably grand and lovely specimen of Lombard architecture, with its blind arcading and trademark cross-shaped window. The best part, the broad, arcaded apse, recalls the contemporary churches of Milan or Pavia. The façade, facing an ancient, colossal plane tree in the village square, is somewhat blighted by an ungainly tower of cheap stone, built in the 14th century more for defence than for bell-ringing. The interior, lofty and dark, has lost almost all of its original decoration. Some fragments of frescoes survive in the side chapels, and niches in the pillars around the choir once held the relics of St-Guilhem and a bit of the True Cross, a gift from Charlemagne. The organ, built in 1782, is the focus of a summer series of Baroque concerts. The cloister is ruined, and most of its capitals have ended up at the Cloisters

Museum in New York. There are sometimes exhibitions there. The museum in the old refectory contains pieces and sculpture from the church and cloister.

Around St-Guilhem

More medieval relics can be seen along the Hérault: medieval mills, for grain and for oak bark (used in tanning leather), set near the modern trout hatcheries by the river. The hills around St-Guilhem make interesting exploring on foot – a ruined castle and other fortifications, and the **Rue du Bout du Monde** that leads from the back end of the village to a lovely spot with a flowing spring. The steep **Gorges de l'Hérault** extend on both sides of the village and can be followed on the D4.

With all this eroded limestone about, you would expect caves, and there are several. The most impressive, 3km south, is the **Grotte de Clamouse**, one of the big tourist attractions of the Hérault, with its lovely aragonite crystals. Some 500 yards south, don't miss the massive stone bridge of 1030, the **Pont du Diable**.

Grotte de Clamouse
t 04 67 57 71 05, www. clamouse.com; open July–Aug daily 10–7; June and Sept Sun–Fri 10–6; Feb–May and Oct Sun–Fri 10–5; Nov–Jan Sun–Fri 12–5; adm

Aniane and Gignac

Everyone who studies medieval history has trouble untangling the two Benedictine Benedicts. The first, Benedict of Norcia, founded the order. In the time of Charlemagne, Benedict of **Aniane**, St Guilhem's mentor, reformed it, forcing the poor Benedictines back to the original precepts of obedience and hard work. The abbey he built in his home town was thoroughly wrecked by the Protestants and rebuilt in the 17th century, and is now occupied by a school. The church, **St-Sauveur**, was rebuilt under Louis XIV, and in drab little Aniane it comes as quite a shock; with its glorious Baroque façade framed in big volutes, it is one of the best in the south. The interior is typically divided into two parts: one for the monks and one for the villagers. Nearby is a Romanesque church, 12th-century **St-Jean-Baptiste des Pénitents**.

South of Aniane on the D32, the bustling market town of **Gignac** enjoyed a period of prosperity in the 17th and 18th centuries, embellishing itself with an ensemble of Baroque churches and palaces to go with its pretty medieval **Tour de l'Horloge**; its best-known monument, however, is outside town, over the Hérault: the **Pont de Gignac**. This bridge, begun in 1776, is every inch a product of the Age of Enlightenment, strong and functional architecture without a trace of Bourbon curlicues.

Mouldering Castles and a Rotten Borough

The monasteries of St-Guilhem and Aniane brought considerable prosperity to the surrounding areas. Villages like **St-Jean-de-Fos** and **St-Saturnin** have fine Romanesque churches and buildings. Near the latter, there are views from the ruined early 11th-century castle on the **Rocher des Vierges**. There are two other fascinating ruined castles in this region. **Montpeyroux**, a village between St-Jean and St-Saturnin, grew up around a mysterious abandoned pile called the **Castel Viel**, a long, impressive circuit of walls with nothing inside. Its history is utterly unknown; it may be from the 11th century, the 16th century or anywhere in between, and it was probably less a military post than a protection for livestock in times of war. Southeast of Gignac, off the main N109, the **Château d'Aumelas** occupies a romantically isolated hilltop. This castle, built some time before 1036 by the lords of Montpellier, is on a dirt track and hard to reach, but it's a wonderful place to explore; parts of the noble residence, chapels and other buildings are still quite intact.

The castle is located in one of the biggest completely blank spots on the French map. It is part of a real, old-fashioned rotten borough, a *commune* without a town and hardly any inhabitants; it does have a mayor, who has a say in deciding representatives to the French Senate – two centuries after the Revolution, such things are still common in rural France. Another attraction in this *Commune d'Aumelas*, south of the château on a rocky track, is a beautiful and austere Romanesque church, **St-Martin-de-Cardonnet**, set amidst the ruins of the monastery that once surrounded it. To the west, back towards civilization on the D139, the circular fortified village of **Le Pouget** is just north of the colossal **Dolmen Gallardet**.

Clermont-l'Hérault to Lodève

Clermont is a peacefully bovine and prosperous town, living off the wine and table grapes of this more fertile part of the Hérault valley. Its medieval centre, on a hilltop, is large and well preserved, including a tall and graceful Gothic church, **St-Paul**, begun in 1276. The 10th–11th-century **castle** around which the town grew up is also in good shape, including the gates, prisons and keep. Clermont holds the big weekly market in this region, every Wednesday, and has done since the year 1000.

West of Clermont, you leave the green valley for more peculiar landscapes around the **Lac du Salagou**, a man-made sheet of water surrounded by hills that is much more natural-looking and attractive than most artificial lakes. Circumnavigating it, you'll pass some singular cliffs and weirdly eroded rock formations, and also the village of **Celles**, on the water's edge, now almost completely abandoned. The oddest formations lie to the south, in the **Cirque de Mourèze**, a long, stretched-out cirque with the dusty village of **Mourèze** and its ruined castle at the centre.

Between the cirque and Clermont lies **Villeneuvette**, founded only in 1670. The 'little new town' was a manufacturing centre for *londrins*, printed linen cloth. Though the works are now closed (since 1954), Villeneuvette is still the very picture of an old French paternalistic company town. The manufactories remain – behind the gate with the big inscription '*Honneur au Travail*' – along with some of the workers' housing, a school, a church, warehouses and gardens. Lately, artists and artisans have been re-colonizing the place, and there are art galleries and handicraft shops.

North of Clermont, the N9 heads into the *causses* of deepest France, passing **Lodève**, a comfortable, somewhat isolated town wedged between two rivers. Like Clermont-l'Hérault, Lodève has an impressive Gothic church with a lofty tower as its chief monument: **St-Fulcran**, named after a 9th-century bishop who became the city's patron, was begun in 1280 and turned into a fortress during the Hundred Years' War. It is one of the few churches in France with a chandelier – a present from Queen Victoria to Napoléon III. Lodève's textile-manufacturing past is recalled in a local workshop of the famous Parisian tapestry factory, the **Atelier National de Tissage de Tapis de Lodève** at 48 Av Général de Gaulle. Lodève was a Roman town, and its **Musée Fleury** on Square Georges Auric has finds from that age, along with dinosaur bones and footprints, and fossil trilobites, paintings and sculptures.

East of Lodève, a narrow but very pretty country road, the D153, takes you 9km to the **Prieuré St-Michel-de-Grandmont**. The Order of Grandmont, founded in the Limousin in the 12th century, was a monastic reform movement like that of Cluny or Cîteaux; it faded away five centuries ago and no one even remembers it today. This priory is its only surviving monument, gradually restored by private owners over the last century. The austere church and cloister, begun in the 12th century, are remarkably well preserved, and there are concerts and art exhibitions throughout spring and summer, but the real attraction here is a group of dolmens in the grounds, colossal works shaped like *cèpe* mushrooms, from *c.* 2000 BC.

St-Fulcran
open summer 9–7; winter 9–5.30

Atelier National de Tissage de Tapis de Lodève
t 04 67 96 41 34; open Tues, Wed and Thurs 1.30–3.30 by appt only

Musée Fleury
t 04 67 88 86 10; open Tues–Sun 9.30–12 and 2–6; closed Mon

Prieuré St-Michel-de-Grandmont
t 04 67 44 09 31, www.prieure-grandmont.fr; open for guided tours June–Sept daily at 10.30, 3, 4 and 5; Oct–May at 3; closed mid-Dec–mid-Jan; adm

(i) Gignac >>
3 Parc d'Activités de Camalce, t 04 67 57 58 83; open Mon–Fri

(i) St-Guilhem-le-Désert >
2 Rue Font du Portal, t 04 67 57 44 33, www.saint-guilhem-le-desert.com; open daily all year

Market Days in the Valley of the Hérault

Gignac: Sat.
Clermont-l'Hérault: Wed.

Where to Stay and Eat in the Valley of the Hérault

St-Guilhem-le-Désert ✉ 34150
In St-Guilhem, rooms are scarce.
**Hostellerie St-Benoit, Aniane, t 04 67 57 71 63 , www.hostellerie-saint-benoit.com (€€). A comfortable motel with a pool and a good restaurant (€€) using local produce. *Closed for a month in winter.*

*La Taverne de l'Escuelle, Place de la Liberté, t 04 67 57 72 05 (€). *Closed Dec and Jan.*

Auberge sur le Chemin, 38 Rue Font du Portal, t 04 67 57 75 05, www.restaurant-languedoc.com (€€€–€€). Medieval inn with tasty regional food.

Gignac ✉ 34150
Les Liaisons Gourmandes de Capion, 3 Bd de l'Esplanade, t 04 67 57 50 83 (€€€–€€). Popular restaurant with an outdoor terrace, worth a visit for its inventive regional and seasonal cooking such as chicken with truffles. *Closed Sat lunch, Sun eve and Mon.*

ⓘ Clermont-
l'Hérault >>
*9 Rue Doyen René
Gosse, t 04 67 96 23 86,
www.clermont-
l-herault.com;
open Tues–Sat*

★ Auberge
Campagnarde de
la Vallée du
Salagou >>

★ Le Mimosa >

ⓘ Lodève
*7 Place de la
République,
t 04 67 88 86 44,
www.lodeve.com; open
Mon–Fri and Sat am*

Ferme-Auberge de Pélican, Domaine de Pélican, *t* 04 67 57 68 92, *http://perso.orange.fr/domaine-de-pelican* (€€). This place (which also has rooms, €€) has wonderful dishes on a single set menu with choices – *pintade* (guinea hen) stuffed with olives, duck in honey vinegar – and their own wines. *Closed Sept and Oct; restaurant open Mon–Wed and Fri–Sat eves and Sun lunch in July and Aug; Nov–June open Sat eve and Sun lunch.*

St-Saturnin ✉ 34725

Ostalaria Cardabela, 10 Place de la Fontaine, *t* 04 67 88 62 62 (€€). A gorgeous small hotel run by a British couple, all tastefully restored stones and tiles and modern furniture. Very comfortable bedrooms. No restaurant but excellent breakfast with fresh orange juice and home-made jam. *Closed Nov–mid-Mar.*

Le Mimosa, in the next village of St-Guiraud, *t* 04 67 96 67 96 (€€). Run by the owners of the Ostalaria and long a pilgrimage for *cognoscenti* from Montpellier. An 18th-century wine-grower's house, beautifully decorated and offering superb cuisine. Eat outside in summer. *Closed Mon, Tues–Sat lunch and Sun eve, plus Nov–mid-Mar.*

Auberge Au Pressoir, Place de la Fontaine, *t* 04 67 88 67 89, *www.pressoir-auberge.com* (€€). Good regional cooking such as fresh trout, *poulet fermier*, lamb and grills, and 130 wines, in a friendly artistic atmosphere; regular art and photography exhibitions are held, as well as jazz and theatre evenings. *Closed Jan–mid-Feb, Sun–Wed eves, Mon lunch and Sat lunch.*

Clermont-l'Hérault ✉ 34800

Clermont-l'Hérault will be the most likely place to find a room if you haven't booked.

**La Source, Place Louis XIV, Villeneuvette, 4km southwest, *t* 04 67 96 05 07, *www.hoteldelasource.com* (€€–€). A charming rural retreat with a swimming pool and tennis courts, and a restaurant (€€€–€€) serving salmon and truffles. *Closed Nov–early April; restaurant closed Wed lunch and Tues.*

Auberge Campagnarde de la Vallée du Salagou, at Salasc on the D8, *t* 04 67 88 13 39, *www.aubergedusalagou.fr* (€). A comfortable B&B with lovely views; the restaurant (€€) serves a filling menu, offering grilled lamb or steaks and wine from nearby Octon.

**Les Hauts de Mourèze, 8km from Clermont, *t* 04 67 96 04 84 (€). Overlooking the cirque, with beautiful views. *Closed Nov–late Mar.*

The Northern Fringes: Monts de l'Espinouse

If you continue along the northern fringes of the Hérault, you'll get an idea of what France is like for the next hundred miles northwards, through Aveyron and Lozère into the Auvergne – rough canyons and rough villages, an occasional dusting of snow, trout streams and chestnut groves. The natural beauty of the Espinouse did it little good in former times; even 40 years ago, this was a poor area, losing its population to the cities. The creation of the Parc Naturel Régional du Haut Languedoc in the 1960s has made all the difference; *tourisme vert*, as the French call it – hiking and canoeing or just relaxing under the pines – increases every year. It's no strain on the kind and hospitable folk in the villages, and right now the Espinouse is as happy and content as a patch of mountains can be.

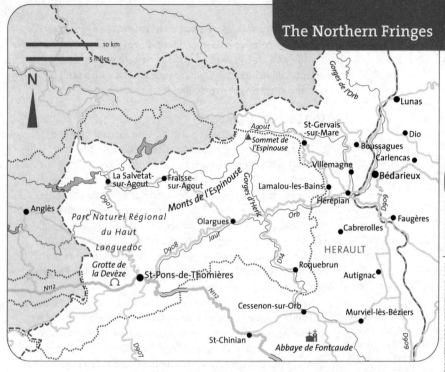

Bédarieux and Lamalou-les-Bains: the Pays d'Orb

The only big road in this region, the D908, runs west from
Clermont-l'Hérault across the base of the mountains, following
the valleys of the Orb and the Jaur. The first town on the way is
Bédarieux, a humble enough agricultural centre and market town.
Humility stops, however, with Bédarieux's famous son, Pierre-
Auguste Cot, one of the 19th-century kitsch-realist artists so
popular with the Academicians, the sort that made the
Impressionist revolution necessary. They've named the main
square after him, and you can see his work in the **Espace Culturel**,
created on the site of an old hospice; it includes a modern art
centre with temporary exhibitions, the **Maison des Arts** (where you
can find Cot's work along with fossils, railway memorabilia and
exhibitions re-creating past country life and costumes), plus a
media centre, a music school and the town's archives.

Espace Culturel
*t 04 67 95 48 27; open
Mon–Fri 9–12 and 2–6,
Sat and Sun 3–6; adm*

Lamalou-les-Bains, 10km further west, is a sort of museum in
itself. A thermal spa since the 17th century, Lamalou made it big
when the railroad came through in 1868. The prosperity of the next
three decades – dukes and counts, famous actresses, even a sultan
of Morocco checked in for the *cure* – built it into a sweet little
resort of Belle Epoque hotels and villas, cafés and a casino with a
chocolate-box theatre. Today, Lamalou is bidding to become
fashionable once again. Its restored 19th-century centre makes a

perfect setting for the big event on its calendar, an important festival of operettas (and opera) that is held in summer and again in winter. Inside the cemetery, on the eastern edge of town, is an exceptional 11th-century Romanesque church with a sculpted portal and apse, **St-Pierre-de-Rhèdes**.

The Eastern Espinouse

Either of the above towns is a good base for exploring the eastern half of the Espinouse. North of Bédarieux, the upper valley of the Orb starts out plagued by industry and power lines, but you can escape into the hills on either side, to **Dio** or to **Boussagues**, both delightful medieval villages with ruined castles; the latter's highly picturesque, stone-roofed Renaissance **Maison du Bailli** once belonged to Toulouse-Lautrec. Persevere northwards and you'll come to the **Gorges de l'Orb**, ending in a big dam and artificial lake at **Avène**. East of Bédarieux, there's another pretty village, **Carlencas**, famous for chickpeas; to the south is **Faugères**, centre of a small wine region.

Hérépian, between Bédarieux and Lamalou, has one of Europe's last bell foundries, the **Fonderie de Cloches**, in business since 1605; it has created a museum of bells. Hérépian offers another medieval detour, north on the D922 to **Villemagne**. Villemagne-L'Argentière it was in the 12th century, when a Benedictine abbey here looked after a rich silver mine owned by the Trencavels of Béziers and Carcassonne. Most of the abbey and its fortifications are in ruins, and sadly neglected. There are two lovely churches, Romanesque **St-Grégoire**, which has an archaeology museum, and Gothic St-Majan, along with a richly decorated 13th-century building believed to have been the mint, the **Hôtel des Monnaies**.

Just to the north of Villemagne is a humpbacked medieval bridge called, like that of St-Guilhem and so many others, the **Pont du**

Fonderie de Cloches
t 04 67 95 07 96; open for guided tours only, July and Aug Mon–Sat 10–12 and 2–6

St-Grégoire archaeology museum
t 04 67 23 06 79; open May–Oct Wed, Sat and Sun 3–6

Wine: Faugères and St-Chinian

It's the mix of limestone and schist in this beautiful, mountainous corner of Languedoc that creates the dark, beefy red wines of Faugères and St-Chinian. The French currently view these wines as the ascendant stars of the country's lesser-known regions, views borne out by the concentration of talented wine-makers to emerge from the area.

The wines require a few years in the cellar to reveal their true personalities; AOC Faugères, *www.faugeres.com*, has a high percentage of syrah, as well as grenache, old carignan stock and mourvèdre grapes – 2000s are excellent. Pick up a few bottles at **Domaine Gilbert Alquier**, Route de Pézenas, in Faugères, t 04 67 95 15 21, *www.gilbert-alquier.fr (open afternoons)*; and **Château des Estanilles**, in Cabrerolles, t 04 67 90 29 25 *(call ahead; closed Sun)*, which produces delightful variations in all three colours (including a fine white Coteaux du Languedoc of maccabeu and grenache).

St-Chinian, *www.saint-chinian.com*, encompasses 20 villages, but you can try nearly all the labels of fruity, dark, cherry-red St-Chinian (especially the 2000, 2001 and 2005) at St-Chinian's **Maison des Vins**, Avenue de la Promenade St-Chinian, t 04 67 38 11 69 *(open Mon–Sat 9–12 and 2–6.30, plus July and Aug Sun 10–12)*. Or visit the **Château Cazal-Viel**, in Cessenon, t 04 67 89 63 15. The very pleasant **Château Grand Burgas** 2006 is part of the JeanJean stable of wines, *www.jeanjean.fr*.

Diable – it must have been hard for the medieval peasant imagination to see how such things could stand up without divine or infernal aid.

Continuing west from Lamalou, at **Moulin** the Orb turns south, away from the road; there's a choice of directions and of scenery: the **Gorges d'Heric** to the north, a hiker's paradise with no roads, and another gorge to the south, leading towards **Roquebrun**. Sheltered by the mountains, this village grows mimosas and likes to call itself 'Little Nice'. South of Roquebrun, it's a clear shot along to Béziers and the sea, with nothing to detain you along the way.

The Parc Naturel Régional du Haut Languedoc

The loveliest village of the Espinouse, **Olargues**, is dominated by two medieval monuments, a romantic 11th-century bell-tower set up above on a hill surrounded by swooping swifts, and a hump-backed bridge. Next, **St-Pons-de-Thomières** is the little capital of the Espinouse, surrounded by forests. St-Pons probably gets more snow than anywhere in Languedoc east of the Pyrenees, giving it a decidedly Alpine air. Its landmarks are a **cathedral**, with a Romanesque portal and a tremendous 18th-century organ, and its **Musée Municipal de Préhistoire Régionale**. Never suspecting they were in a future Regional Park, Neolithic people made St-Pons and the Espinouse one of their favourite haunts in France; archaeologists go so far as to speak of a *civilisation saintponienne*. This museum documents their career, but the star attractions are the statue menhirs, the true cultural totems of this part of the Mediterranean, similar to those found in the Gard, in Tuscany and in Corsica, from 3000 BC to Roman times.

St-Pons is the perfect base for visiting the **Parc Naturel Régional du Haut Languedoc**, spread over a wide area of the Espinouse on the borders of the Hérault, Tarn and Aveyron. It's an extremely well-organized park; all you need do is visit the Maison du Parc in St-Pons (*see* p.158). There is a wide choice of hiking trails in the mountains through wild areas that have, among other things, what is said to be the largest population of *mouflons* in Europe.

From **Prat-d'Alaric**, the valley of the Agout spreads across the heart of the park; the roads that follow it, the D14 and D53, make a delightful tour, through beautiful villages like **La Salvetat-sur-Agout** and **Fraisse-sur-Agout**, which has a curious **statue-menhir** *in situ*, carved with a serpent and egg, a universal symbol found as far afield as the prehistoric Indian mounds in Ohio. The D53 continues towards the summit of the Espinouse (3,652ft). A little further on – over the Lauze pass on the D180 – there is a stone enclosure, a vestige of a Roman army camp, and beyond – on the D922 – **St-Gervais-sur-Mare**, full of medieval and Renaissance buildings.

Musée Municipal de Préhistoire Régionale
*t 04 67 97 22 61;
open summer daily
10–12 and 3–6; call for
winter times; adm*

Parc Naturel Régional du Haut Languedoc
*t 04 67 97 38 22,
www.parc-haut-languedoc.fr*

Grotte de la Devèze
t 04 67 97 03 24; open July–Aug 10.30–6; Mar–June and Sept 2–5; adm

Much closer to St-Pons, there is the **Grotte de la Devèze**, another gorgeous cave of delicate stalactites and shining crystals. To climb down from the Espinouse, there is the choice of the D907 out of St-Pons towards Minerve, or the N112 for Béziers and the Canal du Midi (*see* pp.172–9). On this route, you'll pass through **St-Chinian** and its wine region (*see* p.156); about 9km east of that village is the Romanesque **Abbey of Fontcaude**.

ⓘ **St-Pons-de-Thomières »**
Place du Foirail, t 04 67 97 06 65, www.saint-pons-tourisme.com

ⓘ **Maison du Parc Naturel**
13 Rue du Cloître, St-Pons-de-Thomières, t 04 67 97 38 22, www.parc-haut-languedoc.fr

ⓘ **Lamalou-les-Bains »**
1 Av Capus, t 04 67 95 70 91, www.ot-lamaloulesbains.fr; open June–mid-Sept Mon–Sat and Sun am; mid-Sept–May Mon–Fri and Sat am

ⓘ **Bédarieux**
Rue de la République, t 04 67 95 08 79, www.bedarieux.fr

ⓘ **Olargues »**
Av de la Gare, t 04 67 97 71 26, www.olargues.org

★ **Domaine de Rieumégé »**

Market Days in the Northern Hérault Fringes

Lamalou-les-Bains: Tues.
La Salvetat: Thurs and Sun.

Where to Stay and Eat in the Northern Hérault Fringes

Lamalou-les-Bains ✉ 34240

***L'Arbousier, 18 Av A. Daudet, t 04 67 95 63 11, *www.arbousierhotel.com* (€€–€). This 100-year-old hotel has been prettily renovated; it serves old French favourites in the restaurant (€€).

**Belleville, 1 Av Charcot, t 04 67 95 57 00, *www.hotelbelleville.com* (€). Excellent value for relative luxury: some bathrooms come with Jacuzzi and there's a restaurant (€€).

Faugères ✉ 34600

La Vigneronne, Rte de Pézenas, t 04 67 95 78 49, *www.shopics.be/vigneronne* (€€) Handsome B&B with a pool and *bouldrome*, in the centre of the wine region. Evening meals available (€€). *Mid-June–mid-Sept minimum 3 nights.*

Villemagne ✉ 34600

Auberge de l'Abbaye, next to the church, t 04 67 95 34 84 (€). Dine in the garden or in the 12th-century dining room. Specialities include *profiteroles de foie gras. Closed Mon, Tues lunch and Nov–early Feb.*

Olargues ✉ 34390

***Domaine de Rieumégé, 3km out on the St-Pons road, t 04 67 97 73 99,

www.domainederieumege.com (€€€–€€). Enchanting 17th-century building set in a 20-acre estate – peace guaranteed. Twelve nice rooms, two pools and tennis, and a separate farmhouse with its own pool for a big splurge. If you don't stay, at least eat in the superb restaurant (€€) in the beautifully restored *grange. Closed mid-Dec–Feb.*

St-Pons-de-Thomières ✉ 34220

**Le Somail, 2 Av de Castres, t 04 67 97 00 12 (€). A simple place in town, with a restaurant (€€–€).

**Les Bergeries de Ponderach, about 1km outside St-Pons towards Narbonne, t 04 67 97 02 57, *www.bergeries-ponderach.com* (€€€–€€). A haven of peace in the hills, with a charming owner. There is a rustic restaurant (€€€), rooms with terraces and country views, a pool, summer concerts and even an art gallery.

**Le Cabaretou, on the D907 towards La Salvetat, t 04 67 95 31 62 (€). Up in the heart of the mountains, 10km from St-Pons, is this plain but comfortable motel with a surprisingly ambitious restaurant (€€), its cuisine based entirely on seasonal ingredients.

La Route du Sel, 15 Grand-Rue, t 04 67 97 05 14 (€€–€). A little restaurant specializing in original, well-prepared dishes such as *foie gras* with jerusalem artichokes (*topinambours*) when they're in season. *Closed Sun in winter and Mon in summer.*

Ferme-Auberge du Moulin, Le Soulié, 4km from La Salvetat, t 04 67 97 22 27 (€€). Good farm cooking, specializing in cold meats, farm veal and mushrooms. *Book ahead. Closed Dec–Easter and Wed.*

The Hérault Coast

West of the Camargue (*see* pp.117–22), the lagoons continue for another 80km, dotting the coast like beads on a string. Unlike the Camargue, almost all of this coast is easily accessible by car; there are beaches and resorts in abundance, and attractions like salty Sète and medieval Maguelone and Agde. Only a few kilometres from the walls of Aigues-Mortes (*see* pp.120–22), the Hérault coast begins with a bang, with an uncanny skyline of tall holiday ziggurats, a resort town straight from science fiction.

La Grande Motte

At the same time as the huge industrial complex at Fos was going up on the eastern edge of the Camargue (in Provence), something even stranger was happening on the west. It almost seems as if France's planners wanted an appropriate book-end to Fos's weird mill furnaces and refinery towers. Making the Languedoc resort plan in 1963, they decided that one of the new holiday towns was to be boldly modernist, and they picked 'the big lump', an empty swath of sand on the Golfe d'Aigues-Mortes, for the experiment.

Jean Balladur, the original architect, and his successors gave them more than they bargained for. La Grande Motte looks like no other resort in the world, its hotels and apartments rising in colourful triangles and roller-coaster curves, its public buildings in jarring, amoeboid shapes like a permanent 1960s World Fair. The 'modernism' of the Motte is more surface than substance; there are no real innovations in architecture or design. The buildings themselves, like all the experiments of the kitschy 1960s, already look a bit dated. But La Grande Motte is a great success as a resort, a proper city with room for over 100,000 space-age holidaymakers.

The fun starts at **Point Zéro**, the name Balladur whimsically gave the central square on the waterfront. In season 'little train' tours around the town start from here. The first clutches of ziggurats (the Grande Mottois prefer to call them *pyramides*) rise to the west, around the marina; to the east are the outlandish buildings of the civic centre, including the *mairie* and congress hall. Beyond that, the planners ensure you will be entertained to death, with broad beaches, thalassotherapy, 30 tennis courts, golf courses (three, designed by Robert Trent Jones), marinas, windsurfing, diving, a big water park, Scrabble clubs, a casino and all the rest. Summer is packed with festivals, concerts and sporting events, and there are masses of opportunities to learn how to sail, to hire boats and to take trips out to sea. The deep waters off La Grande Motte are frequented by fin whales (*rorquals*), the world's second

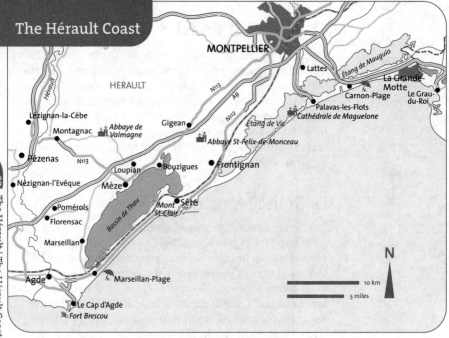

largest mammal after the blue whale, measuring up to 70ft in length. Many of the whales migrate in the autumn, which makes it the best time to spot one; **Orphrys**, a wildlife conservation agency, runs whale-spotting trips during September (although adverse weather conditions may lead to their cancellation).

Orphrys
t 04 67 56 63 01

Just to the south of La Grande Motte the 1960s planners cooked up another artificial playground, **Port-Camargue**. This one, a Florida-style nest of holiday homes and marinas, isn't nearly as interesting (though the beaches are great, and there are 18km of them). To the south of this stretches the **Plage de l'Espiguette**, a remarkable stretch of natural sand dunes that go on and on and on, the only building in sight a lighthouse (the road ends there, by the *phare*, in an enormous car park). Between the two, the holiday complex has swallowed up the old fishing village of **Le Grau-du-Roi**, eight kilometres southwest of Aigues-Mortes, with its 18th-century lighthouse. No resort strip would be complete without a flashy fish show, and **Seaquarium** here, on Av du Palais de la Mer, is one of the Mediterranean's biggest: seals and orcas, the obligatory glass tunnel through the shark tanks, and a small museum dedicated to Le Grau-du-Roi and its seagoing traditions.

Seaquarium
t 04 66 51 57 57,
www.seaquarium.fr;
open July and Aug daily
10–midnight; May, June
and Sept daily 10–8;
Oct–April daily 10–7;
adm exp

West of La Grande Motte, a narrow strip of land separates the sea from the **Etang de Mauguio**, towards Montpellier. A more old-fashioned beach holiday can be spent here at **Carnon-Plage** or **Palavas-les-Flots**, 15km down the dune-lined coast. Built around a narrow canal full of boats, Palavas is an endearing resort with some 8km of good beaches, where grocery clerks from Montpellier come to flash their polyester in the frowzy waterfront casino. The old centre has a wonderfully casual air about it, toured by a silly tourist train dedicated to French humorist Albert Dubout, whose works, if you are curious, are displayed in the **Musée Albert Dubout**, in the 18th-century Redoute de Ballestras, built to defend Palavas' fishermen. Palavas is proud of its **Phare de la Méditerranée**, a modern 45m tower (formerly a *château d'eau*) with panoramic views from the restaurant at the top and the tourist office in the bottom. You can also see bullfights in the arena.

Inland, towards Montpellier, in the village of **Lattes**, you can visit Roman necropolises and the **Musée Archéologique Henri Prades** at 390 Av de Pérols, with recent discoveries from the ongoing excavations at the adjacent Bronze Age site of **Lattara**.

Maguelone

To balance La Grande Motte, a town without a history, here we have a history without a town. Maguelone, 4km from Palavas, may have begun as a Phoenician or Etruscan trading post. It prospered under the Romans and Visigoths, becoming the seat of a bishop. After that the history is obscure. Old maps show the place as 'Port Sarrasin', suggesting Arab corsairs were using it as a base in the 8th century, and there is a record of Charles Martel coming down from Paris to chase them out, destroying the town in the process. But Maguelone still had one attraction – salt – and the rights were owned by a powerful and progressive multinational, the Church. In the 1030s, when demand was high, a cleric named Arnaulf oversaw the town's rebuilding and added a monastery. The enterprise prospered; Urban II, the first of many popes to visit (1096), called Maguelone the 'second church of Rome', and gave its restored bishops special privileges. Later, Maguelone became a papal holding, a key base both politically and ideologically in the difficult 12th century. It gradually dwindled after that, and the see moved to Montpellier in 1536.

Though almost no trace of the town remains today (its very stones were hauled off by the canal-builders), the impressive **Cathédrale de Maguelone** was saved from ruin and restored in the 1870s. Built, and built well, by Lombard masons in the 1170s, it is an austere building. The main decorative feature – reliefs around the main portal – show Christ in Majesty with the four Evangelists. Inside, there are fragments of the bishops' tombs, inscriptions and furnishings, and you can climb the surviving bell-tower for views down the coast.

Except at the height of summer, Maguelone makes a peaceful place to escape to; there are plenty of beaches around it, a bit rocky but good for seashells. The lagoons in this stretch of coast, from

---

Musée Albert Dubout
t 04 67 68 56 41; open July–Aug daily 4pm– 11pm; spring and autumn Tues–Sun 2–6; school hols and weekends only in winter; adm

Musée Archéologique Henri Prades
t 04 67 99 77 20, http://musee.lattes. free.fr; open 10–12 and 2–5.30; closed Tues

Cathédrale de Maguelone
t 04 67 50 63 63; open daily 9–7

La Grande Motte to Frontignan, are rich in waterfowl, especially pink flamingos, but little else. Most are stagnant and lack oxygen; decomposing water plants in hot summers cause a phenomenon called the *malaïgue*, making the air smell like rotten eggs. The vineyards (*vin de sable*, 'sand wine', and others, run by the Compagnons de Maguelone) don't mind the occasional pong; there's a *cave* for tasting next to the cathedral car park.

Cave
www.espace-maguelone.com

Frontignan

From Maguelone, you'll need to backtrack to Palavas and continue around the landward side of the lagoons, rejoining the coast at Frontignan, an industrial town with a good 12th-century church, **St-Paul**, with a frieze of fish and boats over the door. Frontignan claims to be nothing less than the world capital of muscat, beloved by the ancient Romans and Thomas Jefferson. It comes in a screwy bottle, in honour of Hercules, who stopped here for a drink while performing his Twelve Labours; the big fellow liked the wine so much that he twisted the bottle to squeeze out the last drop.

Market Days around La Grande Motte

Palavas-les-Flots: Sun am April–Nov, Mon, Wed and Fri; Sat am, flower market and flea market.

La Grande Motte: Sun am, and Thurs am June–Sept.

Festivals around La Grande Motte

Palavas-les-Flots: *Feria*, first weekend of May and last weekend of Sept.

Where to Stay and Eat near La Grande Motte

La Grande Motte ✉ 34280

The bad news about La Grande Motte is that you can't stay there; all the hotels in the centre are overpriced to the point of absurdity.

***Hôtel-Restaurant Les Corallines, Quartier Point Zéro, **t** 04 67 29 13 13 (€€€€). The fanciest hotel, right on the front, with a thalassotherapy centre (*www.thalasso-grandemotte.com*) and balconied rooms with good sea views. *Thalassotherapy centre closed mid-Dec–Jan.*

***Mercure Port, Rue du Port, **t** 04 67 56 90 81, *www.accorhotels.com* (€€€€–€€€). The splashy status address on the Big Lump, looming over the marina like a concrete refugee from Miami Beach; rather charmless, but a chance to meet that segment of the fast crowd who choose to avoid the Riviera, and it does have a nice terrace regional food restaurant.

Alexandre, Presqu'île du Port, **t** 04 67 56 63 63, *www.alexandre-restaurant. com* (€€€). A splurge for refined regional specialities in an especially elegant setting. *Closed Mon.*

La Cuisine du Marché, 89 Rue du Casino, **t** 04 67 29 90 11 (€€€). Good fresh fish served in classic style. It's small, so you'll need to book. *Closed Mon lunch in summer, all day Mon and Tues rest of year.*

Palavas-les-Flots ✉ 34250

Palavas has plenty of inexpensive, undistinguished hotels. The restaurants have few pretensions, but there are some gratifying, no-nonsense seafood joints.

L'Escale, 5 Bd Sarrail, north of the canal on the seafront, **t** 04 67 68 24 17, *www.restaurant-lescale.com* (€€€). Here you can have *sèche à la rouille* for starters, or extravaganzas like the

ⓘ **La Grande Motte ›**
*Place de la Mairie, **t** 04 67 56 42 00, www. ot-lagrandemotte.fr; open daily all year*

ⓘ **Palavas-les-Flots ››**
*Phare de la Méditerranée, **t** 04 67 07 73 34, www. palavaslesflots.com; open daily all year*

mixed shellfish plate they call *panaché de coquillages* – beware: the bill can skyrocket. *Closed Wed.*

La Passerelle, Quai Paul Cunq, t 04 67 68 55 80 (€). This couldn't be simpler, its menu limited to piles of fresh, inexpensive shellfish. *Closed Oct–April.*

Lattes ✉ 34250

**Mas de Couran, Route de Fréjorgues, t 04 67 65 57 57, *www.mas-de-couran.com* (€€). It's worth coming inland to Lattes for this special place, set in a beautiful park, with pool and restaurant (€€€). *Closed Sun eve.*

Sète

 Sète

After the glitzy candy-land of the planned 1960s resorts, you may have despaired by now of finding anything really Mediterranean on these shores; you can find it almost anywhere along the coasts of Spain, Italy or Greece, but in southern France it is as rare as snowmen. Just in time, there's gritty, salty, workaday Sète, France's biggest Mediterranean fishing port. After the rather depressing and sometimes smelly town entrance, you can stroll along the Canal Maritime and watch businesslike freighters carrying French sunflower and rapeseed oil to every corner of the globe, along with dusty cement boats, gigantic tankers of Algerian natural gas (if one ever goes off, it will take the whole town with it) and Algerian wine (marginally less dangerous), and rusty trawlers jammed full of woebegone sardines or some of the 138 other fish caught by Sétois fishermen. After that, perhaps a leisurely tour of the city's historic monuments? Go ahead and try; in this infant city, younger even than Boston or New York, there isn't a single one.

Boat tours
www.sete-croisieres.com,
t 04 67 46 00 46

For entertainment, there are the sailors' bars, or you might try one of the **boat tours** (from along the Quai de la Résistance) through the Bassin de Thau, with a stop at an oyster farm. The tourist office has plenty of information on boats to rent and opportunities to dive. Or take in an American football match and watch the **water-jousting**, from 25 June and ending with the grand Saint Louis tournament on 25 August. If you can stand a little modern madness, Sète will be great fun. It's an attractive town, laced with canals, and livelier and more colourful than any place on France's Mediterranean coast, save only Marseille.

Along the Grand Canal

The city's arms show a field of *fleurs-de-lis* with a whale – *cetus* in Latin – one of the possible explanations for the name, which is first mentioned in a Carolingian document of 814. In 1666, Louis XIV's minister, Colbert, began construction of the port, the terminus for the Canal du Midi, which was begun in the same year. In 1673 the new town was declared a free port. The pesky English first came to visit in 1710, occupying the city during the War of the Spanish Succession; out in the harbour, you can see **Fort St-Pierre**, which failed to keep them out. Little has happened since. Despite its booming port, Sète never grew into a major city; hedged between Mont St-Clair, the lagoons and the sea, there simply isn't room.

Sète should be the twin city of Livorno (Leghorn) in Italy. Both grew up at the same time; both have canals (Sète likes to call itself the 'Venice of Languedoc') and a winsome architectural anonymity. And they have both made their offbeat contributions to modern culture: Livorno was the birthplace of Modigliani, Sète of the poet Paul Valéry, singer-composer Georges Brassens and Jean Vilar, father of the Avignon festival. The bustling centre is its 'Grand Canal', the **Canal de Sète**, lined with quays where the ambience ranges from boatyards and ship chandlers to banks and boutiques and waterside cafés. A block west, on Place Aristide Briand in front of the *mairie*, Sète has what is undoubtedly the world's biggest cast-bronze octopus, writhing over a modern fountain.

At the southern end of the canal, the **Vieux Port** handles most of the fishing fleet, as well as offering tourist fishing boats and excursions around the Thau lagoon. From the Vieux Port, it's a bit of a climb up to the **Cimetière Marin**, celebrated in a famous poem by Paul Valéry, who was buried here in 1945, his family tomb (under the name Grassi – like Brassens, his mother was Italian) bearing an inscription from the poem (*Ô récompense après une pensée/Qu'un long regard sur le calme des dieux*). The adjacent Musée Paul Valéry contains exhibits on the poet, and on the history of Sète, as well as a good collection of modern paintings, older works by Courbet and even a minor Botticelli. Just below, the open-air **Théâtre de la Mer**, with a lively programme of summer concerts, is dedicated to Jean Vilar; just above begins a network of paths up to **Mont St-Clair** (600ft), once the Sunday promenade of the Sétois.

Sète's other contribution to French culture, Brassens (d. 1981), is buried in the **Cimetière de Py**, under the Pierres Blanches, overlooking the Etang de Thau; fans or the merely curious can learn much, much more in the nearby Espace Georges Brassens at 67 Boulevard Camille Blanc, where you'll not only see photos and exhibits relating to Brassens' life, but hear it as well on the headphones, accompanied by his hit songs and words of wisdom. At 23 Quai Maréchal de Lattre de Tassigny there is also a Musée International des Arts Modestes, an eclectic collection of day-to-day items from over the past 50 years, imaginatively displayed. At 26 Quai Aspirant Herber there is a modern local art centre, the Centre Regional d'Art Contemporain Languedoc-Roussillon.

In summer, the tourist office offers 1hr tours of the **Criée**, the extraordinary fish wholesale market on Quai Maximin Licciardi.

The Bassin de Thau

Sète's Bassin de Thau is one of the largest lagoons along the Mediterranean shore. There have always been saltpans here,

Musée Paul Valéry
*t 04 67 46 20 98;
open July and Aug
daily 10–12 and 2–6;
Sept–June Wed–Mon
10–12 and 2–6;
closed Tues; adm*

**Espace Georges
Brassens**
*t 04 67 53 32 77,
www.sete.fr/brassens;
open July and Aug daily
10–12 and 2–7; June and
Sept daily 10–12 and
2–6; Oct–May Tues–Sun
10–12 and 2–6; adm*

**Musée
International des
Arts Modestes**
*t 04 67 18 64 00; open
10–12 and 2–6; closed
Mon out of season; adm*

**Centre Regional
d'Art Contemporain**
*t 04 67 74 94 37, http://
crac.lr.free.fr; open Mon
and Wed–Fri 12.30–7,
Sat and Sun 2–7*

though today most of the lagoon has found a more lucrative employment as a huge oyster and mussel farm.

There are two roads south from Sète. Taking the coastal route, passing quickly through the unhappy concrete piles of La Corniche, you'll pass 15km of narrow grey beach next to the road. Since there is no room for development, this is your best chance on the entire coast to find some empty beach space, even in the height of summer, if you don't mind the cars. At the southern end, the beach piles up into an expanse of partly overgrown dunes, near the small resort of **Marseillan-Plage**. **Marseillan** itself, another fishing/oyster port, was founded in the 6th century BC by the Greeks and is made of the same black basalt as Agde. By the port at 1 Rue Noilly you can find out the secret ingredients of Marseillan's own *apéritif*, Noilly-Prat.

Noilly-Prat visits
*t 04 67 77 20 15,
www.noillyprat.com*

The other, longer route passes around the back of the lagoon. Along the way, it passes a small, modern thermal resort, **Balaruc-les-Bains**, with its ancient parent up on a hill above, the medieval village of **Balaruc-le-Vieux**. Here you may detour north towards **Gigean** and the 11th–13th-century Benedictine (later Cistercian) **Abbaye St-Félix-de-Montceau**, accessible on a dirt road from the village. Romantically ruined on its hilltop site, with a lagoon view, the abbey includes both a Romanesque and a Gothic church.

Abbaye St-Félix-de-Montceau
*call t 04 67 34 81 to
check opening hours,
www.abbaye-st-felix.new.fr*

In Languedoc's oyster capital, **Bouzigues**, you can learn everything about shellfish-breeding and -fishing, at the Musée de l'Etang de Thau.

**Musée de
l'Etang de Thau**
*t 04 67 78 33 57;
open July–Aug 10–12.30
and 2.30–7; Mar–June
and Sept–Oct 10–12
and 2–6; Nov–Feb
10–12 and 2–5*

Loupian, an attractive village with remnants of its old walls and palaces, has an unusually vaulted 12th-century church; the real attraction here, however, is a recently unearthed Gallo-Roman villa. As with many such villas in France, this one started out as a modest rural manor and gradually grew to palatial proportions – a reminder of how the land-owning families burgeoned through the imperial centuries until they owned nearly everything in Gaul. Many villas eventually became feudal castles or abbeys; others, like this one, disappeared completely, though the excavations here have brought to light an exceptional set of mosaics, covering what was the villa's entire ground floor. These are largely geometric decorative patterns, in the style of Roman Syria, though they also include a peach tree, and an allegory of the Four Seasons. A museum contains finds from the site and explains the history and economic role of the villa.

Gallo-Roman villa
*t 04 67 18 68 18, http://
villaloupian.free.fr; site
open for guided tours of
mosaics on the hour
2–5 (2–6 in July
and Aug); museum
open 2–5; adm*

Further south, the ancient lagoon port of **Mèze** still makes a go of it as a fishing village, though nowadays the money comes from the less romantic chores of oyster-farming. It's a quiet place, with a pleasant harbour lined with cafés and a small beach. Just north of Mèze is an open-air dinosaur park, **Musée-Parc des Dinosaures**, on the N113, where in 1996 they found the biggest cache of dinosaur

**Musée-Parc des
Dinosaures**
*t 04 67 43 02 80, www.
musee-parc-dinosaures.
com; open July–Aug
daily 10–7; Feb–June
and Sept daily 2–6;
Oct–Dec Sat, Sun and
hols 2–6*

eggs ever discovered in Europe. Life-size models and skeletons can be glimpsed among the trees, including a complete skeleton of a brachiosaurus, and you can see the ongoing archaeological dig. There is also a section on the evolution of Mankind.

Abbaye de Valmagne

⭐ **Abbaye de Valmagne**
t 04 67 78 06 09,
www.valmagne.com;
open mid-June–Sept
daily 10–12 and 2.30–6;
Oct–mid-Dec and mid-
Feb–June daily 2–6;
mid-Dec–mid-Feb
Wed–Mon 2–6,
closed Tues

It might try the patience of some readers, dragging them on another detour to another ruined abbey – but this, 8km north of Mèze on the D161, is the best one of all. Valmagne was an early Cistercian foundation, begun in 1138 and financed by Raymond Trencavel. Being one of the richest houses, it also gradually became one of the most decadent; the records mention a 16th-century Florentine abbot named Pietro da Bonzi, who built himself a palace on the site, plus a French garden with a statue of Neptune, and who threw the best dinner parties in Languedoc. Thoroughly trashed in the Revolution, the abbey has survived only by good luck: one owner proposed to dismantle it to provide building stone for a new church in Montpellier, but the canons there found the price too high. For the past century, the vast church has served as

Valmagne wine cellar
open mid-June–Sept
daily 10–12 and 2.30–6;
Oct–mid-Dec and mid-
Feb–June daily 2–6;
mid-Dec–mid-Feb Wed–
Mon 2–6, closed Tues, or
ring t 04 67 78 47 32

the biggest **wine cellar** in the Hérault, with some of the best fruity red AOC Coteaux du Languedoc, and a traditional lemon-coloured white and rosé.

Valmagne is not your typical Cistercian church. St Bernard would have frowned on architectural vanities like the porch, the big bell-towers and the sculpted decoration – grapevines, representing less the scriptural 'labourer in the vineyard' than the real vineyards that made Valmagne so rich. Its size is astonishing: a 370ft nave, and great pointed arches almost as high as Narbonne cathedral's. Most of the work is 14th-century, in a straightforward but sophisticated Late Gothic; note how the nave columns grow slightly closer together towards the altar, a perspective trick that makes the church seem even longer (St Bernard wouldn't have fancied that either). The relatively few monks who lived here would hardly have needed such a church; here, too, architectural vanity seems to have overcome Cistercian austerity.

Both the chapterhouse and the refectory are well preserved, around a pretty cloister that contains the loveliest thing in the abbey, an octagonal Gothic pavilion with a tall flowing fountain inside, a fantasy straight from a medieval manuscript or tapestry; an 18th-century poet, Lefranc de Pompignan, named it right: a *fontaine d'amour*.

Market Days in Sète

Ask the tourist office about night markets and craft fairs.
Daily: Les Halles, Rue Gambetta.

Wed am: Place A. Briand, Place Léon Blum and Rue A. Lorraine.
Fri am: Av V. Hugo, opposite station.
Sun am: Place de la République, flea market.

Festivals in Sète

Aug 22–28: Saint Louis jousting tournament. Ask the tourist office about dates of other tournaments throughout the summer.

Shopping around Sète

Local Wine

Skalli Fortant de France winery, 278 Av du Maréchal Juin, **t** 04 67 46 70 00, *www.skallifamilywines.com*. Guided visits and tastings.

Where to Stay in and around Sète

ⓘ **Sète** ›
60 Grand-Rue Mario Roustan, **t** 04 67 74 71 71, www.ot-sete.fr; open daily all year

Sète ✉ 34200

★★★Grand Hôtel, 17 Quai Maréchal de Lattre de Tassigny, **t** 04 67 74 71 77, *www.legrandhotelsete.com* (€€€€–€€). Right on Sète's 'Grand Canal', it almost deserves its name, with plenty of original décor from the 1920s. If you can't swing the Danieli in Venice, this will do fine: nice people and very reasonable rates. The hotel's **Quai 17** restaurant, **t** 04 67 74 71 91 (€€€), is refined and serves rewarding menus. *Closed mid-Dec–early Jan.*

★★★L'Orque Bleue, 10 Quai Aspirant-Herber, **t** 04 67 74 72 13, *www.hotel-orquebleue-sete.com* (€€). Renovated hotel in central Sète beside the Royal canal. Parking for a small charge.

★★★Terrasses du Lido, Rond-Point de l'Europe, along the Corniche road, **t** 04 67 51 39 60, *www.lesterrasses dulido.com* (€€). A pretty Provençal-style villa with a pool and near the beach, with a good restaurant (€€€) open to non-residents, serving authentic Mediterranean dishes from

bourride to bouillabaisse. *Closed Sun eve and Mon except in July and Aug.*

Eating Out in and around Sète

Sète

La Palangrotte, Rampe Paul Valéry, **t** 04 67 74 80 35 (€€€–€€). Quality seafood on the lower end of the Canal de Sète: grilled fish and several styles of fish stew, including the local *bourride sétoise. Closed Sun eve, Wed eve and Mon, except in July and Aug.*

Le Chalut, 38 Quai Maximin Licciardi, **t** 04 67 74 81 52 (€€). The seafood, including Sétois specialities, is as tasty as the décor. *Closed Wed in Sept–June.*

La Péniche, 1 Quai des Moulins, **t** 04 67 48 64 13 (€€). For lunch with the dockhands, try this place serving simple stuff on an old barge in the harbour. *Closed Sat lunch and Sun eve.*

Bouzigues

Côte Bleue, Av Louis Tudesq, **t** 04 67 78 30 87, *www.la-cote-bleue.fr* (€€€). A large family restaurant overlooking the Bassin de Thau which is the best place to sample a vast variety of shellfish, mussels, langoustines and the local oysters. *Closed Wed in winter, plus Jan and mid-Feb–early Mar.*

Meze

La Marmitiere, 38 Rue du Port, **t** 04 67 43 84 99, *www.lamarmitiere.fr* (€€€–€€). In a narrow street in old Mèze, with evidence of the village's past in its old stone arches. The harbour is nearby and you can eat fish, but also traditional meat dishes such as *filet de bœuf au beurre persillé*. A small terrace faces the street. *Closed Mon–Fri lunch, Sun eve and Mon in winter.*

Agde, the 'Black Pearl of Languedoc'

If Sète is a brash young upstart, Agde has been watching the river Hérault flow down to the sea for some 2,500 years. Founded by Greeks from Phocis, not long after Marseille, its name was originally Agatha, after Agatha Tyche, the 'good spirit' of popular Greek religion, usually portrayed carrying a cornucopia; the people of Agde are still called Agathois. In medieval times it was an important port, despite occasional visits by Arab sea-raiders. The last few centuries have left Agde behind, but it is still a good town, and a grey one – built almost entirely of volcanic basalt from nearby Mont St-Loup. Its road system can be a little bemusing.

With the massive new tourist development at nearby **Cap d'Agde**, this lovely town does not get much peace in summer; parts of the old quarter have almost as many restaurants as houses. **Grau d'Agde**, where the Hérault meets the sea, is pleasant along the riverbanks, with fishing boats and fishermen.

A Stroll Around Town

The tiny **old quarter** is defined by its walls, now largely demolished for a promenade; a bit of the old **ramparts** remains, near the river, resting on Greek foundations (now below street level). Overlooking the Hérault, Agde's stern basalt **Cathédrale St-Etienne** was begun about 1150. Its fortress-like appearance – it looks like a baddie's castle in a Hollywood movie – is no accident; Agde's battling bishops used it as their citadel (the outworks have been demolished). Previous cathedrals had been wrecked in battles, once at the hands of Charles Martel himself. It's open during mass; the only original feature is the 12th-century marble altar. You can climb the Donjon in summer if you ask at the tourist office.

From the quay along the Hérault, Rue Chassefière leads into the *bourg*, or medieval addition to the city. On Rue de la Fraternité, the

Musée Agathois
t 04 67 94 82 51; open July and Aug Mon–Fri 9–7.15, Sat and Sun 12–7; April–June and Sept–early Nov Mon–Sat 9–12 and 2–6, Sun 2–6; rest of Nov–Mar Mon and Wed–Sat 9–12 and 2–5, Sun 2–5, closed Tues; adm

Musée Agathois is one of the best of the south's town museums, encapsulating nearly everything about Agde's history and traditions in a few well-arranged rooms: archaeological finds, religious art, costume exhibits, dances and festivals, an old-fashioned kitchen and fishermen's gear. Behind the museum, Agde's market shares Place Gambetta with the church of **St-André**, where important Church councils were held in the days of the Visigoths; of the present building, though, the oldest part is the 12th-century tower. Another church, **St-Sever** on Rue St-Sever, contains a fine Renaissance painting of Christ on wood, a little the worse for wear from having been thrown into the Hérault during the Revolution.

A Fishy Saint and a Synthetic Resort

The road to Cap d'Agde, only 4km away, passes the ancient, extinct volcano **Mont St-Loup**, its top disfigured by pylons. Agde's black basalt comes from here. Whoever St Loup, or 'Holy Wolf', might have been is not clear (although there is a northern saint by that name, a 5th-century bishop of Troyes). *Loup* is also the name for sea bass, the favourite fish in Agde's restaurants.

Cap d'Agde, built around a small harbour and a lovely black basalt sand beach and black cliffs, is the biggest beach playground in all Languedoc and another triumph of French holiday efficiency. Like La Grande Motte, it began in the 1960s as a planned resort fostered by the government, and it looks it: a freshly built 'traditional' centre, with plenty of parking, broad boulevards and everything in its place. The original plan even accommodated *naturistes*, in a camp called **Héliopolis** on the northern edge of town at Port-Ambonne. Over the last 20 years, this has become the real story at Cap d'Agde; the camp has grown into a **Quartier Naturiste**, the biggest nudist colony in Europe, with a futuristic semicircular central building that includes shopping malls, banks and even a *naturiste* supermarket, where German has become the second language. It was the Germans who provided most of the clientele in the early days, but today 'Naked City' attracts people from all over the world – as many as 40,000 of them on any given day in July and August. Lifestyles of all sorts have found a welcome, and the nightlife, both gay and straight, is legendary: swingers' clubs, S&M clubs and everything else. Anything goes here, though in daytime the families, the old folks and the faster crowd each keep to their own parts of the beach. There's only one hotel in the complex, Hôtel Eve, and a large campground; everyone else who stays in the compound rents one of the holiday flats. To visit for the day, you'll have to buy a card at the entrance (*about €3; €10 per car*).

Cap d'Agde has plenty of other attractions: a first-rate golf course, championship tennis courts and matches, and other sports facilities (they hosted the Mediterranean Games in 1993); a wildlife sanctuary at the nearby **Etang de Bagnas** with rare waterfowl (purple heron, grand bittern); a **casino**; an aquarium specializing in live coral at 11 Rue des Deux Frères; a **Luna Park**; and the inevitable **Aqualand** with water slides. One surprising attraction is a fine, small archaeological collection at the Musée de l'Ephèbe, the star of which is the *Ephèbe d'Agde*, a Hellenistic bronze of a boy, discovered in 1964 in the bed of the Hérault. And from Centre Port you can take a boat trip (ask at tourist office) out to the **Ile du Brescou** to see one of Vauban's 17th-century forts.

Hôtel Eve
t 04 67 26 71 70, www.hoteleve.com or www.villagenaturiste-agde.com

Golf course
t 04 67 26 54 40

Tennis courts
t 04 67 01 03 60

Wildlife sanctuary
t 04 67 01 60 23

Aquarium
t 04 67 26 14 21, www. aquarium-agde.com

Musée de l'Ephèbe
t 04 67 94 69 60; open all year daily 9–12 and 2–6; adm

⭐ La Galiote >>

ⓘ Agde >
Espace Molière, t 04 67 94 29 68, www.agde-herault.com; open July and Aug daily; Sept–June Mon–Sat

Market Days in Agde

Agde: Thurs am.

Cap d'Agde: June–Sept Mon am, Tues am, Wed am and Sat am, and a flea market Sun am.

Where to Stay and Eat in Agde

Agde ✉ 34300

You won't regret stopping over at Agde if you're passing anywhere nearby. It's a sweet town, and the hotels and restaurants are as good as you'll find on the coast, although parking can be difficult.

**La Galiote, 5 Place Jean Jaurès, t 04 67 94 45 58, *www.lagaliote.fr* (€€). Some of the rooms in this old bishop's palace overlook the river; there's an excellent restaurant (€€) serving seafood or roast lamb with thyme. *Restaurant closed Sun and Mon in winter.*

**Le Donjon, Place Jean Jaurès, t 04 67 94 12 32, *www.hotelledonjon.com* (€€–€). The second choice in town, with old-fashioned, comfortable rooms. Parking is available.

(i) **Cap d'Agde >>**
Rond-Point du Bon Accueil, t 04 67 01 04 04, www.capdagde. com; open daily all year

Grau d'Agde ✉ 34300

**Le Château Vert, 25 Quai Commandant Méric, t 04 67 94 14 51, *www. lechateauvert.com* (€€). Reasonable hotel in a good spot by the river and 150m from the beach. There's a restaurant (€€) offering seafood and some surprises, like kangaroo. *Closed Oct–mid-Mar; restaurant closed Wed and Thurs except July and Aug.*

Cap d'Agde ✉ 34300

***Hôtel du Golfe, Ile des Loisirs, t 04 67 26 87 03, *www.hotel-du-golf. com* (€€€). A luxury option, modern with a hint of Morocco. Close to the beach and the golf course. There is a pool, garden, spa and gastronomic restaurant (€€€€–€€€). *Closed Jan and Feb.*

The Southern Hérault

Pézenas

⭐ **Pézenas**

The area inland from Agde, behind the Bassin de Thau, is one of the duller stretches of the Hérault, a rolling plain dotted with a score of agricultural villages – up-to-date and businesslike rather than picturesque and cosy. Right in the centre is Pézenas. If Carcassonne is Languedoc's medieval movie set, this town has often been used for costume dramas set in the time of Richelieu or Louis XIV (most famously, *Cartouche*). Few cities have a better ensemble of buildings from what the French (rather over-enthusiastically) used to call the 'Golden Age'. In summer, the Piscénois live out a lingering *ancien régime* fantasy, with a series of festivals, concerts and exhibitions called the *Mirondela dels Arts* in July and August.

Mirondela dels Arts
www.mirondela delsarts.com

History

Roman Piscenae was known for wool, the best in Gaul. In the 13th century, it became a possession of the French Crown and renewed its prosperity by royally chartered merchants' fairs. Later, the troubles of Béziers and Narbonne in the Albigensian Crusade and the Hundred Years' War would prove lucky for Pézenas. Besides

Wine: More Coteaux du Languedoc

One of the best pockets of this AOC label (*see* p.147) is here. Pézenas is the home of some excellent wines, especially those of the **Prieuré de St-Jean de Bebian**, t 04 67 98 13 60 (*ring in advance*), *www. bebian.com*. For a unique, golden-hued clairette wine from the fragrant, thyme-covered slopes to the north, try the **Château St-André**, Route de Nizas at Pézanas, t 04 67 98 33 46, *www.vins-languedoc-saint-andre.com* (*open Mon–Fri 9–12 and 2–6*).

Pomérols, near Pézenas, is the centre of a traditional but obscure, minuscule growing area on the west shore of the Bassin de Thau called Picpoul de Pinet, producing an unusual soft white wine with sea-green highlights that goes well with freshwater fish; try some at the **Cave Coopérative Les Costières**, in Pomérols, t 04 67 77 01 59, *www.cave-pomerols.com* (*open Mon–Sat 8.30–12 and 2–6*). Lézignan-la-Cèbe, just north of Pézenas, is the mild onion capital of France and also has the **Château d'Ormesson**, t 04 67 98 29 33 (*ring in advance*), run by a count devoted to perfecting his white and red Vins de Pays d'Oc that have surpassed not a few proud AOC labels – especially a red called L'Enclos made of merlot and cabernet sauvignon.

draining off trade and commerce from those cities, the royal town replaced Narbonne as seat of the Estates-General of Languedoc after 1456. The royal governors of the region followed in 1526, bringing in their wake a whole wave of wealthy nobles, clerics and jurists, who rebuilt Pézenas in their own image with new churches, convents, government buildings and scores of refined *hôtels particuliers*. For the next two centuries they remained, preferring their aristocratic little town to decaying Narbonne or to Montpellier, full of untidy industry and Protestants.

All this came to an end with the Revolution, but meanwhile Pézenas has done its best to keep up its monuments while making a living from agriculture and tourism.

A Walk around Town

The tourist information office is the place to start. They offer a brochure with a detailed walking tour of the town and its 70-odd listed historical buildings. From the Renaissance through to the 18th century, Pézenas really did develop and maintain a distinctive architectural manner; this can best be seen in the ***hôtels particuliers***, with their lovely arcaded courtyards and external staircases. It was an eclectic style, incorporating elements as diverse as Gothic vaulting and Italian Renaissance balustrades, tasteful, if not ambitious.

The **tourist office** was also once the shop of a barber named Gély. The playwright Molière spent some seasons in Pézenas in the 1650s, when his troupe was employed by the governor, the Prince de Conti, and he liked passing the afternoons in Gély's salon, doing research for his comedies – watching the comings and goings and listening to the conversations. Across Place Gambetta, the former government palace, the **Maison Consulaire**, has been rebuilt so many times since the 13th century that it is in itself a little museum of Pézenas architecture. Around the corner on Rue Alliés, the Musée de Vulliod-St-Germain contains memorabilia of Molière and his time in Pézenas, along with collections of tapestries, faïence, paintings and the bric-a-brac of Pézenas' past.

Musée de Vulliod-St-Germain
t 04 67 98 90 59; open July–mid-Sept Tues, Thurs, Sat and Sun 10–12 and 3–7, Wed and Fri 10–12, 3–7 and 9–11pm; June and end of Sept Tues–Sun 10–12 and 3–7; mid-Feb–May and Oct–early Nov Tues–Sat 10–12 and 2–5.30; closed mid-Nov–mid-Feb; adm

West of Place Gambetta are some of the best streets for peeking inside the courtyards of the *hôtels particuliers*: Rue Sabatini, Rue François-Oustrin (the **Hôtel de Lacoste**, with an elegant staircase, is at No.8), Rue de Montmorency, and especially **Rue de la Foire**, the status address of the old days, with a number of palaces, including the Renaissance **Hôtel de Carrion-Nizas** at No.10. Just down the street, note the charming relief of child musicians at No.22. At the northern end of the street, a left takes you into Rue Emile Zola; the **Hôtel de Jacques Cœur** (the famous merchant of Montpellier; *see* pp.134–5) is at No.7, with an interesting allegorical sculpted façade. It faces the **Porte Faugères**, a 1597 remnant of the town walls, and

Market Days in Pézenas

Pézenas: Sat.

Where to Stay and Eat in Pézenas

ⓘ Pézenas >
*Place Gambetta,
t 04 67 98 36 40, www.
pezenas-tourisme.fr;
open July–Aug daily;
Sept–June Mon–Sat
and Sun pm*

Pézenas ✉ 34120

★★★Hostellerie de St-Alban, 31 Route d'Agde, Nézignan l'Evêque, just south of Pézenas, t 04 67 98 11 38, *www. saintalban.com* (€€€–€€). A quiet 19th-century villa in the vines, with a pool, tennis and restaurant (€€€). *Closed mid-Nov–mid-Feb.*

★★Genieys, 9 Av Aristide Briand, t 04 67 98 13 99 (€). Outside the historic centre, but a good hotel in town, with a restaurant (€€).

Le Pré St-Jean, 18 Av du Maréchal Leclerc, t 04 67 98 15 31 (€€€–€€). Has a pretty terrace and serves stuffed squid and *carré d'agneau. Closed Sun eve, Mon, and Thurs eve.*

Côté Sud, Place du 14 Juillet, t 04 67 09 41 74 (€€). For a shellfish feast, this place comes up with the goods.

Maison Alary, 5 Rue St-Jean, t 04 67 98 21 39. This *boulangerie* makes Pézenas' spool-shaped *petits pâtés*. They often take French visitors by surprise ('What is this, half sweet and half mutton?'), but if you're British you may not find them that shocking: the recipe was introduced in 1770 by the Indian chef of Lord Clive, Governor of India. Eat them warm. *Closed Mon.*

Museum of Doors and Ironwork
t 04 67 98 35 05; open mid-June–mid-Sept Mon–Fri 10.30–12.30 and 3–7, Sat 11–12.30 and 3–7, Sun 3–7; July and Aug also open Wed and Fri 9pm–11pm; mid-Sept–mid-June Tues–Fri 10–12 and 2–5, Sat 11–12 and 2–5, Sun 2–5

the nearby entrance to the small Jewish **Ghetto**, a single poignant lane closed in by two gates in the 14th century. At 5 Rue Montmorency, in keeping with the town's architectural heritage, there is a museum of doors and ironwork.

The broad **Cours Jean Jaurès**, site of the market, divides Pézenas in two. It, too, has its palaces: an especially good row of them at Nos.14–22, including the **Hôtel de Grasset**. The Cours leads into Place de la République, and the church of **St-Jean**, with profuse 17th- and 18th-century marble decoration that proves Pézenas' artistic instincts were much sounder in secular matters. South of the Cours, there are more palaces: the **Hôtel de Malibran** and **Hôtel de l'Epine**, with a lavish sculptural façade, both on Rue Victor Hugo; the **Hôtel Montmorency**, the Pézenas home of one of 16th-century France's most illustrious noble houses, on Rue Reboul; and, best of all, the **Hôtel d'Alfonse** on Rue Conti, which has a delightful courtyard loggia on three levels, built in the 1630s.

Béziers

This city's history is succinct: a rude interruption and a second chance. Béziers is older than the Romans; its site, a commanding, defensible hill on a key part of the Mediterranean coast, seems promising, but Béziers' long career has produced little distinction and only one famous anecdote. In 1209, at the beginning of the Albigensian Crusade, Cathars took refuge in the city and were besieged. When the besiegers offered the Cathars a chance to leave the city, they refused. The troops stormed the city and found that the entire population had taken refuge in the churches. The

Getting to and around Béziers

Béziers is on the main coastal **rail** line, **t** 04 67 49 63 38, and it's easy to get from Narbonne, Sète, Montpellier or points beyond, with trains never much more than two hours apart.

The *gare routière* is on Place du Général de Gaulle, **t** 04 67 28 36 41, with regular **bus** connections to Pézenas , and less regular ones to villages of the eastern Hérault. City bus 16 runs from here to nearby Valras, the popular lido of the Biterrois.

Crusaders' ayatollah, the Abbot of Cîteaux, had ordered the massacre of all the Cathars. Asked how to distinguish them from the Catholics, he replied, 'Kill them all; God will know his own.' From all accounts, that is exactly what happened; in his report to Rome, the papal legate bragged that 20,000 people were put to death.

Not surprisingly, Béziers languished for centuries. The second chance came in the 1660s, with the building of the Canal du Midi (*see* pp.175–9). A new Béziers has grown up since then, a busy port and industrial town of some 70,000, known best for its crack rugby squad and bullfights. Approaching it from the surrounding plains, you'll see its heroic hilltop skyline from miles away, crowned by its impressive cathedral; seen from inside, unfortunately, Béziers will not sustain your initial expectations, a pigeon-grey city with plenty of traffic, but also three good museums.

Allées Paul Riquet and the Cathedral

Life in Béziers centres around the the **Allées Paul Riquet**, a broad promenade of plane trees named after the city's great benefactor, the builder of the Canal du Midi. Besides a statue of Riquet, there is a handsome 19th-century theatre, and a monument to Resistance hero Jean Moulin (another Biterrois) at the top of the **Plateau des Poètes**, a romantic garden with ponds and swans and statues by local sculptor Jean-Antoine Injalbert that descends gracefully down to the train station. From the other end of the Allées Paul Riquet, any of the streets to the west will take you up to the top of the hill and the medieval centre.

Someone must have been left in Béziers after 1209, for the city spent the next two centuries working on its grandiose **cathedral**, replacing the original that was wrecked in the sack. Its grim, fortress-like exterior, similar to Narbonne's, seems a foreign presence, the citadel of an occupying force. The inside is more graceful; in clean, warm ashlar masonry with plenty of stained glass, it creates a light and airy effect, especially in the apse, where large windows of blue and white decorative glass (behind a dreadful Baroque altar) are the prettiest feature in the church. In two chapels (second right and second left) there are fragments of Giotto-esque frescoes, and, at the west front, there is a magnificent organ almost as good as the one in Narbonne, carved in walnut in 1623 by Guilhaume Martois, who is buried next to it.

09

The Hérault | The Southern Hérault: Béziers

Architectural fragments from the earlier church can be seen in the beautiful vaulted cloister, a work of the late 14th century.

Behind the cathedral, the Hôtel Fabrégat, in Place de la Révolution, houses Béziers' fine arts museum, the **Musée des Beaux-Arts**, founded in 1859, with something for every taste: a 16th-century *Virgin and Child* by Martin Schaffner of Ulm, a portrait by Hans Holbein the Younger, 17th-century Italian works (including a Domenichino), a Richard Bonington *Storm*, and 18th- and 19th-century French paintings. Many of the fine modern works were purchased by Jean Moulin; the great Résistance leader posed as a designer and art dealer under the name of Romanin.

Just north, the **Musée Fayet**, in a delightful 17th-century *hôtel particulier* at 9 Rue du Capus, contains several rooms of 18th- and 19th-century paintings and decorative arts, and several rooms dedicated to the sculptures of Injalbert.

If you have time for more churches, the Romanesque **Madeleine**, north of the cathedral and market on Place de la Madeleine, was one of the sites of the massacre of 1209, when the population sought to take refuge in its walls. **St-Aphrodise**, further north, hidden behind newer buildings in Place St-Aphrodise, was Béziers' cathedral in the 8th century. 'St Aphrodise', if it isn't Aphrodite herself, would be the legendary first bishop, who rode into Béziers one day on a camel (now the city's symbol). The Romans naturally chopped off his head and threw it into a well – but the water rose miraculously to the surface, floating the head with it. Aphrodise fished it out and carried it under his arm to the site of this church, and then disappeared into the ground. It's more likely, however, that pagan Aphrodite had a temple on or near this site. Almost nothing remains of the original building, but a 4th-century sarcophagus has been recycled for use as a baptismal font.

A third Romanesque church, simple **St-Jacques**, is on a belvedere on the south side of Béziers, by a third museum, the **Musée du Biterrois**, housed in an 18th-century barracks on Rampe du 96ème (from the top of Av Gambetta, turn down Av de la Marne). The museum divides its space between regional archaeological finds, medieval capitals and other bits (including St Aphrodise with his head), ethnography, science and ceramics. If you like bullfighting visit the exhibition in summer on *tauromachie* at 1 Av President Wilson. The **Château St-Bauzille** on Route de Bessan has a large collection of pianos, heralded by the tourist office as the largest piano museum in Europe.

Musée des Beaux-Arts
t 04 67 28 38 78; open July and Aug Tues–Sun 10–6; April–June and Sept–Oct Tues–Sun 9–12 and 2–6; Nov–Mar Tues–Sun 9–12 and 2–5; closed Mon; adm

Musée Fayet
t 04 67 49 04 66; open July–Aug daily 10–6; April–June and Oct 9–12 and 2–6; Nov–Mar 9–12 and 2–5; closed Mon; adm

Madeleine
open Wed and Fri 10–12, Thurs 3–6, Sat 10–12 and 2–5, Sun 10–12.30 and 2–4, but check with tourist office as times change often

Musée du Biterrois
t 04 67 36 81 61; open July and Aug Tues–Sun 10–6; April–June and Sept–Oct Tues–Sun 9–12 and 2–6; Nov–Mar Tues–Sun 9–12 and 2–5; closed Mon; adm

Market Days in Béziers

Fri: flowers, antiques, food and clothes in Allées Paul Riquet, Place David d'Angers, and around.

Sat and Sun: Place de la Madeleine, flea and produce markets.

Where to Stay in Béziers

*Palais des Congrès, 29 Av St-Saëns, **t** 04 67 76 84 00, www.beziers-tourisme.fr; open mid-June–Aug daily; Sept–June Mon–Sat*

Béziers ✉ 34500

***Impérator**, 28 Allées Paul Riquet, **t** 04 67 49 02 25, *www.hotel-imperator.fr* (€€). This has the best location in town, and there's a garage.

****Champ de Mars**, 17 Rue de Metz, **t** 04 67 28 35 53, *http://hotel-champ demars.com* (€). A good-value place, central but set on a quiet street.

Eating Out in Béziers

L'Ambassade, 22 Bd de Verdun, **t** 04 67 76 06 24 (€€€€–€€€). Dine well and elegantly while watching the progress of your meal (the kitchen has a large window). *Closed Sun and Mon*.

Café Mondial, 2 Rue Solférino, **t** 04 67 28 22 15. Packed most evenings, not so much for its food but for its free concerts (several eves per month). *Open eves Tues–Sat*.

The Hérault-Aude Borders

The Canal du Midi

🏆 Canal du Midi

The best thing to do in Béziers is go west for one of Languedoc's best-kept secrets. The waterways of other parts of France are well-enough known; this, one of very few in the south, remains serene and still relatively unburdened by tourism, planted its entire length with parallel rows of plane trees (not just for decoration; they hold the soil and help keep the canal from silting up). Shady and idyllic, the canal Paul Riquet built (*see* **Topics**, pp.44–6) is also an early monument of economic planning, from the days of Louis XIV's great minister Colbert, when everything in France was being reformed and modernized. Begun in 1667, as many as 12,000 men worked on the project, which required over 100 locks and runs for 145 miles. The section from the Mediterranean to Toulouse was completed 14 years later; Riquet, the man who planned and financed it, died a few months before the opening.

No one has shipped any freight on the Canal du Midi for years, but it is still kept up for the benefit of holidaymakers. Some of the locks are tended; at others you'll have to figure out the mechanism yourself. You can take a slow cruise from Béziers all the way to Toulouse, or just rent a rowing boat or canoe in one of the villages and spend a drowsy day under the plane trees.

The Canal West of Béziers

The canal connects Sète, on the Mediterranean, with Toulouse – where it still flows right past the central railway station – and thence to the Atlantic, by way of the river Garonne. The best parts of it are west of Béziers, where it passes through a score of lovely old villages, fitting so well into the landscape that it seems to have been there all the time. Pick it up just outside Béziers at the **Ecluses de Fonsérances**, just off the N113 for Narbonne. This is a series of seven original locks, a watery stair that facilitated the biggest drop in altitude along the canal's length.

Getting around the Canal du Midi

By Car or Bike

You'll need a **car** to get around here, or better still a **mountain bike** (*VTT* in French); the shady towpaths are lovely for cycling.

By Boat

Best of all, hire a small **boat**, or spend a week on a **canal barge** (the canal is usually open to navigation Mar–Nov). Reputed firms include **Rive de France** in Colombiers, southwest of Béziers along the canal, **t** 04 67 37 14 60, *www.rivedefrance.com*. Also try **Crown Blue Line**, in Castelnaudary, **t** 04 68 94 52 72, *www.crownblueline.com*; **Connoisseur Cruisers**, 7 Quai d'Alsace, Narbonne, **t** 04 68 65 14 55, *www.connoisseur boating.co.uk*; or **Locaboat Plaisance**, in Argens-Minervois, **t** 04 68 27 03 33, *www.locaboat.com*. No previous experience is required, and most people bring bikes along for outings along the way. Most luxurious of all are the barge hotels (*péniches hôtels*). For more information, contact the **Comité Regional du Tourisme**, 417 Rue Samuel Morse, ✉ 34000 Montpellier, **t** 04 67 22 81 00, *www.sunfrance.net/canal*.

No one road follows the canal for long, but with a good map and some careful navigation you can stay close to it, on the back roads through **Colombiers**, first of the canal villages, then to **Nissan-lez-Ensérune**, a busy place with a 14th-century Gothic church. You will already have noticed this landmark in the flat countryside; signs from Nissan will lead you up to it, and to the remains of one of the most important pre-Roman towns of southern Gaul, the Oppidum d'Ensérune. The Canal du Midi passes right under it by way of the 567ft Malpas tunnel (1679), the first canal tunnel ever, dug by Riquet, who knew best, in spite of considerable controversy at the time.

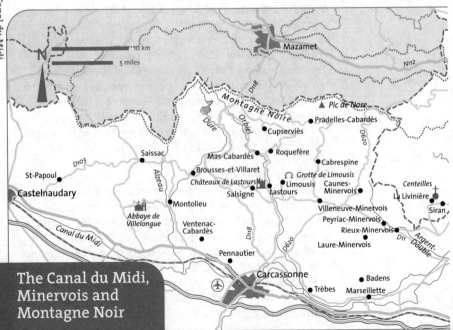

The Canal du Midi, Minervois and Montagne Noir

Oppidum d'Ensérune

Oppidum
d'Ensérune

*t 04 67 37 01 23, www.
oppidumdenserune.com;
open May–Aug daily
10–7; April and Sept
Tues–Sun 10–12.30 and
2–6; Oct–Mar Tues–Sun
9.30–12.30 and 2–5.30;
last entry 1hr before
closing; guided tours
possible; adm*

The site is a relic of the time when these coasts were first coming into the mainstream of Mediterranean civilization. Initially settled in the 6th century BC, it began as a fortified trading village under Greek influence, closely connected to Marseille. By 250 BC it may have had as many as 10,000 people, though later in that century it was wrecked, possibly by Hannibal on his way to Italy during the Punic Wars. Under Roman rule it revived again, refounded as a Roman colony, but in peaceful, settled times it could not survive. The cramped, difficult site was good for defence; when this was no longer necessary, people and trade gradually moved down to the plains and the coast, and Ensérune was largely abandoned by the 1st century AD.

Not much remains of the town: the foundations of the wall, cisterns and traces of habitations can be seen. The excellent **museum** in the centre of the excavations has a collection of ceramics, including some fine Greek and Etruscan works, along with local pieces that show the strong influence of the foreigners. Just outside the town, where an ancient column with an unusual trapezoidal capital has been re-erected, you can take in one of the oddest panoramas in France, a gigantic surveyor's pie, neatly sliced. This was the **Etang de Montady**, a roughly circular swamp reclaimed in the 13th century, when the new fields were precisely divided by drainage ditches radiating from the centre.

09 The Hérault | The Hérault-Aude Borders: The Canal du Midi

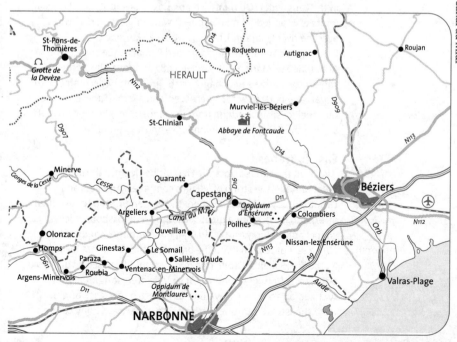

Canal Villages

Most of these have at least one restaurant, some have guest-houses and boat rentals; all of them are agreeable spots to while away an afternoon. From Nissan, the D37 takes you to **Poilhes**, a lovely, sleepy village built around one of Paul Riquet's graceful brick canal bridges. **Capestang**, the next one, has a landmark visible for miles around: the tall, unfinished Gothic **Collégiale St-Etienne**, a monument to unfulfilled ambition, like Narbonne cathedral, which indeed is believed to have been the work of the same architect. They'll let you climb the tower for the view. Capestang's rugged **château** is the summer home of the Archbishop of Narbonne; the interior includes a Renaissance ceiling fancifully painted with caricatures, but it is currently not open to the public. A detour south of Capestang and just west of the village of **Ouveillan** will take you to an unusual medieval monument, the **Grange de Fontcalvy**. A testament to the wealth of the Cistercian order, this was a key stronghold of Fontfroide Abbey (*see* pp.202–203), a fortified barn of considerable architectural sophistication, 66ft square, with ogival vaulting. Today it hosts the summer theatre and music Festival de Fontcalvy (*www.festival-fontcalvy.com*).

Collégiale St-Etienne
open June–Sept 10–12 and 4–7; tower visits by guided tour, summer 11, 5 and 6; adm

Quarante

All along, the lands around the canal have been packed full with vineyards. Further west, this continues but the countryside becomes greener and lusher, with some of the cosiest landscapes in the Languedoc. Quarante isn't on the canal (although there's an impressive aqueduct nearby, one of Vauban's last works (1693), over the river Quarante), but it is worth a 4km side trip, north on D36/D37E, for its severe and dignified Romanesque church, the **Abbatiale Ste-Marie**, built between 982 and 1053. The *trésor* contains a marble sarcophagus of the 3rd century, decorated with angels and portraits of the deceased, and a remarkable example of Montpellier silversmithing from the 1440s: a very leonine bust of St John the Baptist with almond eyes and a Gallic nose.

East to Trèbes

Musée du Chapeau
t 04 68 46 19 26; open summer Mon–Sat 9–12 and 2–7; winter Sun 2–6; adm

Back on the canal, across the Hérault border into the *départe-ment* of Aude, the string of villages continues: **Argeliers** and **Le Somail**, a sweet hamlet where the bargemen stop to take their afternoon naps. It has a great second-hand bookshop, an ice house, chapel and a quirky **Musée du Chapeau**, with thousands of hats.

Musée Amphoralis
t 04 68 46 89 48; open July–Sept daily 10–12 and 3–7; Oct–Dec and Feb–June Tues–Sun 2–6; closed Jan; adm

Just east of Le Somail, on the branch of the canal that leads to Narbonne, **Sallèles d'Aude** thinks you might like to see its dusty old pots at the **Musée Amphoralis**. It's more interesting than that. Archaeologists have excavated a large factory complex on this site from the 1st–3rd centuries AD, one that made everything ceramic from roof tiles to amphorae. The Romans of those days complained that the Gauls were underselling local Italian production in everything from wine to pottery; here is evidence of a little bit of globalization from far-off antiquity. There is a potters' market in August, and you will find the **European Centre of Patchwork**, no less, at 32 Quai de Lorraine.

Further west are **Ventenac-en-Minervois**, **Paraza**, **Roubia** and **Argens-Minervois**, a once-fortified village with a ruined castle. The canal at this point runs parallel to the river Aude, and in places the two are only a few hundred feet apart. Near Roubia, the canal passes over a small stream on the **Pont-Canal de Répudre**. Paul Riquet designed this, too; it is the oldest canal bridge in France.

Further west comes **Homps**, with another ruined castle, built by the Knights Hospitallers, and then a long, empty scenic stretch leading towards **Marseillette** in the Minervois, followed by **Trèbes**, a fortified village with a triple set of locks and an impressive canal bridge over the Orb built by Vauban in 1686. Have a look inside the village church, **St-Etienne**; its impressive single nave holds a real curiosity: high up on the corbels that support the roof, where only God can see them well, are 320 small paintings of human and animal faces from the 14th century. No one knows who painted them or why; they were only discovered in 1977 when some of the plaster that covered them fell. Now they are restored, and a few of the best have been detached and displayed in one of the chapels.

Market Days by the Canal du Midi

ⓘ **Capestang**
Bd Pasteur,
t 04 67 93 34 23,
www.capestango-t.com

Capestang: Wed and Sun am.

Where to Stay and Eat by the Canal du Midi

Most of the villages have at least one eating place with a terrace view.

ⓘ **Nissan-lez-Ensérune >**
t 04 67 37 14 12, www.
nissanlezenserune.com;
open Mon–Fri and
Sat am

Nissan-lez-Ensérune ✉ 34440

**Résidence, 35 Av de la Cave, t 04 67 37 00 63, www.hotel-residence.com (€€). Antiquated charm, with a pool and restaurant (€€€–€€) and a more modern annexe. Closed mid-Dec–Jan; restaurant closed lunch, Sat and Mon.

**Via Domitia, Colombiers, t 04 67 35 62 63 (€). A hotel that is part of a medical clinic but takes healthy guests too. Café open Mon–Fri 9–8.30.

★ **Château de Floure >>**

Homps and Le Somail ✉ 11120

**Auberge de l'Arbousier, 50 Av de Carcassonne, Homps, t 04 68 91 11 24, www.aubergearbousier.com (€€). A charming hotel-restaurant in an old mas on the banks of the canal; the kitchen specializes in cooking with local Minervois wine. Closed Mon and Tues lunch and Sun eve.

Bed and breakfast, Le Somail, t 04 68 46 16 02, www.canalmidi.com/bernabeu.htm (€). In a charming 17th-century house. There is also a gîte. Closed Nov–Feb.

Les Tonneliers, by the port in Homps, t 04 68 91 14 04 (€€). The terrace is a favourite stop. Closed mid-Nov–Feb.

Trèbes ✉ 11800

***Château de Floure, 1 Allée Gaston Bonheur, Floure, t 04 68 79 11 29 (€€€€€). Just east of Trèbes, this ivy-covered château was a Romanesque abbey converted into a home by writer Gaston Bonheur; now a Relais du Silence hotel, it has an elegant French garden, with pool and tennis, comfortable rooms and a good restaurant (€€€). Closed mid-Nov–Feb.

The Minervois

This is a *pays* with plenty of character, though not many people.
With typical French irony, the Minervois suffered grievously from
poverty and rural depopulation throughout the 20th century –
then, just when everyone was gone, vintners improved the quality
of their Minervois wines. They have become popular across France
and the region's prosperity has returned. The Corbières, just over
the Aude (*see* pp.203–11), tells much the same story. In other ways,
too, the Minervois is a prelude to the Corbières: the sharp contrast
of tidy vineyards with ragged country and outcrops of eroded
limestone, the sense of strangeness and isolation – in a region of
France that has been inhabited for more or less 200,000 years.

From the Canal du Midi to Minerve

Olonzac, just north of the canal, is the centre of the wine district
and the closest thing the eastern Minervois has to a town. It is an
attractive place with cafés under the trees and a holiday feel on
warm days. To the northwest, some of the most civilized
landscapes in the Minervois lie around the village of **Siran**, with
three little-known attractions: to the east, an impressive dolmen
called the **Mourel des Fades** ('fairy dolmen') and the 12th-century
country church of **St-Germain-de-Cesseras**, with a beautifully
sculpted apse. Both are signposted off the D168. Another country
church, the **Chapelle de Centeilles**, north of Siran, is a unique
survival, entirely covered inside with frescoes from the 13th to the
15th centuries, with a fragment of Roman mosaic, found nearby.

From Olonzac, the narrow D10 will take you up into the heights
of the Minervois, to **Minerve**, a town as old as any in Languedoc.
Minerve is a natural place for a defensible settlement, on a steep
rock between two rivers, but that does not explain why the area
around it should have been so popular for so long. Traces of habitation dating back 170,000 years have been found in its caves, and
Neolithic dolmens abound. The Celts and the Romans built the
town itself, and in the Middle Ages it was a feudal stronghold with
a Cathar slant. Minerve accepted refugees from the sack of Béziers
in 1209; Simon de Montfort followed them and took the town after
a two-month siege, followed by the usual butchery and burning of
140 Cathars at the stake.

Minerve today counts little over a hundred inhabitants; nothing
has been done or built since Unspeakable Simon's visit, and the
medieval relic on its dramatic site has become a peaceful and
unambitious tourist attraction, with potters, artists and souvenir
stands filling the spaces left by all the folk who have moved to the
cities in the last 80 years. Parts of the walls are still in good nick,
but all that is left of the château is a single, slender, octagonal

Getting around the Minervois

Autorail Touristique Minervois usually connects Bize-Minervois with Narbonne in summer, running old trains from the 1950s. There are stops along the way at Sallèles-d'Aude for the Amphoralis museum, at the *pont-canal* over the Canal du Midi, at Le Somail, and at Cabezac for a tour of an olive-oil press. However, the service was suspended in 2007 for work on the line and it is uncertain whether it will reopen; call the Narbonne tourist office (*see* p.198) for information.

---

09 The Hérault | The Hérault-Aude Borders: The Minervois

Minerve archaeology and palaeontology museum
t 04 68 91 22 92; open May–mid Nov daily

Musée Hurepel
t 04 68 91 12 26

tower; the Minervois call it the *'candela'*. There are narrow medieval alleys, gates and cisterns, a simple 12th-century **church** with a white marble altar from 456, said to be the oldest in Europe, and a small **archaeology and palaeontology museum** with some fossils and prehistoric finds, across from a *caveau de dégustation* of Minervois wines. The **Musée Hurepel** in Rue des Martyrs tells the Cathar story (*see* pp.41–2) with figurines.

Wine: Minervois

Rough and arid, protected from the cold winds of the north by the mountains, the sun-bleached region of AOC Minervois stretches from Carcassonne almost to St-Chinian. Its glories are supple but powerful red wines, dominated by mourvèdre, grenache, syrah and carignan, and with a lingering bouquet reminiscent of the *maquis* that have long been one of the gems of Languedoc – the best wines may require several years in the cellar to reach their best. Along with Fitou, Minervois is the region's wine that has built the best reputation for itself in recent years; it can be found in shops all over France and is also widely available in British supermarkets. In particular, seek out wines from the *appellation* Minervois La Livinière, a sunny, spicy red and to a lesser extent white wine based in seven villages in the semi-arid limestone plateau around La Livinière; try the wines from the excellent wine co-operative there or **Clos Centeilles** (in Centeilles, north of Siran, **t** 04 68 91 52 18), owned by wine pioneers Patricia and Daniel Boyer-Domergue – sample their rich red Part des Anges.

Try the excellent wines produced by the **Château Ste-Eulalie** (which looks more like a farm than a château) at La Livinière (call first on **t** 04 68 91 42 72, *www.chateausainteeulalie.com*). Also at La Livinière is the **Château Laville Bertrou** (**t** 04 68 91 49 20) which produces the delicious, smooth and flavoursome La Réserve 2005; it is one of former rugbyman Gérard Bertrand's vineyards; *www.gerard-bertrand.com*. At Laure-Minervois taste the dark, exquisite Cuvée Alexandre at **Château Fabas**, on the Rieux road, **t** 04 68 78 17 82, *www.chateaufabas.com* (*open 8–12 and 2–7*); also try the **Cave Coopérative de Vinification Tour St-Martin** at Peyriac, **t** 04 68 78 11 20. If you're passing by the Canal du Midi, you can stop to try some Minervois wines right by the canal at two spots: the **Domaine de Sérame**, **t** 04 68 27 02 47, an old *mas* just outside Argens, or the *cave cooperative* at the **Château de Ventenac**, Ventenac-en-Minervois **t** 04 68 43 27 34, *www.chateaude ventenacminervois.com* (*closed Sun, and mornings*). Another estate worthy of mention is **Château de Paraza**, high above the canal in Paraza, ✉ 11200 Lézignan, **t** 04 34 44 42 27, *http://chateau-de-paraza. com*, run by the Baronne Dominique de Girard Passerieux. The white wines of Minervois are among the revelations of recent years, clean and packed with character. Good examples are to be found at **Château La Grave** at Badens, **t** 04 68 79 16 00, *www. chateau-la-grave.net* (*open Mon–Fri 8–12 and 1.30–6; call at weekends*), and **Château de Paraza** again.

One of the most innovative producers in Minervois is **Château Maris**, based at La Livinière and part of the Comte Cathare group, **t** 04 68 91 42 63, *www.comtecathare.com*. Their vineyards are all in conversion to organic viticulture and the wines are notable for their depth and purity of flavour.

In this area north of Carcassonne there is a relatively new *appellation* called Cabardès. Here, mainly red wines are produced from Bordeaux grape varieties, resulting in rounded, quite stylish wines. Producers to look out for in this area are another, different **Château de Ventenac**, in Ventenac-Cabardès, **t** 04 68 24 93 42, and **Château Pennautier**, **t** 04 68 25 63 48, *www.vignobles-lorgeril.com*. You can sample the wines with food at the café in the wine shop.

The real attractions, however, are out in the country. A short walk from town, there are 'natural bridges' – really more like tunnels, eroded through the limestone by streams. To the west extends the narrow, blushing pink **Canyon de la Cesse**, and determined hikers can seek out a collection of caves and dolmens north of this, at **Bois Bas**, off the D147.

The Seven-Sided Church of Rieux-Minervois

West of Siran, the Minervois flattens out into the valley of the Argent-Double ('silver water'; *dubron* was a Celtic word for water, and the Romans made it *Argentodubrum*). A handsome old bridge spans it for the village of Rieux, built around one of the most uncanny medieval monuments in France.

The seven-pointed star is the recurring mystic symbol of the Midi. The Cathar castle at Montségur, in Ariège, was laid out subtly to fit inside its angles, the Félibres of Provence used it as part of their emblem, and it has been a recurring theme in folk art. Just what it means has never been adequately explained; neither has anyone ventured an explanation for the presence in this unremarkable Minervois village of what may be the only seven-sided church anywhere. Dedicated to the Virgin, the church was built some time

⭐ Rieux-Minervois
t 04 68 78 13 98; open 9–12 and 2–6

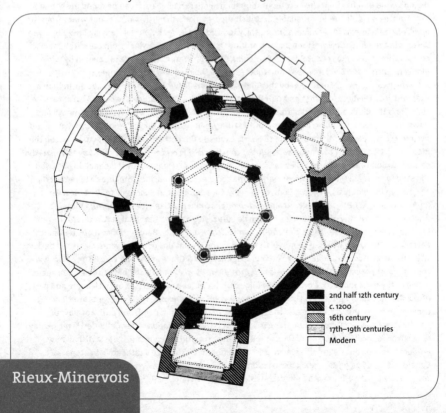

2nd half 12th century
c.1200
16th century
17th–19th centuries
Modern

Rieux-Minervois

in the late 12th century, exactly when, why and by whom, no one knows. A medieval scholar would have cited Scripture: 'Wisdom has built her house; she has set up her seven pillars' (*Proverbs* 1:9), also recalling that the Divine Wisdom was identified (at the time) with the Virgin Mary. Clearly, this temple opens a deep vein of intellectual medieval mysticism, full of geometry and allegory and not entirely recoverable by our minds. Its builders, pressed to explain why the central heptagon around the altar has four squat pilasters and three columns, might have mumbled something about the 'Marriage of Heaven and Earth' – the four-square world and the spiritual triangle. Modern investigators have also discovered various series of ley lines based on this site; according to them, the line of the midsummer sunrise passes from an altar inside the church through a (now closed-up) window and begins an alignment that goes as far as Minerve and St-Guilhem-le-Désert, passing several chapels dedicated to St John along the way.

The ambition of the builders of this church, and their resources, are seen in the sculptural detail inside, entrusted to the Master of Cabestany. Most of the capitals carved with fanciful foliage are by his workshop, while the Master himself is believed to have done the capitals with the reliefs of lions and the Assumption of the Virgin. Building in heptagons certainly must have tried the patience and mathematical know-how of a 12th-century mason; we can admire their careful work, especially the seven-sided belfry, directly over the altar, and the tricky toroid vaulting that connects the heptagon with the 14-sided exterior wall. Over the centuries, a number of chapels have been built along the edges of the church; its exterior aspect, along with the original portal, are now lost.

Caunes-Minervois

The marble for Rieux's church came from **Caunes-Minervois**, just up the Argent-Double, which is also the source of the marble for the Paris Opera and parts of Versailles. It is rare for good stone in so many tints, from green to pink to reddish-orange, to occur in one place. The **quarries**, neatly geometrical excavations around Caunes, make an unusual sight. There is a path along the edge of the quarries with huge chunks of marble left lying around (signposted from the village). Over the centuries they have made Caunes more prosperous and open to the world than its neighbours. Its streets show some modest palaces, such as the Hôtel d'Alibert on the main square, along with the former abbey church of **St-Pierre-et-St-Paul**, founded by Benedict of Aniane, a hotchpotch of Gothic, Romanesque and later styles, conserving some odd capitals from the Carolingian original and a good 13th-century portal. You can also visit the cloister. North of town, the D620 leads past the quarries into the narrow and scenic **Gorge de l'Argent-Double**.

St-Pierre-et-St-Paul
t 04 68 78 09 44; open 10–12 and 2–7; adm

09 The Hérault | The Hérault-Aude Borders: The Minervois

(★) Auberge de
St-Martin >>

(i) Rieux-
Minervois >>
*Place de l'Eglise
Romane*, t 04 68 78 13
98; open daily all year

(★) Château de
Violet >>

(i) Minerve >
9 Rue des Martyrs,
t 04 68 91 81 43, www.
minerve-tourisme.
com; open Tues–Sat

Minervois Market Days

Olonzac: Tues.
Laure-Minervois: Sun.
Rieux-Minervois: Tues, Thurs and Sat.

Where to Stay and Eat in the Minervois

Siran ✉ 34210

***Château de Siran**, Av du Château,
t 04 68 91 55 98 (€€€–€€). Offers
charming comfortable rooms and a
good restaurant (€€€). *Closed Jan;
restaurant closed Sun eve and Mon.*

Olonzac ✉ 34210

Restaurant du Minervois, 2 Rue des
Ecoles, Olonzac, t 04 68 91 20 73,
www.belminervois.com (€€). *Closed Sat
lunch, and eves in winter.*

Minerve ✉ 34210

***Relais Chantovent**, 17 Grand-Rue,
Minerve, t 04 68 91 14 18 (€). The only
hotel in Minerve, with seven rooms;
also a fine restaurant (€€€–€€) with a
terrace overlooking the gorge, serving
truffles. *Closed mid-Nov–mid-Mar;
restaurant closed Sun eve and Mon.*

Auberge de St-Martin, south of
Minerve in Beaufort, t 04 68 91 16 18
(€€). A sweet old *mas* with a shady
terrace, offering wood-fire grilled
meat and fish and a variety of
regional dishes which change
seasonally. *Closed Mon in May–Sept;
Sun eve, Mon and Tues eve in Oct–April.*

Rieux-Minervois and Around ✉ 11160

***Château de Violet**, Route de
Pépieux, outside Peyriac-Minervois,
t 04 68 78 10 42, *www.chateau-de-
violet.com* (€€€–€€). The Minervois'
luxury resort: a restored farmhouse,
elegant and sumptuous, with pool
and gardens, a wine museum with
tastings, and a restaurant (€€€).

****Hôtel d'Alibert**, Place de la Mairie,
Caunes-Minervois, t 04 68 78 00 54
(€€). A sweet little place to stay or
eat, with good regional food in the
restaurant. *Closed mid-Nov–mid-Mar,
and Sun eve and Mon.*

Logis de Mérinville, Av Georges
Clemenceau, Rieux-Minervois, t 04 68
78 12 49 (€€€–€€). An atmospheric
19th-century stone inn in the village
centre, serving good food. *Closed Nov,
Jan–Mar, Tues eve and Wed.*

The Montagne Noire

Even wilder than the Minervois, if not as unusual, the bleak,
brooding Black Mountain is an 18-mile-wide stretch of peaks, taller
than their neighbours and difficult to access until modern times.
The long ridge in fact divides two climates: its north face, looking
towards the Massif Central (the Montagne Noire is the southernmost point of the range), has an Atlantic climate, while the south
is Mediterranean. Its slate-roofed villages have a solemn air, and
their people are bent to serious mountain pursuits – mining and
quarrying, logging and paper-making. In the old days they
scratched iron and copper out of the mountain; this still continues,
along with a bit of silver and gold – the deposits at Salsigne,
discovered a century ago, yield around a tonne of gold each year.
The trees are even more important; you'll see chestnut groves,
some planted in the Middle Ages when chestnuts were a
mountain staple, and also stands of foreign intruders – Scots pine
and Douglas fir, important to the lumber business. An area as
dramatic and authentic as the Montagne Noire in the UK would
attract day-trippers by the thousand in the summer with traffic

jams to match. But here you can drive the winding mountain roads in August, and hardly see a soul. It is also excellent walking country. In the larger tourist offices, look out for the guide *Balades et Randonnées a pied et à VTT Montagne Noire* published by Chamina.

The Clamoux Valley

All the routes into the mountains follow narrow parallel valleys leading up from the river Aude; the first is the Argent-Double, from Caunes. Next comes the Clamoux (on the D112), with equally impressive gorges, north of Villeneuve-Minervois; 6km up the Clamoux is **Cabrespine** with its lofty castle (Simon de Montfort slept here) and deep abyss, the Gouffre Géant de Cabrespine, part of it accessible to all, including wheelchairs, and part of it left as it was, explored in four–five-hour excursions guided by Les Safaris Souterrains. Further up is the **Gorge de Clamoux** in **Pradelles-Cabardès**, where the people used to make a living by shipping ice down to the cities of the valley. Their sunken ice chambers are still a feature of the landscape. Above Pradelles looms the **Pic de Nore**, at 3,937ft the highest point of the Montagne Noire.

Gouffre Géant de Cabrespine
t 04 68 26 14 22; open July–Aug 10–7; Mar–June and Sept–Nov 10–12 and 2–6; closed Dec–Feb; **Les Safaris Souterrains,** *t 04 67 66 11 11*

The Orbiel Valley and Châteaux de Lastours

The next valley, that of the **Orbiel** (D101), is the most populous of the region, and perhaps the most beautiful. It also contains the region's landmark, the Châteaux de Lastours – not one but four castles, in various states of picturesque ruin, all on the same hilltop to defend the Montagne Noire's mineral richness. The lords of Cabardès, bosses of the Montagne Noire before the arrival of Simon de Montfort in 1211, built the first of them, the castles of **Cabaret** and **Quertinheux**; the two between these, **Surdespine** and **Tour Régine**, were added by the French kings in the 13th century. Remember the Drac, in Beaucaire? (If not, *see* p.113.) Apparently, after his embarrassment there he took refuge in the Hérault. The legendary knight Roland himself was on his trail near Lastours, and his horse left a hoof-print in a great boulder near the Châteaux, a place still called the *Saut de Roland*.

Châteaux de Lastours
t 04 68 77 56 02; open July and Aug daily 9–8; April, May, June and Sept daily 10–6; Oct daily 10–5; Feb, Mar, Nov and Dec weekends and hols only 10–5; closed Jan; adm

Salsigne, with its gold mine, lies just to the west of Lastours. To the east is a remarkable cave, the Grotte de Limousis, with unique formations of gleaming white aragonite crystals, one of which, called the *Lustre* (chandelier), is over 30ft across. Further up the valley are two of the most beautiful and unspoiled villages of the region: **Roquefère** and Mas-Cabardès; north of Roquefère, a 5km detour will take you up to a high, lovely waterfall at a place called **Cupserviès**. **Mas-Cabardès** has some half-timbered houses and a 16th-century church with a rugged octagonal belfry. In the village centre, note the pretty, carefully carved stone cross, a typical decoration of Montagne Noire villages. This one was a 16th-century gift of the weavers' guild; with its abundance of water, this region

Grotte de Limousis
t 04 68 26 14 20; open July and Aug daily 10–6; April–June and Sept daily 10.30–5.30; Mar and Oct daily 2.30–5.30; Nov Sun and hols 2.30–4.30; closed Dec–Feb; adm

Musée du Moulin à Papier
t 04 68 26 67 43, www. moulinapapier.com; open for guided tours July–Aug daily on the hour 11–6; Sept–June 11am and hourly 2.30–5.30; Oct–June Mon–Fri 11 and 3.30, Sat, Sun and hols 11am and hourly 2.30–5.30; adm

Montolieu
www.montolieu.net

Musée Michel Braibant
t 04 68 24 80 04; open April–Dec Mon–Sat 10–12.30 and 2–6, Sun 2–6; Jan–Mar daily 2–5; adm

Abbaye de Villelongue
t 04 68 76 92 58; open May–Oct 10–12 and 2–6.30; rest of the year by appt; guided tours, English spoken; adm

z
Musée Goya
t 05 63 71 59 30; open July and Aug Tues–Sat 10–6; Sept–June Tues–Sat 9–12 and 2–5; Sun 10–12 and 2–5; closed Mon; adm

had a thriving textile trade before the black-hearted English Industrial Revolutionaries started underselling them in the 18th century. Another water-powered trade was paper; in **Brousses-et-Villaret**, west of Mas-Cabardès, you can visit an 18th-century paper mill and learn the history of paper and how to make it by hand at the **Musée du Moulin à Papier**.

The Western Montagne Noire

Further west, the crown of the Montagne Noire is dotted with artificial lakes, part of a big hydroelectric scheme; the Bassin de Lampy is particularly attractive. In the valley of the Vernassonne, **Saissac** is another lovely village, built over a ravine and surrounded by forests. Saissac, too, has its romantically ruined, overgrown fortress, and a 10ft menhir, just to the north off the D4.

To the south, **Montolieu**, balanced over the gorges of the Alzeau and Dure, has become the '*Village du Livre*', a centre of the local book-making trade: in the middle of this pretty floral village the **Musée Michel Braibant** traces the history of bookbinding and printing, and there are a dozen or so bookshops, and summer book fairs. West on the D64, the 13th-century **Abbaye de Villelongue** has little artistic interest, but is one of the best preserved monastic complexes in Languedoc; you can stay here, *see* below.

For regions further to the west (around Castelnaudary) and south, *see* the following chapter. North of Pic de Nore, the Montagne Noire descends to rolling hills, in a vast forested area that is part of the Parc Régional Naturel du Haut-Languedoc.

Beyond the boundaries of this book, in the Tarn, **Castres** even further north offers its **Musée Goya**, a small collection of paintings by the Spanish magician, and other minor works by Velázquez, Murillo, Valdes Leal and Alonso Cana. At 2 Place Pélisson there's also a museum devoted to socialist hero Jean Jaurès. In nearby **Sidobre** you can see giant granite boulders fashioned by nature into uncanny shapes such as three cheeses and a goose.

Where to Stay and Eat in the Montagne Noire

Accommodation up here is basic, partly because Carcassonne is close enough for the Montagne to be a day trip. But you'll always eat well.

Lastours ☒ 11600

Le Puits du Trésor, Route des Quatre Châteaux, t 04 68 77 50 24, *www. lepuitsdutresor.com* (€€€€–€€€). For a gastronomic splurge, visit this renovated textile factory by the river Orbiel, which is partly an elegant restaurant

(there is also a cheaper *auberge*). Chef Jean-Marc Boyer offers mouth-watering seasonal dishes. *Closed from Sun eve through to Wed lunch.*

Saissac ☒ 11310

Montagne Noire, Av Maurice Sarraut, t 04 68 24 46 36 (€). Has rooms and serves tasty food under its century-old trees. *Closed Oct–April.*

Montolieu ☒ 11170

Abbaye de Villelongue, St-Martin-le-Vieil, west of Montolieu, t 04 68 76 92 58 (€). Simple *chambres d'hôtes*. Book at least 2 weeks ahead in summer.

Narbonne, the Corbières and the Valley of the Aude

This southern corner of Languedoc, mostly in the département of Aude, is famous for two things – wine and castles – and it has more of them than any other part of France. Western Languedoc traditionally fills an ample bay of the European Union's wine lake, and provides the raw materials for much of the vin ordinaire on French tables. After centuries of complacency, it is also beginning to produce some really good wine. The castles, on the other hand, are strictly AOC.

10

Don't miss

⭐ **A fine Gothic cathedral**
Cathédrale St-Just, Narbonne p.195

⭐ **Beach cottages on stilts**
Gruissan p.200

⭐ **A medieval walled vision**
Carcassonne p.217

⭐ **A castle atop a mountain**
Château de Peyrepertuse p.207

⭐ **The capital of Templar mysteries**
Rennes-le-Château p.212

See map overleaf

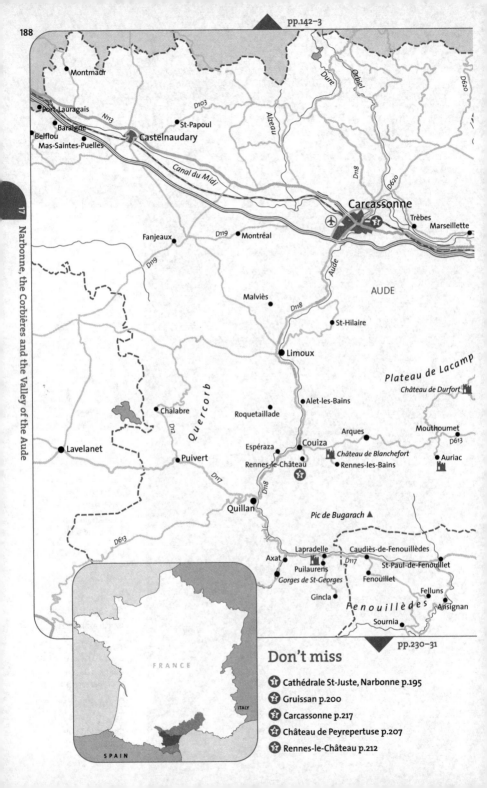

17

Narbonne, the Corbières and the Valley of the Aude

pp.142–3

Montmaur

Port-Lauragais
Baraigne
Belflou
Mas-Saintes-Puelles

St-Papoul

Castelnaudary

Canal du Midi

N113

D103

Alzeau

Dure

Orbiel

D620

D118

D620

Carcassonne

Trèbes

Marseillette

Fanjeaux

D119

Montréal

Aude

AUDE

D119

Malviès

D118

St-Hilaire

Limoux

Plateau de Lacamp

Château de Durfort

Quercorb

Chalabre

Roquetaillade

Alet-les-Bains

Arques

Mouthoumet

D613

Lavelanet

Puivert

Espéraza

Couiza

Château de Blanchefort

Auriac

Rennes-le-Château

Rennes-les-Bains

D12

D117

D118

Quillan

Pic de Bugarach ▲

D613

Lapradelle

Caudiès-de-Fenouillèdes

Axat

Puilaurens

D117

St-Paul-de-Fenouillet

Gorges de St-Georges

Fenouillet

Felluns

Gincla

Fenouillèdes

Ansignan

Sournia

pp.230–31

FRANCE

ITALY

SPAIN

Don't miss

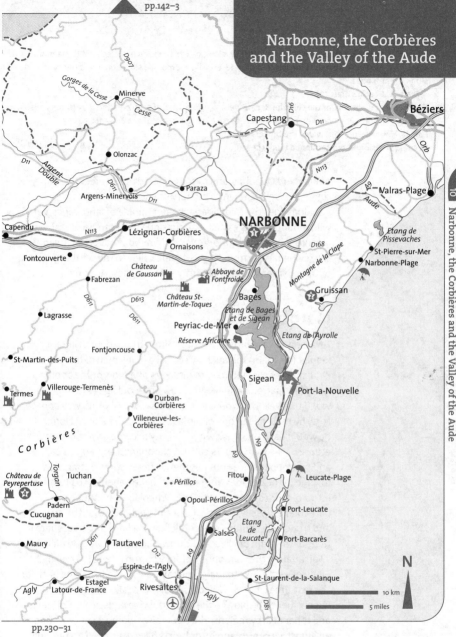

pp.142–3

Narbonne, the Corbières and the Valley of the Aude

Gorges de la Cesse
Minerve
Cesse
D907
Capestang
D16
Béziers
D11
Orb
Olonzac
D11
Argent Double
D611
Paraza
N113
Valras-Plage
Argens-Minervois
D11
Aude
A9
NARBONNE
Etang de Pissevaches
Capendu
N113
Lézignan-Corbières
D168
St-Pierre-sur-Mer
Narbonne-Plage
Ornaisons
Fontcouverte
Château de Gaussan
Abbaye de Fontfroide
Montagne de la Clape
Gruissan
Fabrezan
D611
D613
Château St-Martin-de-Toques
Bages
Lagrasse
D611
Étang de Bages et de Sigean
Peyriac-de-Mer
Fontjoncouse
Réserve Africaine
Étang de l'Ayrolle
St-Martin-des-Puits
Sigean
Termes
Villerouge-Termenès
Durban-Corbières
Port-la-Nouvelle
Villeneuve-les-Corbières
Corbières
N9
Château de Peyrepertuse
Torgan
Tuchan
Périllos
Fitou
A9
Leucate-Plage
Padern
Opoul-Périllos
Port-Leucate
Cucugnan
Maury
D611
Tautavel
D12
Salses
Étang de Leucate
Port-Barcarès
Espira-de-l'Agly
Agly
Estagel
Latour-de-France
Rivesaltes
Agly
St-Laurent-de-la-Salanque
D81

N

10 km
5 miles

pp.230–31

Before the border with Spain was definitively drawn in 1659, the Languedoc was a hotly contested region for a thousand years, disputed first by Visigoths and Saracens, and finally by Madrid and Paris. The French determination to hold it has left us Carcassonne, queen of all medieval castles, cloud-top Cathar redoubts like

Beaches

From Narbonne south into Spain is really just one long beach. The sand is perfect and the lagoons often give you the feeling of being isolated on a desert island, amongst sand dunes and flocks of summer flamingos.

The **best beaches** are:

Gruissan Plage: setting for the cult film *Betty Blue*; a wide expanse of sand populated by curious raised houses on stilts. Popular with motor-homers; there is a big car park at the entrance.

Port-la-Nouvelle: un-chic; watch the tankers roll by.

La Franqui: a simple, old-fashioned family beach.

Aguilar and Quéribus, and over a hundred others, in every shape, colour and style known to military science.

Seldom does the Midi offer a greater jumble of landscapes, with wild mountain gorges just an hour's ride from sandy coastal lagoons where the *tramontane* can blow your hat off; in greenness the region ranges from the lush Aude valley to the scrubby plateau of Opoul, where the French Army enjoys its desert training.

Narbonne

Narbonne gave birth to the last of the troubadours, Guiraut Riquier (d. 1292). A melancholy soul, like many men of his time, Riquier never seemed to earn his lady's affection, or the appreciation of his patrons, and he grew to a bitter old age watching his world unravel. *'Mas trop suy vingutz als derriers'* ('But I was born too late') he mourned in one of his last songs. If he had lived longer, he would have seen his own proud city become a symbol for the eclipse of the Midi and its culture. Narbonne, Languedoc's capital and metropolis since Roman times, suffered some outrageous fortune in the decades after Riquier's death, enough to plunge it into a centuries-long decline. The symbol for Narbonne's own particular eclipse is its majestic unfinished cathedral, the arches and truncated columns of its skeletal nave haunting the square in front of the plain brick façade thrown up when ambition died.

Fortunately, the Narbonne of today has no interest in melancholy whatsoever. Thanks to roads and railroads, trade has come back for the first time since the Middle Ages. The local economy is still largely fuelled by plonk – the bountiful vineyards of the Corbières and other nearby regions. The city is also finding a new vocation as an industrial centre, and its outskirts have developed accordingly. With a population of only 50,000, Narbonne can nonetheless sometimes fool you into thinking it a metropolis. With its impressive medieval monuments, boulevards and lively streets, it is quite a happy and contented town – one of the Midi's most agreeable urban destinations – with an excellent museum and the best cathedral in the south.

Getting to and around Narbonne

By Train

Narbonne is an important rail junction, in the middle of the main Bordeaux–Toulouse–Nice route across the Midi; there are frequent connections (about six a day) to Perpignan and Toulouse, and to Béziers and the other coastal cities to the east. The **railway station** is just north of the centre, on Bd Frédéric Mistral.

By Bus

The *gare routière*, on Av Carnot, offers coach services that largely duplicate the trains; there will also be a bus or two a day to Gruissan, Leucate and along the coast, and more frequently to local beaches.

By Boat

If you haven't any particular destination in mind, take a trip on the **canal boat** (*coche d'eau*) that traverses the Canal de la Robine and the coastal lagoons; in season it leaves from Cours Mirabeau, and goes as far as Port-la-Nouvelle on the coast (**t** 04 68 49 12 40; book). Otherwise, in mid-June–mid-Sept you can hire an **electric boat**, from Cours de la République, **t** 06 03 75 36 98.

History

Colonia Narbo Martius, a good site for a trading port along the recently built Via Domitia, began by decree of the Roman Senate in 118 BC. The colony rapidly became the most important city of southern Gaul, renowned for its beauty and wealth. Under Augustus it was made the capital of what came to be known as the province of Gallia Narbonensis. After 410, it briefly became the headquarters of the Visigoths, and continued as their northern-most provincial capital until the Arab conquest of Spain in the 8th century; the Arabs took Narbonne but could not hold it, and Pépin the Short reclaimed it for the Frankish Kingdom in 759.

In the 12th century, Narbonne entered its second golden age. Under a native dynasty of viscounts the city maintained its independence for two centuries and began its great cathedral (1272). The famous Viscountess Ermengarde, who ruled for five decades after 1134, managed the ship of state with distinction while presiding over a 'court of love' graced by troubadours such as Bernart de Ventadorn. The troubled 14th century was murder on Narbonne, however. As if wars and plagues were not enough, the harbour began to silt up; finally, even the river Aude decided to change its course and desert the city, ruining its trade. By the end of the century, the city had shrunk to a mere market town, albeit one with an archbishop and a very impressive cathedral.

Stagnation continued until the 20th century, despite the efforts of the indefatigable Paul Riquet in the 1680s; though his Canal du Midi (*see* pp.175–9 and 44–6) met the sea further north, Riquet began a branch canal, the Robine, that followed the old course of the river through Narbonne. Powerful interests in Béziers and Sète, however, kept it from being completed until 1786; the man who finally saw it through was Narbonne's last archbishop, an Irishman, Arthur Dillon, who played an important role in the city's

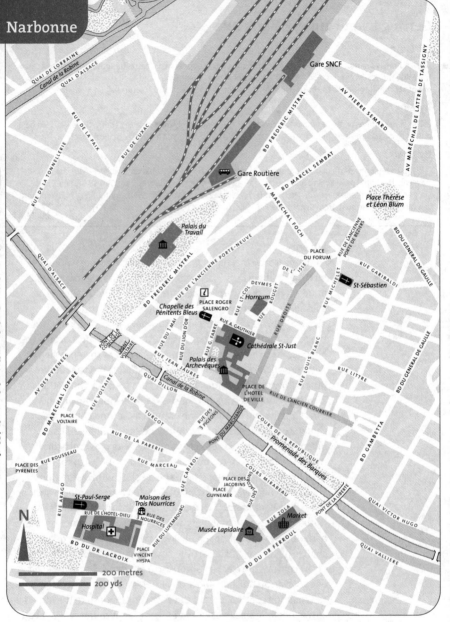

history (his remains were returned to Narbonne cathedral in 2007, after his coffin came to light during excavation work for the new Eurostar station in London's St Pancras). Only in the last hundred years has Narbonne started to revive, thanks to industry and the wine trade; since the Second World War it has overtaken Carcassonne as the largest city of the Aude *département*.

The City Centre

Narbonne is a city of surprises. If you come by train or bus, the first thing you're likely to see is the gargantuan, horrific **Palais du Travail** on Bd Frédéric Mistral, a full-blown piece of 1930s Stalinist architecture. Turn the corner on to Rue Jean Jaurès, though, and you'll be following the **Canal de la Robine** into the centre of the city, lined with a delightful park called the **Jardin Entre Deux Villes**. Behind the Hôtel de Ville, the **Pont des Marchands** is covered with shops, a charming miniature version of Florence's Ponte Vecchio.

Palais des Archevêques

Narbonne's centre is the busy **Place de l'Hôtel de Ville**; in the middle of the square a section of the Via Domitia is cleverly displayed in its original bed and alignment. Standing over this countersunk exhibit and looking at the entrance to the Rue Droite on the northeast side of the square and the Pont des Marchands opposite, you see a pair of steel strips, set in the ground, tracing the edge of the old highway to the two streets. This gives the rather eerie feeling that only a dust cover has been thrown over ancient Narbo Martius.

Facing the square, the twin façades of the **Palais des Archevêques** were blessed with a romantic Gothic restoration by the master himself, Viollet-le-Duc, in the 1840s; opinion is divided over whether this 19th-century fancy was an improvement on the austere 13th-century original it replaced. The passage between the two buildings (the **Palais Neuf** on the left, and the **Palais Vieux** on the right) leads to a small courtyard, and the entrances to Narbonne's two excellent museums, the **Musée d'Art et d'Histoire** and the **Musée Archéologique**. The parts of the Archbishops' Palace not used for museums house Narbonne's **Hôtel de Ville**. In the Palais Neuf, the 1628 Hall of the Synods has original Aubusson tapestries. Now a reception room for the city, it was once the political centre of the region; Narbonne's archbishop had the right of presiding over the *Etats-Généraux*, or parliament, of Languedoc, although it moved to Pézenas in 1456.

Musée d'Art et d'Histoire

Musée d'Art et d'Histoire
t 04 68 90 30 54; open daily April–Sept 9.30–12.15 and 2–6; Oct–Mar Tues–Sun 10–12 and 2–5; joint adm with Musées Archéologique, Horreum and Lapidaire valid for three days

This museum occupies the old archbishops' apartments; it is reached by an elegant stair from the 1620s, decorated with a bust of the Venetian historian Andrea Morosini and a bronze Capitoline Wolf, sent by the city of Rome for Narbonne's 2,000th birthday. These reminders of Italy are perfectly fitting, for this museum could easily pass for one of the great aristocratic galleries of Rome. Most of the collection belonged to the archbishops; they must have acquired a Roman taste on sojourns there. The sumptuous rooms of these princes of the Church have been well preserved, beginning with the chapterhouse, or **Salle des Audiences**, where there is a portrait of the redoubtable Archbishop Dillon (the last of the line – his period of office was rudely interrupted by the Revolution in 1792), and an *Equestrian Louis XIV* by Van der Meulen – a pompous, quite offensive portrait, typical of the Sun King's use of art as political propaganda. Louis slept here in 1642, in the adjacent **Chambre du Roi**. The 1632 ceiling frescoes are by local talent the Rodière brothers: harmless *Muses* that look more like nursery-school teachers. Note the floor, a restored Roman mosaic in a labyrinth pattern.

The third room, the **Grande Galerie**, contains some of the best paintings: a gloomy landscape by Gaspard Dughet and an intense *St Jerome* by Salvator Rosa (both artists were favourites in Rome), a Canaletto and, among many Dutch and Flemish pictures, *Wedding Dance* by Pieter Breughel the Younger. The 16th- and 17th-century enamelled plaques come from Limoges, with portraits of French kings. Opposite these, a collection of lovely faïence apothecary jars from Montpellier makes a proper introduction to the next room, the **Salle des Faïences**. These 18th-century painted ceramics come mostly from well-known French centres like Moustiers and Varange, though many are from cities such as Marseille and Montpellier, where the art has since died out.

The archbishops' chapel, the **Oratoire**, harbours a few surprises: 14th-century carved alabaster from Nottingham, an odd Byzantine icon from the Aegean, and a perfect, incandescent 15th-century Florentine *Madonna*; though anonymous (once falsely attributed to Piero della Francesca), it gracefully upstages everything else in the museum. The rest of the apartments are a grab bag: Archbishop Dillon's library, with his well-thumbed St Augustine, and his dining room. You will encounter an *azulejo* tile floor from Portugal, François Ier's vinegar pot, Beauvais tapestries with scenes from La Fontaine's fairytales, and more good painting: a luscious Veronese (*The Anointing of King David*), portraits by Nattier and by Venice's favourite 18th-century celebrity portraitist Rosalba Carriera, a sprinkling of native and foreign followers of Caravaggio, and a tortured *St Andrew* by Ribera. There are also 19th-century works, and two rooms showing works representing the Orient.

If you don't mind climbing 162 steps, they'll let you up into the 13th-century **Donjon Gilles Aycelin**, a Gothic defence tower with a collection of medieval sculpture and good views from the top.

Donjon Gilles Aycelin
open July–Sept daily 10–6; Oct–June daily 10–12 and 2–5; adm

Musée Archéologique

Musée Archéologique
same hours as Musée d'Art et d'Histoire; joint adm

It is only luck that made Nîmes the 'French Rome' while none of Narbonne's monuments has survived; the ambitious viscounts and archbishops of medieval Narbonne obviously had a greater appetite for recycling old building stone. There is, however, no shortage of remaining bits and pieces, and the best have been assembled here: reliefs from Narbonne's three triumphal arches and the gates of its walls, milestones from the Via Domitia, funeral monuments and a model of a Roman house. The **Chapelle de la Madeleine**, where Greek and pre-Greek ceramics are displayed, retains some fragments of its original 14th-century frescoes; it also offers the best view of the apse and buttresses of the adjacent cathedral, which is almost completely surrounded by buildings.

Christianity seems to have come late to Narbonne; the first bishop, Paul, is recorded in the 3rd century. Nevertheless, there are some Christian sarcophagi, and an unusual reliquary in the form of the Church of the Holy Sepulchre in Jerusalem. The products of other faiths here are more interesting: a Greek statue of a *Drunken Silenus*, altars dedicated to Cybele and Attis, and an image of Priapus, that mythological embarrassment, this time at least decently covered. Recent excavations in and around the city have enriched the Roman collection greatly, with sculptures, mosaics, and some of the finest examples of Roman painting in France.

Cathédrale St-Just

⭐ Cathédrale St-Just
open July–Sept daily 10–7; Oct–June daily 10–12 and 2–6

This can be entered through the fine 14th-century **cloister**, near the entrance to the museums, a Gothic quadrangle with gargoyles. A better way, though, is to circumnavigate the huge bulk of the cathedral and palace complex towards the west front and the **Cour St-Eutrope**, a spacious square that occupies the unfinished two-thirds of the cathedral itself. On every side rise truncated pilasters, walls and arch-bases, witness to medieval Narbonne's ambition and the 14th-century disasters that stopped it cold.

This is the third church to occupy the site; the first was a basilica from the reign of Emperor Constantine, the second a Carolingian rebuilding of AD 890. The present church was begun in 1272, at the height of the city's fortunes. Funds were hardly lacking; the cornerstone was sent by Pope Clement IV, a former Archbishop of Narbonne, and he probably contributed a little more besides. To extend the new cathedral to its planned length, it would have been necessary to rebuild a section of the city wall; in 1340 a lawsuit over this broke out between the city and the Church – a good, old-fashioned French lawsuit, just what was needed in those bad times to put an end to construction forever.

Just the same, this one-third of a cathedral is by any measure the finest in the Midi, the only one comparable to the magnificent Gothic structures of the Ile-de-France. The short nave, in fact, heightens the exuberant verticality of the 130ft apse and choir, exceeded in height only by those of Amiens and Beauvais. Throughout, the structural lines are accented with ribbing or with protruding stone courses, as if the builders wanted to leave a gentle reminder of the extraordinary technical skill that made such a building possible. The whole is done in a clean and elegant stone, grey perhaps, but a grey that here bids to be included among the colours of the spectrum.

Inside, most of the best features are in the ambulatory and its chapels. Near the altar, facing the chapels, are two remarkable archiepiscopal tombs. The **tomb of Cardinal Briçonnet** (1514) is a decorative mix of Renaissance refinement and ghoulish, grinning skeletons, typical of that age. The other, the **tomb of Cardinal Pierre de Jugie**, is an exquisite Gothic work of 1376; though much damaged, some of the original paint remains. The ambulatory chapels are illuminated by lovely 14th-century glass: the *Creation* (left chapel), the *Infancy of Christ* in the centre, and *Sts Michael, Peter and Paul* (right chapels). Some faded original frescoes can be seen in the far right chapel, and also around the main altar. But the central **Chapelle de la Vierge** has something really special: unique polychrome reliefs of the late 14th century. Ruined and covered in a Baroque remodelling of 1732, these were rediscovered in the 19th century, and currently they are being restored and replaced. On the upper band (left to right): an *Annunciation* and *Kings of France*, the *Presentation at the Temple, Palm Sunday* and *Crucifixion*. Lower band: *Purgatory, Hell* and *Limbo*. The side chapels provide little to see but tapestries; in the first right is a 16th-century polychrome *Entombment of Christ* from Bavaria. Almost the entire west wall is covered by a spectacular **organ**, a mountain of carved wood and statuary that took over 100 years to complete (1741–1856).

Cathedral Treasury

Cathedral
Treasury
*open July–Sept
Mon–Sat 11–6, Sun
2–6; Oct–June daily
2–6; adm*

Don't miss the entrance to the treasury, through a tiny door in the right ambulatory chapel. Arranged in a domed chamber with odd acoustics, formerly housing the cathedral archives, the collection includes medieval reliquaries, books and a 10th-century carved ivory plaque. Here also are the most outlandish of all Narbonne's surprises: two early 16th-century Flemish **tapestries** unlike any others you're ever likely to see. Originally a set of 10, belonging to Archbishop François Fouquet, eight and a half have disappeared, probably ending up as insulation, mattress-stuffing and a bed for the dog. The half-tapestry depicts Adversity, from an *Allegory of Prosperity and Adversity*. Amidst a landscape of shipwrecks and earthquakes you will notice Cleopatra, Antiochus Seleucis and other celebrities of antiquity who met bad ends (all conveniently labelled), while Vulcan grinds out strife on his forge and a grinning Penury exults over the unfortunates. Part of the centrepiece also survived (on the left), dominated by an uncanny Goddess of Fortune on horseback, her face veiled.

The other tapestry, much better preserved, is a strange account of the *Creation*. The seven days of Genesis are arranged in tableaux, each with figures of the Holy Trinity, represented as three crowned, bearded old men. The iconography is unorthodox in the extreme; the symbolism seems to hint at some concealed vein of medieval mysticism. In any case, the artists who created it produced a true *tour de force*, filling every corner with delightful naturalistic detail – a forest, the firmament, spring flowers and the Kingdom of the Sea. Bring the children, and see if they can spot the elephant.

Roman Narbonne

Horréum
*open April–Sept
Tues–Sun 9.30–12.15
and 2–6; Oct–Mar
Tues–Sun 10–12 and
2–5; closed Mon; adm;
joint adm with Musées
Archéologique, d'Art et
d'Histoire and Lapidaire
valid for three days*

There isn't much of it. The centre of the ancient city, north of the cathedral, is a dowdy, blank-faced quarter, with a neighbourhood development group trying to interest people in fixing up the many abandoned houses. Small signs on the street corners direct you to the only Roman monument left – a warehouse or **Horréum** on Rue Lt. Col. Deygmes. Typical of the state-run warehouses of any Roman city, this is the only complete one anywhere. Just a small part has been excavated, a maze of tiny chambers; the original structure was over 500 feet long. Among the ancient fragments displayed in the various rooms is a charming relief of bear trainers and their bears bathing together. To the west, on Rue de l'Ancienne Porte Neuve, there is a 17th-century **powder-house** converted into a centre for temporary exhibitions.

From the Place de l'Hôtel-de-Ville, Rue Droite runs northeastwards, roughly following the route of the Roman main street; it ends at **Place du Forum** – the former Forum, though nothing remains but some re-erected columns, a modern mural and a copy of a 17th-century fountain. One block east is the 15th-century Flamboyant church of **St-Sébastien**, built over the (apocryphal) birthplace of the saint himself. A favourite of artists across southern Europe (usually depicted stuck full of arrows), Sebastian was always a popular saint owing to the belief that he could intercede against the plague.

The Bourg

Musée Lapidaire
*t 04 68 90 30 54;
open April–Sept
Tues–Sun 9.30–12.15
and 2–6; Oct–Mar
Tues–Sun 10–12 and
2–5; closed Mon; adm;
joint adm with Musées
Archéologique, d'Art et
d'Histoire and Horréum
valid for three days*

This is Narbonne's medieval extension across the river (now across the canal). Cross over by the bridge in the **Promenade des Barques**, the elegant park along the canal. On the other side, the city's covered **market** is a rare sensory experience even by French market standards. The Narbonnais take great pride in it, and it once won an annual award as the best in France.

Behind it, the deconsecrated 13th-century church of Notre-Dame-de-Lamourguie now houses the **Musée Lapidaire**, a large collection of architectural fragments from ancient Narbonne, displayed more or less at random. The fragments are here thanks to François Ier; on a visit, he recommended to the Narbonnais that they incorporate the vast heaps of antique rubble lying about into the new walls they were building. The walls themselves thus became an open-air museum, much commented on by travellers, until they were demolished in the 19th century and the old bits assembled here.

Follow the boulevards west, along the course of the demolished medieval walls; the modern city hospital on Boulevard du Dr Lacroix incorporates the old one, the **Hôtel-Dieu**, with a grand Baroque chapel decorated by Narbonnais painters of the 1780s. Behind this, the **Maison des Trois Nourrices**, on the street of the same name, is the best surviving example of a Renaissance palace in the city; the 'three nurses' are the three classical caryatids holding up the main window.

Narbonne's other ancient church, the **Basilique St-Paul-Serge**, was first built in the 5th century, and dedicated to the first bishop of Narbonne. The present building was begun in 1229, an imposing monument that was one of the first in the south to adopt the new Gothic architecture. Three early Christian sarcophagi remain from the first church, an introduction to the catacomb-like **cemetery-crypt** beneath (ask for the key from the vestry). This subterranean necropolis was begun in the time of Constantine. Such burials were not peculiar to the Christians. In Rome, pagan and Christian catacombs exist side by side; parts of this one are decorated with pagan symbols, raising the intriguing possibility that this cemetery was for a time non-denominational. Also spot the frog squatting in a stoop – petrified, so legend has it, by an archbishop, in punishment for having croaked God's praises.

Services in Narbonne

Post office: 19 Bd Gambetta.

Market Days in Narbonne

Daily am: Les Halles.
Thurs: outdoor market.

Shopping in Narbonne

Local Wine
For a wide selection of Languedoc wines, the **Cave du Palais** at Domaine de St-Crescent on the Route de Perpignan outside Narbonne, t 04 68 41 49 67, *www.lacavedupalais.com*, can't be beaten.

Activities in Narbonne

On a wet day, you could do worse than head out of town on the N9 towards Perpignan to **Espace de Liberté** (t 04 68 42 17 89, *www.espace liberte.com*; *open daily*), a giant aquatic park with three huge swimming pools, slides, tenpin bowling and ice skating.

Where to Stay in Narbonne

Narbonne ✉ 11100
Most of the cheaper places are around the station, especially on or around Av Pierre Sémard.
***La Résidence**, 6 Rue du 1er Mai, t 04 68 32 19 41, *http://hotelresidence. fr* (€€). Near the cathedral in an old *hôtel particulier*, with calm, well-equipped rooms and a garage. *Closed mid-Jan–mid-Feb.*

ⓘ **Narbonne >>**
*31 Rue Jean Jaurès,
t 04 68 65 15 60,
www.mairie-
narbonne.fr;
open daily*

***Grand Hôtel du Languedoc, 22 Bd Gambetta, **t** 04 68 65 14 74, *www. hoteldulanguedoc.com* (€€). A formerly gracious old establishment, now a little down-at-heel. It has a good restaurant and bar-crêperie.

France, 6 Rue Rossini, **t 04 68 32 09 75, *www.hotelnarbonne.com* (€€–€). On a quiet side street near the covered market.

Will's Hôtel, 23 Av Pierre Sémard, **t 04 68 90 44 50, *http://willshotel-narbonne.com* (€). It's not run by a Will, and the owners can't imagine who Will might have been, but it is still a comfortable and friendly place.

*Hôtel de la Gare, 7 Av Pierre Sémard, **t** 04 68 32 10 54 (€). Nice for its price.

Eating Out in Narbonne

As you might expect after a tour of their wonderful market, the Narbonnais are a gastronomically fastidious lot; their restaurants reflect this, with a minimum of pretension.

La Table St-Crescent, Rte de Perpignan, **t** 04 68 41 37 37 (€€€€–€€). One of Narbonne's top restaurants is outside town at the Palais du Vin. A vine-covered terrace shelters a modern stylish establishment specializing, of course, in the best regional wines and dishes. *Book. Closed Sat lunch, Sun eve and Mon.*

Le Billot, 22 Rue de l'Ancienne Porte de Béziers, **t** 04 68 32 70 88, *www. lebillot.com* (€€€). Northeast of the centre, near a delightful park called the Place Thérèse et Léon Blum. Specializes in meat dishes – beef, lamb, duck and pork. *Closed Mon, and Tues lunch.*

L'Ecrevisse d'Alsace, 2 Av Pierre Sémard, **t** 04 68 65 10 24, *www. restaurant-narbonne.com* (€€€–€€). This friendly brasserie with a veranda is a good source of fresh seafood. *Closed Sun eve and Wed.*

Le Petit Comptoir, 4 Bd du Maréchal Joffre, **t** 04 68 42 30 35 (€€). A 1930s-style *bistrot* for some adventurous dishes. *Closed Sun and Mon.*

Le Castel, 26 Bd du Dr Lacroix, **t** 04 68 41 35 07 (€). Specializes in grilled meats. *Closed Sat lunch and Sun.*

Narbonne's Coast

The coastal road, more or less along the path of the Roman Via Domitia, cannot follow this complicated shoreline, a miasma of marshes and lagoons; some detours on the back roads will be necessary to see it. One big obstacle is the mouth of the Aude, northeast of Narbonne; this pretty and amiable river comes all the way from the high Pyrenees to meet an inglorious end in a boggy landscape called (literally) 'Piss-cow Swamp'.

Narbonne-Plage to Port-la-Nouvelle

South of the Etang de Pissevaches, one of the rare fishing villages in these parts, **St-Pierre-sur-Mer**, has been swallowed up by the bright, modern, characterless resort of **Narbonne-Plage**, with plenty of sand and its full whack of seaside amusements. Just to the north, near **Oustalet**, is Languedoc's answer to the Fontaine de Vaucluse, a 'bottomless' pool called the **Gouffre de l'Œil Doux** – the 'seductive eye' – always full of pure, fresh water, though only a mile from the sea. Beyond Narbonne-Plage, the landscape rises into the **Montagne de la Clape**, once an island and still a world in itself. Parts are lush and pine-clad, others rugged and desolate, reminiscent of a Greek island; on the lower slopes vineyards produce small quantities of a very good Coteaux du Languedoc wine. Near the

Notre-Dame-des-Auzils
key from Gruissan tourist office

 Gruissan

top, the chapel of Notre-Dame-des-Auzils has a fascinating collection of sailors' *ex votos* – ship models, paintings and the like.

Most of those sailors came from Gruissan, south of La Clape. One of Narbonne's ports in the Middle Ages, Gruissan today is surrounded by lagoons and salt pans; the charming village is set in concentric rings around a ruined 13th-century castle, built to defend the approaches to Narbonne. Its tower, the **Tour de Barbarousse**, possibly takes its name from a visit by the famous Turkish pirate-admiral Barbarossa; in the 1540s the Ottoman sultan's fleet was briefly based in Toulon, helping the French against the Holy Roman Emperor Charles V. To Gruissan's fine beaches the government has added a marina, resulting in one of the more agreeable resorts on these coasts. Gruissan's other landmark is the **Plage des Pilotis**, where neat rows of beach cottages hang in the air. The sea regularly covers the sand, so over a century ago people began the habit of building their holiday retreats on stilts. The houses and beach gained romantic notoriety as the setting for Jean-Jacques Beineix's cult 1986 film, *Betty Blue*.

To go further south, you'll have to return to Narbonne and circle around the **Etang de Bages et de Sigean**. This broad lagoon, with its many islands and forgotten, half-abandoned hamlets, is especially rich in waterfowl, including flamingos, cormorants, egrets and herons. For the best view, drive across part of the Etang on the narrow D105 between **Bages** and **Peyriac-de-Mer**. Boat trips can be arranged, starting from the dock of a vanished medieval village, **Port-Mahon**, near **Sigean**, a pleasant if rather forgotten village that began as a station on the Via Domitia. Wildlife of an entirely different sort co-exists peacefully nearby at the Réserve Africaine north of Sigean, a big zoo, flamingo lake and drive-through safari park with the only white rhinoceroses, most likely, in all Languedoc.

Boat trips
*contact the Cercle Nautique des Corbières
t 04 68 48 44 52, www. port-mahon-voile.com*

Réserve Africaine
t 04 68 48 20 20, www. reserveafricaine sigean.fr; open April–Aug daily 9–6.30; Sept daily 9–5; Oct–Mar daily 9–4; adm

When the builders of the Canal de la Robine laid out their coastal port in 1820, they gave it the strikingly original name of **Port-la-Nouvelle**. Now France's third-largest Mediterranean port, it is a gritty, no-nonsense town of Communist stevedores, where the most prominent restaurant is called 'Le Chicken Shack', and where the waterfront promenade takes in a panorama of shiny oil tanks. It has good beaches, and for a long time it was also a resort; there are, incredibly, still some holiday motels in town. If you didn't fancy the palms and ice cream of La Grande Motte or Cap d'Agde (*see* pp.159–61 and 168–9), a day on the beach here, watching cement barges and tankers sail past, might be just the thing. If you're sticking around, don't miss the Domaine de Jugnes et sa Baleine, a skeleton of a dead whale that washed up on the beach, which has been carefully reconstructed in a wine warehouse. If you know your plants, cross the Canal de la Robine to the 250ha Ile Ste-Lucie, abandoned and overgrown with 100 rare specimens.

Domaine de Jugnes et sa Baleine
t 04 68 48 00 39; open daily 10–12 and 3–7

Tourist Information on Narbonne's Coast

The tourist office at **Sigean** includes a little museum with stuffed birds and archaeological titbits.

(i) Sigean >
Pl de la Libération,
t 04 68 48 14 81,
www.sigean.fr;
open summer Mon–Fri
plus Sat am and Sun
am; winter Tues–Sat am

Shopping on Narbonne's Coast

Local Wine

Coteaux du Languedoc-La Clape (see p.147): Château Rouquette-sur-Mer, off the D168 southwest of Narbonne-Plage in Gruissan, t 04 68 49 90 41, http://chateaurouquette.com. They also rent out *gîtes* and an apartment.

Château de Pech Redon, Rte de Gruissan, Narbonne, t 04 68 90 41 22. See p.147.

Domaine du Fraisse, at Autignac, t 04 67 90 23 40. For whites.

Quatourze: A noble variation on Corbières, www.vitis.org/QUATOURZE. html, made along the back roads around Bages and Peyriac-de-Mer.

Caves des Vignerons de Fitou, on the N9, t 04 68 45 71 41.

Les Maitres Vignerons de Cascastel, Grand Rue, Cascastel, t 04 68 45 91 74, produce a red Fitou, Seigneurie d'Arse, which despite its unfortunate name is a real fruity delight; try the 2004. *Open Mon–Fri 8–12 and 2–6.*

(i) Gruissan >>
1 Bd Pech Maynaud,
t 04 68 49 09 00,
www.gruissan-
mediterranee.com

Where to Stay and Eat on Narbonne's Coast

Narbonne-Plage ✉ 11100

***Château l'Hospitalet, Rte de Narbonne-Plage, t 04 68 45 36 00,

(★) Château
l'Hospitalet >

www.chateau-hospitalet-na
federal-hotel.com (€€€€–€€
Gérard Bertrand (see p.181;
gerard-bertrand.com) property, this
wine *domaine* on the Clape Massif
incorporates a renovated hotel with
22 pretty rooms, a *bistrot*-style
restaurant, pool, *caves* and wine-
tastings and craft workshops, all in
an idyllic setting of vineyards overlooking the sea.

**Hôtel de la Clape, 4 Rue des Fleurs, t 04 68 49 80 15 (€€). Hardly upmarket, but a great address from which to write home, and it does have a pool. *Closed Jan–mid-Mar.*

Gruissan ✉ 11430

**Le Corail, Quai Ponant in Gruissan Port, t 04 68 49 04 43 (€€). Has a fine restaurant (€€) specializing in *bouilla-baisse. Closed Nov–Jan.*

**Les Trois Caravelles, Av Front de Mer, Gruissan Plage, t 04 68 49 13 87 (€€). Also pleasant, with a snack bar serving pancakes and salads. *Closed mid-Sept–April.*

L'Estagnol, Quai de l'Etang, t 04 68 49 01 27 (€€). Popular converted fisher-man's cottage at the entrance to the village, offering sumptuous seafood and fish. *Closed Sun eve, Mon and Tues, and Oct–Mar.*

Bages ✉ 11100

Bages is a tiny fishing villlage overlooking the Etang de Bages, now a fashionable haunt of art galleries and fish restaurants.

Portanel, Passage du Portanel, t 04 68 42 81 66 (€€€–€€). One of the best fish restaurants here, Portanel specializes in serving eel in every imaginable way. *Best to reserve.*

Around Narbonne: Inland

Attractions within a short drive of the city include, 11km to the north, the **Oppidum de Montlaures**, the site of a pre-Roman town, similar to the Oppidum d'Ensérune (see p.177) and set on the same sort of hilltop. Better still, take the N113 west from the city and turn south on the D613. The first sight, to the left, is the derelict, frequently overlooked castle of **St-Pierre-des-Clars**. In its grounds, Roman coins with the images of Pompey and Brutus have been found, but the present building probably dates from the late 12th or 13th centuries. The purpose of this ineffably romantic ruin was probably to protect sheep in wartime. This is not as daft as it may sound: after iron, sheep were the most valuable commodity of the Middle Ages, the wool-on-the-hoof that made the banking fortunes of so many medieval cities.

Three kilometres further down the D613, you'll see another impressive castle in the distance, madly perched on a perpendicular cliff. A perfect introduction to the fortified wilderness of the Corbières (*see* below), **St-Martin-de-Toques** was gradually built between the 10th and 13th centuries by the viscounts of Narbonne, to guard the route into the Corbières. Recently restored, it is now a private residence.

Abbaye de Fontfroide

Abbaye de Fontfroide
t 04 68 45 11 08, www.fontfroide.com; open daily for guided tours only, July and Aug 10–5.30, every half-hour; April–June and Sept–Oct 10–4.45, every 45mins except 1pm; Nov–Mar 10–4, every hour except 1pm; adm

Further along the D613 towards Narbonne, a marked side road leads to the Abbaye de Fontfroide. When the tour reaches the monks' **refectory**, the guide will take pains to point out that the fireplace is a recent addition; heating of any kind was a little too posh for medieval Cistercians. On the other hand, after inspecting the lavish church and grounds it is hard to believe the monks were giving much away to the poor – a typical medieval enigma: power and wealth, without the enjoyment of them. One of the most important Cistercian abbeys in the south, Fontfroide was founded in 1145 on the site of an earlier Benedictine house. Until its suppression in 1791, it was one of the richest and most influential of all Cistercian houses. It was largely in ruins when a local family, the Fayets, bought it early in the 20th century; they have been fixing it up a little at a time ever since, and today the national and regional government are finally helping them to meet the costs.

The best part of the tour is Fontfroide's lovely 13th-century **cloister**; its style of broad arches inset with smaller ones was much copied in later cloisters in Languedoc. The 12th-century **church** impresses with its proportions and Romanesque austerity: following Cistercian custom, simple floral patterns constitute the only decoration. The art of making stained glass, once one of France's proudest achievements, had nearly died out by the 19th century. There has been a modest revival in the last century; one of its first productions was the excellent set of windows here, a *Last Judgement* and signs of the zodiac done in the 1920s. More glass can be seen in the **dormitory** – fascinating abstract collages of old fragments, brought here from northern French churches wrecked during the First World War. Behind the cloister is a nursery of roses where medieval varieties are grown by a local firm. The abbey also produces its own wine, which you can taste and buy.

To protect the produce of its vast estates, the abbey maintained a network of fortified farms and storehouses all over the region. The

Château de
Gaussan
t 04 68 25 19 92

most impressive is near Capestang (*see* p.178); the closest, 8km west of Fontfroide, is the Château de Gaussan at Bizanet. Followers of Viollet-le-Duc restored it in the 19th century, with plenty of neo-Gothic ornament and frescoes inside. In 1994 it became the home of some Benedictine monks from the abbey of Fontgombault in Indre, who cultivate vines and sell honey and goat's cheese.

The Corbières

Thanks to wine, the Corbières has finally found its vocation. This scrubby, mountainous area, where landscapes range from classic Mediterranean to rugged Wild West, has been the odd region out since ancient times. As a refuge for disaffected Gauls, it was a headache to the Romans. In the Middle Ages, sitting astride the boundaries of France and Aragon, it was a permanent zone of combat. Local *seigneurs* littered the landscape with castles in incredible, impregnable mountaintop sites. Some of these became the last redoubts of the persecuted Cathars; nearly all of them are ruined today. For anyone with clear lungs and a little spirit, exploring them will be a challenge and a delight. Amid the lonely landscapes of limestone crags and hills carpeted in *maquis*, the vineyards advance tenaciously across every dusty, sun-bleached hectare of arable ground.

Lézignan-Corbières and Lagrasse

Musée de la Vigne
et du Vin
*t 04 68 27 07 57;
closed until mid-2008*

Musée
Charles Cros
t 04 68 27 81 44

The Corbières' 'capital', Lézignan-Corbières, lies halfway between Carcassonne and Narbonne, and offers, besides a few places to flop, an introduction to what the *pays* does best: the Musée de la Vigne et du Vin, at 3 Rue Turgot. Just south of Lézignan, on the other side of the *autoroute*, Fabrezan remembers the Corbières' most famous son in the Musée Charles Cros in the *mairie*. Cros (1842–88) was a poet and would certainly be better known had he not also been the unluckiest inventor ever. In 1869 he invented a process of colour photography at exactly the same time as Ducos de Hauron, who got the credit for it, and in 1877 he invented the phonograph and discovered how to record sounds at the same time as Edison, who beat him to the patent office.

Lagrasse abbey
*t 04 68 43 15 99; open
July–Aug daily 10.30–
6.15; May and June daily
10.30–12.30 and 2–6.15;
Sept daily 10.30–11.45
and 2–6.45; April and
Oct daily 10.30–12.30
and 2– 5.15; mid-Feb–
Mar and Nov–mid-Dec
daily 2–5.15; mid-Jan–
mid-Feb Sat and Sun
2–4.30; closed mid-Dec–
mid-Jan; guided tours*

This northern part of the Corbières has more monasteries than castles. The greatest of these was the Abbey de Fontfroide, just west of Narbonne (*see* left). Continuing in that direction on the D613/D3 takes you to **Lagrasse**, a walled medieval village that grew up around a Benedictine abbey founded in the 8th century and chartered by Charlemagne himself. Some of the houses date back to the 14th century, while the walls and the graceful arched **Pont Neuf** are from the 12th. The bridge leads to the abbey, partly in ruins and partly the restored home of a Byzantine Catholic

Getting around the Corbières

By Train

SNCF rail lines make a neat square around the Corbières – they define its boundaries almost exactly, but none of them ventures inside the region. The only useful one is from Carcassonne, following the Aude and then turning east through the Fenouillèdes, stopping at Limoux, Alet-les-Bains, Couiza and Quillan on its way to Perpignan. A local association, the **TPCF**, runs the narrow-gauge **Train du Pays Cathare et du Fenouillèdes**, offering excursions from Rivesaltes or Espira de l'Agly through some lovely scenery to St-Paul-du-Fenouillet, Caudiès, Puilaurens and Axat (regular schedule in summer, a few trains out of season; for information and reservations, call t 04 68 59 99 02, *www.tpcf.fr*).

By Bus

Don't count on **buses** either. There are some services from Perpignan's *gare routière* up the Agly valley to Maury, St-Paul and Quillan, t 04 68 35 29 02, or try **Roussillon Voyages Autocars Cayrol**, t 04 68 34 35 35, *www.roussillonvoyages.fr*.

By Car

If you're driving, keep the tank full. The Corbières is the badlands of France, and its unique fascination comes from traversing spaces as empty as central Anatolia with all the specific charms of France close at hand. There are few good roads.

Here are two possibilities for a quick *tour*: from Narbonne, the D613/D3 passing Fontfroide and Lagrasse, then south on the scenic D212, rejoining the D613 and ending up in Couiza. Alternatively, the N9/D611A/D611/D14/D10/D7 from south of Narbonne passes the best of the wine country, the castles of Aguilar, Peyrepertuse and Quéribus, and the Gorges de Galamus, ending up on the main D117 route for Perpignan.

---

monastic community, with a permanent exhibition on the 12th-century sculptor, the Master of Cabestany (*see* p.35)

St-Martin-des-Puits
ask at the mairie, t 04 68 43 11 66, for the key

Southwest of Lagrasse, in one of the remotest corners of the Corbières, there is a remarkable country church at **St-Martin-des-Puits**. The oldest part, the choir, was built in the 10th century, and the nave has some still older capitals, recycled Merovingian pieces. The fanciful frescoes all around are 12th-century.

Aguilar and Quéribus

The humble, two-lane D611 and D14 were the medieval main routes through the Corbières, connecting with the passes over the Pyrenees to Spain. Castles occur with the frequency of petrol stations on a motorway; before the kings of France asserted their authority, one wonders how many times the poor merchants had to pay tolls. Even the landscape is suggestive of castles, with limestone outcrops resembling ruined walls and bastions.

All of the real strongholds are in ruins today. The first, one of the smaller models, is at **Durban-Corbières**, in the centre of the wine-growing region; it was built by the kings of Aragon.

Tuchan, another typically stark and dusty Corbières village, has no fewer than three ruined castles. The best of them, the impressive

Château d'Aguilar
t 04 68 45 51 00; open mid-June– mid-Sept 10.30–12.30 and 3.30–7; adm

Château d'Aguilar – one of the 'five sons of Carcassonne', along with Puilaurens, Quéribus, Peyrepertuse and Termes – saw plenty of action: Simon de Montfort stormed it in 1210, but the French had to take it again from rebellious barons 30 years later; over the next 200 years the Spaniards knocked at the gate with regularity.

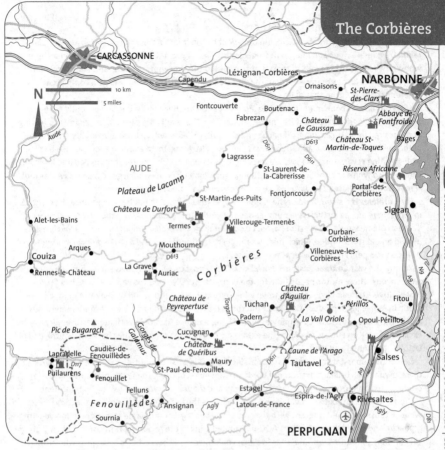

West of Tuchan, the landscapes become higher and wilder. **Padern** has another castle, ruined despite rebuilding work in the 18th century, and so does **Cucugnan**, a colourful little village. Both these towns offer scenic detours – from Padern, north through the **Gorges du Torgan**, and from Cucugnan, south through the spectacular **Grau de Maury**, the Corbières' back door.

Cucugnan's landmark is obvious from a distance, the picture-postcard **Château de Quéribus**, balancing nonchalantly on a slender peak, half a mile in the air over the gorge. Quéribus was the last redoubt of the Cathars; a small band of bitter-enders held out against the French for months here in 1255. Probably the best maintained of the Corbières castles, it takes about 10 minutes to walk up to – watch your step. Admission includes an optional stop at the Achille Mir theatre to hear the famous speech of the parish priest of Cucugnan, from the story in Alphonse Daudet's *Lettres de mon moulin*. And who was Achille Mir? The local scribe who wrote the story that Daudet shamelessly plagiarized for his own.

Château de Quéribus
t 04 68 45 03 69; open July and Aug daily 9–8; April–June, Sept daily 9.30–7; Oct daily 10–6.30; Nov–Jan daily 10–5; Feb daily 10–5.30; Mar daily 10–6; closed Jan except school hols; adm

Wine: Corbières, and Some Others

The Corbières has a singular microclimate, swept by the *tramontane* and with a sparse, irregular rainfall. Under its vines and *maquis* lies a geological jigsaw puzzle of Liassic, Triassic, Urgonian and who-knows-what-other kinds of rocks, not to mention the Urgo-Aptian debris and Villefranchean scree. There are just as many variations of soil, often giving wine from one village a completely different character from that of its neighbour.

Wine has always been made here – the land isn't good for much else – but only recently have producers really tried to exploit its unique possibilities. The results have been more than encouraging. Corbières red (mostly carignan, grenache and cinsault) varies widely in price and quality: from some of the best 12 per cent *appellation contrôlée* plonk you'll ever taste, to truly excellent, estate-bottled wines costing seven times as much. Always, though, it will be dark ruby red, full-bodied and intense. There is also white and rosé Corbières, although you won't often see them; good rosé (as well as red) comes from the **Château La Baronne**, near Fontcouverte, t 04 68 43 90 20.

The Corbières is a stronghold of the village co-operative cellar, and has been ever since the troubles in 1907. There are, nevertheless, a number of strictly private producers. Along the D611A, you may visit **Château Gléon-Montanié**, west of Portel, t 04 68 48 28 25, *www.gleon-montanie.com*, a lovely estate behind an old stone bridge, which makes a fine, very traditional red and a striking Corbières white, based on 100 per cent malvoisie, as well as rosé.

Nearby, the vast **Château Lastours**, Portel-des-Corbières, t 04 68 48 64 74, is set among the *garrigues* and canyons where motor-heads train for the Paris–Dakar rally – you too can have a go in a four-wheel-drive. Château Lastours has grown wine since the 12th century, and was revived in 1970 by a group in Marseille to produce Corbières and special *cuvées* according to the most modern methods, and at the same time to offer employment and independence to people with mental disability (try the excellent Cuvée en Fûts de Chêne or the extremely unusual Vendange Tardive harvested at the end of October, perfumed and rich).

One of the superstars of Corbières is **Domaine Cascadais**, at St-Laurent-de-la-Cabrerisse, t 04 68 44 01 44, owned by a brilliant producer of Bordeaux, Philippe Courrian. The first vintage was 1992. He produces red only, from carignan, grenache, syrah and mourvèdre; you can visit by appointment.

The stretch of D611 between Villeneuve and Tuchan is the heartland of one of Languedoc's finest wines, Fitou; strong and fragrant with the scent of the *garrigue*, dominated by carignan (mixed with grenache and syrah), it was the first AOC-designated wine in the region (1948). It isn't sold until after a year or more of maturation, and after five years or longer in the bottle takes on a spicy, wild aroma.

At the **Château de Nouvelles**, on a side road north of Tuchan, t 04 68 45 40 03, *http://chateaude nouvelles.com*, try the delicious 2002–2003 Fitous, drinking well now (*see* also p.201). They also produce Rivesaltes and Muscat. Another good bet is **Château L'Espigne** in Villeneuve-les-Corbières, t 04 68 45 91 26. This ancient estate was originally a *'moulin à huile'*. It is planted with 80-year-old vines that produce tiny amounts of grapes, resulting in wines of enormous concentration and complexity. The **Château de Boutenac**, Maison des Terroirs en Corbières, t 04 68 27 73 00, is a showcase for Corbières AOC wines, *www.aoc-corbieres.com*, with a wide range of wines to taste and buy, along with other local products. Also look out for wine from the **Château St-James** in Nevian, t 04 68 27 00 03, one of the Gualco family properties.

In the valley of the Agly, just over the boundary between Languedoc and Roussillon, the wine scene changes completely. Like most of Roussillon, the area around Maury and Estagel produces sweet dessert and *apéritif* wines called VDNs, or *vins doux naturels* – but it makes what many consider the best of them: Maury. Like its chief rival Banyuls, Maury is made from grenache noir, but it has a distinctive character of its own, a more consistent colour and spicy, leathery aroma, especially as it ages (1994 was a great year); a fragrant well-aged Maury Chabert is one of the few French wines that goes well with curries. Most of the 40,000 hectolitres produced each year pass through Maury's village co-operative, the **Vignerons de Maury**, on Av Jean Jaurès in Maury, t 04 68 59 00 95, *www.vigneronsdemaury.com*. Also look out for wines from the excellent estate of **Mas Amiel**, t 04 68 29 01 02, isolated in the middle of the dry schist vineyards surrounded by cypress and olive trees under the grey jagged peaks. You can see the Maury being exposed to the sun in a collection of glass jars (*bonbonnes*). Call to visit and get directions from Maury village.

Château de Peyrepertuse

⭐ **Château de Peyrepertuse**
t 06 71 58 63 36, www.chateau-peyrepertuse.com; open July and Aug daily 9–8.30; June and Sept daily 9–6.30; April–May and Oct daily 9–7; Nov–Dec and Feb–Mar daily 10–5; closed most of Jan; adm

Castles atop mountains will be nothing new by now, but nowhere else, perhaps, is there a bigger castle atop a taller, steeper mountain. If the air is clear, and you know where to look for it, you can see Peyrepertuse from any bit of high ground as far away as the coast. From Cucugnan it is an unforgettable sight, a white limestone cliff rising vertically up to the clouds, crowned by a stretch of walls and towers over 777ft long. Close up, from the bottom of the cliff, you can't see it at all.

Probably begun in the 10th century, Peyrepertuse was expanded to its present dimensions by Saint Louis in the 1240s. As important to the defence of France's new southern border as Carcassonne, Peyrepertuse was intended as an unconquerable base, big enough to hold a large force that could come down and attack the rear of any Aragonese invader. As you will see when you climb up to it, attacking it would be madness; no one ever tried. The vertiginous road to the castle starts from the village of **Duilhac**; from the car park, it's an exhausting 20-minute struggle up to the walls.

The entrance leads into the **Château Vieux**, the original castle, rebuilt by Saint Louis. Here you'll discover one of Peyrepertuse's secrets: the castle may indeed be long, but, conforming to its narrow site, in places it is only a few yards across. Nearly everything is in ruins; the keep is still in good shape, and a large cistern and the ruined chapel can be seen directly behind it. Further up is a vast open space that held most of the barracks and stores; and

Château St-Georges
t 04 68 45 69 40

Château de Termes
t 04 68 70 09 20; open July and Aug daily 9.30–7.30; April–June and Sept–Oct daily 10–6; Nov–mid-Dec and Mar Sat, Sun and hols 10–5; closed mid-Dec–Feb; adm

Château de Villerouge-Termenès
t 04 68 70 09 11; open July and Aug daily 10–7.30; April–June and Sept–mid-Oct Mon and Wed–Fri 10–1 and 2–6, Sat and Sun 10–6; mid-Oct–Dec and Mar Sat, Sun and hols 10–5; closed Jan–Feb; adm

above this, Louis added yet another citadel, the **Château St-Georges**, with another keep and chapel. There is a medieval festival in August, and falconry demonstrations in summer.

Do you need more castles? North of Peyrepertuse, in the wildest, least-travelled part of the Corbières, there are at least four more, starting with one at **Auriac**, an old copper-mining village; nearby, at **La Grave**, is an unusual 9th- to 12th-century country church, the Chapelle St-André. A bit further north, the castles at **Termes** and **Durfort** are less than 5km apart. Both the strongholds of local barons, both were besieged and taken by Simon de Montfort under the pretext of the Albigensian Crusade; Termes held out for four months, until lack of water resulted in a surrender. Montfort also conquered the **Château de Villerouge-Termenès**, 14km east, where there is an audiovisual display, 'The World of Guilhem Bélibaste, the last Cathar *parfait*', evoking 13th-century life and Bélibaste's story.

There are no easy roads in any other direction from Peyrepertuse, but, if you're heading west, rejoin the main route by way of the D7 and the white cliffs of the **Gorges de Galamus**, the most impressive natural wonder of the Corbières, a deep gorge with wonderful stone pools for swimming and canyoning.

The Plateau d'Opoul

The southern border of the Corbières is a long rocky wall, crossed by the Gorges de Galamus and the Grau de Maury. Near the sea it spreads into a *petit plateau*, one of the most barren and isolated places in France. Don't be surprised to find tanks and suchlike growling across your path. The western half of the Plateau d'Opoul is one of the French Army's zones for manoeuvres, the closest France can get to desert conditions. Most of the time, however, you won't see anyone at all, save old farmers half-heartedly trying to keep their ancient Citroëns on the road, on their weekly trip to the village to get a haircut or a goose.

The village is **Opoul-Périllos**, a cosy place that shuts itself off from the surrounding void. It is a relatively new settlement; its predecessor, **Périllos**, is an eerie ruined village higher up on the plateau, now inhabited only by praying mantises, with another **castle** nearby. Both castle and village have enormous stone cisterns. Water was always a problem here – indeed, everything was a problem, and the 14th-century Aragonese kings who built both village and castle had to bribe people with special privileges to live on the plateau. Today there are vineyards, but until very recently the only real occupation was smuggling.

Near the castle, a rocky side road leads west into the most desolate part of the plateau; at a spot called **La Vall Oriole** you'll see a massive, lonely limestone outcrop with a locked door at the bottom. It seems that some time in the early Middle Ages this rock was hollowed out by a community of cave-dwelling monks, like the famous Cappadocia ones in Turkey. There are plenty of other strange things up on this plateau, and in its history: connections with Bérenger Saunière and André Malraux, dragon legends, ley lines, an odd ruin called the 'Seat of Death', a lord of Périllos who became grand master of the Knights of Malta, a mysterious plane crash and UFO sightings, rumours of secret government installations. Enough material, in fact, for Périllos to have become a little vortex of mystery, a kind of bargain-basement Rennes-le-Château (a website, *www.perillos.com*, provides a suitably murky introduction).

Tautavel and the Fenouillèdes

Descending from Opoul to the southwest, the D9 passes through some romantically empty scenery towards **Tautavel**, a pretty village under a rocky escarpment. Throughout Europe, prehistoric man picked the unlikeliest places to park his carcass. Around Tautavel, human bones have been found from as far back as 450,000–680,000 BC, making 'Tautavel Man' a contender for the honour of First European; the only older finds come from Isernia, an equally unpromising spot in southern Italy. Back then, the climate was quite different, and Tautavel Man had elephants, bison and even rhinos to keep him company. Palaeolithic bones have become a cottage industry – over 430,000 have been found, especially in a cave called the Caune de l'Arago, north of the village – the best being displayed in the village's Musée de la Préhistoire, which shares a car park with the wine co-operative. There is now a camera link from the museum to the cave. A second exhibition, '*Les Premiers Habitants de L'Europe*', in the Palais des Congrès on Av Anatole France, describes the lives of the first Europeans.

From Tautavel, the D9 continues south into the valley of the Agly, joining the D611 and finally the D117 west, the main route inland from the coast to Foix and the Ariège. This road passes **Maury**, famous for its dessert wines and its pottery of deep blues and greens, and **St-Paul-de-Fenouillet**, known for almond cookies.

The next village, **Caudiès-de-Fenouillèdes**, has become something of an art centre, especially in summer. To the north, you will see the **Pic de Bugarach**, the highest crag in the Corbières. Three kilometres to the south, the village of **Fenouillet** is guarded by three more ruined castles, all within a few hundred yards of each other (for the crow, anyhow). Beneath them, the simple medieval chapel of **Notre-Dame-de-Laval** has a wonderful polychrome wooden altarpiece, dated 1428.

Higher into the mountains, there's yet another mountaintop castle to climb (in about 20 minutes): Puilaurens. Even Simon de Montfort couldn't get into this one; its fortifications were the most complete and sophisticated of any in the region. The Cathars who took refuge here only surrendered in 1256, after Montségur's fall.

The Agly valley and the mountains around it make up the **Fenouillèdes** – Fenouillet in Catalan, the northernmost region of medieval Catalunya. Though equally mountainous, its scenery makes a remarkable contrast to the dry and windswept Corbières. Here, limestone gradually gives way to granite, the true beginning of the Pyrenees. Much is covered by ancient virgin forest, broken by quick-flowing streams and scenic ravines. The best parts are the **Forêt d'Ayguesbonnes-Boucheville**, southwest of Fenouillet, and the **Forêt des Fanges**, in the steep mountains behind Puilaurens.

The D619 south from St-Paul-de-Fenouillet is the only good road through the Fenouillèdes, passing through **Sournia** on the Desix river, the only real town. Along the way, be sure to stop at **Ansignan** to see its Roman **aqueduct**, a rustic, seldom-visited version of the famous Pont du Gard. An arcade of 551ft, with 29 arches, carries it over the Agly; it is still in use, carrying water to the vineyards, and you can walk over it, or follow the channel towards the village. The question is why the Romans built it, with no nearby towns to serve. It is unlikely that agriculture on the coastal plains was ever so intensive as to merit such a work. One possibility is an important

---

Caune de l'Arago
open July and Aug to groups only

Musée de la Préhistoire
t 04 68 29 07 76; open July and Aug daily 9–9; April–June and Sept daily 10–6; Oct–Mar daily 10–12.30 and 2–6; adm

Palais des Congrès de Tautavel
t 04 68 29 07 76; open July and Aug daily 11.30–7.30; April–June and Sept daily 11.30–1 and 2.30–6.30; Oct–Mar daily 11.30–1 and 2.30–5.30

Puilaurens
t 04 68 20 65 26; open daily April–June and Sept 10–6; July and Aug 9–8; Oct–mid-Nov 10–5; mid-Nov–Mar Sat, Sun and school hols only 10–5; closed mid-Nov–Jan; adm

patrician villa – such things were often cities in themselves – but no traces of one have been discovered. Signs in Ansignan point the way up to a dolmen and to **Felluns**; there are wide-ranging views over the mountains just beyond, on the D7 south to Sournia.

(i) **Lagrasse »**
6 Bd de la Promenade, t 04 68 43 11 56, www.lagrasse. com; open daily

★ **Château Haut-Gléon »**

(i) **Lézignan-Corbières ›**
9 Cours de la République, t 04 68 27 05 42; open July and Aug Mon–Sat and Sun am; Sept–June Mon–Fri

Market Days in the Corbières

Lézignan-Corbières: Wed.
Lagrasse: Mon.
Tuchan: Thurs.

Where to Stay and Eat in the Corbières

For tourism, the Corbières is virgin territory. Not only will you have trouble finding a petrol station, but accommodation is scarce. Most people make day trips from nearby towns such as Narbonne and Quillan.

Lézignan-Corbières ✉ 11200

Le Tassigny, Rond-Point de Lattre de Tassigny, t 04 68 27 11 51, *http://hotel-le-tassigny.com* (€). Has a restaurant, **Le Tournedos (€€€–€€). *Closed Sun eve and Mon.*

Stromboli, 43 Cours Lapeyrouse, t 04 68 27 00 81. A popular, better-than-average pizzeria, also with pancakes.

Ornaisons ✉ 11200

***Relais du Val d'Orbieu, on the D24, t 04 68 27 10 27, *www.relaisduval dorbieu.com* (€€€€). Modernized *mas* among the fields north of the village, it has tennis, a pool and all amenities, including an excellent restaurant (€€€) serving fish baked with rosemary and more. *Closed Dec and Jan; restaurant closed Mon.*

Auberge du Vieux Puits, Av St-Victor, Fontjoncouse (off the D611, south of Thézan-des-Corbières), t 04 68 44 07 37, *www.aubergeduvieuxpuits.fr* (€€€€). Join the Narbonnais who make a special trip here to feast on the gorgeous cuisine of Gilles Goujon, who learned a trick or two at the Moulin de Mougins. There are also 14 rooms (€€€€–€€€) and a pool. *Closed June–Sept Mon lunch; Oct–May Sun eve, Mon and Tues; plus Jan and Feb.*

Lagrasse ✉ 11220

L'Hostellerie des Corbières, 9 Av de la Promenade, t 04 68 43 15 22 (€€). A Logis de France hotel in a *maison de maître*, with a decent restaurant looking out over the vines (€€). *Closed Jan; restaurant closed Thurs.*

Villesèque-des-Corbières ✉ 11360

Château Haut Gléon, t 04 68 48 85 95, *www.hautgleon.com* (€€). A wine estate in the Corbières hills, with comfortable stylish accommodation (rooms and a *gîte*) in the renovated stable wing and works of art in the garden. There's no restaurant (most go to the Auberge du Vieux Puits, *see* left), but wine-tasting is offered.

Cucugnan ✉ 11350

**Auberge du Vigneron, 2 Rue Achille Mir, t 04 68 45 03 00, *www.auberge-vigneron.com* (€€). A good hotel, with just six cosy rustic rooms and a restaurant (€€) in a former wine cellar. *Closed mid-Nov–Feb; restaurant closed Sat lunch and Sun in summer, Sun eve and Mon in winter.*

Tautavel ✉ 66720

Le Petit Gris, Route d'Estagel, t 04 68 29 42 42 (€€€). A very popular family restaurant with great views of the plain from big windows; they serve traditional Catalan fare. *Closed Mon.*

Estagel ✉ 66310

**Le Plein Sud, 9 Bd Jean Jaurès, Estagel, near Tautavel on the D117, t 04 68 29 00 84, *http://hotelpleinsud. aglyservices.com* (€). If you're passing by, you can eat and/or sleep well and economically at this hotel; Catalan specialities (€€–€) are served.

Caramany ✉ 66720

Auberge du Grand Rocher, Rue Eloi Tresserres, Caramany, t 04 68 84 51 58, *www.auberge-du-grand-rocher-bb.com* (€€€–€€). Simply furnished restaurant in a pretty hill town, a 20min drive from Maury; the terrace has valley views. Local specialities such as boar casserole. *Book. Closed Sun eve and Mon in summer and Sun eve and Thurs in winter, plus Jan and Feb.*

St-Paul-de-Fenouillet ✉ 66220

Le Châtelet, Rte de Caudiès, t 04 68 59 01 20, *www.hotel-lechatelet.com* (€€–€). A Logis de France hotel, with a pool and restaurant (€€). *Closed Nov–Mar; restaurant closed lunch.*

*Relais des Corbières,** 10 Av Jean Moulin, t 04 68 59 23 89 (€). Smaller, central and with a restaurant (€€).

Duilhac ✉ 11350

L'Hostellerie du Vieux Moulin, 24 Rue Fontaines (entrance to the village),

t 04 68 45 02 00 (€€–€). Run by the same people as the Auberge du Vigneron in Cucugnan (*see* p.210). They have entirely renovated this old house near Peyrepertuse to create equally welcoming rooms. No restaurant, but breakfast available. *Closed mid Nov–Easter.*

Gincla ✉ 11140

Hostellerie du Grand Duc, 2 Route de Boucheville, t 04 68 20 55 02, *www. host-du-grand-duc.com* (€€). A handsome old mansion near Puilaurens with a shady garden; the restaurant (€€€) serves tasty French classics. *Closed Nov–Mar; restaurant closed Wed lunch except July and Aug.*

St-Paul-de-Fenouillet ›
26 Bd Agly, t 04 68 59 07 57, www. st-paul66.com; open July–Aug Mon–Sat; Sept–June Tues–Sat

The Valley of the Aude

The Upper Aude Valley

Near the castle of Puilaurens, the D117 joins the course of the Aude, passing northwards through a spectacular canyon, the **Défilé de Pierre-Lys**. The *pays* that begins here is called the **Razès**, a sparse, scrubby, haunted region, the back door to the Corbières. As Rhedae, it has been known to history since the time of the Visigoths; according to author Henry Lincoln, the uncanniness begins with the Razès' sacred geometry: its five most prominent peaks, including the perch of Languedoc's conspiracy headquarters, Rennes-le-Château, describe a unique, perfect natural pentangle. The precise measurements were repeated in the Middle Ages, in the geomantic placing of churches around Espéraza. Even in the off season you'll see cars with number plates from faraway countries, cruising about looking for goodness knows what.

Quillan, Espéraza and Couiza

Quillan, the first town after the Pierre-Lys canyon, makes its living from manufacturing shoes and Formica; it has an odd, perfectly square castle from the 1280s, a ball and three *quilles* (bowling pins) on its coat of arms. Dinosaurs were fond of the Aude valley and especially **Espéraza**, just north, where they left a nest of eggs, now displayed with fossils, skeletons, dioramas and more Jurassic-era souvenirs at the really quite good **Dinosauria**, Av de la Gare. In later years the village was no less than 'the world's second-greatest maker of hats in the first half of the 20th century' and curses the day JFK set the fashion for going without. The village's glory days are recalled in the **Musée de la Chapellerie**.

Dinosauria
t 04 68 74 26 88, www.dinosauria.org; open July and Aug daily 10–7; early Feb–June and Sept–early Nov daily 10–12 and 2–6; early Nov–Jan Mon–Fri 2–5, Sat and Sun 10–12 and 2–5; adm

Musée de la Chapellerie
t 04 68 74 00 75; open July and Aug daily 10–7; Jan–June and Sept–Oct daily 10–12 and 2–6; Nov and Dec daily 2–6; adm

Arques château
t 04 68 69 84 77;
www.chateau-arques.fr;
open July and Aug daily
9.30–7.30; April–June
and Sept daily 10–6;
Oct–Mar daily
10.30–12.30 and 1.30–5;
closed Nov–Feb; adm

Maison de
Déodat Roché
t 04 68 69 85 62;
open July and Aug daily
9.30–8; June and Sept
daily 10–7; Oct and Mar
daily 10.30–12 and
1.30–5.30; April–May
daily 10.30–6.30; Nov
daily 10.30–12 and
1.30–5; closed Dec–Feb

 Rennes-le-
Château

This is a
terrible place
Abbé Saunière's
inscription over the
door of Ste-Marie-
Madeleine

The Razès' biggest town, gritty and peculiar **Couiza**, makes even more shoes, and plastic panelling, too. Its landmark is the imposing Renaissance **château** of the Ducs de Joyeuse, who made nuisances of themselves on the Catholic side during the Wars of Religion; their descendants have turned the old homestead into a hotel (*see* p.214). To the east of Couiza are **Rennes-les-Bains**, a small spa in business since the time of the Romans (finds from the ancient baths are in the Villa Marie), and **Arques**, where a few Cathars still go about their business. Arques has a tall, elegant, Gothic 13th-century **château** – or just the keep of one, framed in turrets, as Simon de Montfort took it from the Termes family in 1231 and gave it to one of his lieutenants. The same ticket admits you to the **Maison de Déodat Roché**; a famous Cathar historian, Roché (1877–1978) was born in Arques, and his house in the centre of the village has a permanent exhibition on Catharism in the 19th and 20th centuries.

Rennes-le-Château

Whatever is haunting the Razès, it resides here, in a woebegone mountaintop village above Couiza that is possibly familiar to more people in Britain and America than in Carcassonne. The fun began in the 1890s, when the young parish priest Bérenger Saunière began spending huge sums of money on himself and on embellishing his church. The story, and the speculation, hasn't stopped unfolding since. In a nation addicted to secret conspiracies, preferably with a medieval pedigree, every sort of shadowy religious cult and fantastico-political faction has got its oar in, from neo-fascists to neo-Jews, along with monarchists, satanists, dilettante Cathars and dress-up Templars.

With its few dusty streets, spectacular views over the Aude valley and a superabundance of mangy dogs, Rennes-le-Château is an unsurpassed vortex of weirdness. Its one permanent business is an occult bookshop, where you can pick up a copy of the 1970s best-seller *Holy Blood, Holy Grail*, the first and best account in English that attracted international attention to Rennes, describing Jesus' problematical but well-publicized western European tour, an escape from Palestine after a faked crucifixion. It's been a recurring theme in French and English legend from the beginning ('And did those feet in ancient time,' etc.). Here, the idea is that Jesus came to Gaul with his wife Mary Magdalene; both may have been buried in Rennes and their descendants were the French Merovingian kings, deposed in the 8th century by a shady deal between the popes and Carolingians. Supposedly, the bloodline survives to this day.

It hardly matters that the entire story has been revealed as a hoax, perpetrated on the poor authors of *Holy Blood, Holy Grail* by some devilishly clever Frenchmen. The recent worldwide success of

Dan Brown's novel *The Da Vinci Code* has got the whole occult fairytale machine wound up and running again. Did Saunière discover proof of Jesus' tomb in Rennes and make his fortune by blackmailing the Vatican to keep his mouth shut? Or did he find the Holy Grail, or the treasure of the Visigoths, the Merovingians or the Templars? The most fashionable theory these days leans towards the fabulous treasure of the Jews, stolen from Jerusalem by Titus in AD 10 and pillaged in turn by the Visigoths, who carted it off from Rome to Carcassonne in the 5th century. When Clovis, King of the Franks, took the Visigoths' capital of Toulouse, the treasure was supposedly removed for safekeeping to the impregnable fortress at Rennes (today, the whole area around the village is lined with stern 'no digging' signs). Rennes became the capital of the region when Amairic, a Visigothic prince, married a Frankish princess, and it is claimed to have eventually had a population of 30,000 – 3,000 would be closer to reality – before it was definitively sacked by the Aragonese in 1170, only to be destroyed again for good measure in Simon de Montfort's *blitzkrieg*.

When Bérenger Saunière was appointed parish priest of Rennes-le-Château, the village was in a sorry state; even the 12th-century church was falling over. During the repairs on the church in 1891, Saunière supposedly found, under a statue of the Virgin (she stands on a stone carved with a cross set upside down – perhaps a Visigothic altar), a parchment in a glass phial. Not long after, Saunière was spotted by the villagers, digging furtively most evenings in the local cemetery. One of his activities was the systematic defacement of the inscription on the tomb of the last Lady of Rennes, Hautpoul de Blanchefort (d. 1781), not knowing that someone had already copied it out in the early 1820s (it had Greek letters reading '*Et in Arcadia ego*', i.e. death is present, even in Arcadia). Hautpoul, who died without heirs, had in her last hours of life confided some great secret to the parish priest, who left the enigmatic epitaph on her tomb. The same inscription, by apparently no coincidence at all, appears on the tomb in one of Nicolas Poussin's best-known paintings. The background of his painting shows – surprise! – the distinctive profile of Rennes-le-Château.

After his nocturnal digs, Saunière began spending money like nobody's business, paving the road up to Rennes, and redoing the church, dedicated (naturally) to Mary Magdalene, in a style the French have labelled 'St-Sulpicien' after the garish church in Paris. This hardly seems to have been Saunière's main concern in his decorative schemes; rather, the somewhat unorthodox imagery of his bevy of plaster statues apparently distils a secret message to the initiated (note, for instance, that in the Holy Family both Mary and Joseph hold babies). Even Saunière got into hot water with the Church over the demonic figure that supports the font by the door,

Ste-Marie-Madeleine
open May–mid-Sept daily 10.30–6; mid-Sept–Oct daily 11.30–1 and 2–5; Nov–mid-Jan Sat and Sun 11.30–1 and 2–5; Mar–April daily 11.30–1 and 2–4; closed mid-Jan–Feb; adm

representing not Satan but Asmodeus, the guardian of the treasure of Solomon.

Outside the church, the statue of the Virgin still stands on her mysterious stone. An adjacent museum relates some of this to the Cathars, who had a mysterious treasure of their own that they slipped out of Montségur and hid in parts unknown before the bitter end (see pp.41–2).

Museum
t 04 68 74 72 68;
same hours as church

You can visit the **Domaine de l'Abbé Saunière**, the genteelly dilapidated bourgeois villa and garden that Saunière built for himself with his secret loot (lately, there have been suggestions that the priest really made his bundle by selling masses). Under the Abbé's peculiar library-belvedere, the **Tour Magdala**, you'll find documents and photos relating to his doings and the whole history of Rennes. Saunière died in 1917, leaving everything to his housekeeper, Marie Dénaraud, who took his secrets with her to the grave in 1953. From the top of the belvedere you can see a number of towers, fortresses and other ruins, their origin and purpose a matter of conjecture; the largest of them, the **Château de Blanchefort**, was probably wrecked by Simon de Montfort.

Domaine de l'Abbé Saunière
www.rennes-le-chateau.fr; same hours as church; adm

Further up the Aude, and Down into the Earth

Quillan tourist office arranges visits to the **Grotte de l'Aguzou**, 27km up the Aude on the D118. This is a spectacular stalactite cave, full of lovely delicate formations and crystals, but unlike others open to visitors. It hasn't been fitted out with walkways and lights; rather, small groups from eight to ten (children must be at least 10 years old) are taken in with lighted helmets, overalls, belts and lights to explore. Die-hard couch potatoes should abstain.

Grotte de l'Aguzou
t 04 68 20 45 38, www. grotte-agouzou.com; visits strictly by appt, with one-day tours, including lunch, for small groups, and half-day tours for individuals

Market Days in the Upper Aude Valley

Quillan: Wed and Sat.
Espéraza: Thurs and especially Sun.
Couiza: Tues and Sat.

Where to Stay and Eat in the Upper Aude Valley

ⓘ Quillan >
Square André Tricoire, t 04 68 20 07 78, www. ville-quillan.fr; open mid-June–mid-Sept Mon–Sat and Sun am; mid-Sept–mid-June Mon–Fri and Sat am

Quillan ✉ 11500
***La Chaumière**, 25 Bd Charles de Gaulle, t 04 68 20 02 00, www.pyren.fr (€€). Cosy rooms and mountain food featuring trout. *Closed mid-Nov–Mar.*
****Hôtel Cartier**, 31 Bd Charles de Gaulle, t 04 68 20 05 14, www.hotel cartier.com (€). Near the train station

and Quillan's indoor pool, with restaurant (€€). *Closed mid-Dec–mid-Mar; restaurant closed Sat lunch.*
****La Pierre Lys**, Av François Mitterrand, t 04 68 20 08 65 (€). At the north end of town, this modern hotel offers comfort, quiet and the best meals in the town (€€€–€€), with sea perch, confits, etc. *Closed mid-Nov–mid-Dec.*
Le Terminus, 45 Bd Charles de Gaulle, t 04 68 20 93 33 (€). Inexpensive restaurant near the train station.

Couiza ✉ 11190
Château des Ducs de Joyeuse, off the main road, set amid playing fields, t 04 68 74 23 50, www.chateau-des-ducs.com (€€€). A handsome 16th-century place with attractive rooms; the elegant restaurant serves the best meals around. *Closed mid-Nov–Feb; restaurant closed Sun eve and Mon eve.*

Into the Limouxin

Before its right turn at Carcassonne, the Aude traverses a lovely, modest stretch of open rolling country, the Limouxin. Most of the roads here are still graced with their long arcades of plane trees – there isn't enough traffic yet to threaten them.

Alet-les-Bains

Continuing down the Aude from Couiza, Alet-les-Bains is one of the most beautiful and best-preserved medieval villages of Languedoc. A small spa since Roman times, Alet owes its prominence to the popes, who made it a bishopric in 1318. Its two jewels are the 14th-century church of **St-André**, with frescoes and a fine west portal, and the impressive Benedictine abbey, founded in the 9th century and wrecked in the Wars of Religion. The narrow streets of the village itself are an equal attraction, with a score of 13th- and 14th-century buildings, such as the colonnaded house called the **Maison Romane**. Alet is still a thriving spa; it bottles its water to clean out your digestive tract, and runs a casino to clean out your pockets. There's a pretty river to paddle in.

Benedictine abbey
open July–Aug daily 10–12 and 2.30–7; Sept–June Mon–Sat 10–12 and 2.30–6, closed Sun

Limoux and the Quercorb

Even before you notice the vineyards, the civilized landscapes suggest wine. Limoux, the capital, is an attractive town, with a medieval bridge across the Aude, the **Pont Neuf**; this meets the apse and steeple of **St-Martin**, a good piece of Gothic, if anachronistic – although the church was begun in the 14th century, most of the work is from three centuries later. The centre is the arcaded **Place de la République**. Like Carcassonne's Ville Basse, Limoux was a *bastide*, and this was its market square; the streets of the old town around it make a pleasant stroll. Rue Blanquerie, named for the tanneries that once were Limoux's main business, is one of the streets with 15th- and 16th-century houses, like the 1549 **Hôtel de Clercy**, with a lovely and unusual courtyard of interlocking arches.

On the Promenade du Tivoli, a broad boulevard that replaced the town walls, the tourist office shares the home of the Petiet family with the Musée Petiet, which contains a collection of 19th-century paintings, and canvases by the museum's founder, Marie Petiet, a talented, neglected artist of the 1880s. A woman painter, and a woman's painter, her work brings a touch of magic to very domestic subjects, nowhere better than in the serene, luminous composition called *Les Blanchisseuses* (*The Washerwomen*). There is also a **Musée du Piano** at the Chapelle St-Jacques, Place du 22 Septembre, with 50 instruments. Limoux's final attraction sounds like something P. T. Barnum would think up: Catha-Rama (47 Av F. d'Eglantine), two 30-minute audiovisual spectaculars on the history of the Cathars, in languages from Catalan to Japanese.

Musée Petiet
t 04 68 31 85 03; open July–Aug daily 9–7; Sept–June Mon–Fri 9–12 and 2–6, Sat and Sun 10–12 and 2–5; adm

Musée du Piano
t 04 68 31 85 03; open July and Aug daily 10–12 and 2–5, otherwise call for times

Catha-Rama
t 04 68 31 48 42, www. d-av.com/catharama; open July–Aug Mon–Fri 3–6; Easter–June and Sept–Oct call for times; closed Nov–Easter; adm

Wine: Blanquette de Limoux

Available in London or New York, Blanquette de Limoux may already be familiar under the Aimery label and others, popularly recognized as the poor man's champagne. The Limouxins wouldn't care to hear it put that way; they would point out that their Blanquette was the world's first sparkling wine, produced at least since 1531, when it was first recorded – long before anyone ever heard of champagne. Blanquette, made from mauzac, chenin and chardonnay, may not have the depth or ageing ability of its celebrated rival, but you should certainly give it a try while you're here, especially as it is excellent value. Locals like to drink it as an *apéritif*, with little cakes called *pebradous*, flavoured with pepper.

You'll have little trouble finding Blanquette (along with the other, non-classified *vins de pays*, white and red) on the roads around Limoux, starting with the big firm **Sieur d'Arques**, Av Mauzac (from Limoux, follow signs to Chalabre and you will see it indicated, t 04 68 74 63 00, *www.sieurdarques.com*). They have a big tasting room filled with local wines and offer tours to see how it is produced; they also produce an excellent, slightly less sparkling wine called Crémant de Limoux, such as the Grande Cuvée Renaissance. Among the best producers of Blanquette is the **Domaine Antech**, at Domaine de Flassian, on the D118 towards Carcassonne, t 04 68 31 15 88, *www.antech-limoux.com* (*closed weekends*). Maison Antech is a producer of several special *cuvées* and fine Crémants. Those interested in tasting some excellent organic Blanquette should visit **Cave Beirieu** at Roquetaillade, t 04 68 31 60 71, *beirieu@blanquette-bio.com* (contact them first).

Northwest of Limoux you'll find an estimable but little-known red wine called La Malepère, which only received AOC status in 2007, making it the youngest Languedoc AOC. It is produced in a small area, but the closest one in Languedoc to Bordeaux – hence the use of varieties like cot, merlot and cabernet franc. You'll find it around Malepère, Brugairolles, Malviès and Lauraguel: look out for the **Château Guilhem**, 1 Bd Malviès, t 04 68 31 14 41, *www.chateauguilhem.com*.

St-Hilaire
t 04 68 69 62 76, www.perso.orange.fr/abbayedesainthilaire; open July and Aug daily 10–7; April–June and Sept–Oct daily 10–12 and 2–6; Nov–Mar daily 10–12 and 2–5

Musée du Quercorb
t 04 68 20 80 98; open mid-July–Aug daily 10–7; April–mid-July and Sept daily 10–12.30 and 2–6; Oct daily 2–5; adm

Château de Puivert
t 04 68 20 81 52, www.chateau-de-puivert.com; open summer daily 9–7; winter Sun–Fri 10–5, closed Sat; closed mid-Nov–mid-Dec; adm

In the sculpted countryside around Limoux, you can combine picnics and piety with a tour of three sites. The chapel of **Notre-Dame-de-Marceille**, just to the northeast, houses a 'Black Virgin', an 11th-century icon. To the east, an exceptionally pretty side road (the D104) takes you to St-Hilaire, an abbey founded in the 8th century; its Benedictine monks invented the bubbly Blanquette de Limoux. A graceful, double-columned Gothic cloister survives, along with the Romanesque abbey church, containing the white marble sarcophagus of St Sernin (d. 250), the patron of Toulouse, sculpted by the Master of Cabestany – one of his masterpieces.

South of St-Hilaire, the monastery of **St-Polycarpe** is just as old, though not as well preserved. Its Romanesque church retains some bits of early frescoes and Carolingian carved altars.

Southwest of Limoux, you may venture into one of the most obscure *pays* in all France. Very few French people, even, have heard of the **Kercorb** (or Quercorb), a sleepy region with plenty of sheep and plenty of trees. **Quercorb** is known for its apple cider, and little else. **Chalabre**, an attractive village of old stone houses with overhanging windows, is its capital. At **Puivert**, 8km south, the Musée du Quercorb will tell you everything there is to know (a reconstructed kitchen and other rooms, cow bell manufacturing, and crafts). It also includes reconstructions of 14th-century musical instruments, based on the sculptures of musicians found in the *donjon* of the Château de Puivert; its lords were famous as patrons and protectors of the troubadours. Puivert also has a popular lake.

Limouxin Festivals

Limoux' carnival, steeped in local folklore and the longest in France (weekends Jan–Easter) makes it worth visiting in winter; ask tourist office.

ⓘ **Chalabre**
Cours d'Aguesseau,
t 04 68 69 65 96,
www.quercorb.com

ⓘ **Alet-les-Bains ›**
Av Nicolas Pavillon,
t 04 68 69 93 56, http://
info.aletlesbains.free.fr

★ **Maison de la Blanquette ››**

ⓘ **Limoux ›**
Promenade du Tivoli,
t 04 68 31 11 82,
www.limoux.fr

Limouxin Market Days

Limoux: Fri; flea market 1st Sun.
Chalabre: Sat.

Where to Stay and Eat in the Limouxin

Alet-les-Bains ✉ 11580

**L'Hostellerie de l'Evêché, t 04 68 69 90 25, *www.hotel-eveche.com* (€). The riverside former bishop's mansion; rather plain, it nevertheless has a huge garden with century-old cypresses. *Closed Nov–Mar.*

Limoux ✉ 11300

***Grand Hôtel Moderne et Pigeon, Place Général Leclerc, t 04 68 31 00 25, *www.grandhotelmodernepigeon.fr*

(€€–€). The most luxurious choice. It has served as a convent, a *hôtel particulier* and a bank. The restaurant (€€€) is good, appropriately serving pigeon dishes. *Closed Jan; restaurant closed Mon, Tues lunch and Sun eve.*

**Hôtel des Arcades, 96 Rue St-Martin, just off Place de la République, t 04 68 31 02 57 (€). With comfortable rooms and a restaurant (€€). *Closed mid-Dec–Jan; restaurant closed Wed.*

*Auberge de la Corneilla, just off the D118 at Cournanel, south of Limoux, t 04 68 31 17 84 (€). An unpretentious restored farmhouse with nice rooms, a restaurant (€€) and a garden and pool. *Restaurant closed Sat lunch and Sun eve out of season.*

Maison de la Blanquette, 46 bis Promenade du Tivoli, t 04 68 31 01 63 (€€€–€€). Wine-sampling and relaxed home cooking, from Limoux's *charcuterie* to *confits* to the people's choice, a variation on *cassoulet* called *fricassée* (Limoux even has an 'Association pour la Promotion de la Fricassée'). *Closed Wed eve.*

Carcassonne

ⓘ **Carcassonne**

Standing before the great eastern gate of the walled city, the writer had his notebook out and was scribbling furiously. It was market day, and rustic villeins in coarse wool tunics were offering hung pheasants and great round cheeses from their wooden carts. Geese honked from cages made of twigs and rushes, while pigs and hounds poked about in the cobbled gutters. 'This is medieval indeed,' the writer mused – and just then the director and his entourage appeared over the drawbridge. 'Lovely, everyone, but we'll want more sheep; lots more sheep!'

Plenty of obscure costume dramas have been shot here, drawn by Viollet-le-Duc's romantic restoration. Even without pigs in the gutters, Carcassonne is the Middle Ages come to life. The people of the city do their best to heighten the medieval atmosphere: every August there are various medieval-themed events with artisans in costume, music and jousts. Reality intrudes in the history of the place. Today a dour manufacturing town, Carcassonne was once the strategic key to the Midi; the castle built here by Saint Louis (Louis IX) was a barrier to invaders greater than the Pyrenees.

History

After running north down from the Pyrenees, the river Aude makes a sharp right turn for the sea, thus conveniently providing

Getting to and around Carcassonne

By Air

There are direct flights from the UK (*see* **Planning Your Trip**); a bus shuttle service links the **airport** to the Cité, Place Gambetta and the station.

By Train and Bus

From the **train station**, on Av du Maréchal Joffre at the northern edge of the Ville Basse, there are regular connections to Narbonne, and from there to all the coastal cities; there are also trains down the Aude valley to Limoux and Quillan.

There are several **bus** companies going to towns and villages outside Carcassonne; contact **Cars Teissier**, **t** 04 68 25 85 45, *www.teissier.fr*, or **Trans Aude**, 2 Bd Paul Sabatier, **t** 04 68 25 13 74.

To get up to the Cité from the lower town, take the no.8 city bus from Place Gambetta.

By Car

There is a big **car park** outside Porte Narbonnaise, but expect to pay €6 a day. Otherwise, you need to be up at the crack of dawn to find a space in summer.

Bike and Boat Hire

You can hire **bicycles** at **Evasion 2 Roues**, 85 Allée d'Iéna, **t** 04 68 11 90 40. You can hire a **boat** by the week to cruise the Canal du Midi at **Nautic**, 15 Quai Riquet, **t** 04 67 94 78 93, *www.nautic.fr*. If you prefer letting someone else do the work for a couple of hours, contact **Lou Gabaret**, for trips up and down the river from the port, April–Oct (except Mon out of season), **t** 04 68 71 61 26, *www.carcassonne-croisiere.com*.

Other Ways of Seeing the Cité

Carriage rides leave from Porte Narbonnaise for a trot around Les Lices, April–mid-Nov, **t** 04 68 71 54 57; a **tourist train** leaves from the same area for a visit of the towers and ramparts, May–Sept, **t** 04 68 24 45 70.

---

not only an easy natural route into the mountains, but also one across the 'French isthmus', between the Mediterranean and the Atlantic. The river's angle, one of the crossroads of France since prehistoric times, is an obvious site for a fortress; there seems to have been one nearby since the 8th century BC. The Tectosage Gauls occupied the site of the present Cité in the 3rd century BC; a century later the Romans established a fortified veterans' colony on it called Carcaso, which gradually grew into a town. With the coming of the Visigoths in the Germanic invasions of the 5th century AD, Carcassonne began to assume its historic role as a border stronghold between France and Spain – the Frankish and Visigothic kingdoms. The action started as early as AD 506, when the Frankish King Clovis unsuccessfully besieged the town.

Arabs from Spain arrived about 725, one of the high-water marks of the Muslim tide in Europe. Pépin the Short chased them out 30 years later. Not that the Franks could hold it either. With the collapse of the Carolingian Empire, local viscounts attained a *de facto* independence. From 1084 to 1209, Carcassonne enjoyed a glorious period of wealth and culture under the Trencavels, a family who were also viscounts of Béziers and Nîmes. Under them, the cathedral and the Château Comtal were begun. Simon de Montfort, realizing the importance of the town, made it one of his first stops in the Crusade of 1209. The last viscount, Raymond-

Roger Trencavel, was no Cathar but a gentleman and a patriot, determined to oppose the planned rape of Languedoc by the northerners. His famous declaration is still remembered today: 'I offer a town, a roof, a shelter, bread and my sword to all the persecuted people who will soon be wandering in Provence.' Unfortunately, Trencavel allowed himself to be tricked outside the Cité walls on pretence of negotiation; he was put in chains and the leaderless town surrendered soon after. Raymond-Roger died in prison three months later, probably poisoned by Montfort, who declared himself viscount and used Carcassonne as his base of operations until his death in 1218. His son, Amauri, ceded the town and the rest of Montfort's conquests to King Louis IX. The last of the Trencavels, Raymond-Roger's son and heir, also named Raymond, fought to reclaim his lands until 1240, without success despite popular revolts. Under Louis and his son, Philip III, the outer walls were built, making the entire town into the greatest fortress in Europe, the impregnable base of French power in the south. No attempts were ever made on it; even the Black Prince, passing through in 1355, declined to undertake a siege.

When France gobbled up the province of Roussillon in 1659, this mighty bastion no longer had any military purpose and it was allowed to fall into disrepair. While the lower town, with its large textile industries, prospered until English competition ruined the trade in the 19th century, the Cité gradually decayed into a half-abandoned slum. It was the writer Prosper Mérimée, France's Inspector-General of Historic Monuments in the 1830s, who called attention to this sad state of affairs. Viollet-le-Duc, fresh from sprucing up Narbonne, got the job of restoring the Cité in 1844, and work continued according to his plans for the rest of the century.

Today's Carcassonne has a split personality: up on its hill, the pink towers of the lovingly restored Cité glitter like a dream, no longer impregnable; its few hundred inhabitants (all of whom, it seems, have opened Ye Olde tourist shops or snack bars) are invaded by over 200,000 visitors each year while, down below, the workaday Ville Basse gets on with the job. This is one place where you really should try to come outside high season.

The Cité and its Walls

Most visitors come in through the back door, by the car parks and the bus stop at **Porte Narbonnaise**. This is not the best introduction to the impressive military sophistication of Carcassonne's defences. It's probably the weakest point along the walls, though there may have been outworks that have since disappeared. Still, it looks strong enough, with two stout rounded bastions on the inner wall from which to mow down any attackers fortunate enough to have got through the outer wall.

Gare

Port

AV MARECHAL JOFFRE

AV MARECHAL FOCH

RUE TOURTEL

ALLEE D'IENA

Canal du Midi

BOULEVARD OMER SARRAUT

RUE ANTOINE MARTY

BOULEVARD DE VARSOVIE

RUE DE LA LIBERTE

RUE DE LA LIBERTE

VILLE

BASSE

BOULEVARD JEAN JAURES

RUE DE 4 SEPTEMBRE

RUE ALBERT TOMEY

Gare
Regionale

RUE DE 4 SEPTEMBRE

St-Vincent

RUE DE LA REPUBLIQUE

RUE DE LA REPUBLIQUE

ALLEE D'IENA

RUE VICTOR HUGO

RUE VICTOR HUGO

PLACE
CARNOT

BD VARILLA

PL DAVILLA

RUE DE VERDUN

RUE DE VERDUN

SQUARE

← To
Airport

BOULEVARD MARCOU

RUE JULES SAUZEDE

RUE ALBERT TOMEY

Maison des Mémoires

Musée des
Beaux Arts

BOULEVARD CAMILLE PELLETAN

GAMBETTA

RUE DU PONT

Halles aux
Grains

RUE AIME RAMOND

Cathédrale
St-Michel

RUE VOLTAIRE

BOULEVARD BARBES

BOULEVARD BARBES

BOULEVARD CDT ROUMENS

R. DES TROIS COURONNES

Aude

N

250 m
250 yds

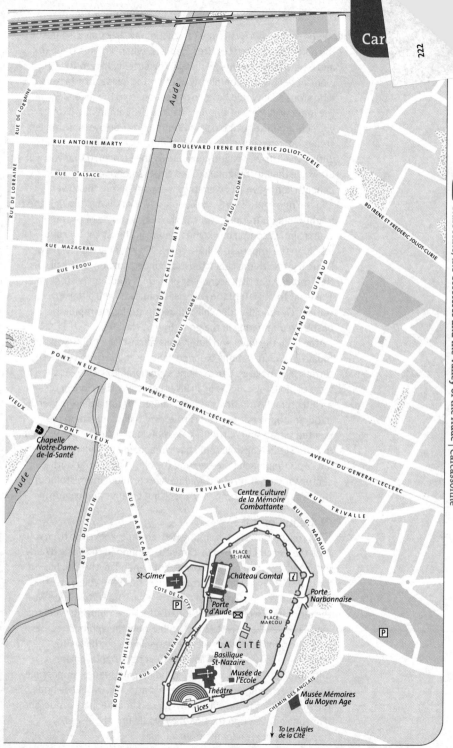

RUE DE LORRAINE

RUE ANTOINE MARTY

RUE D'ALSACE

RUE DE LORRAINE

RUE MAZAGRAN

RUE FEDOU

Aude

BOULEVARD IRENE ET FREDERIC JOLIOT-CURIE

RUE PAUL LACOMBE

AVENUE ACHILLE MIR

RUE PAUL LACOMBE

RUE ALEXANDRE GUIRAUD

BD IRENE ET FREDERIC JOLIOT-CURIE

PONT NEUF

AVENUE DU GENERAL LECLERC

VIEUX

PONT VIEUX

Chapelle
Notre-Dame-
de-la-Santé

Aude

AVENUE DU GENERAL LECLERC

RUE TRIVALLE

Centre Culturel
de la Mémoire
Combattante

RUE G. NADAUD

RUE TRIVALLE

RUE DUJARDIN

RUE BARBACANE

PLACE
ST-JEAN

St-Gimer

COTE DE LA CITÉ

P

Porte
d'Aude

Château Comtal

i

Porte
Narbonnaise

PLACE
MARCOU

P

ROUTE DE ST-HILAIRE

RUE DES REMPARTS

LA CITÉ

Basilique
St-Nazaire

Musée de
l'Ecole

Théâtre

Lices

CHEMIN DES ANGLAIS

Musée Mémoires
du Moyen Age

To Les Aigles
de la Cité

Between the two walls, you can circumnavigate Carcassonne by the open space called **Les Lices**, the 'lists', where knights trained and where tournaments were held. The **outer wall** is Louis IX's work; note how it is completely open on the inside, so attackers who stormed it would have no protection from the defenders on the **inner wall**. Parts of this date back to the Romans – wherever you see large, irregular blocks without mortar, or layers of smaller stones interspersed with courses of thin brick. The ground level within the lists was slightly lowered by the French, so that you will often see their rectangular stones, either smooth or rusticated, beneath Roman work, where they had to underpin the towers.

To the right of the Porte Narbonnaise, the first large tower is the mighty **Tour du Trésau**. Beyond it, the northern side of the inner wall is almost completely Roman, begun in the 1st century and rebuilt in the Imperial decline of the 4th century, like the walls of Rome itself, with the characteristic rounded bastions used all over the Empire. Near the second-last of them is a Roman postern gate. The walls to the left of the Porte Narbonnaise were almost completely rebuilt under Philip III, a long stretch of impressive bastions culminating in the great **Tour St-Nazaire**.

Atop both the inner and outer walls, almost everything you see today – the crenellations, wooden galleries (*hourds*) and pointed turrets that make up Carcassonne's memorable skyline – is the work of Viollet-le-Duc. As in all his other works, the pioneer of architectural restoration has been faulted for not adhering literally to original appearances. This is true, especially concerning the pointed turrets and northern slate roofs, but Viollet-le-Duc worked in a time before anyone could have imagined our own rigorous, antiseptic approach to re-creating the old. His romantic, 19th-century appreciation of the Middle Ages resulted in a restoration that was not only essentially correct, but creative and beautiful.

Château Comtal

Approaching the Cité from the western side, above the river, you pass the Gothic church of **St-Gimer**, ascending to the **Porte d'Aude**. In the old days, you couldn't come empty-handed; the Cité has no natural source of water and commoners from the Ville Basse had to bring up two buckets each time to get in. The Porte d'Aude was the ultimate discouragement for an attacker, employing every trick in the medieval bag. Note, for example, how the approach comes from the right; to protect themselves, soldiers on the way up would have to keep their shields in their right hand, making it difficult to do anything else. The winding path made it impossible to use a battering ram on the gate, and attackers would be under fire from the walls the entire way; there is another gate inside, and if anyone got through the first they would find themselves trapped in a box, under fire from all sides.

The defences are strongest on the western side because here the Cité's three lines of defence are closely compressed – the outer and inner walls and the citadel, the Château Comtal. Probably the site of the Roman governors' palace, the château was rebuilt by the Trencavels for their own palace, and expanded by King Louis IX. You have a choice of guided tours of the walls and towers, which begin with a room-sized model and continue, in fascinating, excruciating detail, through an advanced course in medieval military architecture. Louis' builders laid as many traps for invaders inside the walls as without – for example, the stairways where each riser is a different height. Be careful.

Château Comtal
t 04 68 11 70 70; open April–Sept 9.30–6.30; Oct–Mar 9.30–5; closed most public hols; adm; guided tours last 40 or 90 mins, usually on the hour, schedule posted at the entrance

Your ticket also includes the **Musée Lapidaire**, which fills much of the château. The collection includes ancient and medieval fragments: from Roman inscriptions and milestones to Merovingian sarcophagi and country roadside crosses (in local folklore, erroneously believed to be tombstones of the Cathars). Old prints and paintings give an idea of the half-ruined state of the Cité before Viollet-le-Duc went to work on it, with houses half-filling Les Lices and windmills along the walls. Two medieval works saved from the town's churches are especially worth a look: an unusual 15th-century English alabaster of the Transfiguration, and an excellent sculpted altarpiece, with a host of expressive faces in attendance.

Basilique St-Nazaire

In 1096 (the year after he declared the First Crusade), Pope Urban V visited here, giving his blessing to the beginning of the works. The building took shape as an austere, typically southern Romanesque cathedral, and stayed that way until 1270. The French conquerors had more ambitious plans and rebuilt the transepts and choir in glorious perpendicular Gothic. The best features can be seen from outside: two tremendous rose windows and a tall apse with acres of windows and gargoyles projecting like cannons, although these are now awaiting restoration.

Basilique St-Nazaire
open summer Mon–Sat 9–11.45 and 1.45–6, Sun 9–10.45 and 2–5; winter Mon–Sat 9–11.45 and 1.45–6, Sun 9–10.45 and 2–4.30

The windows illuminate the interior with beautiful 16th- and 17th-century stained glass depicting the Tree of Jesse and Life of Christ. In the right aisle, pay your respects to the devil himself at the **tomb of Simon de Montfort**, marked by a small plaque. Understandably, Montfort is no longer present; six years after his death, his descendants took him back up north, where he would be less in danger of desecration.

The Ville Basse

Before Saint Louis, the Cité was surrounded by long-established suburbs. In 1240 these were occupied by Raymond Trencavel, son of the last viscount. With the help of the townspeople, he besieged the Cité and nearly took it back. Louis pardoned the rebels, but did find it necessary to knock their houses down, to deprive any future attackers of cover. To replace the old *bourg*, he laid out a new town across the river, in the strict (and here, rather drab) grid pattern of a *bastide*. Don't confuse this with the *bastides*, or old farmhouses, in Provence and Languedoc; as you approach the former English possessions of Aquitaine, *bastide* takes on the meaning of a medieval new town, one of hundreds built by the French and English rulers during the Hundred Years' War; this Ville Basse (or Bastide Saint-Louis, as it's sometimes called, especially by the tourist office) has gradually replaced the Cité as the centre of modern Carcassonne.

Descending from the Cité through the Porte d'Aude, you'll pass some streets of houses that managed to creep back despite the royal decree. **Rue Trivalle**, with a pair of elegant Renaissance *hôtels particuliers*, leads down to the long, 14th-century **Pont Vieux**. At the far end, there once was a sort of triumphal arch, as can be seen in the old prints in the Château Comtal. Now there remains only the chapel of **Notre-Dame-de-la-Santé**, built in 1538.

The Ville Basse proper begins two streets further down, with a circle of boulevards that replaced the old walls. In 1355, during the Hundred Years' War, the walls failed to keep out the Black Prince, who burned the *bastide* to the ground after he was unable to take the Cité. Only the street plan survived and, at the north and south ends, two huge, mouldering Gothic churches: **St-Vincent** and **St-Michel**, both begun under Louis IX, both on Rue Dr Tomey. St-Michel was restored by Viollet-le-Duc and serves as co-cathedral with St-Nazaire in the Cité.

A *bastide* was always built around a central market square (here, **Place Carnot**), while one street over, off Rue de Verdun, you can see the handsome 18th-century **Halles aux Grains**.

Museums and Sights

You can learn all about the famous heretics at the **Centre for Cathar Studies** in the **Maison des Mémoires**, 53 Rue de Verdun, in the Ville Basse; this was the home of Carcassonne's contribution to Surrealism, Joë Bousquet, and there's a display about him, and another organization dedicated to the study of folk traditions in the Aude. At 1 Rue de Verdun, the 17th-century **Présidial** houses the **Musée des Beaux Arts**, with paintings and decorative arts from the 17th–19th centuries. Museums dedicated to all things medieval include the **Musée Mémoires du Moyen-Age**, just outside the Cité, near Porte Narbonnaise, with videos and models of the Cité, costumes, weapons and so on, and the **Musée de la Chevalerie**, in Rue Porte d'Aude, about knights and their arms. Rushing forward in history, there's the **Centre Culturel de la Mémoire Combattante**, a museum on French military exploits from 1870 on, outside the Cité at 102 Rue Trivalle, and the **Musée de l'Ecole**, on the history of French schools, in the Cité at 3 Rue du Plô.

Centre for Cathar Studies
t 04 68 72 45 55; open Tues–Sat 9–12 and 2–6

Musée des Beaux Arts
t 04 68 77 73 70; open mid-June–mid-Sept daily 10–6; mid-Sept–mid-June Tues–Sat 10–12 and 2–6, first Sun of month 2.30–5.30

Musée Mémoires du Moyen-Age
t 04 68 71 08 65; open all year except Xmas hols 10–7; adm

Musée de la Chevalerie
t 04 68 72 75 51; open Easter–early Nov Tues–Sun 10–7; closed Mon

Centre Culturel de la Mémoire Combattante
t 04 68 72 40 16; open Mon–Fri 9–12 and 2.30–5

Musée de l'Ecole
t 04 68 25 95 14; open summer daily 10–7; winter daily 10–6; closed Jan

Cité des Oiseaux
t 04 68 47 88 99, www. citedesoiseaux.com; open April–early Nov 2–6; phone or see website for show times; adm

Parc Australien
t 04 68 25 05 07; http:// leparcaustralien.free.fr; open July and Aug daily 10.45–7.30; April–June and mid-Sept–mid-Nov 2–7

Parc Acrobatique Forestier
t 06 07 96 04 55; open summer daily 1–6; winter Wed, Sat, Sun and hols 1–6; closed Dec–Feb

ⓘ **Carcassonne >**
Ville Basse: 28 Rue de Verdun, t 04 68 10 24 30, www.carcassonne-tourisme.com; open daily

Cité: Porte Narbonnaise, t 04 68 10 24 36; open daily

Between Easter and 1 November, you can watch an exhibition of falconry, the **Cité des Oiseaux**, at Colline Pech-Mary, 1km from the Cité, signposted off the road to Narbonne; it also now has some wolves and a mini-farm. Learn about animals, art and music from Down Under at the **Parc Australien**, Chemin des Bartavelles, on the way out to Lac de la Cavayère. And in the same direction, there's the **Parc Acrobatique Forestier** at the **Complexe de Loisirs Raymond Chésa**, where there's also a lake, pedalos, picnic area and mini-golf.

Market Days in Carcassonne

Tues, Thurs and Sat: Pl Carnot, flowers, fruit and veg, and Bd Barbès, clothes.

Where to Stay in Carcassonne

Carcassonne ✉ 11000

Stay in the Cité if you can, though it won't be cheap. Otherwise, the hotels are down in the Ville Basse, near the train station or around Bd Jean Jaurès. There are some real dives, but most are respectable enough. *Book early.*

Luxury (€€€€€)
****Hôtel de la Cité**, Place Auguste-Pierre Pont, t 04 68 71 98 71, *www.hoteldelacite.com*. In a pretty garden beside the walls of the Cité, this hotel occupies the former episcopal palace, grandly restored in 1909, with marble baths, a pool and three restaurants. You can now also rent a three-bedroom villa – for a price. *Closed end Nov–Dec and Feb.*

****Domaine d'Auriac**, Rte St-Hilaire, south of town, t 04 68 25 72 22, *www.domaine-d-auriac.com*. A luxury alternative to staying in the Cité is this Relais & Châteaux hotel, a stately, ivy-covered 18th-century mansion set in a large park. There's a pool, tennis court and even a golf course close by. Also an elegant and highly rated restaurant (€€€€), featuring mostly traditional dishes of the Aude, such as pigeon, served here with truffles. *Closed Jan; restaurant closed Mon lunch, Tues lunch, Wed lunch, plus Sun eve and Mon eve out of season.*

Very Expensive (€€€€)
***Terminus**, 2 Av Maréchal Joffre (lower town), t 04 68 25 25 00, *www.*

hotels-du-soleil.com. For a touch of class; the building has been used as a set in a number of French films. There is a gym and a pool, and a buffet-style restaurant. Try to get one of the rooms that have not been 'renovated'. *Closed Nov–Mar.*

Expensive (€€€)
***Hôtel du Donjon**, Rue du Comte Roger, t 04 68 11 23 00, *www.hotel-donjon.fr*. About as medieval as it gets, an atmospheric old mansion in the Cité filled with suits of armour, with a small garden and a fine restaurant.

Expensive–Moderate (€€€–€€)
***Château de Cavanac**, Cavanac, 4km south on the Rte St-Hilaire, t 04 68 79 61 04, *www.chateau-de-cavanac.fr*. A big old wine-maker's house in a quiet garden, with an excellent restaurant in the former stables which serves a unique four-course menu, starting with a peach kir. You can also taste and buy their wines. *Closed Jan–Feb and 2 weeks Nov; restaurant closed Sun eve and Mon.*

Moderate (€€)
***Trois Couronnes**, 2 Rue des Trois Couronnes, t 04 68 25 36 10, *www.hotel-destroiscouronnes.com*. Modern hotel by the river in the lower town; makes up for its unprepossessing appearance with a superb view of the Cité, an indoor pool on the 4th floor and a very good restaurant.

***Bristol**, 7 Av Foch, t 04 68 25 07 24. A grand 19th-century hotel near the station, with rooms overlooking the Canal du Midi. *Closed mid-Dec–mid-Jan; restaurant closed Sat lunch and Sun eve.*

Hôtel du Pont Vieux, 32 Rue Trivalle, t 04 68 25 24 99, *www.lacitedecarcassonne.fr*. One of the best and closest hotels to the Cité. No restaurant.

Inexpensive (€)

Au Royal Hôtel , 22 Bd Jean Jaurès (lower town), t 04 68 25 19 12. Not really very royal. *Closed Dec–early Jan.*

Hôtel Central, 27 Bd Jean Jaurès (lower town), t 04 68 25 03 84, *www. medievalhotellerie.com.* Cheap, but quite nice.

Astoria, 18 Rue Tourtel (lower town), t 04 68 25 31 38, *www.astoria carcassonne.com.* A friendly, family-run place, with comfy décor. *Closed Feb.*

Auberge de Jeunesse, Rue Raymond Trencavel, t 04 68 25 23 16. In the Cité; reserve in summer, or book online at *www.fuaj.org. Closed mid-Dec–Jan.*

Eating Out in Carcassonne

Château St-Martin, Montredon (take Bd Jean Jaurès to Rue A. Marty and follow the signs), t 04 68 71 09 53, *www.chateausaintmartin.net* (€€€). If you have a car, this is situated in a handsome *gentilhommière* with a huge terrace over a park, offering a choice of traditional dishes and fresh market cuisine; delicious seafood salad, *cassoulet* and langoustines. *Closed Wed, plus Sun eve in winter.*

Le Languedoc, Hôtel Montségur, 32 Allée d'Iéna (lower town), t 04 68 25 22 17, *www.hotelmontsegur.com* (€€€–€€). A popular restaurant with a patio, serving regional cuisine but particularly famed for its *cassoulet* with *confit de canard* and salad of *foie gras. Closed Sun eve and Mon out of season, and mid-Dec–mid-Jan.*

Brasserie Le Donjon, 4 Rue Porte d'Aude (Cité), t 04 68 25 95 72, *www. hotel-donjon.fr* (€€). The best of Languedoc cooking – here the humble *cassoulet* reaches new heights. *Closed Sun eve from Nov–Mar.*

Au Jardin de la Tour, 11 Rue Porte d'Aude (Cité), t 04 68 25 71 24 (€€). A pretty, idiosyncratic restaurant with garden dining and authentic regional dishes and fish. *Book.*

L'Escalier, 23 Bd Omer Sarraut (lower town), t 04 68 25 65 66 (€€). Something of an institution in Carcassonne, with Tex Mex, pizza and moussaka.

Dame Carcas, 3 Place du Château, t 04 68 71 23 23, *www.damecarcas.com* (€€). Delicious wood-fired cooking, with Provençal options like grilled piglet with honey sauce. *Closed Wed, and 2 weeks late Dec.*

Le St-Jean, Place St-Jean (Cité), t 04 68 47 42 43 (€€–€). A varied menu at this popular lunchtime restaurant serving *cassoulet*, meat and fish dishes. The *cassoulet* has hearty chunks of meat. *Closed Tues out of season, plus early Jan–mid-Feb.*

L'Œil, 32 Rue de Lorraine, t 04 68 25 64 81 (€). You can also find wood-fired food down in the Ville Basse. *Closed most of Aug, and Sun.*

In most of Carcassonne's *pâtisseries* you can satisfy your sweet tooth on the local favourite, *boulets de Carcassonne*, which are made with peanuts and honey. There's also an interesting local wine, Vins de Pays de la Cité de Carcassonne. Look out for the gold-medal-winning Heretic 2003, a light and lively red.

The Aude's Northwest Corner: The Lauragais

West of Carcassonne and the Montagne Noire lies a region called the Lauragais, an undulating expanse of serious farming of the humbler sort: beans, barley and pigs, and in some villages a substantial chicken-plucking trade. Windmills are a chief landmark, as is the shady, blue and nearly straight ribbon of the Canal du Midi en route to Toulouse. Rugby makes the juices flow in these parts, but in the old days it was religion: here stands St-Félix-de-Caraman (today 'de-Lauragais'), where the doctrines of Catharism were born.

Castelnaudary, Famous for Beans

To be authentic, a *cassoulet* requires four things: 'white beans from Lavelanet, cooked in the pure water of Castelnaudary, in a casserole made of clay from the Issel, over a fire of furze from the Black Mountain'. Every French book ever written on the area mentions this, so we felt obliged to pass it on. Having finally penetrated to deepest France, what you find is not always what you might expect. Here, the precious insight into the folk soul is a cherished mess of beans, lard, goose fat and miscellaneous pork parts. The clay pot of *cassoulet* in Castelnaudary's kitchen is the town's Eiffel Tower, its Acropolis, its very identity. Back in the 1570's, Castelnaudary's *cassoulet* was prescribed to Queen Margot as a cure for sterility, unfortunately without success.

With *cassoulet*, the charms of Castelnaudary are nearly exhausted. There is the 14th-century church of **St-Michel**, with a tall steeple dominating the city; the **Moulin de Cugarel**, a restored 17th-century windmill, one of over 30 that once spun in the vicinity, and the port and turning basin of the Canal du Midi. Next to the **Présidial** (now a school) you can visit the **local museum** in the old prison. You can also see an 18th-century **apothecary** with its original pots and utensils, at the hospital on Av Monseigneur de Langle.

Moulin de Cugarel
open July–mid-Aug; ask tourist office for times

Musée du Lauragais
t 04 68 23 00 42; open July–mid-Sept Tues–Sat 10–12.30 and 3–6.45, Sun 3–6.30; closed Mon; adm

Abbaye de St-Papoul
t 04 68 94 97 75, http:// saintpapoul.free.fr; guided tours July and Aug 10–6.30; April–June and Sept 10–11.30 and 2–5.30; Oct 10–11.30 and 2–4.30; Nov–Mar Sat, Sun and hols 10–11.30 and 2–4.30

The Medieval Lauragais

In the Middle Ages, **St-Papoul**, 8km east of Castelnaudary on the D103, was the centre of the Lauragais and the home of its bishop. An **abbey** has been here since the time of Charlemagne; in 1317 Pope John XXII turned the abbot into a bishop and the monks into canons – the better to keep an eye on local heretics. In decline for centuries, this forgotten town still has some of its walls and half-timbered houses, as well as a fine Romanesque **cathedral** – from the 14th century, a typically archaic building in a region that disdained the imported Gothic of the hated northerners. Though remodelled in trashy Baroque inside, the exterior has remained largely unchanged, including a beautiful apse with carved capitals attributed to the Master of Cabestany. Other good Romanesque churches with carvings are west of Castelnaudary at **Mas-Saintes-Puelles** and **Baraigne** (take the D33 and D218 from Castelnaudary), and at **Montmaur**, north of the D113 on the D58; the latter two preserve examples of small circular roadside crosses. In medieval times this region had hundreds of them; almost all have been destroyed or moved.

West of Castelnaudary, the Canal du Midi loses most of its tranquillity, as both the *Autoroute des Deux Mers* and the N113 move in to keep it company on the way to Toulouse. On the borders of the *département*, at **Port-Lauragais**, the canal passes its highest point. Figuring out how to cross it was Paul Riquet's biggest challenge; he solved it with an elaborate system of smaller canals and reservoirs, carrying water to the locks from as far as 30 miles away, in the Montagne Noire. Near Port-Lauragais there is a large obelisk in Riquet's honour (erected by his descendants in 1825, the year the canal turned in a profit!) and a small museum-cum-information centre about the canal, accessible from the *autoroute*.

South of Castelnaudary are more reminders of the Cathars and their oppressors. **Fanjeaux**, on the D119, began its career as Fanum Jovis, from an ancient temple of Jupiter; from that you can guess that the town, like almost all the sites dedicated to the god of thunder and storms, is on a commanding height, with a wide view over the Lauragais plains. Fanjeaux was a hotbed of Catharism and gained its fame in 1206, when St Dominic himself came from Spain to live here as a missionary to the heretics – quite peacefully and sincerely, though his Dominican followers would be the Church's chief inquisitors and torture-masters for centuries to come. They bequeathed Fanjeaux a 14th-century Gothic church, in the former Dominican monastery; a better work, the parish church of 1278, has a *trésor* full of unusual old reliquaries. St Dominic founded a monastery in nearby **Prouille**, after a vision in Fanjeaux, and it became a pilgrimage site. Unfortunately, it was wrecked in the Revolution and charmlessly rebuilt in the 19th century.

South of Fanjeaux, on the way to Limoux, the villages are often laid according to a circular or even elliptical plan: **Ferran**, **Brézilhac** and **La Digne**, among others. They are medieval new towns, or *bastides*; no one knows exactly why the medieval planners decided to depart from their accustomed strict rectangularity here, but there are clusters of them in Languedoc. They even have their own association, the **Association des Villages Circulaires**.

Association des Villages Circulaires
Mairie de Paulhan
✉ 34230, **t** 04 67 25 31 42, www.circulades.com

ℹ **Castelnaudary >**
Place de Verdun,
t 04 68 23 05 73, www.castelnaudary-tourisme.com; open Mon–Sat

Market Day in the Lauragais

Castelnaudary: Mon.

Where to Stay and Eat in the Lauragais

Castelnaudary ✉ 11400

Centre et Lauragais, 31 Cours République, **t 04 68 23 25 95, www.hotel-centre-lauragais.com (€€–€). A family-run hotel in the centre, with nice big rooms, a terrace and a restaurant (€€–€) serving *cassoulet*, of course. *Restaurant closed Sun eve.*

*Grand Hôtel Fourcade, 14 Rue des Carmes, **t** 04 68 23 02 08 (€). Family-run, remodelled but still nicely old-fashioned. Its restaurant (€€) is the best in town: gourmet *cassoulet* with goose *confits*, and the like. *Closed Sun eve and Mon out of season, and Jan.*

Around Castelnaudary

Auberge Le Cathare, Château de la Barthe, Belflou ✉ 11410, **t** 04 68 60 32 49, www.auberge-lecathare.com (€). West of Castelnaudary, on an artificial lake off the D217. Home cooking, peace, and nice if basic rooms. There is also a campsite with mobile homes for hire and chalets. *Closed Fri eve and Sat lunch in winter.*

Les Deux Acacias, Villepinte (11km southeast of Castelnaudary on N113), **t** 04 68 94 24 67, www.lesdeuxacacias.com (€). Another highly respected pot of beans is dished up here; they also have rooms (€€–€). *Closed Fri.*

Roussillon

Crossing the Agly river, bound for the southernmost angle of the French hexagon, you'll begin to notice a certain non-Gallic whimsy in the names of the towns. The further south you go, the stranger they become: Llivia, Llous and Llupia, Eus and Oms, Molitg, Politg and Py, Ur and Err. You'll also notice that some malcontents have decorated the yellow diamond 'priority road' signs with four red stripes, making them into little escutcheons of the long-ago Kingdom of Aragon. Street signs appear in two languages. On your restaurant table, impossibly sweet wines and peculiar desserts will appear, and you may begin to suspect that you are not entirely in France any more.

You are in fact among the Catalans, in the corner of Catalunya that, for military considerations in the 17th century, was destined to become part of France.

11

Don't miss

⭐ **An inspiration for artists**
Collioure p.236

⭐ **A fine cloister**
Elne cathedral p.235

⭐ **A delight of a modern art museum**
Céret p.264

⭐ **An unnerving** *Dévôt Christ*
Cathédrale St-Jean, Perpignan p.247

⭐ **The holy mountain of the Catalans**
Canigou p.251

See map overleaf

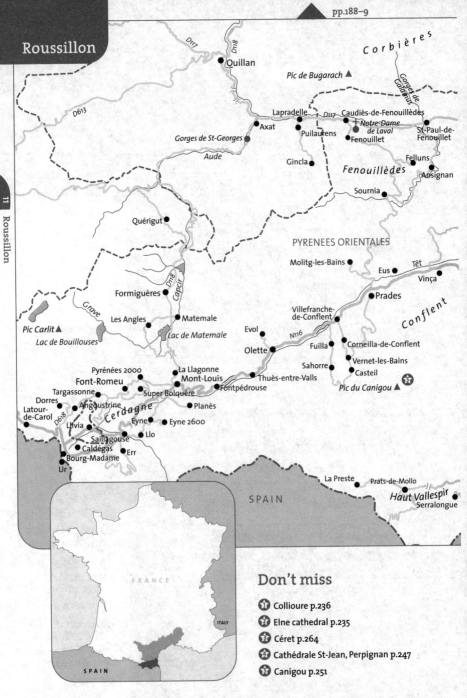

Roussillon

Corbières

Quillan

Pic de Bugarach ▲

D117

D118

Gorge de Galamus

D613

Lapradelle
Caudiès-de-Fenouillèdes
D117
Notre-Dame
de Laval
St-Paul-de-
Fenouillet
Axat
Puilaurens
Fenouillet
Gorges de St-Georges
Fenouillet
Felluns
Aude
Gincla
Fenouillèdes
Ansignan

Sournia

Quérigut

PYRENEES ORIENTALES

Molitg-les-Bains
Eus
Têt
Vinça

Formiguères
D118
Capcir
Prades

Pic Carlit ▲
Grave
Les Angles
Matemale
Villefranche-
de-Conflent
Conflent

Lac de Bouillouses
Lac de Matemale
Evol
N116
Fuilla
Corneilla-de-Conflent
Olette
Vernet-les-Bains
Pyrénées 2000
La Llagonne
Sahorre
Casteil
Font-Romeu
Mont-Louis
Thuès-entre-Valls
Pic du Canigou ▲
Targassonne
Super Bolquère
Fontpédrouse
Dorres
Planès
Latour-
de-Carol
Angoustrine
Cerdagne
D618
Llívia
Eyne
Eyne 2600
Saillagouse
Llo
Caldégas
Err
Bourg-Madame
Ur

La Preste
Prats-de-Mollo
SPAIN
Haut Vallespir
Serralongue

FRANCE

ITALY

SPAIN

Don't miss

Like the other captive nations of the Hexagon – the Bretons and
Corsicans, for example – most of Roussillon's people have rationally
decided that being French isn't such a terrible fate after all. Catalan

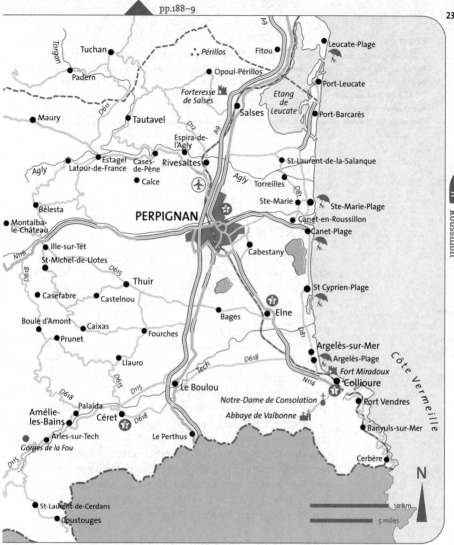

is spoken by relatively few (though numbers are growing), but this culturally passionate people stays in close touch with the rest of Catalunya, over in Spain, and in the squares of many villages they still perform a weekly *sardana*, the national dance and symbol of Catalan solidarity.

Perpignan is the capital; around it stretches the broad Roussillon plain, crowded with the dusty, introverted villages that make all that sweet wine. The real attractions are on the periphery: Collioure and the delectable Côte Vermeille on one side and, on the other, valleys that climb up into the Pyrenees. The scenery is tremendous, even an hour's drive from the coast; among the pine forests and glacial lakes you can visit Vauban fortresses, ride the

Beaches

The sand continues into Roussillon, to beaches favoured by beach bum Pablo Picasso. From Port-Barcarès southwards, beach follows beach, some less accessible than others (these tend to be haunted by overweight nudists). Picasso's favourite was Collioure, with its three small stretches of sand.

The **best beaches** are:

South of Port-Barcarès: empty miles of sand.

Collioure: for the bell-tower and because Picasso can't be wrong, but be prepared to share the space.

famous Little Yellow Train (*see* p.252), and get an introduction to the surprising architectural and sculptural monuments of Catalunya's brilliant Middle Ages.

The Roussillon Coast

A geographical oddity, this run of coastline is almost perfectly straight and runs due north–south for 40km from Port-Barcarès to Argelès. It isn't the most compelling landscape, but it is almost solid beach, and has been much developed since the 1940s.

Port-Barcarès and Around

South of Port-la-Nouvelle, the hill of **Cap Leucate** anchors the northern end of this coast, with government-planned resorts at **Leucate-Plage** and Port-Leucate. These initiate perhaps the most animated but least attractive of Languedoc's resorts, beginning with Port-Leucate and continuing for 8km down to **Port-Barcarès**. You might like it; there's mini-golf, shopping centres, thalasso-therapy, horse-riding, model aeroplanes, folkloric spectacles, windsurfing and other activities. **Port-Leucate** is mostly holiday bungalows, built around man-made canals so that everyone can park their boat at the front door. Further south, the beaches are less cluttered but harder to reach; back roads lead off the D81 to **Torreilles-Plage** and **Ste-Marie-Plage**.

Forteresse de Salses and Around

The alternative to traversing this inferno means a voyage through the back end of the lagoon, the **Etang de Salses** (also called the **Etang de Leucate**). The divorce of land and sea here is startlingly complete. Until the last few decades, the malarial coast was utterly deserted and no one in the region gave it a second thought; from the landward side of the lagoon, in a few minutes you can be up in the rugged, dusty hills of the Corbières and Opoul (*see* previous chapter), where it is hard to believe any sea could be within a hundred miles. The only village on this side of the lagoon is **Fitou**, justifiably famous for one of the finest wines of Languedoc-Roussillon (though most Fitou wine comes from a nearby area of the Corbières).

Getting around the Roussillon Coast

By Train

The coastal railway from Narbonne to Spain passes through Leucate, Salses and Rivesaltes, dipping inland for Perpignan before returning to the coast. There are frequent services from Narbonne and Perpignan to Elne, and then Collioure and Cerbère.

By Bus

There are buses from the station in Perpignan to resorts where the train doesn't go, such as Canet and Port-Barcarès, as well as frequent services to Collioure and the Côte Vermeille. There are buses between Barcarès and nearby beaches; call the tourist office at Barcarès, t 04 68 86 16 56.

Forteresse de Salses
t 04 68 38 60 13; open June–Sept 9.30–7; Oct–May 10–12.15 and 2–5; adm

After another 7km of total emptiness appears the last, lowest and least spectacular of all this region's many castles – but the **Forteresse de Salses** was the most important of them all. Built in 1497 by Ferdinand the Catholic, first king of united Spain, Salses was the last word in castles for its time, the masterpiece of a great military architect named Ramiro Lopez. Set squarely on the then French–Spanish border, Salses was meant to guard Perpignan and the coastal road. It did not have a chance to do so until 1639, and sadly then it was not up to the task. The Spaniards, caught by surprise, had only a small garrison at Salses; nevertheless, it required 18,000 Frenchmen and a month's siege to take it. The same year, a Spanish army spent three months winning it back. Both sieges were serious operations; the locals still go out cannonball-hunting for fun in the surrounding hills. When France acquired Roussillon in 1659, Salses no longer had a role to play.

At first glance, Salses looks strikingly streamlined and modern. It is a product of a transitional age, when defenders were coming to terms with the powerful new artillery that had made medieval castles obsolete. Salses is all curves and slopes, designed to deflect the cannonballs; its walls are not only incredibly thick (28ft on average, 50ft thick at the base), but also covered with heavy stone barrel vaulting to protect the walkway at the top. Renovation plans include a restaurant and artists' workshops by 2009.

Musée du Maréchal Joffre
t 04 68 38 59 59; open mid-June–mid-Sept Tues–Sat 9.30–12.30 and 3–7; adm

The region around Salses and **Rivesaltes**, to the south, is famous for its inexpensive sweet wines, sold throughout France (*see* box, overleaf). Rivesaltes was the home of Marshal Joffre, and now houses the small **Musée du Maréchal Joffre**, dedicated to the Battle of the Marne. In nearby **Espira-de-l'Agly** stands the impressive fortified Romanesque church of **Ste-Marie**, built in 1136 as part of a monastery by the bishops of Urgel in Spain (powerful Catalan clerics whose successors, along with the presidents of France, are still the joint tributary lords of Andorra). The business-like exterior has one fine carved portal, but the lavish interior still comes as a surprise, with polychromed marbles and elaborate altarpieces from the 16th century.

Wine: Rivesaltes and Côtes du Roussillon

Catalans have a notoriously sweet tooth, and some 90 per cent of the dessert wine (*vin doux naturel*) of France comes from this *département*, spilling over into the Corbières to the north. Mostly from grenache, muscat or maccabeu grapes, these wines are made simply by stopping the fermentation at the right moment, leaving more sugar in the wine; usually a small amount of pure alcohol is added at the same time. Since the 13th century, Rivesaltes (*www.rivesaltes.com*) has been known for its fruity muscat, a wine to be drunk young, with sorbets or lemon tarts. Its AOC status, awarded in 1972 along with other Rivesaltes red and white *apéritif* wines, covers 99 *communes* in the eastern Pyrenees. Try some in Rivesaltes itself, at the **Domaine Cazes**, 4 Rue Francisco-Ferrer, t 04 68 64 08 26, *www.cazes-rivesaltes. com*; the talented brothers Bernard and André Cazes not only produce some of the finest muscat but also AOC Côtes du Roussillon and Côtes du Roussillon Village, plus some excellent white, rosé and red *vin de pays*. In the past, few wine writers ever had anything good to say about this old *vin de pays* but, as in Languedoc, a number of producers like the Cazes brothers have been creating notable, individualistic wines from fine blends of syrah, carignan, grenache and mourvèdre.

Côtes du Roussillon is made all over the *département*, often in village co-operatives that also produce Rivesaltes or sweet muscat, but there are a few good estates to visit. In the hot corner around Perpignan, **Domaine Sarda-Malet**, Chemin de Ste-Barbe, t 04 68 56 72 38, *www.sarda-malet.com*, puts out three labels of red, two whites, a rosé, several *vins de table* and four dessert wines. Or visit the **Château de Jau** on the D117 in Cases-de-Pène, t 04 68 38 91 38, which produces Côtes du Roussillon of surprisingly high quality. In summer they also host art exhibitions and have a restaurant that offers good value fixed-price-menu lunches (*June–Sept only*) featuring local specialities and a wide range of wines. Some of the finest red and white wines can be found at **Domaine Gauby** in Calce, t 04 68 64 35 19: wines of rare concentration and full of local character. The **Cellier des Albère** at St-Genis-des-Fontaines, t 04 68 89 81 12, produces a honey-sweet, fresh, lively rosé, Château Montesque des Albères.

Canet-en-Roussillon to Argelès

Back on the coast, **Canet-en-Roussillon** has long been the favourite resort of the Perpignanais. After taking a beating in the last war, it has been rebuilt without much distinction. There is an

Aquarium
t 04 68 80 49 64; open July and Aug daily 10–8; Sept–June Tues–Sun 10–12 and 2–6; closed mornings Christmas–New Year; adm

Aquarium by the port, where the star attraction is that impossibly unlovely living fossil from the depths of the Indian Ocean, the coelacanth. You can also jet-ski, dive and do other water-based activities; see *http://aquatile.free.fr*, and the tourist office organizes tours of the medieval **castle** in summer.

South, past a long stretch of wild beach, good for windsurfing and kite-flying, you'll find **St-Cyprien-Plage**, which looks just like Canet only more so, with fancier restaurants, an attractive 27-hole golf course with a backdrop of Pyrenean peaks, tennis courts and a

Centre d'Art Contemporain
t 04 68 21 32 07; open July–mid-Sept daily 10–12 and 3–7; mid-Sept–June Wed–Mon 10–12 and 2–6, closed Tues; adm

summer chamber music festival. It has two museums of its own, set back in **St-Cyprien** proper, 3km from the beach: the Centre d'Art Contemporain in Rue J. Romains, dedicated to Catalan artists such as Maillol, Delfau and Bonel; and the Musée François Desnoyer in

Musée François Desnoyer
t 04 68 21 06 96; open same hours as art museum

Rue Emile Zola, with a small collection of lesser works by Picasso, Dufy, Chagall, Miró and especially François Desnoyer, who spent time here; plus an exhibition of primitive art such as African masks.

South of St-Cyprien, **Argelès**, the largest of the French Catalan resorts with 7km of sand and 3km of rocky shoreline, makes some claim as the European Capital of Camping, with 56 sites and a capacity for 100,000 happy campers. Divided in two parts, the old town of **Argelès-sur-Mer** and the modern beach strip of **Argelès-Plage** with its wide promenade popular with dog-walkers, this has become the second biggest resort in the region and one of the blandest, with nothing of particular interest. Four km inland, **St-André** has a lofty 12th-century church and, opposite it, the small **Maison Transfrontalier de l'Art Roman**, with sculpture from this and other Romanesque churches in the area.

**Maison
Transfrontalier de
l'Art Roman**
*t 04 68 89 04 85;
open summer Tues–Sat
10–12 and 2.30–7; spring
and autumn Tues–Sat
10–12 and 3–6; closed
Sun and Mon, and mid-
Nov–mid-Mar; adm*

Elne and its Cloister

Between these last two resorts, set a little way inland atop a steep hill, the citadel of Elne has guarded the Roussillon plain for at least 2,700 years. Its ancient name, Illiberis, is said to come from the Iberians. Hannibal sojourned here on his way to Italy, waiting to negotiate an alliance with the Celts to guard his rear; the locals, apparently unimpressed even with the elephants, made him pay a toll to pass through. The name-change came in the time of Constantine, to Castrum Helenae, after the emperor's mother, St Helen, legendary discoverer of the True Cross. Through the Middle Ages, and until the 16th century, Elne remained the most important city in Roussillon and seat of the archbishops. The town is now reduced to some 6,000 souls (and 70,000 tourists a year), having lost all its honours and status to Perpignan.

But they couldn't take away its **cathedral**, a fortified church begun in 1069; it has a wonderful stage presence, with its crenellated roof-line and stout, arcaded tower. Inside, in a chapel on the right, is an Italianate 14th-century altarpiece of St Michael and there are some fine tombs, especially that of Ramon de Costa (1310). The **cloister** is perhaps the best in the Midi, and also the best preserved. Capitals and pillars are decorated with imaginative, exquisitely carved arabesques and floral patterns. The four sides were completed in different periods, at roughly 50-year intervals; that closest to the cathedral is the earliest, from the 12th century, and its capitals show the influence of the sculptors of St-Michel-de-Cuxa (*see* p.254). Oddly, each generation of sculptors chose to repeat the subjects of their predecessors: all but the north gallery have central pillars carved with serpentine dragons and mermaids spreading their forked tails; other capitals repeat scenes from the Old Testament. The little **history museum** tells the history of the cathedral and cloister, including its lost upper gallery, dismantled in 1827 and sold off at an auction in 1960. There is also a **museum of archaeology** in the cloister, with finds from the area dating from Neolithic times to the Middle Ages.

Admission to the cloister includes the chance to climb the steps up to the terrace which dominates the cloister, and admission to the **Musée Terrus** across the square; the painter Terrus was a friend of Matisse and Derain and the museum contains mainly his works.

**Cathedral
cloister**
*t 04 68 22 70 90; open
daily except during
services June–Sept
9.30–6.45; April–May
9.30–5.45; Oct
9.30–12.15 and 2–5.45;
Nov–Mar 9.30–11.45
and 2–4.45; adm*

Musée Terrus
*t 04 68 22 88 88; open
same hours as cloister*

(i) **Port-Barcarès**
Pl. de la République,
t 04 68 86 16 56, www.
portbarcares.com;
open daily

(i) **Elne** >>
Place Sant Jordi, t 04
68 22 05 07, www.ot-
elne.fr; open July and
Aug daily; June and Sept
Mon–Fri and Sat pm;
Oct–May Mon–Fri

(i) **St-Cyprien** >
Quai Arthur Rimbaud,
t 04 68 21 01 33,
www.saint-cyprien.
com; open daily

Where to Stay and Eat on the Northern Roussillon Coast

St-Cyprien ✉ 66750

Two of the area's class resort hotels are here.

****L'Ile de la Lagune**, Bd de l'Almandin, **t** 04 68 21 01 02, *www. hotel-ile-lagune.com* (€€€€). Air-conditioned rooms, tennis and a swimming pool, all set on its own little island, L'Ile de la Lagune. The restaurant (€€€€–€€€) is considered one of the best on the coast, with stylish treatment of Catalan dishes, such as *blinis aux anchois de Collioure à la tapenade et caviar d'aubergine. Restaurant closed Mon and Tues in Oct–mid-April.*

***Le Mas d'Huston**, **t** 04 68 37 63 63, *www.golf-st-cyprien.com* (€€€€). By

the golf course and an easy walk to the beach, with a pool, restaurant and cheaper brasserie. A modern, relaxing place. *Restaurant closed lunch; brasserie closed eves.*

Elne ✉ 66201

****Hôtel Cara Sol**, 10 Bd Illibéris, **t** 04 68 22 10 42, *www.hotel-carasol.com* (€€). Hotel with eight rooms set in the old ramparts of the town. Bedrooms have views across the Roussillon plain to the mountains. The British owner caters to homesick palates, offering apple crumble in the restaurant (€€), as well as Mediterranean dishes. There's a terrace for eating out..

Argelès-sur-Mer ✉ 66700

*****Auberge du Roua**, Chemin du Roua, **t** 04 68 95 85 85, *www.auberge duroua.com* (€€€–€€). A little Catalan *auberge* with a terrace restaurant (€€€). *Closed mid-Nov–Feb.*

The Côte Vermeille

For anyone with the determination to follow France's long Mediterranean coast all the way to the end, there is a lovely surprise. After Argelès, the shoreline changes dramatically, climbing into the Pyrenees and a delicious southern world of crystalline rock, olive trees and uncanny sunlight, a 30km prelude to Spain's Costa Brava. Forgive yourself for cynically thinking that the name 'Vermilion Coast' might have been cooked up by tourist promoters – of course it was, just like the 'Côte d'Azur', 'Costa Smeralda' and all the rest. The red clay soil of the ubiquitous olive groves does lend the area a vermilion tint, but as far as colours go that is only the beginning.

Every point or bend in the Mediterranean coast is a sort of meteorological vortex, given to strange behaviour: the Fata Morgana at the southern tip of Italy, the winds of the Mani in the Peloponnese or the glowing, subdued light of Venice. The Côte Vermeille gets a strong dose of the *tramontane* wind, but also a remarkable mix of light and air, inciting the coast's naturally strong colours into an unreasonably heady and sensual Mediterranean spectrum. Henri Matisse spent one summer here, at Collioure, and the result was a milestone in the artistic revolution known as Fauvism.

Collioure

⭐ **Collioure**

If the tourists would only leave it in peace, Collioure would be quite happy to make its living in the old way, filling up barrels with anchovies. As it is, the town bears their presence as gracefully as possible, though in summer there's a throng and parking is nigh on impossible (try the station car park). In a way, Collioure *is* unspoiled – if it has 17 hotels for its 2,700 inhabitants, it does not have a casino, a miniature golf course or a water slide, or all the hype projected on St-Tropez, that other unaffectedly beautiful resort discovered at the beginning of the 20th century by the Fauves. Instead, you'll find every other requisite for a civilized Mediterranean resort: a castle, a pretty church by the sea, three small beaches, a shady market square with cafés – and warehouses full of anchovies. Its narrow streets are lined with boutiques and tall, shuttered houses painted in pink, green, blue and yellow.

It's hard to believe, looking at the map, but in the Middle Ages this village was the port for Perpignan; with no good harbours on the dismal and (then) unhealthy coast to the north, Perpignan's fabrics and other goods had to come to the Pyrenees to go to sea. In the 14th century, Collioure was one of the biggest trading centres of Aragon, but nearly the whole town was demolished by the French after they took possession in 1659. They weren't angry with the Colliourencs; the town was merely in the way of modernizing its castle's fortifications. Our own century has no monopoly on twisted military logic: Collioure had to be razed in order that it could be better defended.

The population moved into the part that survived, the steep hillside quarter called the Mouré, where they have made the best of it ever since. Collioure was discovered in 1905 by Matisse and Derain. Many other artists followed, including Picasso, but these two were the most inspired by the place, and they put a little of Collioure's vermilion tint into the deep colours of their first Fauvist experiments. Fourteen sketches by Matisse are in Céret 30km away, but his best works are in private collections, or in the Hermitage in St Petersburg. There is none in Collioure. To rectify the lack, the village has created the *Chemin du Fauvisme,* placing copies of Matisse and Derain's works on the spots where the two set up their easels. The **Espace Fauve** is on Quai de l'Amirauté; there is also the **Musée d'Art Moderne,** in a peaceful villa on the south edge of town with a terraced olive grove, which has works by lesser-known artists in the style of the Fauves, as well as an intriguing collection of Moorish ceramics and a programme of temporary exhibitions sometimes including Matisse works.

Collioure (or as the locals call it, Cotllures) is a thoroughly Catalan town, and the red and yellow striped Catalan flag waves proudly over the **Château Royal,** which dominates the harbour. With its outworks it is nearly as big as the town itself. First built by the Templars in the 13th century, it was expanded by various Aragonese kings. The outer fortifications, low walls and broad banks of earth,

Espace Fauve
t 04 68 98 07 16; open June–Sept daily 9.30–12.30 and 3–7; Oct–May Tues–Fri 10–12 and 3–6, Sat and Sun 3–6

Musée d'Art Moderne
t 04 68 82 10 19; open July and Aug Wed–Mon 10–12 and 2–7; Sept–June Wed–Mon 10–12 and 2–6; closed Tues; adm

Château Royal
t 04 68 82 06 43; open June–Sept daily 10–5.15; Oct–May daily 9–4.15; adm

were state-of-the-art in 1669. The great Vauban, Louis XIV's military genius, oversaw the works and the demolition of the old town. Collioure's fate could have been even worse; Vauban had wanted to level it completely and force everyone to move to Port-Vendres. The older parts of the castle have been restored and are open for visits, along with several small exhibitions on local specialities from whip-making to espadrilles. From the castle, cross the small stream called the Douy (usually dry and used as a car park) into the **Mouré**, the old quarter that is now the centre of Collioure. There is an amiable shorefront, with a small beach from which a few anchovy fishermen still ply their trade; several brightly painted fishing smacks are usually pulled up to complete the effect.

At the far end you'll see Collioure's landmark, painted by Matisse and many others: the church of **Notre-Dame-des-Anges**. The Colliourencs built it in the 1680s to succeed the original church destroyed by Vauban; they chose the beach site to use the old cylindrical lighthouse as a bell-tower. The best thing about the church is that you can hear the waves of the sea from inside, a profound *basso continuo* that makes the celebration of mass here a unique experience. The next best are the retables, five of them, done between 1699 and 1720 by Joseph Sunyer and others. Catalan Baroque at its eccentric best, influenced by the Spanish *churrigueresque*, often concentrated its finest efforts on these towering constructions of carved wooden figures, dioramas of scriptural scenes with intricately painted stage-drop backgrounds. Sunyer's are especially lifelike.

The second of Collioure's beaches lies right behind the church; really an old sand bar that has become part of dry land, it connects the town with a former islet, the **Ilôt St-Vincent**, crowned with a tiny medieval chapel. A scenic footpath called the Sentier de la Moulade leads from near the church along the rocky shore north of Collioure. High above, you'll see **Fort Miradoux**, the Spanish King Philip II's addition to Collioure's defences, and still in military use.

If you want to see how local anchovies are prepared, visit the Roque family anchovy business at 17 Route d'Argelès. There's also a shop. Few of us, probably, give any thought to how anchovies are apprehended in the open sea. It isn't, in fact, a terribly difficult operation. The diabolical Catalans have boats called *lámparos*, with big searchlights. They sneak out on warm summer nights, when the normally shy anchovies are making their promenade, and nab the lot. After spending a few months in barrels of brine, the unfortunate fish reappear, only to be stuffed into olives.

Notre-Dame-des-Anges
open daily 9–12 and 2–6

Roque anchovy business
t 04 68 82 04 99; call first

Port-Vendres and Banyuls-sur-Mer

More of this doubtful anchovy business goes on in **Port-Vendres**. This is a real port, modern-style, with none of the charm of

Collioure. Louis XVI's government had big plans for developing Port-Vendres, all of which were scuppered with the Revolution; some grandiose neoclassical buildings remain from this programme, around the central **Place de l'Obélisque**, along with a 98ft obelisk decorated with propaganda reliefs celebrating poor Louis' glorious reign. Short boat trips leave from Quai Forgas.

From here, the coast juts out east, with a picturesque little promontory called **Cap Béar**, topped by another of this area's many Baroque-era fortresses. Its monument to Sidi-Ferruch was originally erected in Algiers in 1930 to celebrate the centenary of French colonization; after 1962, when the Algerians didn't want the thing any more, it was set up here. There are many isolated **beaches** in the vicinity, though they are hard to reach; most are south of the cape, including the one at **Paulilles**, near an abandoned dynamite factory (a mildly historic one, because it belonged to Alfred Nobel, inventor of dynamite and plywood, who used the profits to finance his prizes).

Banyuls-sur-Mer (Banyuls de la Marenda in Catalan) is the next town along the picturesque coastal N114, a sleepy resort out of season, with a beach and mini-golf right at the centre. The heart of the Banyuls wine region, it is also the home of the **Fondation Arago**, an oceanographic laboratory affiliated to the University of Paris. Their excellent **Aquarium of Mediterranean Species** was built in 1883; don't miss the granddaddy lobster and sea anemones and 250 kinds of birds. The coast between Banyuls and Cerebère forms a 650ha **Marine Reserve**, the oldest in France. You can visit some parts of it through organized **driving trips**.

As for art, Banyuls has a good 11th-century Romanesque church, **La Rectorie** in Av du Puig-del-Mas, and takes credit for Aristide Maillol, perhaps the best-known French sculptor of the last century after Rodin, born here in 1861. He contributed the town's War Memorial, on the waterfront promontory, as well as many other monuments along the Côte Vermeille and in Perpignan; his tomb, documents tracing his life and a few copies of works are in his old farmhouse, La Métairie, now the **Musée Aristide Maillol**, 4km up the Col de Banyuls road.

If you don't care to go to Cerbère, or to Spain, there is an alternative to retracing your steps along the coast – an extremely scenic route through the mountains back to Collioure, along the steep and narrow D86. It begins from the back of Banyuls, beyond the railway overpass, and climbs through ancient olive groves on the lower slopes of the **Monts-Albères**. Several abandoned fortresses come into view, though none is especially easy to reach. This border region rivals even the Corbières for quantity of castles. There is also a ruined monastery, the **Abbaye de Valbonne**, on the heights to the west; the track to it begins at the pilgrimage chapel

Aquarium of Mediterranean Species
t 04 68 88 73 39; open July and Aug daily 9–1 and 2–9; Sept–June daily 9–12 and 2–6.30; adm

Driving trips
t 04 68 88 09 11

La Rectorie
open Sat 10.30–12 and 2–6, Sun 3–6; guided visits arranged by tourist office

Musée Aristide Maillol
t 04 68 88 57 11; open daily 10–12 and 2–5; adm

Wine: Banyuls

A naturally sweet, spicy wine (AOC since 1936), fortified with a dollop of *eau de vie* prior to being aged for 3 to 15 years, Banyuls was first made by the Templars in the 11th century, from the dark grenache grapes grown on the rocky red terraces of the Côte Vermeille. A fine old Banyuls is claimed to be the only wine that can accompany chocolate desserts, but be warned: a cheap young bottle may hardly do justice to a Mars bar.

Collioure, Port-Vendres, Cerbère and Banyuls are the only places allowed to wear the AOC label, and 80 per cent of their wine, as well as the delightful dry red wines of Collioure, pass through the **Grande Cave du Cellier des Templiers** co-operative, Route de Mas-Reig, **t** 04 68 98 36 92 (*open April–Oct daily 10–7.30; Nov–Mar tastings Mon–Sat 10–1 and 2.30–6.30, visits Mon–Fri 2.30–6*), a large concern happy to receive visitors for tastings and a tour at their magnificently vaulted 13th-century *grande cave*; their *cave souterraine* just below has enormous hundred-year-old oak barrels, and a film on the wine. If you have a car you can organize 2hr tours by appt, and there is a tourist train that leaves from Collioure every 2hrs in July and Aug to trundle round the vineyards.

The **Cave de l'Etoile**, 26 Av du Puig-del-Mas in Banyuls, **t** 04 68 88 00 10, is a co-operative where everything is done lovingly in the old-fashioned way; up the same street, one can visit the excellent **Domaine de la Rectorie**, **t** 04 68 88 13 45, *www.la-rectorie.com*.

A good selection of Collioure wine can be found at **Domaine du Mas Blanc**, 9 Av Général de Gaulle, **t** 04 68 88 32 12, *www.domainedumasblanc.com* (*open by appt only out of season*) and in Collioure at **Cellier des Dominicains**, Place Orphila, **t** 04 68 82 05 63, *www.dominicain.com*. If you wish to try the local wines with local food in a delightful setting, book dinner (*May–Sept only*) at the *ferme-auberge* Les Clos de Paulilles at the **Domaine de Valcros**, Port-Vendres, **t** 04 68 82 04 27, *www.domainedevalcros. com* – different wines accompany each course.

of **Notre-Dame-de-Consolation**. A little before this, the **Tour Madeloc** is the climax of the trip; it was a signal tower, part of the sophisticated communications network that kept the medieval kings of Aragon in close contact with their borders.

Cerbère and Beyond

You may well have already been here, but Cerbère won't bring back any pleasant memories – being herded from one train to another in the middle of the night (because Spanish railways still use a different track gauge) under the gaze of soldiers with sub-machine-guns and impossible customs men who do their best to make this seem like an old Hitchcock spy film instead of one of the busiest, most unexciting border rail-crossings in the EU. No one has ever seen Cerbère in daylight, but you might give it a try. The coast here is at its most spectacular (it's especially good for diving) and there are a few pebble beaches, never crowded. With its handful of hotels, Cerbère is a minuscule resort, with a World's End air about it – an impression reinforced by its solar lighthouse.

There is a lot to be said for pressing on even further, into Unoccupied Catalunya (the signs at the border still say 'Spain' for courtesy's sake). **Barcelona**, one of the most vibrant and creative cities in Europe today, is only two hours by train from Cerbère. **Girona**, with its exquisite medieval centre and unique cathedral, is half the distance. If you liked the Côte Vermeille, continue south for more of the same on the **Costa Brava**, often overcrowded though still nice (especially the northern parts). And if you can manage only one unambitious day trip into Spain, try **Figueras**, a short hop by train or a pleasant 50km drive along the C252; the Salvador Dalí Museum here, in the artist's home town, is an unforgettable attraction, the 'temple of Surrealism', where you can water the plants in the garden by feeding coins into a Cadillac.

Market Days on the Côte Vermeille

Collioure: Wed, and Sun am.
Port-Vendres: Sat am.
Banyuls: Thurs and Sun am.

Where to Stay and Eat on the Côte Vermeille

Collioure ✉ 66190

***La Casa Païral**, Impasse des Palmiers, **t** 04 68 82 05 81, www.hotel-casa-pairal.com (€€€). A good place for an agreeable stay in the centre; a dignified, mansard-roofed palace a few streets from the shore. There is a wide choice of rooms, from the simple to the luxurious; also a pool and enclosed garden. No restaurant. Closed Nov–Mar.

Hostellerie des Templiers, Quai de l'Amirauté, **t** 04 68 98 31 10, www.hotel-templiers.com (€€€–€€). Picasso, Matisse, Dufy and Dalí all stayed here, and owner René Pous was friend to them all. Original works cover the walls of this unique hotel, although the Picassos have been locked away since several were stolen by a 'guest' a few years ago. Each room has its own charm; reservations are imperative. The bar is a friendly local hang-out, and the restaurant (€€) is excellent, with a people-watching terrace and imaginative, good-value dishes like paella or their own bouillabaisse. Closed Dec and Jan; restaurant closed Mon–Fri in Feb and Mar.

La Frégate, Av Camille Pelletan, **t** 04 68 82 06 05, www.hotel-lafregate.com (€€). This pink and jolly place is on the busiest corner of Collioure, but has been soundproofed and air-conditioned; it has a good restaurant (€€€–€€), mostly serving seafood. Closed Dec–Jan.

Boramar, 19 Rue Jean Bart, on the Plage du Faubourg, **t** 04 68 82 07 06 (€€–€). A simple hotel overlooking the busiest beach. Closed Dec–Mar.

Ermitage, Notre-Dame-de-Consolation, above Collioure on the D86, **t** 04 68 82 17 66 (€). A pleasant B&B. Closed in winter; call to confirm months.

Dinner in Collioure need not necessarily include anchovies, but the rest of the catch merits attention.

Le Neptune, 9 Rte Port-Vendres, **t** 04 68 82 02 27 (€€€€–€€€). One of the best restaurants in town, with wonderful canopied sea views and the full nouvelle Catalan cuisine; menus change seasonally but you might be offered salade chemin des Fauves, which combines eggs, artichokes, tapenade and tomato confit in highly decorative style, or lobster ravioli with cardamom vinaigrette; desserts are delicious. Closed 2 weeks Dec, Jan and Feb, plus Mon and Wed out of season and Tues lunch and Mon in June–Sept.

La Marinade, 14 Place 18 Juin, **t** 04 68 82 09 76 (€€€–€€). Delectable seafood from simple sardines en papillote to an elaborate Catalan bouillabaisse. Closed Dec–Jan.

Le Trémail, 16 bis Rue Mailly, **t** 04 68 82 16 10 (€€). A small seafood restaurant just off the front, with a good reputation. Catalan specialities.

Le Copacabana, Plage du Boramar, **t** 04 68 82 06 74, www.restaurant-copacabana.com (€€). A tourist option, admittedly, but with good views of the château and bell-tower from the terrace. Closed mid-Jan–mid-Mar.

Banyuls-sur-Mer ✉ 66650

Banyuls lacks Collioure's glamour, but also its high prices.

Les Elmes, Plage des Elmes, **t** 04 68 88 03 12, www.hotel-des-elmes.com (€€€–€€). Pleasant seaside rooms and an excellent restaurant, **La Littorine**

Port-Vendres — Quai François Joly, **t** 04 68 82 07 54, www.port-vendres.com; open daily

Collioure — Place du 18 Juin, **t** 04 68 82 15 47, www.collioure.com; open July and Aug daily; April–June and Sept Mon–Sat; Oct–Mar Tues–Sat

⭐ **Le Neptune** ≫

⭐ **Hostellerie des Templiers** ›

Banyuls-sur-Mer ≫ — Av de la République, **t** 04 68 88 31 58, www.banyuls-sur-mer.com; open July–Aug daily; Sept–June Mon–Sat

(€€€), serving Catalan dishes; half-board is excellent value. There's also a hammam and training pool.

El Llagut, 18 Av du Fontaulé, t 04 68 88 00 81, *www.hotel-banyuls.com* (€€). Logis hotel opposite the port with a good restaurant, **Al Fanal (€€€–€€), which has a summer terrace *Closed 3 weeks Feb, 2 weeks Dec; restaurant closed Wed and Thurs out of season.*

La Plage, at the centre of the beach strip, t 04 68 88 34 90 (€€). Serves satisfying seafood dinners.

Cerbère ✉ 66290

**La Vigie, on the N114, t 04 68 88 41 84, *www.lavigiebb.fr* (€). The choice spot in Cerbère, built on the sea cliffs, with a fine view; it has a restaurant (€€). *Closed mid-Nov–mid-April.*

Perpignan

There's a little craziness in every Catalan soul. In *Perpinyà* (as its residents call it), former capital of the kings of Majorca and the counts of Roussillon, this natural exuberance was until recently rather suppressed by French centralization, but the spate of building works, the busy calendar of festivals and activities and the lively outdoor cafés suggest that the city is now springing into life in its own way. The tourist office certainly wants it on the European cultural map, filling the streets with information panels pinpointing historical sites, sights, and even shops; in 2008 the city will even hold the title 'Capitale de la Culture Catalane'.

The king of kookiness himself, Salvador Dalí, set off the first sparks when he passed Perpignan's train station in a taxi, and 'it all became clear in a flash: there, right before me, was the centre of the universe!' The otherwise ordinary Gare SNCF has been a hot destination for Surrealist pilgrims ever since; the street leading to the station, Av du Général de Gaulle, has undergone a *traitement dalinien*, which includes the installation of benches shaped like Mae West's lips and a Dalinien railway carriage suspended in front of the station. The city worships Dalí like a hero.

History

Perpignan is named after Perperna, a lieutenant of the great 1st-century BC populist general Quintus Sertorius. While Rome was suffering under the dictatorship of Pompey, Sertorius governed most of Spain in accordance with his astonishing principle that one should treat Rome's provinces decently. The enraged Senate sent out five legions to destroy him, but his army, who all swore to die if he was killed, defeated each one until the villainous Perperna invited his boss to a banquet in the Pyrenees and murdered him.

In 1197, Perpignan became the first Catalan city granted a municipal charter, and governed itself by a council elected by the three estates or 'arms'. Its merchants traded as far abroad as Constantinople, and the city enjoyed its most brilliant period in the 13th century when Jaime I, king of Aragon and conqueror of Majorca, created the Kingdom of Majorca and County of Roussillon

Getting to and around Perpignan

By Air

Perpignan's **airport**, *www.perpignan.cci.fr*, is 5km northwest of the city and linked by shuttle bus *navettes* from the bus station an hour before each flight (info on **t** 04 68 55 68 00 and schedules on the airport website). There are regular flights from London and other UK cities (*see* **Planning Your Trip**).

By Train

The **train station**, Dalí's 'centre of the universe', is at the end of Av du Général de Gaulle and has frequent services down to the Spanish border at Port Bou and a TGV service to Paris taking six hours.

By Bus

The *gare routière* is to the north of the city, on Av du Général Leclerc, **t** 04 68 35 29 02.

Car and Bike Hire

You can hire a **car** at the airport, or from **Europcar**, 1 Av Général de Gaulle, **t** 04 68 34 89 80, near the train station, or **Avis**, 13 Bd du Conflent, **t** 04 68 34 26 71, which also has an office at the station, **t** 04 68 34 26 71. **Bicycle** hire is available at **Cycles Mercier**, 20 Av Gilbert Brutus, **t** 04 68 85 02 71.

for his younger son, Jaime II. This little kingdom was absorbed by the Catalan kings of Aragon in the 14th century, but continued to prosper until 1463, when Louis XI's army came to claim Perpignan and Roussillon as payment for mercenaries sent to Aragon. Besieged, the Perpignanais ate rats rather than become French, until the king of Aragon himself ordered them to surrender. In 1493, Charles VIII, more interested in Italian conquests, gave Perpignan back to Spain. But in the 1640s Richelieu pounced on the first available chance to grab back this corner of the mystic Hexagon, and French possession of Roussillon and the Haute-Cerdagne was cemented in the 1659 Treaty of the Pyrenees.

Perpignan made little noise after that. Long-standing social problems, ethnic rivalries and political corruption have made it one of the more troubled cities of France. Worries over immigration have led to an increase in support for the Front National over recent years. A lot of the trouble resides in the city-centre St-Jacques quarter, inhabited by communities of North Africans and Catalan Gypsies. Though relations between the two are generally good, both have their drug-involved gangs, and the murder of a young Moroccan in May 2005 touched off 10 nights of rioting in which 43 people were wounded. Having said that, Perpignan is a sunny, attractive town, popular with visitors.

Le Castillet

When most of Perpignan's walls were destroyed in 1904, its easy-going river-cum-moat, **La Basse**, was planted with lawns, flower-beds, mimosas and Art Nouveau cafés. The fat brick towers and crenellated gate of **Le Castillet** in Place de Verdun were left upright for memories' sake; built in 1368 by Aragon to keep out the French, it became a prison once the French got in, especially during the

BD EDMOND MICHELET

Auberge
de Jeunesse

Gare Routière

P

RUE CLAUDE MARTY

AV DE GRANDE BRETAGNE

AV JOSEPH ROUS

AV

JEAN-BAPTISTE LULLI

Musée
Puig

AV DES PALMIERS

G

COURS

LAZARE

ESCARQUET

BOULEVARD

REMPART

RUE

RUE

BD DU CONFLENT

RUE VALETTE

RUE CABRIT

RUE FRANKLIN

RUE RIQUET

PLACE DE
CATALOGNE

R. DE LA
REPUBLIQUE

RUE VAUBAN

AV DU GENERAL DE GAULLE

RUE D'IENA

QUAI BOURDAN

QUAI VAUBAN

Gare
P

RUE COURTELINE

RUE PIERRE LEFRANC

RUE PAUL BOILEAU

RUE MESSOT

RUE

OLIVA

QUAI NOBEL

QUAI BARCELONE

Q. DE LATTRE DE TASSIGNY

Palais de
Justice P

RUE DE PARIS

La Basse

AV DU LYCÉE

P

BOULEVARD DES PYRENEES

RUE PIERRE CARTELET

RUE DE TAMENHOFE

FOCH

RUE H ABBADIE

RUE DE VENISE

QUAI DE HANOVRE

QUAI DE GENEVE

RUE DU PET DEUMAR

MARECHAL

RUE DE LA LANTERNE

AV RIBERE

RUE DE CERDAGNE

RUE

DU

RUE DU FOUR ST. FRANCOIS

P

RUE

DUG

RUE LA FAYETTE

BOULEVARD

FELIX MERCADER

RUE DES LICES

RUE

AV JULIEN PANCHOT

RUE DU DR GEORGES

RUE PAULIN TESTORY

AV GILBERT BRUTUS

JOGLARS

AVENUE DES BALEARES

RUE PIERRE RENAUDEL

RUE DE L'EMPORDA

Ganganell

AV VICTOR DALBIEZ

RUE MARCELIN ALBERT

RUE

RUE BOND

RUE ALAIN LESAGE

RUE RODIN

RUE DES ROMARINS

Revolution. In 1946 a mason broke through a sealed wall in
Le Castillet and found the body of a child, which on contact with
the air dissolved into dust; from the surviving clothing fragments
the corpse was dated to the end of the 18th century. And ever since,
people have wondered: could it have been Marie-Antoinette's son,

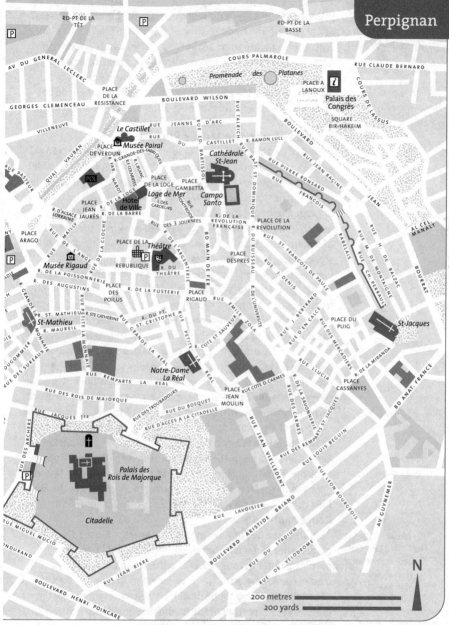

the *dauphin* Louis XVII? After all, the child buried in the Temple in Paris was known to be a substitute, and there have always been rumours that the Revolutionaries used the *dauphin* as a secret bargaining chip in dealing with his Bourbon relatives in Spain.

Musée du Castillet Casa Pairal
t 04 68 35 42 05; open May–Sept Wed–Mon 10–6.30; Oct–April Wed–Mon 11–5.30; closed Tues; adm

Along with this mysterious ghost, Le Castillet houses a museum of Catalan art and traditions, the Musée du Castillet Casa Pairal, with items ranging from casts of Pau (Pablo) Casals' hands to a kitchen from a Catalan *mas*, complete with a hole in the door for the Catalan cat. **Place de Verdun**, nearby, is one of Perpignan's liveliest squares, while just outside the gate the **Promenade des Platanes** is lined with rows of magnificent plane trees and palms.

Loge de Mer to the Musée Rigaud

From Le Castillet, Rue Louis Blanc leads back to **Place de la Loge**, where the cafés provide a grandstand for contemplating Aristide Maillol's voluptuous bronze *Venus* and Perpignan's most beautiful building, the Gothic **Loge de Mer** or Llotja, built in 1397 by the king of Aragon to house the exchange and the Consolat de Mar, a branch of the Barcelona council founded by Jaime I to resolve trade and maritime disputes. This proud and noble building of ochre stone, with its Venetian arches and loggia and ship-shaped weathercock, fell on hard times, and at one point the city rented out the Llotja to a fast-food chain, but things have moved slightly upmarket and it is now a nice *bistrot*-grill (*see* 'Eating Out', p.250).

The neighbouring 13th-century **Hôtel de Ville** has been spared the Llotja's humiliation, probably because it still serves its original purpose: on Saturday mornings, when its courtyard fills with blushing brides posing for photos by Maillol's allegory of the Mediterranean (as a naked woman, of course). It is built of rounded river pebbles and bricks in the curious layer-cake style of medieval Perpignan; three bronze arms sticking out of the façade are said to symbolize Perpignan's three estates, or *bras*. To the right, the **Palais de la Députation Provinciale** (1447) is a masterpiece of Catalan Renaissance, formerly the seat of Roussillon's parliament and now housing dismal municipal offices. **Rue des Fabriques-d'en Nabot**, opposite the palace, was once the street of drapers: note the **Hôtel Julia** (No.2), a rare survival of a 15th-century town house, with a Gothic courtyard.

Musée Rigaud
t 04 68 35 43 40; open May–Sept Wed–Mon 12–6.30; Oct–April Wed–Mon 11–5.30; closed Tues; adm

South of the Députation, in Rue de l'Ange, the Musée Rigaud is named after Perpignan native Hyacinthe Rigaud (1659–1743), portrait-painter to Louis XIV. Hyacinthe, master of raising the mediocre and unworthy to virtuoso heights of rosy-cheeked, debonair charm and sophistication, is well represented, most famously in his portrait of the Cardinal de Bouillon, who beams with self-satisfaction as chubby *putti* wallow in his worldly loot. All the hypersensitive alarms, however, are around the *Retable de la Trinité* (1489) by the Master of Canapost, painted for the 100th anniversary of the Consolat de Mar and showing, underneath, a fanciful scene of the sea lapping at the base of the Llotja. Works by Picasso, Dufy, Maillol, Miró and a score of others are upstairs.

The tangle of narrow streets near here and around **Place de la République** is full of interesting stalls and small shops.

Cathédrale St-Jean and the *Dévôt Christ*

⭐ **Cathédrale St-Jean**
open daily 9–12 and 3–6.30

Just east of Place de la Loge unfolds **Place Gambetta**, site of Perpignan's pebble and brick cathedral, topped by a lacy 19th-century wrought-iron campanile. Begun in 1324 but not ready for use until 1509, the interior is a success because the builders stuck to the design provided in the 15th century by Guillem Sagrera, architect of the great cathedral of Palma de Mallorca. Typical of Catalan Gothic, it has a single nave, 157ft long, striking for its spacious width rather than its soaring height.

The **chapels**, wedged between the huge piers, hold some unique treasures, the oldest of which is a mysterious marble **baptismal font** (first chapel on the left). Pre-Romanesque, perhaps even Visigothic in origin, and carved from the drum of a Roman column to look like a tub bound with a cable, it bears a primitive face of Christ over an open book. Further up the left aisle, the massive **organ** was decorated in the 15th century with painted shutters and sumptuous carvings. On the pendentive under the organ, note the Moor's head – a common Catalan conceit symbolizing wisdom, taken from the Templars, who exerted a powerful influence over the kings of Aragon. The jaw was articulated, to vomit sweetmeats on holidays; now it's stuck, gaping open. Beyond the Moor's head, in an 11th-century **chapel** from the original cathedral, is a pawn shop window of dingy reliquaries and the effigy of the cathedral's founder, Jaime's son Sancho, his feet resting on a Chinese lion.

The cathedral is proudest of its exquisite **retables**: on the high altar, the marble *Retable de St-Jean*, carved in a late Renaissance style in 1621 by Claude Perret; at the end of the left crossing, the *Retable des Stes Eulalie et Julie* (1670s); in the apsidal chapels, the painted wood *Retable de St-Pierre* (mid-16th century), and, to the right, the lovely *Notre-Dame de la Mangrana* (1500) – its name, 'of the pomegranate', comes from an earlier statue of the Virgin, which held a pomegranate, a symbol of fertility.

A door in the right aisle leads out to a 16th-century chapel constructed especially to house an extraordinary wooden sculpture known as the ***Dévôt Christ***. Carved in the Cologne region in 1307, this wasted Christ, whose contorted bones, sinews and torn flesh are carved with a rare anatomical realism, is stretched to the limits of agony on the Cross. Almost too painful to behold, it comes straight from the gloomy age when Christendom believed that pain, contemplated or self-inflicted, brought one closer to God. It is an object of great veneration, and the Perpignanais claim that when the Christ's bowed head sags another quarter-inch to touch His chest, the world will end.

11 Roussillon | Perpignan

Nearby in Place Gambetta is the entrance to the cathedral's

Campo Santo
*open April–Sept
Tues–Sun 12–7;
Oct–Mar Tues–Sun 11–5;
closed Mon*

Campo Santo of 1300–30, the only cloister-cemetery of its kind of France, the tombs decorated with fine bas-reliefs; this being Perpignan, until the late 1980s it was used as offices by the local *gendarmerie*. A door from the cloister leads into the striking 15th-century **Salle Capitulaire**, its complex ogival vaulting attributed to Guillem Sagrera. To the left of the cathedral's façade is Perpignan's oldest church, **St-Jean-le-Vieux** (1025), converted into an electrical generating station in 1890. Its Romanesque portal offers a very different view of Jesus from the German *Dévôt Christ*: the imperious and typically Catalan *Majestat* (Christ in Majesty).

Quartier St-Jacques

The piquant neighbourhood south of the cathedral, built on the slopes of **Puig des Lépreux** (Lepers' Hill), was once the *aljama*, or Jewish quarter of Perpignan. In its happiest days, in the 13th century, it produced a remarkable body of literature – especially from the pen of the mathematician and Talmudic scholar Gerson ben Salomon (author of the philosophical *Gate of Heaven*) – as well as rare manuscripts and calligraphy, all now in Paris. After the Jews were exiled, the quarter was renamed St-Jacques, and inhabited by working men's families and Gypsies, and most recently by

St-Jacques
*open daily
afternoons only*

North Africans. The 12th- to 14th-century church of **St-Jacques** is opulent and rich inside: there's a 'Cross of Insults' as in Elne, a statue of St James in Compostela pilgrimage gear (1450), and more fine retables, especially the 15th-century *Notre-Dame de l'Espérance*, featuring a rare view of the pregnant Virgin. In the early 15th century, while the fire-eating Dominican preacher St Vincent Ferrer was in Perpignan to advise in the dispute between Antipope Benedict XIII and Rome, he founded in this church the confraternity of the Holy Blood (*de la Sanch*) to bring religious comfort to prisoners condemned to death. As in Seville, the confraternity reaches a wider audience during Holy Week, when it dons spooky Ku Klux Klan-like hoods and bears a procession of holy floats (the *misteri*) while singers wail dirges from the crowd.

The Palace of the Kings of Majorca

**Palace of the
Kings of Majorca**
*t 04 68 34 48 29;
open daily June–Sept
10–6; Oct–May
9–5; adm*

Enclosed in a vast extent of walls, originally medieval and later enlarged by Vauban, the Palais des Rois de Majorque (entrance in Rue des Archers) is the oldest royal palace in France, begun in the 1270s by Jaime the Conqueror and occupied by his son Jaime II after 1283. Yet for all its grandeur, only three kings of Majorca were to reign here before Roussillon, Montpellier, the Cerdagne and the Balearic islands were reabsorbed by Aragon in 1349. The scale of magnificence that they intended to become accustomed to survives, but not much else.

A rectangle built around a mastodontic but elegant Romanesque-Gothic courtyard, the palace is now a favourite venue for events, exhibitions and dancing the *sardana*, the Catalan national dance.

The **Salle de Majorque**, or throne room, with its three vast fireplaces, and the double-decker chapels in the **Donjon**, with the queen's chapel on the bottom and the king's on top, both offer hints of the exotic splendour of the Majorcan court. The **sacristy** was the entrance to a network of underground passageways that connected the palace to its enormous 147ft-deep wells, which also afforded Jaime II an escape from his fierce and unwelcome older brother, Pedro III of Aragon. The palace once stood in the midst of what the archives call 'Paradise' – partly enclosed terraced gardens, inspired by Moorish gardens on Majorca. A few traces remain to the right of the mightiest tower, the **Tour de l'Hommage**.

The narrow grid of streets below the palace, around the church of **St-Mathieu**, were designed by the Templar tutors of Jaime the Conqueror, although most of the buildings are 18th-century.

Musée des Médailles et des Monnaies Puig
t 04 68 66 24 86; call for opening times; adm

Lastly, on the northwest side of town at 42 Avenue de Grande-Bretagne, the **Musée des Médailles et des Monnaies Puig** has an excellent collection of coins and medals from antiquity to modern times, with a section on Catalan money.

Perpignan Environs: Cabestany

Of all the villages ingested by Greater Perpignan, none is as celebrated as Cabestany (Cabestanh), 4km to the southeast. It produced a highly original Romanesque sculptor known as the Master of Cabestany (*see* p.35), who worked as far afield as Tuscany and left his home-town church a **tympanum** of the *Dormition and Assumption of the Virgin*, and a scene of the Virgin in heaven, handing her girdle down to St Thomas.

Cabestany was also the home of the troubadour Guilhem de Cabestanh, who wrote some of the most popular love poems of the Middle Ages. He is most famous for a legend that reached even Boccaccio (*Decameron*, Day 4: 9). Guilhem loved and was loved by the wife of a knight, one Raymond of Castel-Rossello. When Raymond learned of their affair, he ambushed Guilhem, murdered him and cut out his heart, which he gave to his cook to prepare with plenty of pepper. His wife ate it and praised the dish. 'I am not surprised,' said her husband, 'as you loved it so well when it was alive.' And he told her what she had eaten. But the lady kept her *sang-froid*. 'Sir,' she said, 'you have given me such an excellent thing to eat that God forbid any other food should again pass my lips.' And she leapt out of the window to her death.

Services in Perpignan

Post office: Rue Dr Zamenhof.

Perpignan Market Days

Daily am: Place Cassanyes.

Sat am: Place de la République, regional produce.

See www.mairie-perpignan.fr for a full list.

(★) La Casa Sansa >>

(ⓘ) Perpignan >
Palais des Congrès, Place Armand Lanoux, t 04 68 66 30 30, www. perpignan tourisme. com; open mid-June–mid-Sept daily; mid-Sept–mid-June Mon–Sat and Sun am

Information point: Espace Palmarium, Place Arago; open Mon–Sat

(★) La Galinette >>

Where to Stay in Perpignan

Perpignan ✉ 66000

****La Villa Duflot**, Rond-Point Albert Donnezan, t 04 68 56 67 67, *www.villa-duflot.com* (€€€). The only four-star hotel is near the Perpignan-Sud-Argelès motorway exit, in the middle of an industrial zone! However, you can pretend to be elsewhere in the comfortable air-conditioned rooms and garden, or in the popular restaurant (€€€) overlooking the pool.

***Park Hôtel** , 18 Bd Jean Bourrat, near tourist office, t 04 68 35 14 14, *www. parkhotel-fr.com* (€€€–€€). Plush, air-conditioned, soundproofed rooms and restaurant (€€€€–€€; *see* 'Eating Out') with an old Spanish feel and flair.

***Kyriad Perpignan Centre**, 8 Bd Wilson, t 04 68 59 25 94, *www.kyriad-perpignan-centre.fr* (€€). Small, central, modern hotel, good value and clean if a little lacking in Catalan atmosphere.

****Hôtel de la Loge**, 1 Rue des Fabriques-d'en Nabot, t 04 68 34 41 02, *www.hoteldelaloge.fr* (€€–€). The nicest in the centre, in a 16th-century building, this has pretty rooms, some with TV and air-conditioning, and a lovely inner courtyard.

***Le Berry**, 6 Av du Général de Gaulle, t 04 68 34 59 02 (€).

Auberge de Jeunesse, Parc de la Pépinière, Av de Grande-Bretagne, t 04 68 34 63 32, *www.fuaj.org*. A small youth hostel, with breakfast available. Book in summer. *Closed mid-Dec–mid-Jan.*

Eating Out in Perpignan

Le Chapon Fin, Park Hôtel (*see above*), t 04 68 35 14 14 (€€€€–€€). Perpignan's finest restaurant for years, as well as one of the prettiest, with its Catalan ceramics. But it's the *aiguillettes de saumon cuisinées en trois façons*

(smoked, roasted and marinated) and *daube de bœuf* that keep its clients coming back for more, even all the way from Spain. *Closed Sun, plus first 2 weeks in Jan and 2 weeks Aug.*

La Casa Sansa, 3 Rue Fabriques Couvertes, near Le Castillet, t 04 68 34 21 84 (€€€–€€). Lively, with excellent food served in a 14th-century cellar – with dishes from Catalan *escargots* to rabbit with *aïoli*; occasional live music, and more than its share of Catalan flair. *Book Fri and Sat nights.*

Les Antiquaires, Place Desprès, t 04 68 34 06 58 (€€€–€€). A local favourite for reliable French cooking. *Closed Sun eve and Mon, and 3 weeks in June.*

La Galinette, 23 Rue Jean Payra, t 04 68 35 00 90 (€€€–€€). The current talk of the town. Christophe Comes' gastronomic restaurant delights palates with fresh and seasonal products including vegetables from the chef's own garden. Excellent value. *Book first. Closed Sun and Mon, plus mid-July–mid-Aug.*

Le France, Place de la Loge, t 04 68 51 61 71 (€€). The *bistrot*-grill under the Loge, a relaxed place with pink and white floor tiling to match the outside. Eat inside or on the terrace; there are good meat and fish menu choices. *Closed Mon eve and Jan.*

Brasserie Arago, Place Arago, t 04 68 51 81 96 (€€). Packed day and night; good food and pizza – not always a strong point with the Catalans.

Le Vauban, 29 Quai Vauban, t 04 68 51 05 10 (€). A sure bet, with well-prepared *plats du jour. Closed Sun.*

Les Expéditeurs, 19 Av du Général Leclerc, t 04 68 35 15 80 (€). Catalan cooking.

Entertainment and Nightlife in Perpignan

On evenings from June to September in Place du Castillet, the Perpignanais come to dance *sardanas*, the national Catalan circle dance. Outside summer, nightlife is mostly concentrated on students.

Every year in September, Perpignan is host to **Visa pour l'Image**, *www.visa pourlimage.com*, the annual world festival of photo-journalism.

Le Zinc, 8 Rue Grande des Fabriques, t 04 68 35 08 80. Jazz and cocktails; especially animated during the Perpignan Jazz Festival in October, called *Jazzèbre*.

Cinéma Mega-Castillet, zac Mas Balande, t 04 68 28 08 08.
Cinéma Rive Gauche et Centre-Ville, 29 Quai Vauban, t 04 68 51 05 00.

Southern Roussillon and the Pyrenees

Pyrenean Valleys: The Conflent

⭐ Canigou

Two important valleys, the **Conflent** (the valley of the river Têt) and the **Vallespir** (of the river Tech), slope in parallel lines towards the Spanish border. Don't think that this butt end of the Pyrenees consists of mere foothills; in between the two valleys stands snow-capped **Canigou**, not the highest (a mere 9,134ft) but certainly one of the most imposing peaks of the chain, jauntily wearing a Phrygian cap of snow until late spring. The *muntanya regalada* ('fortunate mountain') of the Catalans is one of the symbols of the nation, the subject of one of the best-known Catalan folksongs. Every summer solstice Catalans from both sides of the frontier ceremoniously light a huge bonfire on its summit, the signal for surrounding villages to light their own, all at the exact same time. Legends and apparitions abound on Canigou. Fairies and 'ladies of the waters' are said to frequent its forested slopes, and King Pedro of Aragon climbed it in 1285 and met a dragon near the top.

From Perpignan to Ille-sur-Têt

The fish-filled Têt, before passing through Perpignan, washes a wide plain packed full of vineyards and fat villages. The fattest, **Thuir**, puts up signs all over Roussillon inviting us over to see the **World's Biggest Barrel**, in the cellars of the famous *apéritifs* Byrrh and Dubonnet – wine mixed with quinine, invented here over a century ago. After a few *apéritifs*, head 6km west for golden-hued **Castelnou**, a perfectly preserved medieval village on winding, pebble-paved lanes and steps under the 10th-century **castle** of the counts of Cerdagne. Restored after the roof caught fire in 1981, this castle, unlike most military castles in France, never graduated into a lordly residence, and the rooms are empty today.

The narrow D48 wiggling west of Castelnou is unabashedly beautiful: if you have a couple of hours to spare, you can circle around to the Prieuré de Serrabonne (*see* overleaf) by way of the D2 to **Caixas** and **Fourques**, then on to the D13 for **Llauro** and **Prunet-et-Belpuig**, where the ruins of the **Château de Belpuig** offer a superb view and the 11th-century **Chapelle de la Trinité** has sculpture by the same school as Serrabonne.

World's Biggest Barrel
www.byrrh.com; tours July and Aug daily 10–11.45 and 2–6.45; May–June and Sept daily 9–11.45 and 2.30–5.45; April and Oct Mon–Fri 9–11.45 and 2.30–5.45; adm

Castelnou castle
t 04 68 53 22 91; open July and Aug daily 10–7; April–June and Sept daily 11.30–6; Oct–Dec and Feb–Mar daily 11–5; Jan Sat and Sun 11–5; last ticket 1hr before closing; adm

Getting around the Pyrenean Valleys

The bus and train service is probably better here than in any other rural region in this book – only it won't help you see rural monuments like St-Michel or Serrabonne.

By Little Yellow Train

You can pick up **Le Petit Train Jaune, t** 04 68 96 63 62, *www.trainstouristiques-ter.com/train_jaune.htm*, at Villefranche-de-Conflent. It's a scenic narrow-gauge train that runs six times a day in July and August into the Cerdagne, unchanged since 1910. One of the most unlikely railways in France, it was entirely a political project, meant to bring some new life into the impoverished mountain valleys. It has kept puffing ever since – only tourism has saved it from closing: when checking the schedule, make sure you don't choose one of the departures taken over by buses. The scenery is striking, even more so in summer when viewed from open carriages. The last station is Latour-de-Carol, where you can get a bus to Andorra and Spain, or a train to Toulouse or Barcelona.

By Bus

Using Perpignan as a base, it's possible to see quite a bit of the Conflent and Vallespir; from the *gare routière* there are 10 or 12 buses a day (**t** 04 68 35 29 02) to Prades and Villefranche-de-Conflent, and a few of these continue to Font-Romeu and Latour-de-Carol. For the Vallespir, there are frequent buses to Céret, Arles-sur-Tech and Amélie-les-Bains-Palalda, and a few press on further to Prats-de-Mollo.

Centre d'Art Sacré
t 04 68 84 83 96; open mid-June–Sept Mon–Fri 10–12 and 2–7, Sun 2–7; Oct–Nov and Feb–mid-June Wed–Mon 2–6, closed Tues; closed Dec and Jan

Les Orgues
t 04 68 84 13 13; site open July–Aug daily 9.30–8; April–June and Sept daily 10–6.30; Oct daily 10–12.30 and 2–6; Nov–Jan daily 2–5; Feb and Mar daily 10–12.30 and 2–5.30; adm

Château-Musée
t 04 68 84 55 55; open mid-June–mid-Sept Wed–Fri and Sun–Mon 2–7; mid-Sept–mid-June Wed–Fri and Sun–Mon 2–5.30; closed Tues and Sat; adm

Prieuré de Serrabonne
t 04 68 84 09 30; open daily 10–6; adm

In **Boule d'Amont**, just up the road, there's another charming church from the same century. A shorter alternative, but on even more dubious roads, is to take the D2 north to **St-Michel-de-Llotes** (site of the **Dolmen de la Creu de la Llosa** and with a museum on local agriculture and wine production) and turn back to Serrabonne by way of **Casefabre**, with its tremendous views.

At **Ille-sur-Têt**, an attractive old village at the gateway to the mountains, neglected art from the 11th to 19th centuries from churches all over Roussillon has been assembled in a 16th-century hospital, the **Centre d'Art Sacré**, with changing exhibitions.

The D2 northwest of Ille to **Montalba-le-Château** takes you very quickly to some surprising scenery: orange eroded 'fairy chimneys' called the **Orgues**, with the forgotten ruin of a 12th-century tower perched on top, and the Pyrenees forming a magnificent backdrop. The fortified church of **Régleille** (from Ille, take the D2 over the river and after a kilometre turn right on to a little road) looks like a castle – a typical example of a monastic church, in an area without any castles, that grew into a fortress to protect the monks and the village. Ille was here before its population drifted to the present site.

Six kilometres north on the D21, in little **Bélesta**, the **Château-Musée** holds the treasure found in a Neolithic tomb in 1983; the superbly restored castle itself is a 13th-century work built by Saint Louis.

Prieuré de Serrabonne

Seeing the finest medieval sculpture in Roussillon requires dedication: the most direct route (for others, see above) requires 13km of hairpin bends on a road where you dread oncoming traffic,

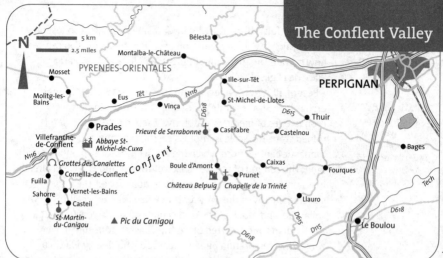

starting from the D618 at Bouleternère, just west of Ille, and ending in a lofty, remote, barren spot on the slopes of a mountain called Roque Rouge. The solemn, spare shape and dark schist of Serrabonne's church are not promising, making the surprise inside that much the greater. The best efforts of the 12th-century Catalan sculptors were concentrated in the single gallery of the cloister, and especially in the **tribune**, in rose marble from Canigou. Perfectly preserved in its isolated setting, this includes a fantastical bestiary, centaurs, a grimacing St Michael, reliefs of the four Evangelists and more. The style of these capitals will become familiar if you spend much time in the Conflent; like most of the works in the region, Serrabonne's was done by the school of artists that grew up at St-Michel-de-Cuxa. Note the small figure of the Virgin; a narrow window allows a ray of sunlight to illuminate it only one day each year – the Feast of the Assumption on 15 August.

Prades, St-Michel-de-Cuxa and Canigou

Prades is known around the world in connection with the music festival founded in 1951 by Pablo Casals, but few people could place it on a map. Casals, in exile after the Spanish Civil War, spent much of the 1940s and '50s here, in the one safe corner of his beloved Catalunya. From the beginning, his **festival** attracted many of the world's greatest musicians. Otherwise, Prades is a typical stolid Catalan town with a rather worrying road system.

There are a couple of things to see. The **Musée Pablo Casals**, in the **Médiathèque de Prades** at 33 Rue de l'Hospice, has a section dedicated to Casals – photos, his piano and pipes, records, letters, etc. There are also paintings by local artist Martin Vivès. In the heart of Prades, the church of **St-Pierre** has a fine Romanesque bell-tower with a pyramid crown and, inside, an operatic Baroque

Prades festival
www.prades-festival-casals.com; late July–mid-Aug

Musée Pablo Casals
t 04 68 96 52 37; open summer Mon–Sat 9–12 and 2–6; winter Tues 10–12 and 3–7, Wed 10–7, Fri 3–7 and Sat 10–1

retable in full 17th-century fig by Catalan chisel virtuoso Joseph Sunyer, along with an exhibition of church treasures. You can see how garnets are made into opulent jewellery at **Casa Perez** in Place de l'Eglise.

Casa Perez
open daily

Best of all, it's only a few kilometres from Prades up through orchards to **St-Michel-de-Cuxa**, one of the most important monasteries of medieval Catalunya. Even in its reduced, semi-ruined state, the scale is impressive; this was one of the great monastic centres from which medieval Europe was planned and built. The coming of the French Revolution found St-Michel already in a state of serious decay. Looted and abandoned, the abbey suffered greatly in the 19th century. One of the two bell-towers collapsed, and much of the best sculptural work went 'into exile' as the Catalans put it, carted off to the Cloisters Museum in New York. When restoration began, the rest of the cloister was in a public bathhouse in Prades, while the altar top was found holding up a balcony in Vinça. Now restored, St-Michel is occupied once again by a small community of Benedictine monks from Montserrat, the centre of Catalan spiritualism and nationalism.

St-Michel-de-Cuxa
t 04 68 96 15 35,
www.cuxa.org;
open summer Mon–Sat
9.30–11.50 and 2–6, Sun
2–6; winter Mon–Sat
9.30–11.50 and 2–5,
Sun 2–5; adm

While much of the inspiration for early medieval architecture in Languedoc came from northern Italy or France, Roussillon was heavily influenced by nearby Spain. Here, the obvious Spanish feature is the more-than-semicircular 'Visigothic' arches in the nave. This style, which goes back almost to Roman times, never became too popular in Christian Europe, though the Muslims of Spain adopted it to create the architectural fantasies of Seville and Granada.

Other notable features of St-Michel include the massive and extremely elegant bell-tower, and an unusual circular **crypt**, built in the 11th century under a building that was later demolished. The crypt is covered by toroid barrel vaulting, with a mushroom-like central column almost unique in medieval architecture. Antonio Gaudí used similar columns in his work in Barcelona – a fascinating piece of Catalan cultural continuity, for Gaudí could not have got the idea here, since the crypt was discovered and excavated only in 1937. In the **cloister**, you can see the galleries and capitals that didn't go to Manhattan: monsters from the medieval bestiary in the corners, intertwined with men on the four faces. There is an obsession with lions, almost Chinese in their stylization, biting and licking each other.

Chalet-Refuge des Cortalets
open May–Sept; call
t 04 68 96 36 19 to
book a bed; €28 a night,
meals €14.50; half-
board €31.30

If **Canigou**'s magnetism is working its juju on you, don't resist the call. You can make two-thirds of the climb – 7,053ft – by car, on a forest road that begins on the east end of Prades. This leaves you at the **Chalet-Refuge des Cortalets**. From here it's a fairly easy 3–4-hour walk to the summit, requiring only a decent pair of walking shoes and a windcheater. There's a second, even more hair-raising forest road up to the refuge from the D27, practical only in a four-wheel drive. The Prades and Vernet-les-Bains tourist offices have lists of operators; leave the driving to them.

Vernet-les-Bains and St-Martin-du-Canigou

The D27, the narrow road that snakes around the lower slopes of Canigou, is an exceptional drive through the mountain forests, with grand views of the big mountain itself; after St-Michel-de-Cuxa, it meets **Vernet-les-Bains**, a bustling modern spa with most of the accommodation in the area and hot sulphuric waters that are good for your rheumatism and respiratory problems. Wear comfy shoes to climb the steep, narrow streets of the old town.

Three kilometres further up, **Casteil**, a little wooded resort with a small museum of mountain life and plenty of picnic grounds, is the base for visiting Canigou's other great medieval monument, the

St-Martin-du-Canigou
t 04 68 05 50 03, http://stmartinducanigou.org; open daily in summer; Oct–April Tues–Sun; guided tours only; adm

abbey of **St-Martin-du-Canigou** – a taxing though lovely 40-minute walk up from the town. A monkish architect named Sclua designed this complex, begun in the early 11th century by a count of the Cerdagne named Guifred Cabreta. Sclua was a designer ahead of his time; he made his monastery a rustic acropolis, spectacularly sited with views around Canigou and surrounding peaks, and arranged as a series of courtyards and terraces on different levels. The church, with its immense, fortress-like bell-tower, has two levels, an upper church dedicated to St-Martin and a lower crypt for a certain obscure subterranean Virgin Mary, Notre-Dame-sous-Terre. Some good white marble capitals can be seen in the cloister, heavily restored in the early 20th century, and medieval tombs, including Count Guifred's, survive in the upper church. But on the whole St-Martin, damaged by an earthquake in 1428, abandoned after the Revolution, restored between 1952 and 1971 and reinhabited, retains relatively few of its former glories.

To complete the tour of Romanesque Canigou, in the village of **Corneilla-de-Conflent** there is another 11th–12th-century church, a former Benedictine priory full of good sculpture. Side roads to the west, in the valley of the Rotja, can take you to several more, including rare 10th-century churches in the tiny villages of **Fuilla** and **Sahorre**.

Not all the area's attractions are on Canigou. Five kilometres northeast of Prades, in the empty, largely forested Pyrenean foothills, **Eus**, 'one of the most beautiful villages in France', is an ambitious place; it also claims to have 'the most sunshine of any *commune* in France'. Spilling down its steep hillside, as you see it from the Têt valley, it makes an elegant composition. The parish **church** has some elaborate 17th-century polychrome retables.

Heading up from Prades in the Castellare valley, on the D14, **Molitg-les-Bains**, on a hill in the forest, has been a spa (specializing in skin disorders) since the Belle Epoque, with a suitably grand hotel with a lake, river and lovely gardens open to the public. Beyond Molitg, the road climbs up to the **Col de Jau**, a pass with stunning views, once the border between France and Spain, and a route to the Aude valley. On the way, you pass the fortified village of **Mosset**, a little haven of artists and potters, where there is a beautifully restored Romanesque chapel, the *capelletta*, in the old village.

At tiny **Escaro** there is a **mining museum**, with trains, tools, old equipment and photos, and organized walks around the mining area on Saturdays in summer, lasting 3½hrs.

Villefranche-de-Conflent

Some villages have their own ideas for welcoming visitors. This one casually points cannons down at you as you pass along the N116, by way of an invitation to drop in. Villefranche, the most logical place from which to defend the Têt valley, has had a castle at least since 1092. In the 17th century it took its present form, as a model Baroque fortress-town, rebuilt and refortified by Vauban. Almost nothing has changed since, and Villefranche remains as a fascinating historical record, a sort of stage set of that era.

Tours of Vauban's **ramparts**, with their walkway built through the wall, are offered and, for those with sufficient puff and military curiosity, there's a steep climb up the remarkable 1,000 subterranean rock-hewn steps (at the end of Rue St-Pierre) to **Fort Liberia**, another Vauban *opus*, further fortified by Napoléon III, dominating the valley and long used as a prison, where you can 'meet the villainous female prisoners' (don't be alarmed – they're made of wax). There's transport up from Villefranche's Café Canigou.

A survivor from the pre-Vauban Villefranche, the church of **St-Jacques** is a fine 12th-century building with the familiar capitals from the workshop of St-Michel-de-Cuxa; inside there's another retable by Sunyer and, by the door, note the measures engraved in the stone, used by drapers who had market stalls in the square. Vauban built its walls and tower into his wall to help with the defence. For all its grim purpose, Villefranche is a lovely town, attracting crafty types, woodcarvers and potters.

One kilometre up the Vernet road, some of the Pyrenees' most peculiar stalactites await your inspection at the **Grotte des Canalettes** and the **Grotte des Grandes Canalettes**.

Mining museum
t 04 68 97 15 34, http://perso.orange.fr/mairie/escaro; open July–Aug daily 2–6; June and Sept–Oct Sat and Sun only 2–6; call for details of organized walk

Ramparts
t 04 68 96 10 40; tours June–Sept daily 9–7; April and May daily 10.30– 12.30 and 2–6; Feb, Mar, Oct and Nov daily 10.30–12.30 and 2–5; closed Dec and Jan; adm

Fort Liberia
t 04 68 96 34 01; open July–Aug daily 9–8; May–June daily 10–7; Sept–April daily 10–6; adm

Grotte des Canalettes
open July and Aug 10.30–5; adm

Grotte des Grandes Canalettes
t 04 68 05 20 20, www.grottes-grandes-canalettes.com; open mid-June–mid-Sept daily 10–6.30; April–mid-June and mid-Sept–Oct daily 10–6; Nov–Mar Sun only 2–5; adm; son-et-lumiere July and Aug at 6.30pm

ⓘ **Ille-sur-Têt**
Square de la Poste, t 04 68 84 02 62, www.ille-sur-tet.com; open July–Aug Mon–Sat and Sun am; Sept–June Mon–Fri

Market Days in the Pyrenean Valleys

Ille-sur-Têt: Wed and Fri; flea market on Sun.
Prades: Tues.

Where to Stay and Eat in the Pyrenean Valleys

Until recently this area has been a gastronomic desert, but it's improving, with imaginative Catalan cuisine and seafood.

Prades >
*4 Rue des Marchands,
t 04 68 05 41 02,
www.prades-
tourisme.com or
www.prades.com;
open Mon–Fri*

**Vernet-les-
Bains >**
*2 Rue de la Chapelle,
t 04 68 05 55 35,
www.ot-vernet-les-
bains.fr; open July–Aug
Mon–Fri and Sat am;
Sept–June Mon–Fri*

**Villefranche-
de-Conflent >>**
*32 bis Rue St-Jacques,
t 04 68 96 22 96, www.
villefranchedeconflent.
com; open June–Sept
daily; Oct–Dec and
Feb–May daily pm;
closed Jan*

**Auberge
St-Paul >>**

Prades ✉ 66500

*Hostalrich, 156 Av Général de Gaulle, **t** 04 68 96 05 38 (€). A big neon sign makes it easy to find the Hostalrich; all rooms have TV and showers and some have balconies. Avoid the restaurant if you can; the food is simple to the point of dullness. There's a wonderful chestnut-shaded garden as compensation.

Le Jardin d'Aymeric, 3 Av du Général de Gaulle, **t** 04 68 96 53 38 (€€). The best bet for stylish regional cooking, though the excess of neon detracts from the atmosphere. *Closed Sun, Mon, and Wed eve in winter.*

L'Hostal de Nogarols, Chemin Nogarols, at Codalet, on the way to St-Michel-de-Cuxa, **t** 04 68 96 24 57 (€€). A good stop before music concerts, serving excellent wood-fired pizzas, as well as Catalan classics like *petit gris* snails, in an airy dining room or pretty, shady garden.

Vernet-les-Bains ✉ 66820

***Le Mas Fleuri, 25 Bd Clemenceau (the road up to St-Martin), **t** 04 68 05 51 94, *www.hotellemasfleuri.fr* (€€€–€€). At the top of the list, this century-old hotel is set in a pretty park, with a pool; rooms are air-conditioned (no restaurant). *Closed mid-Oct–mid-April.*

Princess, Rue Lavandières, **t 04 68 05 56 22, *www.hotel-princess.fr* (€€). A pleasant Logis de France with a better-than-average restaurant (€€). *Closed Feb; restaurant closed Jan–mid-Mar and end of Nov..*

Au Comte Guifred, **t** 04 68 05 51 37 (€€). This modern restaurant is the training ground for the local hotel school. *Open lunchtimes Mon, Tues, Thurs and Fri; closed July.*

Molitg-les-Bains ✉ 66500

****Château de Riell, **t** 04 68 05 04 40, *www.chateauderiell.com* (€€€€€–€€€). Molitg may have only 180 inhabitants, but it can claim Roussillon's top luxury hotel, the sumptuous Relais & Châteaux Château de Riell. This Baroque folly from the turn of the last century is in a theatrically Baroque setting, perched on a rock with exquisite

views of Canigou; it has elegant, luxurious Hollywood-style rooms in the château (from €275) and maison-ettes in the garden (from €144) – both a contrast with the medieval *oubliettes*, which you can visit – and two pools, including one on top of the tower, perhaps the best place in the world to watch the Catalan bonfires go up on the solstice (*see p.251*). Lots of extras, and a restaurant (€€€) worthy of the décor. *Closed Nov–Mar; restaurant closed Mon–Fri lunch except in summer.*

***Grand Hôtel Thermal, **t** 04 68 05 00 50 (€€€). Less pricey, but almost as splendid, with marble spa rooms, swimming pool and marble terrace, glorious views and also a very good-value restaurant (€€). *Closed mid-Nov–Mar.*

Mas Lluganas, just outside Mosset, **t** 04 68 05 00 37, *www.maslluganas. com* (€). Offers rooms and *chambres d'hôtes*, plus meals (€€) based on its own produce of ducks, guinea fowl, veal and *foie gras*. The same family also offers inexpensive *chambres d'hôtes* accommodation at **La Forge**, a peaceful retreat by the river. There is also a *gîte. Closed mid-Oct–Mar.*

Villefranche-de-Conflent ✉ 66500

Auberge du Cèdre, Domaine Ste-Eulalie, outside the walls, **t 04 68 96 05 05 (€). Ten comfortable rooms, an adequate restaurant and two fat, friendly cats in the garden. Restaurant only open to residents. *Closed early Nov–early Dec.*

Auberge St-Paul, Place de l'Eglise, **t** 04 68 96 30 95, *http://perso.orange. fr/auberge.stpaul* (€€€€–€€). The chef at this lovely restaurant fetches from Canigou all the basic ingredients for mountain surprises like *filet mignon de sanglier* (boar) and beef with morel mushrooms. *Closed Sun eve and Mon in summer, Sun eve, Mon and Tues in winter, and 3 weeks Jan, 1 week June and 1 week Nov.*

Au Grill La Senyera, 81 Rue St-Jean, **t** 04 68 96 17 65 (€€). Solid, traditional cuisine. *Closed Tues, Wed, and mid-Oct–mid-Nov.*

The Cerdagne

This is as close as we get, in this book, to the heart of the Pyrenees, but it's far enough for the real thing: mountain rhododendrons and blue gentians, hordes of skiers, herds of horses, and snow on top until May or June. The lofty plateau of the Cerdagne (Cerdanya in Catalan) was an isolated and effectively independent county in the Middle Ages; from the 10th century its counts gradually extended their power, eventually becoming counts of Barcelona – the founders of the Catalan nation. In spite of this heritage, the Cerdagne was split between Spain and France in the 1659 Treaty of the Pyrenees. The building of the Little Yellow Train (*see* p.252) in 1911 brought the French Cerdagne into the modern world; skiing has made it rather opulent today. And besides skiing, you can see some good Romanesque churches, warm up at the world's largest solar furnace, visit the highest railway station in France – and circumnavigate Spain in less than an hour.

To Mont-Louis and the Capcir

After Villefranche, the main N116 climbs dramatically into the mountains. There are a few possible stop-offs on the way: at **Olette**, you can turn off to explore nearly abandoned old mountain villages like **Nyer** and **Evol**.

A bit further up, at **Thuès-entre-Valls**, you can stretch your legs in the beautiful **Gorges de la Carança**, then soak your weary bones in the natural hot springs at St-Thomas-les-Bains, **Fontpédrouse**, where no matter the weather you can take a dip outside or in the Jacuzzi, visit the hammam or have a massage.

Climb, climb, climb, and at last you'll reach the gateway to the Cerdagne, **Mont-Louis**, another work of Vauban's and the highest fortress in France (5,250ft), named after Louis XIV. The army still resides here, though only to look after a pioneer **solar furnace**, built in 1953 and used, not for generating power, but for melting substances for scientific experiments; the huge mirror generates temperatures up to 6,000 degrees. It shares the small space inside the walls with some 350 residents and a few cafés and shops. In the summer you can also visit the **Puits des Forçats** and see the 17th-century wheel which lifted water from the wells dug into the rock.

A 7km detour up into the mountains will take you to tiny **Planès** and its equally tiny and unique triangular 11th-century church. Like the seven-sided model at Rieux-Minervois (*see* pp.182–3), this one has occasioned much speculation; some have claimed it as the centre of a network of ley lines.

The road to Planès is a dead end, but there are better choices from the big crossroads at Mont-Louis. To the north, the D118

Fontpédrouse
*t 04 68 97 03 13,
http://perso.orange.fr/
fontpedrouse; open July
and Aug daily 10–9;
Jan–June and Sept–Oct
daily 10–8; closed Nov;
hammam closed
Mon; adm*

Solar furnace
*t 04 68 04 14 89,
http://mont-louis.net/
foursolaire.htm; guided
tours only; documents
avail. in English; open
summer 10–6; spring
and autumn 10–5;
winter 10–4; closed first
half Dec; adm*

Puits des Forçats
*contact tourist office
for times; adm*

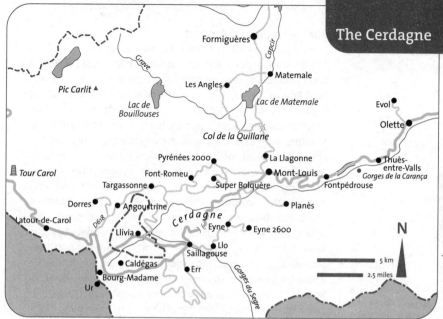

carries you to the isolated plateau of the **Capcir**. It's a perfect place to get away from it all – after a road was built into the Capcir in the 19th century, almost the entire population deserted it, tired of scratching a living from land that would only support a few cows. They left behind beautiful pine forests and a score of little lakes carved out long ago by Pyrenean glaciers. Skiing has brought the Capcir back to life since the 1960s, and the government has transformed the landscape with a number of dams and artificial lakes.

On your way into the Capcir, don't miss the church of St-Vincent in **La Llagonne**, only 3km from Mont-Louis. The centuries have left it in peace, with a remarkable collection of medieval art, including an altarpiece and painted baldachin (12th- and 13th-centuries), and an excellent polychrome *Majestat*.

Further north, **Les Angles**, **Matemale** and **Formiguères** are the main ski centres. Les Angles has, as well as some 30 ski pistes and a whole range of winter sports, a **Parc Animalier**, a partly free-range zoo with native fauna of the Pyrenees, both current and past residents, including bears, reindeer, wolves and bison. Mountain goats are likely to cross your path. A telecabin also runs in summer, affording some great views. **Formiguères** (not the ski station, but the village, 4km away) is one of the prettiest and best-preserved villages in the region, hardly changed since the days when the kings of Majorca sojourned here to relieve their asthma. This region is great for hiking. The best parts lie to the west, on the slopes of the 9,584ft **Pic Carlit**; there you will find the sources of both the Tët and the Aude (above the D60, in the Forêt de Barrès).

Parc Animalier
t 04 68 04 17 20, www. faune-pyreneenne.com; open daily summer 9–6; winter 9–5; adm

Font-Romeu and Around

The western road (D618) will take you through more pine forests to Font-Romeu; along with its new satellite towns, **Super-Bolquère** and **Pyrénées 2000**, this is one of the biggest ski resorts in France. **Font-Romeu** grew up after 1910, around a now-closed *Grand Hôtel*; it prospers today partly from its excellent sports facilities, often used for training France's Olympic teams; it also has a golf course. Stamped from the same mould as every other continental ski resort, it has plenty of fake Alpine chalets, innumerable pizzerias and 460 snow machines to help out when the weather isn't co-operating. But no other resort has the world's largest solar furnace, 'stronger than 10,000 suns!', the successor to the one in Mont-Louis. With its curved mirror, covering an entire side of the nine-storey laboratory building, it reflects the Pyrenees beautifully while helping scientists work out all sorts of high-temperature puzzles; learn all about it at **Heliodyssée** at 7 Rue du Four Solaire. Above the town, the pilgrimage chapel of **Notre-Dame-de-Font-Romeu** has an exuberant altarpiece by Joseph Sunyer and a 12th-century statue of the Virgin. There is a **reindeer park** at Bolquère/Pyrénées 2000 where in winter you can feel like Santa being pulled along on a sledge.

Another solar experiment can be seen at **Targassonne**, west of Font-Romeu on the D618; this big mirror was built to generate electricity, but hasn't quite worked as well as intended. The glaciers that reshaped the Capcir were busy here too, leaving a strange expanse of granite boulders called the **Chaos**. The Cerdagne is famous for its Romanesque churches and chapels, testimony to the mountain Catalans' prosperity and level of culture even in the very early Middle Ages. One of the best of the churches is **St-André**, at **Angoustrine**, west of Targassonne, with fragments of 13th-century frescoes representing the months of the year.

To the west, **Dorres** is a lofty *village perché* with another church, this one from the 11th century, with another Romanesque Virgin inside, and a chance to soak in a **granite hot tub** with a rather sulphurous pong. There is also a **museum** on the granite industry.

Heliodyssée
*t 04 68 30 77 86;
open July–Aug daily
10–7.30; Sept–June daily
10–12.30 and 2–6; adm*

Reindeer park
*t 04 08 30 35 18,
www.territoire-lapon.fr;
open Christmas–Easter
and summer school
holidays*

Granite hot tub
*t 04 68 04 66 87; open
July and Aug 8.30–9.15;
Sept–Oct and May–June
daily 8.30–7.45;
Nov–April 9–7.45*

The Vallée du Carol

From the village of **Ur** (with yet another richly decorated Romanesque church), you can make a northern detour into the Vallée du Carol, the western edge of Roussillon. **Latour-de-Carol** is a romantic name for another great border rail crossing most of us have blinked at in the dark; the name does not come from Charlemagne, as most people think, but the Carol river. Latour's **church** has more work by Joseph Sunyer. The best church in the area, however, is the **Chapelle St-Fructueux** in the minuscule village of **Yravals**, above Latour-de-Carol – with a wealth of medieval art inside, and a magnificent mid-14th-century altarpiece of *St Martha* by a Catalan named Ramon Destorrents.

Further up this scenic valley, you'll pass the tower of the ruined 14th-century **castle** that gives Latour its name. The trees give out as the tortuous road climbs to the **Pass of Puymorens**. From here, if you have a sudden hankering for some tax-free Havanas or a new phonograph, it's only 40km to the Pyrenean Ruritania, the principality of **Andorra**.

Llivia, Llo and Eyne

Bourg-Madame, 'the same latitude as Rome, but sunnier', as its brochure claims, is the crossing point for Spain; just across the border lies **Puigcerdà**, with a 14th-century church and the best ice hockey squad on the Iberian peninsula. The N116 will take you northeast from here back to Mont-Louis, completing your circumnavigation of Spain – or at least the tiny Spanish enclave of **Llivia**, marooned by accident in the Treaty of 1659. The treaty stipulated that Spain must give up the *villages* of the Cerdagne, and everyone had forgotten that Llivia had the legal status of a *ville*; it had been a Roman *municipium*, the capital of the Cerdagne in ancient times. Llivia's historic centre is clustered around a 15th-century fortified church, housing a superb 13th-century sculpture of Christ; opposite, in the **Musée Municipal**, the unlikely attraction is a 16th-century pharmacy, one of the most beautiful, oldest and best-preserved in Europe. East of Bourg-Madame, more Catalan Romanesque churches can be visited: at **Hix**, an impressive edifice of 1177, built when the town was the residence of the counts of the Cerdagne and containing a majestic Romanesque Virgin with a little kingly Christ child on her lap; and at **Caldégas**, where the frescoes include a hunting scene with falcons.

Musée Municipal
open Tues–Sat 10–1 and 3–7, Sun 10–2; closed Mon

Further east along the N116, road signs will startle you with town names like Llo and Err; linguists say they're Basque, evidence that the Basques lived here in remote times. **Llo** has a church with a lovely sculptured portal and an exceptionally sweet cemetery over in nearby **Ste-Léocadie** (home of the highest vineyard in Europe). You can visit the **Musée de Cerdagne** in a 17th-century farm, dedicated to rural life including the pre-ski trades of the great plateau – shepherding and farming.

Musée de Cerdagne
Ste-Léocadie t 04 68 04 08 08; Eyne t 04 68 04 78 66; open July–Aug Wed–Mon 11–7; Sept–mid-Nov and mid-Dec–June Wed–Mon 10–12 and 2–6; closed Tues and mid-Nov–mid-Dec; call before visiting

The other half of the museum is at nearby **Eyne**, and focuses more on the natural history of the area, with a botanical garden. The **Réserve Naturelle d'Eyne** also offers guided tours in summer. Come in May, when it's late enough to avoid the skiers from the resort called Eyne 2600 but just in time for a spectacular display of wild flowers and medicinal herbs in the Vallée d'Eyne, climbing up to the Spanish border. There are opportunities for hiking, southwards into the narrow **Gorges du Sègre**.

Réserve Naturelle d'Eyne
t 04 68 04 77 07

(i) **Les Angles**
2 Av de l'Aude, **t** 04 68 04 32 76, www.les-angles.com; open daily

(i) **Bourg-Madame**
Place Catalogne, **t** 04 68 04 55 35, www.bourg-madame.fr; open Mon–Sat

(i) **Mont-Louis >**
3 Rue Lieutenant Pruneta, **t** 04 68 04 21 97, www.mont-louis.net; open Mon–Sat

(i) **Font-Romeu >**
38 Av E. Brousse, **t** 04 68 30 68 30, www.fontromeu.com; open daily

Market Days in the Cerdagne

Puigcerdà: Sun am, the best market in the area.

Where to Stay and Eat in the Cerdagne

Olette ✉ 66360

La Fontaine, 3 Rue de la Fusterie, **t** 04 68 97 03 67 (€). Nice B&B on the village square in a large house run since 2006 by an English couple. Guest lounge available and terraces for eating out on and relaxation. Evening meals (€€) for guests only.

Mont-Louis ✉ 66210

Le Clos Cerdan, **t 04 68 04 23 29, www.leclosceradan.com (€€). Get a room with a view at this grey stone hotel on a cliff overlooking the valley; modern but very comfortable, with a restaurant (€€). There are also apartments to rent and a spa with gym.

Lou Roubaillou, Rue des Ecoles Laïques, **t** 04 68 04 23 26 (€). In the village, by the ramparts, the family-run Lou Roubaillou is pleasant; no restaurant.

Font-Romeu ✉ 66120

Clair Soleil, 29 Av F. Arago, **t 04 68 30 13 65 (€). With a view, a pool and a restaurant (€€). Closed mid-April–mid-May and late Oct–mid-Dec.

Cal Xandera, Angoustrine, 8km away, **t** 04 68 04 61 67, www.calxandera.com (€€). Completely different: a beautifully restored 18th-century farmhouse serving flavour-packed

traditional mountain cuisine. Also rooms in maison d'hôte style, for 2–6 people: €25–26 per person,half-board €33.50–36 per person per night. Jazz concerts in summer.

Llo and Saillagouse ✉ 66800

***L'Atalaya, Llo, **t** 04 68 04 70 04, www.atalayabb.com (€€€). A rare example of a country inn unconcerned with the skiing business; tranquillity is assured in this setting, close to the wild flowers of the Vallée d'Eyne and infinitely far from anything else, with a pool and an excellent restaurant in summer (€€€). Closed mid-Jan–mid-April and mid-Nov–mid-Dec.

Planotel, Rue de la Poste, **t 04 68 04 72 08, www.planotel.fr (€€). Modern, with a heated pool and restaurant and run by the same family that runs Planes (see below). Closed Oct–May except school hols.

Planes, Place des Comtes de Cerdagne, Saillagouse, **t 04 68 04 72 08, www.planotel.fr (€). Planes has been hosting guests since 1895; the dining room (€€€–€€), with its huge fireplace, is a great place to settle down to a plate of Catalan anchovies and red peppers. Guests can use the facilities at the Planotel. Closed last 2 weeks Mar, and Nov–mid-Dec.

Valcebollère ✉ 66340

***Les Ecureuils, **t** 04 68 04 52 03, www.aubergeecureils.com (€€). Friendly mountain auberge, offering charming rooms and local produce (€€€–€€). Proprietor Etienne Lafitte will take you on guided mountain walks following smugglers' paths. Closed Nov–early Dec.

Pyrenean Valleys: The Vallespir

The valley of the Tech, the southernmost valley of Roussillon, and of France, winds a lonesome trail around the southern slopes of Canigou. Known for its mineral waters since Roman times, it traditionally made its living from these and from ironworking, the basis of Catalan prosperity in the Middle Ages. When the iron gave out, there was smuggling.

Today, as smugglers have become superfluous, the Vallespir lives by tourism, with some euros on the side from cherries and cork oak – the primeurs, the first cherries in the French market each year,

and the *grand cru* corks that have kept the best champagne bubbly for centuries.

Le Boulou and St-Martin-de-Fenollar

From Perpignan, you reach the Vallespir by the A9, getting off at **Le Boulou**, a truck-stop known to every European TIR jockey. The ancient Roman teamsters knew it, too. Le Boulou has been fated by geography as an eternal transit point, today jammed in summer with tourists heading up the N9 into Spain via Le Perthus. It also has a casino and spa, and a fine Romanesque **church** with a superb white marble tympanum sculpted by the Master of Cabestany, portraying the Resurrection of the Virgin. The cornice shows scenes of the Nativity, the Christ Child's first bath (also rarely depicted in art), the Shepherds, Magi and Flight into Egypt.

East of Le Boulou, **St-Genis-des-Fontaines** was one of the important early medieval monasteries of Roussillon. Its church has a remarkable carved lintel dated 1020, with a *Majestat* and stylized apostles shaped like bowling-pins; the cloister was dismantled and sold off in 1924, one of the final scandals of France's traditional lack of concern for its medieval heritage. In 1988 it was rebuilt as it was, with originals and copies; restoration continued until recently and there is now an art gallery to see as well.

The A9 and N9 continue south into Spain, passing **St-Martin-de-Fenollar** and its 9th-century **church**, with some of the most unusual and best-preserved 12th-century frescoes in the Midi. Nine-tenths of all early medieval painting is lost to us, and this is a rare example of the best of what is left: brilliant colours and a confident stylization, with an imagery untroubled by the dogma of later religious painting, as in the *Nativity*, where Mary lies not in a

St-Genis-des-Fontaines
t 04 68 89 84 33; open May–Oct Mon–Fri 10–12 and 2–6, Sat and Sun 9–12 and 2–6; Nov–April daily 9.30–12 and 2–5

St-Martin-de-Fenollar church
t 04 68 87 73 82; open mid-June–mid-Sept daily 10.30–12 and 3.30–7; mid-Sept–mid-June Wed–Mon 2–5, closed Tues; adm

stable but in a comfortable bed under a chequered baldachin. The scene from the Apocalypse, of Christ in Majesty with the four symbols of the Evangelists and the 24 elders, was a favourite 12th-century theme on both sides of the Pyrenees.

Hannibal entered Gaul through **Le Perthus**, the last, or first stop in France. Archaeologists have uncovered, at Panisars, a monumental pedestal, identified as belonging to the **Trophée de Pompée**. Similar to La Turbie near the Italian border, this monument was erected by a victorious Pompey in 71 BC on the Gallo-Hispanic frontier. Part of the stone was used to build a priory in 1011 (the ruins are nearby); the rest was quarried by Vauban in the 17th century to build the **Fort de Bellegarde**.

Fort de Bellegarde
*t 04 68 83 60 15;
open June–end Sept
10.30–6.30; adm*

Céret: the 'Mecca of Cubism'

Back in the valley of the Tech, the D115 streaks from Le Boulou to Céret, centre of the optimal cherry-growing region suspended between the Pyrenees and the sea. Amid the orchards in the hills around, Céret is a laid-back town under enormous plane trees, with perfect little café-lined squares (especially the **Plaça dels Nou Raigs**), medieval gates, the biggest Baroque church in Roussillon, **St-Pierre**, a war memorial by Maillol and an elegant 14th-century bridge over the Tech. Céret takes its bullfighting seriously, with *ferias* in July and September.

✪ Musée d'Art Moderne
*t 04 68 87 27 76; open
July–mid-Sept daily
10–7; mid-Sept–June
Wed–Mon 10–6,
closed Tues; adm*

Have a look around Céret before visiting the **Musée d'Art Moderne** (8 Bd du Maréchal Joffre) and you'll be surprised at how many scenes you'll recognize. Céret found its artistic destiny at the turn of the last century, thanks to Picasso, Braque, Gris, Manolo, Matisse, Soutine, Kisling, Masson, Tzara, Lhote, Marquet and others who spent time here up until 1940, and whose works fill the rooms. Best of all are the works donated by Picasso in 1953, among them 28 little plates painted in a five-day spurt of energy, all with variations on the *corrida* under a blasting sun.

Maison du Patrimoine
*t 04 68 87 31 59, www.
maisondupatrimoine-
ceret.fr; open summer
daily 10–12 and
2–7; winter daily
10–12 and 2–5*

Although not as dazzling, the **Maison du Patrimoine** in the Tour Port d'Espagne houses well-arranged Neolithic, Classical and medieval finds from the Vallespir, as well as temporary exhibitions.

Amélie-les-Bains and Arles-sur-Tech

Musée de la Poste
*t 04 68 39 34 90;
open May–Sept Tues–Fri
10–12 and 2–6.30, Mon
and Sat 2–6.30, closed
Sun; mid-Feb–April and
Oct–mid-Dec Tues–Fri
10–12 and 2–5.30, Mon
and Sat 2–5.30, closed
Sun; closed mid-
Dec–mid-Feb; adm*

Sulphurous waters, good for your rheumatism, have been the fortune of **Amélie-les-Bains** since ancient times; a Roman swimming pool with a vaulted roof has been uncovered, and the spa, rising on either side of the river Tech, still does a grandstand business. Amélie's pretty medieval ancestor, **Palalda**, is piled on a nearby hill, and offers a small **Musée de la Poste** for snail-mail nostalgia from the days of Louis XI to 1900, with a collection of stamps, and telephones; a museum on how the locals lived in days gone by has also moved into the same building.

Just west, **Arles-sur-Tech**, the ancient capital of the Vallespir, is a curious old village built on a narrow maze of lanes and offering some even curiouser hagiography in its 11th- and 12th-century **abbey of Ste-Marie**, originally the centre of an important monastery. Dark Age Arles-sur-Tech got by with an anonymous saint – an empty 4th-century sarcophagus known as *Sainte-Tombe* – until the dreaded *simiots* came to town, ape-like monsters that trampled the crops and violated the women. In despair, the abbot of Ste-Marie went to the pope asking for some holy relics. This was in 957, when demand for saints' bones was at its historic high, and the best the pope could offer was a pair of Persian martyrs named Abdon and Sennen. The abbot brought them back in a false-bottomed water-barrel, to fool the Venetians and Germans and any other relic thieves, and they dealt with the *simiots* as efficiently as if they had been the bones of St Peter himself. The story is portrayed in a 17th-century retable, in the chapel where Abdon and Sennen's relics are kept. The *Sainte-Tombe* itself, once a major pilgrimage attraction, is kept in a little enclosure outside the front door. It fills continually with perfectly pure water – some 500 to 600 litres a year, ceremoniously pumped every 30 July.

Tissages Catalans
t 04 68 39 10 07; open April–Oct Mon–Fri 10–12 and 2.30–5.30

Arles-sur-Tech is the home of **Tissages Catalans**, where they've been making cloth since 1900 (there's a little museum on Rue des Usines), and it was the last redoubt of the valley's famous medieval iron industry; the last working mine in Roussillon, up at Batère, closed down in the early 1990s.

Gorges de la Fou
t 04 68 39 16 21; open April–Nov daily 10–6; adm

Two kilometres northwest along the D44 you can go through the World's Narrowest Gorge, the **Gorges de la Fou**, a giant crack in the rock with sides towering 650ft, with waterfalls and caves along the mile-long walkway. Legend made it the lair of witches, bogeymen and *traboucayres*, robbers who pounced on passing diligences. At **Montferrer**, just west of Arles-sur-Tech, there is a museum which,

Museum
t 04 68 39 12 44; open Mon–Fri 2–6

among other things, tells the story of the *traboucayres*.

Continuing up the valley, just south of the D115, the hilltop village of **Serralongue** has a church dating from 1018, with a fine portal and one of the only surviving examples of a Catalan *conjurador*; this is a small, square pavilion with a slate roof and statues of the four Evangelists facing the four cardinal directions. When a storm threatened, the priest would go up to the *conjurador* and perform certain rites facing the direction of the storm to avert its wrath.

A detour further south, on the D3, will uncover **St-Laurent-de-Cerdans**, famous for making espadrilles, and **Coustouges**, which has a lovely early 12th-century fortified church with a slate roof and two carved portals, one inside the other.

Some towns just ask for it. As if having a name like **Prats-de-Mollo** weren't enough, this tiny spa advertises itself as the 'European Capital of Urinary Infections'. Prats-de-Mollo's other

ⓘ **Prats-de-Mollo-la-Preste**
Place du Foiral, t 04 68 39 70 83, www.pratsde mollolapreste.com; open Mon–Sat; July–Aug also Sun

ⓘ **Céret >**
Av G. Clemenceau, t 04 68 87 00 53, www.ot-ceret.fr; open Mon–Sat

ⓘ **Arles-sur-Tech >>**
Rue Barjau, t 04 68 39 11 99, www.ville-arles-sur-tech.fr, or www.tourisme-haut-vallespir.com; open Mon–Sat

⭐ **Les Glycines >>**

Market Days in the Vallespir

Céret: Sat.
Arles-sur-Tech: Wed.
Prats-de-Mollo: Wed and Fri.

Where to Stay and Eat in the Vallespir

Céret ✉ 66400

****La Terrasse au Soleil, Route Fontfrède, t 04 68 87 01 94, *www.terrasse-au-soleil.com* (€€€€€). A restored, modernized *mas* on a hill above Céret, with a view, a heated pool and tennis court. Its restaurant, **Cerisaie** (€€€), is good, and there is also a cheaper *brasserie*, and a spa. *Closed Dec–Feb.*

Le Mas Trilles, Pont de Reynès, on the Céret–Amélie-les-Bains road, t 04 68 87 38 37 (€€€€–€€). A tastefully renovated *mas* with a heated pool and a charming garden overlooking a trout stream. No restaurant, just snacks, but there are three very near by. *Closed Oct–Easter.*

**Les Arcades, 1 Place Picasso, t 04 68 87 12 30, *www.hotel-arcades-ceret.com* (€). Artistically decorated, with balconies overlooking the market square. You can rent rooms with a small kitchen for €360 per week.

*Vidal, 4 Place Soutine, t 04 68 87 00 85, *www.hotelvidalceret.com* (€). In a charming, if quirky and sometimes noisy, listed building, with a restaurant (€€). *Open all year.*

Les Feuillants, 1 Bd Lafayette, t 04 68 87 37 88 (€€€–€€). Modern paintings and a varied choice of dishes, many Catalan-based. *Closed Mon all year, plus Sun eve except in July and Aug.*

Amélie-les-Bains ✉ 66110

**Castel Emeraude, Route de la Corniche, t 04 68 39 02 83, *www.lecastelemeraude.com* (€€–€). This is the place to get away from it all: a big white manor on the banks of the river, with a good restaurant (€€€–€€). *Closed mid-Nov–mid-Mar.*

**La Pergola, 60 Av du Vallespir, t 04 68 39 05 71, *www.hotel-pergola.com* (€). A good choice which does not require full board. You can also rent rooms with a small kitchen and balcony for €45 per night. *Closed Jan.*

Arles-sur-Tech ✉ 66150

**Les Glycines, Rue Jeu de Paume, t 04 68 39 10 09 (€). Named for the ancient wisteria that shades the garden terrace, Les Glycines has modernized rooms, all with bath, and a wonderful restaurant (€€) where the chef defies every snide remark we've ever made about Catalan cuisine. *Closed Jan.*

claim to fame is a European record for rainfall: 33 inches in 16 hours on 15 October 1940. The baths are really at **La-Preste**, 8km up in the mountains; Prats-de-Mollo itself is an attractive old village, with remains of its walls and medieval buildings that recall the days when it was a textile centre, specializing in Catalan bonnets. Don't miss the whale bone stuck in the church wall. This is as far as we go; the Spanish border is 14km away.

Toulouse

Called 'La Ville Rose' for its millions of pink bricks, Toulouse should have been the rosy capital of a nation called Languedoc, but it was knocked out of the big leagues in the 1220s by the popes and kings of France and their henchman Simon de Montfort. Seven and a half centuries later, the Toulousains are finally getting their rhythm back; the city has around 800,000 lively inhabitants, including more than 110,000 university students, and 70 per cent of the industry in the Midi-Pyrénées region, much of it hi-tech and related to aeronautics and space. It's this big pink dynamo on the cutting edge of the 21st century that keeps southwest France from nodding off in its vats of goose fat and wine.

12

Don't miss

⭐ The biggest Romanesque church on Earth
St-Sernin Basilica p.274

⭐ A Gothic masterpiece
Les Jacobins p.278

⭐ *Pastel* palaces
Hôtels de Bernuy, d'Assézat, and de Pierre pp.279–81

⭐ Cutting-edge art in an old abattoir
Les Abattoirs p.285

⭐ A restaurant revolution
Old Toulouse p.287

See map overleaf

BOUCHURE

BOULEVARD DE LA MARQUETTE

Jardin Compans-Caffarelli

PLACE ARNAUD-BERNARD

BOULEVARD LASCROSSES

RUE LASCROSSES

R. ARNAUD BERNARD

PL. DES TIERCERETTES

ALLEE DE BARCELONE

ALLEE DE BRIENNE

Canal

BOULEVARD MAL. LECLERC

BOULEVARD ARMAND DUPORTAL

RUE DES PUITS CREUSES

Université des Sciences Sociales

PLACE A. FRANCE

RUE DES AMIDONNIERS

de

Brienne

AV PAUL SEJOURNE

EDF Bazacle

St-Pierre des Chartreux

St-Pierre-des-Cuisines ✝

RUE VALADE

RUE PARGAM

Don't miss

⭐ St-Sernin Basilica p.274

⭐ Les Jacobins p.278

⭐ Hôtels de Bernuy, d'Assézat, de Pierre pp.279–81

⭐ Les Abattoirs p.285

⭐ Old Toulouse p.287

PONT DES CATALANS

Garonne

PLACE ST-PIERRE

PONT ST-PIERRE

QUAI LOMBARD

RUE LARREY

No -la

RUE DE L'ABATTOIR

PLACE DES ABATTOIRS

RUE DES FONTAINES

Les Abattoirs

⭐ 🏛

ALLEES

Hospice St-Joseph de la Grave

Hôtel-Dieu St-Jacques *(Musée d'Histoire de la Médecine)*

Ecole Beaux

RUE ADOLPHE COLL

Centre Municipal de l'Affiche, de la Carte Postale, et de l'Art Graphique 🏛

CHARLES

St-Nicolas ✝

RUE RECLUSANE

RUE DE LA PLACE OLIVIER

REPUBLIQUE

Château d'Eau ●

PLACE LAGANNE

PONT-

PLACE ST-CYPRIEN

ROGUET

DE

PLACE

RUE I VIE

AV. ETIENNE BILLERES

FITTE

RUE TEINTURIERS

RUE COUBEFER

LAGANNE

COURS DILLON

PRAIRIE DES FILTRES

Garonne

N

RUE DE CUGNAUX

RUE DES ARCS ST-CYPRIEN

RUE STE-LUCIE

PLACE DU FER-A-CHEVAL

PONT ST-MICHEL

═══ 250 metres
═══ 250 yards

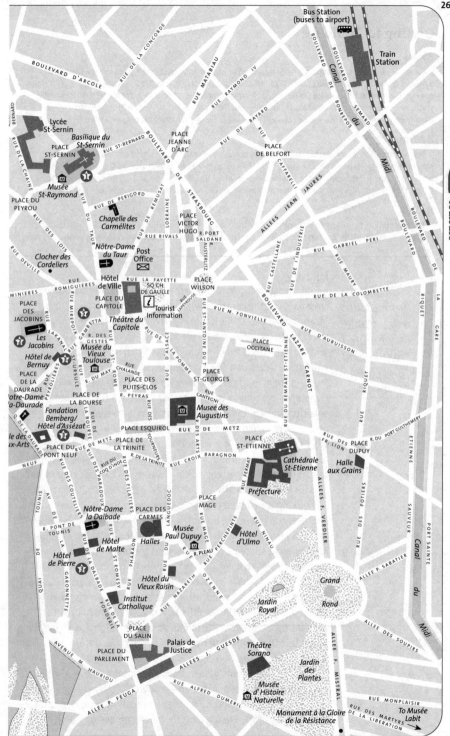

Getting to Toulouse

By Air

Toulouse's international **airport** is at Blagnac, 10km from the centre, **t** 05 61 42 44 00, *www.toulouse. aeroport.fr*. Airlines include Air France (**t** 08 20 82 08 20), British Airways (**t** 08 25 82 54 00), BMI, Flybe and easyJet. The **airport bus**, **t** 05 34 60 64 00, *www.navettevia-toulouse.com*, departs from Toulouse's SNCF station every 20mins from 5am to 8.20pm daily, and from the airport to central Toulouse every 20mins 7.35am–12.30am. Ticket price is €4 one way. The ticket booth at the airport is outside Hall 1.

By Train

The main **station** is Gare Matabiau. Trains run from Paris-Austerlitz through Gourdon, Souillac, Cahors and Montauban to Toulouse in 6hrs 30mins; TGVs from Paris-Montparnasse in around 5hrs, via Bordeaux. Slow trains to Bordeaux, stopping in Montauban, Castelsarrasin, Moissac, Agen and Aiguillon, take 2hrs 30mins. Other links include Albi (1hr), Castres (1hr 30mins), Lille (TGV, 7hrs), Auch, Carcassonne, Nice and Lyon.

By Bus

The **bus station**, **t** 05 61 61 67 67, is next to the train station; there are buses to Foix, Albi, Gaillac, Auch, Nogaro and Montauban. You can also travel by coach to London, Madrid and Barcelona (*www.eurolines.com*).

History

The history of Toulouse is detestable, saturated with blood and perfidy.
Henry James

Toulouse grew up at a ford in the Garonne, a natural strategic crossroads at the centre of what the ancient Greek geographer Strabo called the 'Gallic isthmus' between the Mediterranean and the Atlantic. When the Romans found it, its inhabitants were the Tectosage Gauls, a tribe that had grown rich from mining and the wine trade. After first forcing them into an alliance, the Romans crushed them in 107 BC, gobbling up the Tectosages' fabulous treasure – 100 tons of gold and silver hidden at the bottom of a swamp. As a refounded Roman colony, Palladia Tolosa enjoyed five centuries of peace and quiet, developing into a modest provincial city of some 20,000. The Visigoths took over in 420 AD, but instead of a sacking and burning, Tolosa got a surprising new role to play – as capital of a new Visigothic Kingdom, under warrior king Ataulf and his loving bride, the Roman imperial princess Galla Placidia.

That kingdom lasted only until 507, when Clovis's Franks decisively defeated the Visigoths. They moved over the Pyrenees to found a new kingdom in Spain, while under Clovis's 'do-nothing' Merovingian successors, Toulouse and the rest of the southwest was largely left to itself. And by its own efforts, the city repelled an attack by the Arabs in 721, a decade before Charles Martel chased them out of Gaul for good. After that, the new Carolingian dynasty enjoyed a nominal rule over the southwest, and to hold onto it they set up a branch of the family as Counts of Toulouse, governing a vast territory extending from the Rhône to the Garonne and from the Pyrenees to the Dordogne.

Most of these counts were named Raymond, and over the next two centuries they would become a powerful dynasty, retaining most of these lands and ruling them more as independent princes than vassals of the French king. Toulouse's golden age began in the

Getting around Toulouse

By Métro and City Bus

The *métro* and city buses are run by **TISSEO**, which has an information office at 7 Place Esquirol, **t** 05 61 41 70 70, *www.tisseo.fr*. A new *métro* line, running north to south, from Borderouge to Ramonville, should be fully operational by 2008. Bus and *métro* times coordinate.

Almost all sights are in the compact centre, so you'll hardly ever need to use either the *métro* or the bus, though the *métro* is useful for getting into the centre from the station. There's also a free shuttlebus (*navette*; Mon–Sat 9–7) around the historic quarters – you find a red line and stick your hand out when you see the bus coming. A tramway to the west of the city is scheduled to be up and running by 2009.

By Taxi

If you can't find one cruising around or at a taxi stand, try **t** 05 61 42 38 38, or **t** 05 34 25 02 50.

By Car

Toulouse's rapid growth and narrow streets have led to major traffic problems. Rush hour can be hell – it may be quicker to go around the **ringroad** (*rocade*) and come back into the centre where you need to be.

The most convenient pay **car parks** are at Place du Capitole, Allée J-Jaurès, Place V. Hugo and Place St-Etienne; they cost more than €1 an hour. The Jeanne d'Arc car park tends to be less crowded. Alternatively, battle to find a space in the free parking areas such as Place St-Sernin and Allées Jules Guesde (near the Grand Rond), trawl the streets for a free spot (easiest in summer when people leave for the coast) or park at Joliment or Gramont and take the *métro* in – the price of parking is included in the *métro* ticket (the car parks get full quickly, though, so you need to get there early).

There are quite a few **car hire** companies at the **airport**: ADA, **t** 05 61 30 00 33; Avis, **t** 05 34 60 46 50; Budget, **t** 05 61 71 85 80; Europcar, **t** 0825 82 55 14; Hertz, **t** 0825 80 10 31.

By Bicycle and Motorcycle

Movimento, **t** 05 34 30 03 00, *www.movimento.coop*, has bike-hire kiosks at the bus station and near the tourist office. You can also be driven around on electric tricycles (**t** 06 67 71 17 22; *June–Sept*).

By Boat

The system of aqueducts that enabled the people to paddle around the city in the 6th century is sadly long gone, but you can still see some of the nicest corners of Toulouse by river. In summer, **Toulouse Croisières** (**t** 05 61 25 72 57, *www.toulouse-croisieres.com*) offers **trips on the Garonne** from Quai de la Daurade (*Tues–Sun 10.30, 4.30 and 6, plus some other times*) and wonderful night cruises, to show off the city's illuminated river banks.

Other Means

A **tourist train** tours the main sites in 30mins or so (from in front of the post office on Rue Lafayette; **t** 05 62 71 08 51). You can also hire **tourist taxis** with driver-guides (**t** 05 34 25 02 50; about €40/75mins). The tourist office has some bike and walking routes drawn up by the *mairie*.

11th century, under such mighty counts as Raymond IV, who built the great basilica of St-Sernin and led the Christian armies in the First Crusade in 1095. Raymond V, a princely troubadour, granted the city of Toulouse a large degree of self-rule, and did his best to fight off that eternal troublemaker Richard the Lion-Heart, who invaded his domains in the 1190s.

Under its governing *capitouls*, Toulouse grew wealthy and fat, with one of the biggest grain-milling industries in Europe. But more troubles would soon be coming from outside. Raymond VI, who became count in 1195, was a modern, tolerant soul; the new religion of the Cathars was making great advances in his lands, and Raymond defended them against the powers of the Church. That resulted in a powerful coalition against him, led by Innocent III, strongest of all the medieval popes, and the King of France. The 'Albigensian Crusade', as the attack on the Cathars came to be known, was in reality a massive grab for land and power at Toulouse's expense. A northern army under Simon de Montfort invaded the county in 1209. In 1213, the crushing defeat of Raymond and his Aragonese allies at Muret, just outside Toulouse, ensured the end of Languedoc's independence, and also of southern culture and prosperity. Simon de Montfort entered Toulouse as its new count two years later, while Bishop Folquet de Marseille, a former troubadour who became the most rabid bigot of them all, presided over a grisly Inquisition. Toulouse revolted successfully two years later, and de Montfort died besieging it, but the last two Raymonds of the line were only able to hold out a little longer. King Louis VIII himself led another bloody invasion in 1229, and the county reverted to the French crown when the last count, royal appointee Alphonse de Poitiers, died childless in 1271.

Under French rule, Toulouse gradually lost its rights and privileges, and over the next three centuries it would decline to an economic and cultural backwater. The city was lucky to avoid the calamities of the Hundred Years War, and it even enjoyed a period of prosperity after 1560 thanks to *pastel*, a locally grown crop much in demand across Europe for dyeing. Indigo from the Carolinas put an end to *pastel's* prominence in the 1660s, but at the same time, a new engine of prosperity was taking shape – the Canal du Midi (1666–81), a locally planned and financed effort that linked the Atlantic and the Mediterranean by way of the Garonne, and brought Toulouse a considerable amount of new wealth and trade.

Still, compared with its medieval heyday Toulouse remained little more than a sleepy provincial city; even with the coming of the railroad in 1856. What proved to be the turning point for modern Toulouse literally fell from the sky. The city's surprising aerial adventures began with pioneer aviator Clément Ader, who managed to get a steam-powered plane off the ground in the 1890s. By the First World War Toulouse had an aircraft factory, and afterwards it served as the hub of France's first big air mail service. Another local firm, nationalized in the 1930s, grew to become Aérospatiale. In the 50s the government decided to concentrate all its air and space efforts here, and the last few giddy decades have seen France's City of the Air give birth to the Ariane rockets and Hermès, the European space shuttle, as well as Caravelle, Concorde and Airbus jets. Today, many visitors' startling introduction to the city will be the vast complex of factories, research centres and industrial parks that surrounds the airport at Blagnac.

The new Toulouse has become the fourth-largest city in France, and the capital of the Midi-Pyrenees region, giving it a political role, albeit a limited one, for the first time since the Middle Ages. New building and improvements are everywhere, including a shiny new metro. At times Toulouse may seem all business, but a lively population that includes the descendants of the wave of refugees from the Spanish Civil War and *pieds noirs* from Algeria, along with hordes of students at the bustling University, ensures that it remains one of the most engaging cities of the Midi.

Place du Capitole

This dignified front parlour of Toulouse dates from 1850, when the 200-year-long tidying away of excess buildings was over and the edges rimmed with neoclassical brick façades. As a permanent memorial to the southern kingdom of nevermore, the centre of the pavement is marked by an enormous **Cross of Languedoc**. This same golden cross on a red background hangs proudly from Toulouse's city hall, the **Capitole**, or CAPITOLIUM as it reads, bowing to a 16th-century story claiming that ancient Rome got its Capitol idea from Toulouse's temple of Capitoline Jupiter.

Capitole
t 05 61 22 29 22; historical rooms open Mon–Fri 9–5

Jupiter Poopiter! Everyone knows this Capitole is really named after the *capitouls*. In 1750, flush with money brought in by the Canal du Midi, these worthies decided to transform their higgledy-piggledy medieval buildings into a proper Hôtel de Ville. Parts of the original 12th–17th-century complex were saved, as much as could be masked by the neoclassical façade designed by Guillaume Cammas, who imported stone and marble to alternate with the home-made brick of Toulouse. Cammas's careful polychromatic effects were only briefly admired before the *capitouls* decided to order every building in the city to be whitewashed or covered with white stucco, the better to reflect the moonlight and make up for the lack of street lighting. The first building to get the treatment was the Capitole itself; the entire Place du Capitole lay under this dull make-up until 1946, when Toulouse decided to become the *Ville Rose* once more. Other critics have had trouble with the Capitole's height. '*C'est beau mais c'est bas*' was the only comment of Napoleon, an expert on the subject.

Théâtre du Capitole
t 05 61 22 29 22; open Mon–Fri 9–5

The portal on the right belongs to the **Théâtre du Capitole**, while over the central door eight pink marble columns represent the eight *capitouls*; the extravagant pompous historical rooms upstairs were decorated in the 1800s with busts of famous Toulousains and a painting by Henri Martin called *Jean-Jaurès on the banks of the Garonne*. Behind the great façade, the **Cour Henri IV** gives on to Square Charles de Gaulle, defended by the Donjon of 1525, where the *capitouls* kept the city archives. The building, well restored by Viollet-le-Duc, now houses the city tourist office.

From Place du Capitole to the Basilica of St-Sernin

Running north from Place du Capitole, narrow **Rue du Taur** was the road to Cahors in Roman times. The Taur in its name means 'bull', which features in the life of the city's first saint, Sernin, who died here in the 240s. Sernin (a corruption of Saturnin) was a missionary from Rome who preached in Pamplona and Toulouse. One day, runs the legend, he happened by the temple of Capitoline Jupiter, where preparations were under way for the sacrifice of a bull to Mithras. The priests ordered him to kneel before the pagan idol, and, when Sernin refused, a sudden gust of wind blew over the statue of Mithras, breaking it to bits. In fury the crowd demanded the sacrifice of Sernin instead, and he was tied under the bull, which, maddened by the extra weight, dragged his body through the city streets. Curiously, an identical martyrdom awaited Sernin's disciple Fermin in Pamplona, where he became the patron saint of matadors and is honoured each year by the famous running of the bulls, even though the official hagiography claims that Fermin died peacefully in bed as bishop of Amiens. One wonders: could Fermin really be Sernin, transformed long ago by a slip of a monastic quill?

After turning Sernin to pulp, the bull left his body where the 14th-century **Notre-Dame-du-Taur** now stands, replacing an oratory built over Sernin's tomb in 360. Its 41m *clocher-mur* looks like a false front in a Wild West town; the nave is surprisingly wide, and has a faded fresco of the Tree of Jesse along the right wall. Sernin's tomb attracted so many pilgrims and Christians who desired to be buried near him that in 403 a *martyrium* was built just under 300m to the north. An imperial decree permitted the removal of the saint's relics to this spot, and over the centuries tombs lined Rue de Taur, as in the Alyscamps in Arles. In 1075, just as the pilgrimage to Compostela was getting under way, Count Guilhem decided Sernin deserved something more grand.

The Basilica of St-Sernin

The construction of the Basilique St-Sernin was continued by Guilhem's famous brother Raymond IV, and the building was of such importance that in 1096 Pope Urban II, on tour that year preaching the First Crusade, came to consecrate its marble altar. The whole wasn't finished, however, until 1220.

At 116m, this is the largest surviving Romanesque church in the world (only the great abbey church of Cluny, destroyed in the Revolution, was bigger). It was begun at the same time, and has the exact same plan, as the basilica of St James at Compostela: a

⭐ **Basilique St-Sernin**
*t 05 61 21 80 45;
open June Mon–Sat
8.30–12.30 and 2–6.15,
Sun 8.30–12.15 and 2–7;
July–Sept Mon–Sat
8.30–6.15, Sun
8.30–7.30; Oct–May
Mon–Sat 8.30–11.45
and 2–5.45, Sun
8.30–12.30 and 2–7*

cross, ending in a semicircular apse with five radiating chapels. In the 19th century the abbey and cloister were demolished, and in 1860 Viollet-le-Duc was summoned to restore the basilica. He spent 20 years on the project – and botched the roof so badly that rainwater seeped directly into the stone and brick. A century later the church was found to be in danger of collapse – hence a 22-million-franc 'de-restoration' project to undo Viollet-le-Duc's mischief. Off came his neogothic ornamentation and heavy stone, to be replaced with tiles handcrafted in the 13th-century manner.

The Exterior

The apse of St-Sernin (seen from Rue St-Bernard) is a fascinating play of white stone and red brick, a crescendo culminating in the octagonal bell-tower that is Toulouse's most striking landmark. New York had its war of skyscrapers in the 1930s; 13th-century Toulouse had its war of bell-towers: St-Sernin's original three storeys of arcades were increased to five for the sole purpose of upstaging the bell-tower of the Jacobins. The most elaborate of the basilica's portals is an odd, asymmetrical one on the south side, the **Porte Miège-ville**. It faces Rue du Taur; apparently this street, called Miège-ville or 'mid-city' in medieval times, ran right through the spot before the basilica was built. Devotees of medieval *Toulousain* arcana – a bottomless subject – say that this portal is the real cornerstone of the kingdom of Languedoc that the 11th-century counts were trying to create; books have been written about its proportions and the symbolism of its decoration, even claiming that it is the centre of a geomantic construction, with 12 lines radiating from here across the counts' territories, connecting various chapels and villages and forming – what else? – Raymond IV's Cross of Languedoc. The tympanum was carved by the 11th-century master Bernard Gilduin, showing the *Ascension of Christ*, a rare scene in medieval art, and one of the most choreographic: Christ surrounded by dancing angels, watched by the Apostles on the lintel. On the brackets are figures of David and others riding on lions; the magnificent capitals tell the story of the Redemption (*Original Sin, Massacre of the Innocents, Annunciation*), all from the expressive chisel of Gilduin.

The north transept door, now walled up, was the royal door; the south transept door, the **Porte des Comtes**, is named after the several 11th-century counts of Toulouse who are buried in palaeo-Christian sarcophagi in the deep *enfeu* nearby. The eight capitals here, also by Gilduin (*c.* 1080), are the oldest Romanesque works to show the torments of hell, most alarmingly a man having his testicles crushed and a woman whose breasts are being devoured by serpents, both paying the price for Lust.

The Interior

Begun in 1969, the 'de-restoration' of the barrel-vaulted interior stripped the majestic brick and stone of Viollet-le-Duc's ham-handed murals and fiddly neogothic bits. In the process, some fine 12th-century frescoes have been found, especially the serene angel of the Resurrection in the third bay of the north transept, which also has some of the best capitals. In the south transept, the shrine of St Jude, the patron saint of lost causes, blazes with candlelight in July – when French students take their exams.

Ambulatory
open July–Sept Mon–Sat 10–6, Sun 2–6; rest of year Mon–Sat 10–11.30 and 2–5.30, Sun 2–5.30; adm

For a small fee you can enter the **ambulatory** and make what the Middle Agers called 'the Circuit of Holy Bodies', for the wide array of saintly anatomies stashed in the five radiating chapels. In the 17th century, bas-reliefs and wood panels on the lives of the saints were added to bring the relics to life, and although these were removed in the 1800s they were restored and replaced in 1980. Opposite the central chapel are seven magnificent marble bas-reliefs of 1096, carved and signed by Bernard Gilduin. The *Christ in Majesty* set in a mandorla is as serene, pot-bellied and beardless as a Buddha, surrounded by the four Evangelists; the others show a seraph, a cherub, two apostles and a pair of hierarchic, extremely well-coiffed angels – scholars guess these were perhaps modelled after a Roman statue of Orpheus.

The Holy Bodies circuit continues down into the upper crypt, with the silver shrine of St Honoratus (1517) and the 13th-century reliquaries of the Holy Cross and of St Sernin, the latter showing the saint under the hooves of the bull. The dark, dank lower crypt contains, more bodily, two Holy Thorns (a present from St Louis), 13th-century gloves and mitres, and a set of six 16th-century painted wooden statues of apostles. In the choir an 18th-century baldachin shelters St Sernin's tomb, remade in 1746 and supported by a pair of bronze bulls. In the south transept, note the big feet sticking out of a pillar, all that remains of a shallow relief of St Christopher effaced by the hands of centuries of pilgrims.

Around Place St-Sernin and the Quartier Arnaud-Bernard

At No.3, the Lycée St-Sernin occupies the **Hôtel du Barry**, built by Louis XV's pimp, the Roué du Barry. Du Barry married his charming lover, Jeanne de Bécu, to his brother and then in 1759 introduced her to the king. His pandering earned him the money to build this mansion in 1777; it would later earn the Comtesse du Barry the guillotine in the Terror. (The word *roué*, incidentally, was first used in the 1720s, to describe the bawdy companions of the regent, the Duke of Orléans; it was invented by some disapproving soul who thought they should have been broken on the wheel.)

On the south side of the square stood a pilgrims' hostel, founded in the 1070s by a chanter of St-Sernin named Raymond Gayard, who was canonized for his charity to the poor. His hostel was succeeded by the *collège* of St Raymond (1505) for poor university students, and now by the rich archaeological collections of the **Musée St-Raymond**. This is the antiquities museum of Toulouse, with some exceptional pieces. The top floors concentrate on finds from the Roman region of Narbonnaise and one of its biggest towns, Tolosa, ancient Toulouse. One of the most interesting exhibits is the section of a relief depicting two Amazons in combat, one clearly with the upper hand over a man: this would have formed part of a temple or major monument. The collection of outstanding busts is small compared to the avenue of heads of emperors, men, women and children on the floor below: all found, with the other exhibits here, at Chiragan in Martres-Tolosane, 60km to the south of Toulouse. Don't miss the splendid marbles depicting the *Labours of Hercules*. Digs in the basement of the museum have revealed the presence of a Christian necropolis dating from the 4th century which grew up around the tomb of St Sernin. Several of the tombs have been left not far from where they were found, close to a large, circular 5th-century lime kiln. Ornate sarcophagi from southwest France and other funerary objects are also on display. There are also vestiges of walls from an 11th-century hospital and 13th-century college. Temporary exhibitions allow the public to see other artefacts from the Iron Age to the Middle Ages. The museum's specialist **library** at 11 Rue des Trois Renards can be used by the public .

Musée St-Raymond
t 05 61 22 31 44; open June–Aug daily 10–7; rest of year daily 10–6; **library** Mon–Fri 10–6, Sun 10–1 and 2–6

Musée St-Raymond Library
11 Rue des Trois Renards; Mon–Fri 10–6, Sat and Sun 10–1 and 2–6

Just south of St-Sernin in Rue du Périgord, the southern Gothic **Chapelle des Carmélites** (1643) owes its existence to Anne of Austria, wife of Louis XIII. The walls are covered with paintings, and vaulting has been restored to bring out its lavish ceiling, with an unusual allegory, the *Glory of Carmel*, by Jean-Baptiste Despax.

This northernmost medieval neighbourhood, the lively **Quartier Arnaud-Bernard**, has been the city's Latin Quarter ever since 1229, when the **University of Toulouse** was founded in Rue des Lois (part of it now occupies the old seminary of St-Pierre-des-Chartreux to the west). Although forced down Toulouse's throat by Paris, the university enjoyed a certain prestige in the Middle Ages; among its alumni were three popes and Michel de Montaigne. Rabelais started to study here, where he 'well learned to dance and to play at swords with two hands', but he quickly got out because its regents still had a certain problem when it came to freethinkers; several were burned alive at the stake. 'It didn't please God that I linger,' Rabelais continued, 'me with my nature already rather parched, and not in need of any more heat.'

The three principal squares of the quarter – Place du Peyrou, Place des Tiercerettes and Place Arnaud Bernard – became the centre of immigrant life in the last century; today they are quickly being gentrified but remain quite lively after dark.

Jardin Compans-Caffarelli
open daily 7.45–6

To the north of Boulevard Lascrosses, the neighbourhood's 'lung', the **Jardin Compans-Caffarelli**, was laid out in 1982 and has exotic plants, a Japanese garden and a tearoom.

Les Jacobins

Les Jacobins
t 05 61 22 23 82; open 9–7 daily; adm (cloister)

Just west of Place du Capitole stands the great Dominican mother church, Les Jacobins, the prototype for Dominican foundations across Europe and one of the masterpieces of southern French Gothic. The Spanish priest Domingo de Guzmán had tried hard to convert the Cathars before the Albigensian crusade, although the persuasive powers of one man, even a saint, proved negligible in the face of an intellectual revolt against the openly corrupt, materialistic clergy. In 1206 Domingo had re-converted enough women to found a convent, which became the germ of his Order of Preaching Friars, established in Toulouse in 1215. Promoted by Folquet, the bishop of Toulouse, and confirmed by the pope in 1216, the new Dominican order quickly found adherents across Europe. In 1230, the Dominicans erected this, their third convent in Toulouse, which took the name of the Jacobins from the Dominicans' Paris address, in Rue St-Jacques (the very same convent where the fanatical party of Robespierre would later meet, hence the *Jacobins* of the French Revolution – a fitting name in light of the Dominicans' role as Inquisitors). The magnificent Jacobins in Toulouse so impressed the popes that they made it the last resting place of the relics of the greatest Dominican of them all, St Thomas Aquinas (d. 1274).

Confiscated in the Revolution, the church and convent were requisitioned by Napoleon as a barracks for his artillery, which built an upper floor in the nave. When Prosper Mérimée, inspector of historic monuments, visited Toulouse in 1845, he found the mutilated complex occupied by 500 horses and cannoneers, with a pig-ignorant military administration bent on demolishing the whole thing. In 1865 the military was finally convinced to leave the Jacobins to the city, and Toulouse spent 100 years on its restoration.

The church is the perfect expression of the 13th-century reaction to Rome's love of luxury, which made the great preaching orders, the Dominicans and Franciscans, so popular in their day. Gargoyles are the only exterior sculpture in this immense but harmonious brick pile of buttresses, alternating with Flamboyant windows; its octagonal bell-tower of brick and stone crowned with baby towers is one of the landmarks of the city skyline. The interior is breathtakingly light and spacious, consisting of twin naves divided by seven huge columns, crisscrossed by a fantastic interweaving of ribs in the vault, reaching an epiphany in the massive Flamboyant *palmier* in the apse. The painted decoration dates from the 13th to the 16th century, but only the glass of the rose windows on the west side is original. The 19th-century gilded reliquary shrine of St Thomas Aquinas was returned to the high altar in 1974.

A small door leads out into the lovely garden **cloister** (1309), with brick arcades and twinned columns in grey marble, used in summer for the concert series *Piano aux Jacobins*. The east gallery gives on to the **chapterhouse**, supported by a pair of slender marble columns. The walls of the **Chapelle St-Antonin**, the funerary chapel, were painted in the early 1300s with scenes from the life of St Antonin, while the ceiling is decorated with southwest France's favourite vision from the Apocalypse: the 24 elders and angels glorifying Christ. In Rue Pargaminières, the **Refectory**, more than 60m long, houses temporary historical and cultural exhibitions.

West of Les Jacobins, near the Garonne's hog-backed Pont St-Pierre, are Toulouse's two churches dedicated to St Peter. **St-Pierre-des-Cuisines**, a little Romanesque priory associated with Moissac, is named after its kitchens, where a person's bread could be baked at cheaper rates than at the counts' ovens. **St-Pierre-des-Chartreux**, to the north in Rue Valade, was founded in the 17th century by monks fleeing the Huguenots of Castres; it has fine works from the 17th and 18th century, but is often closed.

Les Jacobins Refectory
open daily 9–7

St-Pierre-des-Cuisines
t 05 61 22 31 44; open July Mon 10–1 with guided tour at 11, Aug daily 10–12 and 2–7, guided tour at 4

Pastel Palaces and Violets of Gold

🛈 **Hôtel de Bernuy**

Just south of Les Jacobins, towards the south end of Rue Gambetta, is one of the city's most splendid residences, the **Hôtel de Bernuy**, built in 1504 by a *pastel* merchant from Burgos, Don Juan de Bernuy, a Spanish Jew who fled Ferdinand and Isabella's Inquisition and became a citizen – and *capitoul* – of Toulouse. Although Gothic on the outside, inside his master mason Loys Privat designed an eclectic fantasy courtyard, a mix of Gothic, Plateresque and Loire château, topped by a lofty tower rivalling those of all the other *pastel* nabobs. De Bernuy had a chance to repay France for the fortune he made when King François I was captured at the battle of Pavia by Emperor Charles V and imprisoned in Madrid; the king fell gravely ill, but no one could afford the ransom of 1,200,000 gold écus demanded by the emperor – until De Bernuy bailed him out. In his distress the king had promised an *ex voto* to St Sernin if he survived, and in the ambulatory you can still see the black marble statue he donated when he came in 1533 to thank the saint and de Bernuy for his generosity. Not long after de Bernuy's time the Jesuits converted his *hôtel particulier* into a college, now the prestigious **Lycée Pierre de Fermat**, named after its star pupil, the brilliant mathematician (1595–1665).

Just east, the 16th-century *hôtel particulier* at 7 Rue du May houses the **Musée du Vieux Toulouse**, with a fascinating collection from the city's history and its former porcelain industry, as well as paintings and etchings. Rue du May gives on to Rue St-Rome, decorated with 16th-century mansions built by the *capitouls* and wealthy merchants. At its south end don't miss triangular **Place de la Trinité**, with a 19th-century fountain supported by bronze mermaids. Near here, you can examine the popular artistic pulse of Toulouse in the ever-changing murals along Rue Coq-d'Inde.

Musée du Vieux Toulouse
t 05 62 27 11 50; open mid-May–mid-Oct Mon–Sat 2–6; guided tours Wed and Fri at 3

One of the finest private residences constructed in Toulouse, the Hôtel d'Assézat, is just west, off Rue de Metz. The *hôtel particulier* was begun in 1555 by another *pastel* magnate, Pierre d'Assézat, who had a near monopoly on the dye in northern Europe. Designed by Nicolas Bachelier, Toulouse's master architect-sculptor-engineer, it consists of two buildings around a large square court, and a curious tower crowned with an octagonal lantern and dome that served the merchant as an observation post over the Garonne. Facing the street, an Italianate loggia has seven brackets decorated with *pastel* pods. Inside, the **Fondation Bemberg** has a fine collection of art, particularly Renaissance work and modern French paintings. Since the 19th century, the *hôtel* has also been home to the **Palais des Académies**, seat of the Académie des Jeux Floraux poetry society (*see* below). Over the portico there's a statue of Dame Clémence Isaure, patroness of the Floral Games.

Hôtel d'Assézat

Fondation Bemberg
t 05 61 12 06 89, www.fondation-bemberg.fr; open Tues–Sun 10–12.30 and 1.30–6; night visits Thurs 9pm; themed visits Thurs 7pm; adm

The Eisteddfod of France

In November 1323, seven burghers of Toulouse met together in a monastery garden. Although not poets, these 'Seven Troubadours' were connoisseurs who regretted that good poetry in their town had died out with the counts of Toulouse. To inspire some new verse, the seven decided to invite all the bards of Languedoc to gather in the monastery garden to recite on 3 May; the poem the seven judged best would receive a violet made of gold. A big crowd showed up, and ever since then 3 May in Toulouse has hosted what has become known as the *Jeux Floraux*. The Seven Troubadours were soon succeeded by the 'Maintainers' of the Collège du Gay Scavoir, the world's oldest literary society, renamed the Académie des Jeux Floraux by Louis XIV.

Early on, the Seven Troubadours added two other prizes, an eglantine and a marigold in silver. To cope with the bewildering disorder of entries in the competition, they commissioned a code from one of Toulouse's top jurists and humanists, Guilhem Molinier; the resulting *Las Leys d'Amors* in 1356 was widely read, and soon copied in Barcelona, which in 1388 started its own *Jocs Florals*. There the first prize was not a gold rose but a real rose, because, like the greatest poetry, a rose can never be imitated. Although any true blue *Toulousain* would deny it, Barcelona's Floral Games actually produced the better poetry; so great was the fear of heresy or challenging accepted moral norms in the home town of the Inquisition that nearly all of Toulouse's entries were safe, bloodless praises of the Virgin Mary that hold little interest today. (Chaucer, a contemporary of the Seven Troubadours, would have told them the poetry might have been better had they chosen a different date for the contest: 3 May is the Invention of the Cross, traditionally the unluckiest day in the year.)

Along the Garonne

Rue de Metz continues to Toulouse's oldest bridge, which, as in Paris, is confusingly known as the new, or **Pont Neuf**. This Pont Neuf, with its seven unequal arches of brick and stone and curious holes (*oculi*), took from 1544 to 1632 to build, and links Gascony – the Left Bank – with the medieval province of Languedoc. Just down the quay is the **Ecole des Beaux-Arts**, its façade larded with allegorical figures (1895). Hidden under the icing is a 17th-century U-shaped monastery connected to **Notre-Dame-la-Daurade**. Only the name recalls what was for centuries one of the wonders of Toulouse, the 10-sided, domed, 5th-century palatine chapel of the Visigothic kings, known as the Daurade ('the golden one') after its shimmering mosaics. Similar to the churches of Ravenna, it was destroyed in 1761, when the nitwitted monks who owned it decided to replace it with a reproduction of the Vatican. Plans for the new church collided with the Revolution and the building was only completed in the mid 19th century. The paintings in the choir are by Ingres's master, Roques. Don't miss the pretty **Place de la Daurade** just north of the church; it overlooked the Garonne until the rebuilding of the quays in the 19th century.

One of the finest views of the Pont Neuf and riverfront is south along the **Quai de Tounis**. Rue du Pont de Tounis, built in 1515 as a bridge over the Garonnette (a now covered tributary of the Garonne), leads back to the original riverbank and **Notre-Dame-la-Dalbade** (Our Lady the Whitened, after its medieval whitewash). This church too has taken some hard knocks. It was rebuilt in the Renaissance with a 85m spire, to show up St-Sernin's bell-tower; this was chopped down in the Revolution and rebuilt in the 1880s, using such cheap materials it fell through the roof in 1926. It has a rich Renaissance door, under the tympanum's ceramic reproduction of Fra Angelico's *Coronation of the Virgin* (1874).

① Hôtel de Pierre

Rue de la Dalbade was the favourite address for the nobility; among its *hôtels particuliers*, the standout is the sooty Hôtel de Pierre (No.25), which, extravagantly for the *ville rose*, is made of stone. In 1538 Nicolas Bachelier designed the façades around the courtyard, the doorway, framed by two bearded old men, and the monumental chimney. In the early 17th century, the next owner, a president of the *parlement*, married a *pastel* heiress and added the grandiose Baroque façade in imitation of one in Italy. Opposite is the grand **Hôtel de Malte** (1680), headquarters of the Knights of St John in Toulouse since 1115; after 1315, they took over the wealth and duties of the Templars (who before their suppression were at No.13).

Musée Archéologique de l'Institut Catholique

t 05 61 36 81 00; open one Sun a month, call for details

At 31 Rue de la Fonderie, the **Catholic Institute** includes an archaeology museum that includes some Gallo-Roman fragments and a number of funerary artefacts.

The Quartier du Jardin

At the south end of Rue de la Dalbade/Rue de la Fonderie in Place du Salin stood the fortified residence of the counts of Toulouse, the celebrated Château Narbonnais; it was also the site of the *parlement*, established in Toulouse in 1443. The whole complex was demolished in the 19th century for the **Palais de Justice**, with only the square brick tower, the 14th-century royal treasury (converted into a Protestant church), as a memory. In the adjacent Place du Parlement is an old house built on the Roman wall, donated to Domingo Guzmán for his new preaching order, and later converted to the use inscribed over the door: 'Maison de l'Inquisition'.

South of Place du Parlement, Allées Jules Guesde replaces the walls torn down in 1752. Here, by the Théâtre Sorano, a plaque marks the spot where the hated Simon de Montfort was brained; nearby, at No.35, is Toulouse's fascinating **Musée d'Histoire Naturelle**. The **Jardin Royal** was planted outside the walls and, in the 19th century, Toulouse's prettiest park, the **Jardin des Plantes**, was added. The garden's grand 16th–17th-century portal on Allée Frédéric-Mistral was salvaged from the original Capitole. Just south of this is the **Monument à la Gloire de la Résistance**, with a crypt aligned to be illuminated by the sun's rays on 19 August, the anniversary of the Liberation of Toulouse. If you are interested in the Resistance, look out also for the **Musée Départemental de la Résistance et de la Déportation** at 52 Allées des Demoiselles.

There is one last museum in this quarter, and it's not to be missed if you're fond of Egyptian, Coptic, Indian and Far Eastern Art – the **Musée Georges Labit**, housed in a neo-Moorish villa off the Allée Frédéric-Mistral. Labit was a 19th-century traveller with plenty of money and a good eye who accumulated a choice Oriental collection, considered the best in France after the Guimet Museum in Paris.

Musée d'Histoire Naturelle
closed for renovation until early 2008; ask at tourist office

Monument à la Gloire de la Résistance
open Mon–Fri 10–12 and 2–5 exc hols

Musée Départemental de la Résistance et de la Déportation
t 05 61 14 80 40; call for times

Musée G. Labit
43 Rue des Martyrs-de-la-Libération, t 05 61 22 21 84; open summer Wed–Mon 10–6; winter Wed–Mon 10–5, exc hols

From Place du Salin to the Musée des Augustins

The parliamentarians liked to build themselves distinguished houses in the unified quarter between the old *parlement* and the cathedral: all pink brick, with light grey shutters and black wrought-iron balconies. In this mesh of quiet lanes, there are a few to pick out during a stroll, such as the sumptuously ornate **Hôtel du Vieux Raisin** (1515) at 36 Rue du Languedoc, built by another *capitoul* in love with Italy. Another *hôtel* houses the **Musée Paul Dupuy**, named after the obsessed collector – every city seems to have one – who left to Toulouse his hoard of watches, automata,

Musée Paul Dupuy
13 Rue de la Pleau, t 05 61 14 65 50; open summer Wed–Mon 10–6; rest of year Wed–Mon 10–5, exc hols

guns, coins, fans, faïence, pharmaceutical jars and gems such as the 11th-century 'horn of Roland' and other exquisite medieval ivories, as well as a silver marigold from the Jeux Floraux of 1762. Some of the exhibits can only be seen by appointment.

Rue Perchepinte and Rue Fermat, lined with antique shops, lead up to Place St-Etienne, with Toulouse's oldest fountain (1546) and the massive archbishop's palace (1713), now used as the Préfecture. All are overpowered by the **Cathédrale St-Etienne**, begun in the 11th century by Raymond IV but completed only in the 17th century. Fashions and finances rose and fell in the three major building campaigns, resulting in a church that seems a bit drunk. Have a good look at the façade: in the centre rises a massive brick bell-tower with a clock, over the Romanesque base. To the right is a worn, asymmetrical stone Gothic façade, where the portal and rose window are off-centre; to the left extends the bulge of the chapel of Notre-Dame, a small church in itself stuck on the north end. It's even tipsier inside. In 1211, Raymond VI inserted the oldest known representation of the Cross of Languedoc as the key in one of the vaults, just before 1215, when Bishop Folquet rebuilt most of Raymond IV's church in the form of a single nave 19m high and 19m wide, with ogival crossings – a style that went on to become the model for southern Gothic.

In 1275, Bishop Bertrand de l'Isle-Jourdaine decided that Bishop Folquet's bit of the cathedral was hardly grandiose enough for Toulouse's dignity and came up with a plan based on northern French Gothic that involved realigning the axis of the church. The choir was built, a fine example of Flamboyant Gothic, with beautiful 14th-century glass on the west side, but the vaults, designed to be 40m high, were cut short at 27m due to limited funds. Money and energy ran out completely when Bishop Bertrand died, leaving a curious dogleg where his choir meets Raymond IV and Bishop Folquet's nave, marked by the massive Pilier d'Orléans, one of four intended to support the transept; it bears a plaque marking the tomb of Pierre-Paul Riquet, father of the Canal du Midi. Although many of the cathedral's best decorations are now stowed away in the Musée des Augustins, there are tapestries, faded into negatives of themselves, from the 15th and 16th centuries, and some interesting grotesques in the choir. The organ, a remarkable instrument from the early 1600s, was at the point of collapsing in the 1970s then restored and bolted high on its wall bracket like an elephant in a flower vase.

Rue Croix Baragnon, opposite the cathedral, has two beautiful Gothic houses, especially No.15, decorated with a band of stone carvings. But the greatest medieval art in this part of town is in the Musée des Augustins, a block north at the corner of Rue de Metz and Rue d'Alsace-Lorraine.

Musée des Augustins

Musée des Augustins
t 05 61 22 21 82,
www.augustins.org;
open Thurs–Mon 10–6,
Wed 10–9; closed
Tues and hols

This museum, one of the oldest in France, is in a beautifully restored 14th-century Augustinian convent. During the Revolution, the *ville rose* gaily smashed up its fabulous architectural heritage, as ordered in 1790 by the Convention, 'to leave standing no monument that hinted of slavery'. Enter Alexandre Dumège, self-taught son of a Dutch actor, who had such a passion for antiquities he singlehandedly rescued most of the contents of this museum and opened its doors in 1794. Gothic sculptures occupy the Augustinians' Flamboyant chapterhouse: the beautiful 14th-century *Virgin and Child* from Avignon, *Notre-Dame de Grasse* from the Jacobins, scenes from a 14th-century retable, the *Group of Three Persons, One of Whom is Strangled by a Monster*, and effigies from tombstones. A crooning choir of gargoyles from Toulouse's demolished Franciscan convent keep company with the sarcophaguses around the cloister; one is said to belong to the Visigothic Queen Ranachilde – *la reine Pédauque*, the goose-foot, maybe because of the web-footed bird carved in the side.

The nave of the convent church is devoted to religious paintings (Van Dyck's *Christ aux anges* and *Miracle de la mule*, Rubens's *Christ entre deux larrons*, and *San Diego en extase* by Murillo) and reliefs by Nicolas Bachelier. Best of all are the Romanesque works, most rescued from demolished cloisters: from St-Sernin, there's a capital sculpted with the *War of Angels* and an enigmatic bas-relief from the Porte des Comtes showing two women looking at one another, one holding a lion in her arms, the other a ram, an image that also appears on the main portal at Compostela. Other capitals stylistically related to those of Moissac are from the Romanesque cloister of the Daurade; the most beautiful are from Raymond IV's 11th-century cloister of St-Etienne – note the delicate, almost fluid scene of the dance of Salome and the beheading of John the Baptist. From the Romanesque portal of St-Etienne's chapterhouse are statue-columns of the Apostles that look ahead to Chartres.

The first floor of the convent is devoted to paintings, including two portraits of *capitouls*; one of their oldest prerogatives was the *droit d'image* – the right to have their portraits painted. In the 13th and 14th centuries this was exceptional: kings, emperors, the doge of Venice and the pope were among the few allowed to leave their likenesses for posterity. Other paintings include a 15th-century Florentine hunt scene, a highly unpleasant *Apollo flaying Marsyas* by the 'Divine' Guido Reni, a typical froufrou portrait by Hyacinthe Rigaud, and works by Simon Vouet, Philippe de Champaigne, Van Dyck, Rubens (in the Augustins' church), the two Guardis, Delacroix, Ingres, Manet, Morisot, Vuillard, Maurice Denis and Count Henri de Toulouse-Lautrec. There's also a medieval garden here.

Toulouse's Left Bank

Although the Left, or Gascon, bank of the Garonne has been settled since the early Middle Ages, the periodic rampages of the river dampened property values until the end of the 19th century, when flood control projects were completed.

The main reason for visiting the area lies just over the Pont Neuf – the round brick lighthouse-shaped tower of a pumping and filtering station, which was constructed in 1817 to provide pure drinking water for the city. In 1974 this found a new role as the **Galerie Municipale du Château-d'Eau**. The hydraulic machinery is still intact on the bottom level, while upstairs you can visit one of Europe's foremost photographic galleries – over and over again, since exhibitions change 15 times a year. An annexe has been installed in a dry arch of the Pont Neuf. There is also a reference **library** on the history of photography .

Galerie Municipale du Château-d'Eau
t 05 61 77 09 40;
open Tues–Sat 1–7
exc hols; **library**
Mon–Fri 1.30–6 and
1st Sat of month; adm

Facing the watertower is the **Hôtel-Dieu St-Jacques**, a medieval pilgrimage hospital rebuilt in the 17th century. The grand Salle St-Jacques and Salle St-Lazare have magnificent ceilings, while down on the ground floor are the **Musée d'Histoire de la Médecine** and a **museum of medical instruments** from the city's hospitals, dating from the second half of the 19th century to today.

Musée d'Histoire de la Médecine
t 05 61 77 84 25;
open Wed–Sun 1–6

Musée des Instruments de Médecine des Hôpitaux de Toulouse
t 05 61 77 82 72;
open Thurs and Fri 1–5

Nearby, a single arch survives of a 17th-century covered bridge over the Garonne, the Pont de la Daurade. Each of France's four great rivers has a nickname, and the Garonne is 'the Laughing'. Often enough, the joke has been on Toulouse. St Cyprien, the original dedicatee of the Left Bank's parish church (behind the Hôtel-Dieu), proved to wield so little celestial influence over the water that when his church was rebuilt in 1300 he was sacked in favour of St Nicolas, patron of sailors and protector of the flooded. **St Nicolas church** is a small southern Gothic version of Les Jacobins and boasts a grand 18th-century altar painted by Despax.

More visual arts, this time in the form of graphics, posters, ads and postcards from the 17th century to the present, are the subject of the changing exhibits at the **Centre Municipal de l'Affiche, de la Carte Postale et de l'Art Graphique**; there's an extensive library of books, films and records, and, most popular of all, French commercials – those that used to be shown in the cinemas – dating from 1904 to 1968, on video cassettes.

Centre Municipal de l'Affiche, de la Carte Postale et de l'Art Graphique
58 Allées Charles de Fitte, *t 05 61 59 24 64,*
St-Cyprien métro;
open Mon–Fri 9–12 and 2–6; library open to public by appt; adm

Just up the road is **Les Abattoirs**, dedicated to art at its most contemporary, with all the main movements from the second half of the 20th century into the 21st represented. Some of it is quite disturbing stuff, such as Alberto Burri's *Sacco IV* with patched and tattered heavy sacking, holes in places resembling sores. The prize exhibit, displayed on and off throughout the year, was created just outside the timeframe for most of the work: a stage curtain for the

⭐ **Les Abattoirs**
76 Allées Charles de Fitte, *t 05 34 51 10 60;*
open Tues–Sun 11–7

play *14 Juillet* by Romain Rolland, painted by Luis Fernandez in 1936 on the request of Pablo Picasso, and copied from the great man's gouache of the corpse of a Minotaur dressed in the costume of a Harlequin. You would never guess the building's original purpose as the city's abattoir (of course): it is now large and airy with a sense of space throughout.

(i) **Toulouse >**
*Donjon du Capitole,
Rue Lafayette,
behind the Capitole,
t 05 61 11 02 22, www.
toulouse-tourisme.com
and www.toulouse.fr.*

Tourist Information in Toulouse

The **tourist office** offers a range of **themed tours**, some in English. If you're around for a while, buy an *En Liberté* card (€10 or €13) which gives discounts on tours, entrance fees, activities, hotels and eating out.

For information on the whole of the Midi-Pyrénées region, go to (call ahead) the **Comité Régional du Tourisme Midi-Pyrénées**, 54 Bd de l'Embouchure, **t** 05 61 13 55 55, *www.tourisme-midi-pyrenees.com*, or the **Maison Midi-Pyrénées**, 1 Rue Rémusat, near Place Capitole (*Mon–Fri 10–7*).

Markets and Shopping in Toulouse

There are regular covered **markets** at **Place des Carmes** (*daily exc Mon*) and at **Les Halles** in Bd Victor Hugo (*Tues–Sun 6am–1pm*). On Tuesday and Saturday mornings, **Place du Capitole** has a lively organic produce market. There is a good fruit and veg market (*daily exc Mon*) along **Boulevard de Strasbourg**, starting near Place Jeanne d'Arc, and Sun (and to a lesser extent Sat) morning sees a huge flea market around **St-Sernin** and along the length of the boulevards, the 'relics' of modern Toulouse that draw thousands of 'pilgrims'.

With many of the major French department stores, the Pink City is the shopping capital of the southwest. You can obtain superb **chocolates** at Maison Pillon, at 2 Rue Ozenne.

The Bookshop, 17 Rue Lakanal, **t** 05 61 22 99 92, has **books** in English. For **posters** and reprints, try the shop in the Centre Municipal de l'Affiche.

If you fancy tasting some of the best **cheese** that France has to offer, head for Betty, 2 Place Victor Hugo;

(★) **Hôtel des Beaux Arts >>**

you smell it from fifty paces. There are 200 different types from all over the country, some of them quite special, such as the Vieux Salers, made in just one village in the Cantal and given a minimum of one year to mature. For fine **preserves** and French classics such as **olive oil** and very dark chocolate, go to La Boutique des Saveurs at 1 Rue Ozenne, **t** 05 61 53 75 21, a delightful shop that bombards you with tantalizing smells.

Toulouse's flower is the **violet** – visit the violet barge on the Canal du Midi near the station, run by a woman potty about the flower.

Where to Stay in and around Toulouse

Toulouse ✉ **31000**

Toulouse has chain hotels galore for business visitors and a few reliable independents in the historic centre. Try to avoid the cheap fleabags near the station. Book early, and check hotel websites for offers, especially at weekends and in summer.

****Grand Hôtel de l'Opéra, 1 Place du Capitole, **t** 05 61 21 82 66, *www.grand-hotel-opera.com* (€€€€€–€€€€). The city's most beautiful hotel, with 50 sumptuous rooms and three suites in an old convent, an indoor pool and a magnificent restaurant (*see p.287*).

***Holiday Inn Capoul, 13 Place Wilson, **t** 05 61 10 70 70, *www.hotel-capoul.com* (€€€€–€€€). A swish member of the chain, with large, light rooms and an excellent brasserie. Adjoining it, **Le Capoul** is a *hôtel-résidence* with quite chic apartments and studios.

***Hôtel des Beaux Arts, 1 Place Pont-Neuf, **t** 05 34 45 42 42, *www.hoteldesbeauxarts.com* (€€€€–€€). An 18th-century *hôtel particulier* with pleasant, cosy, soundproofed rooms overlooking the Garonne.

⭐ **Guest House Josephine >>**

***Mermoz, 50 Rue Matabiau, **t** 05 61 63 04 04, *www.hotel-mermoz.com* (€€€). The best hotel near the station, with delightful air-conditioned rooms overlooking inner courtyards.

***Brienne, 20 Bd du Maréchal Leclerc, **t** 05 61 23 60 60, *www.hoteldebrienne. com* (€€). An ultra-modern, good-value choice with well-equipped rooms.

Arnaud-Bernard, 33 Place des Tiercerettes, **t 05 61 21 37 64 (€€). Good rooms in the centre of the lively popular quarter near St-Sernin.

✡ **Old Toulouse >>**

Castellane, 17 Rue Castellane, **t 05 61 62 18 82, *www.castellanehotel.com* (€€). Light, spacious rooms on a quiet side street, with private parking (for a fee) and a pleasant breakfast area.

Grand Hôtel d'Orléans, 72 Rue de Bayard, **t 05 61 62 98 47, *www.grand-hotel-orleans.fr* (€€–€). A characterful choice near the station, with interior galleries, a garden and satellite TV.

Hôtel de France, 5 Rue d'Austerlitz, **t 05 61 21 88 24, *www.hotel-france-toulouse.com* (€€–€). Traditional rooms and a vaguely funky lounge.

St-Sernin, 2 Rue St-Bernard, **t 05 61 21 73 08, *www.hotel-saint-sernin.new.fr* (€€–€). Good rooms with baths, minibars and TVs, opposite the basilica.

*Anatole France, 46 Place A. France, **t** 05 61 23 19 96 (€). Some of the best low-priced rooms in Toulouse, with showers, near the Capitole.

*Croix-Baragnon, 17 Rue Croix-Baragnon, **t** 05 61 52 60 10 (€). Rooms with bath and shower, by St-Etienne.

*Hôtel des Arts, 1 bis Rue Cantegril, **t** 05 61 23 36 21 (€). Friendly place near lively Place St-Georges, with good rooms with showers but shared WCs.

Foyer des Jeunes Travailleurs, Résidence San Francisco, 92 Route d'Espagne, **t** 05 61 43 23 00, *www.ucjg-monnier.org* (€). A popular youth hostel; book ahead.

⭐ **Les Jardins de l'Opéra >>**

Outskirts of Toulouse

***La Flânerie, Route de Lacroix-Falgarde, Vieille-Toulouse (✉ 31320), 8km south on D4, **t** 05 61 73 39 12, *www.hotellaflanerie.com* (€€€–€€). A pretty country house where the Tectosages once roamed, with grand views over the Garonne. There's a

pool, and tennis and golf nearby. *Closed Sun, Dec, 1 weekend Jan, and 1wk end of Aug.*

Guest House Joséphine, 1 Rue des Ecoles, Villenouvelle (along N113, direction Villefranche-de-Lauragais), **t** 05 34 66 20 13, *http://maison. josephine.free.fr* (€). A sensitively restored 18th-century house run by a welcoming Franco-Irish couple, with airy bedrooms with marble fireplaces, some ideal for those with young kids, a pool and dinner (€€) by request.

Eating Out in and around Toulouse

Toulouse, and in particular its restaurant quarter, Old Toulouse, has enjoyed a restaurant revolution that has trickled down from *les grandes tables* to the corner bistro. Yet along with this leap in the quality of food, the city hasn't quite forgotten its key place in the southwest bean belt, and claims to make a *cassoulet* that walks all over the cassoulets of rivals Carcassonne and Castelnaudry. To the base recipe (white beans, garlic, herbs, goose fat, salt bacon, fat pork and *confits* of goose or duck), they chuck in a foot or two of their famed sausage (*saucisse de Toulouse*), shoulder of mutton, and perhaps ham. This is sprinkled with breadcrumbs and baked. To aid digestion, locals advise a game of rugby, or a tipple of *eau de noix Benoît Serres*, the local walnut *digestif*, or of armagnac.

The first floor of the **Marché Victor Hugo** (Tues–Sun) has a number of cheaper places popular for lunch.

Note that many of the city's restaurants close for all of August.

Toulouse ✉ 31000

Cosi Fan Tutte, 8 Rue Mage, **t** 05 61 53 07 24 (€€€€–€€€). Top Italian food in an operatic setting. *Closed Sun and Mon.*

Les Jardins de l'Opéra, Grand Hôtel de l'Opéra (*see p.286*), **t** 05 61 23 07 76 (€€€€–€€€). Toulouse's finest gastronomic experience, and one of the southwest's most beautiful restaurants. The food matches the hushed, sophicated setting – it includes aromatic mushroom dishes, seafood cooked to perfection, flavourful regional specialities, and delicate desserts. *Closed Sun and Mon, Aug and 1st week Jan.*

Le Pastel, 237 Rue de St-Simon, Mirail, t 05 62 87 84 30 (€€€€–€€€). Some of the finest, most imaginative gourmet food in Toulouse, at some of the kindest prices. Book at lunchtimes. *Closed Sun, Mon, and 2wks in Aug.*

⭐ **Michael Sarran >** Michel Sarran, 21 Bd Armand Duportal, t 05 61 12 32 32 (€€€€–€€€). A superb synthesis of sun-soaked southwest and Provençal cuisines served in an elegant town house. *Closed Wed lunch, Sat, Sun, Aug and Christmas.*

La Belle Chaurienne, Allée de Barcelone, Canal de Brienne, t 05 61 21 23 85 (€€€€–€€). A barge (*péniche*) in a pretty canal location, serving good regional dishes. *Closed Sat lunch, Sun, Mon lunch and Aug.*

Le Bibent, 5 Place du Capitole, t 05 61 23 89 03 (€€€–€€). One of the most beautiful brasseries in Toulouse, with an excellent shellfish selection and southwest favourites.

Le Bon Vivre, 15 Place Wilson, t 05 61 23 07 17 (€€€–€€). A place popular for its authentic southwestern cooking.

Le Bouchon Lyonnais, 13 Rue de l'Industrie (off Rue de la Colombette), t 05 61 62 97 43 (€€€–€€). Delicious dishes from Provence and Lyon, served in an Art Deco setting. *Closed Sat lunch and Sun.*

Les Caves de la Maréchale, 3 Rue Jules Chalande, t 05 61 23 89 88 (€€€–€€). Sophisticated regional dishes served in the vast cellar of a 13th-century priory off Rue St-Rome. *Closed Sat lunch, Sun, and Mon lunch.*

Chez Emile, 13 Place St-Georges, t 05 61 21 05 56 (€€€–€€). Something of a Toulouse institution, serving some of the finest seafood in Toulouse, duck *confit* and other meats. *Closed Sun and Mon lunch, plus Mon eve out of high season.*

⭐ **Le Colombier >** Le Colombier, 14 Rue Bayard, t 05 61 62 40 05 (€€€–€€). Some of the finest cassoulet in Toulouse (the owner's recipe is safeguarded by his lawyer) and other southwest treats. *Closed Sat lunch, Sun, Aug and Christmas.*

Les Ombrages, 48 bis Route de St-Simon, t 05 61 07 61 28 (€€€–€€). Fresh, sunny cuisine: try minced duck with berries and foie gras. It's a bit hard to find – take a taxi. *Closed Sun and Mon eves and 2wks Aug.*

Sept Place St-Sernin, 7 Place St-Sernin, t 05 62 30 05 30 (€€€–€€). A large ivy-covered house opposite the cathedral, with delightful menus featuring the likes of *foie gras* with figs and herb salad. *Closed Sat lunch and Sun.*

La Bascule, 14 Av Maurice-Hauriou, t 05 61 52 09 51 (€€). A popular brasserie a short way from the centre, with good seafood, traditional meat and game, and a few adventurous offerings. *Closed Sat lunch, Sun and Mon.*

Grand Café de l'Opéra, 1 Place du Capitole, t 05 61 21 37 03 (€€). A cosy, elegant brasserie with excellent classics, with the emphasis on seafood. *Closed Sun and Aug.*

Benjamin, 7 Rue des Gestes (off Rue St-Rome), t 05 61 22 92 66 (€€–€). The likes of fennel and courgette terrine and steak with *cèpes*, in the heart of old Toulouse at friendly prices.

La Tantina de Burgos, 27 Avenue de la Garonnette, t 05 61 55 59 29 (€€–€). A zesty tapas bar/restaurant with tasty *zarzuela* (Catalan fish soup) and more. *Closed Sun and Mon.*

A la Truffe du Quercy, 17 Rue Croix-Baragnon, t 05 61 53 34 24 (€€–€). Southwestern home cooking and some Spanish dishes too. *Closed Sun, Mon eve and Aug.*

Outskirts of Toulouse

L'Amphitryon, Chemin de Gramont, ✉ 31770 Colomiers (exit 3 off *rocade*), t 05 61 15 55 55 (€€€€–€€€). Delicate southwestern cuisine, including lamb fillet with mint and citrus fruits, served in a leafy park a short drive out of the city. Desserts are sumptuous.

O Saveurs, 8 Place Ormeaux, Rouffiac Tolosan, on N88 to Albi, t 05 34 27 10 11 (€€€€–€€). A charming restaurant in a delightful, calm square, with very light dishes such as roast scampi with seasonal fruits. *Closed Sat lunch, Sun eve, Mon and 3wks Aug.*

Au Pois Gourmand, 3 Rue E Heybrard, Casselardit (just off *rocade*), t 05 34 36 42 00 (€€€€–€€). A handsome old manor with wooden galleries, serving refined, original cuisine such as red mullet grilled in fig leaves with thyme and lemon. *Closed Sat and Mon lunch, Sun, and several wks Aug.*

Le Cantou, 98 Rue Vélasquez, St-Martin-du-Touch, t 05 61 49 20 21 (€€€). A lovely ivy-covered house in a beautiful garden in the suburbs, offering some of Toulouse's best regional cuisine and a huge southwest wine list. *Closed Sat, Sun, and 2wks in Aug.*

Le Manoir du Petit Prince, Château de Vincasses, Route de Seysses, ✉ 31120 Portet sur Garonne, t 05 61 31 14 14 (€€€–€€). A lovely château serving neglected regional fare like roast beef with thyme and mushroom cream. *Closed Sat lunch, Sun eve and Mon.*

Cafés, Bars and Wine Bars in Toulouse

L'Ancienne Belgique, 16 Rue de la Trinité. A wide selection of beer.

Bar Florida, Place du Capitole, t 05 61 23 94 61. *The* place in central Toulouse to sit and watch the world go by on a warm day, attracting tourists but plenty of *Toulousains* too, with an Art Deco interior. *Open 7am–2am.*

Mon Caf', Place du Capitole, t 05 61 23 14 07. A discreet venue where locals lounge on big maroon seats to enjoy beers, spirits, hot drinks and snacks.

Le Père Louis, 45 Place des Tourneurs, between Rue Peyras and Rue de Metz, t 05 61 21 33 45. A fiercely traditional bar (it's a historical landmark) and magnet for *quinquina* drinkers.

Entertainment and Nightlife in Toulouse

The weekly *Flash*, available at newsstands, will tell you what's on; or pick up the free *Toulouse Cultures*, published by the *mairie*.

Zénith, Av Raymond Badiou, t 05 62 74 49 49, is one of France's largest performance venues; events range from displays of Basque sport to pop concerts, ice-skating competitions to musicals. The nearest *métro* stations are Patte d'Oie and Arènes.

Theatre, Music and Dance

Since the Second World War, the *Toulousains* have discovered **classical music** in a big way, with the *gonfalon* held high by the **Orchestre Nationale du Capitole** (*www.onct.mairie-toulouse.fr*), one of France's top symphony orchestras, who often play in the acoustically excellent **Halle aux Grains**, Place Dupuy (just east of St-Etienne cathedral), t 05 61 63 13 13.

In July and August, the city **music festival** hosts performances by the fine **Orchestre National de Chambre de Toulouse** (*www.orchestredechambredetoulouse.fr*). In September, **Les Jacobins cloister** hosts the **Festival International Piano aux Jacobins**, t 05 61 22 40 05, *www. pianojacobins.com*. There is also a prestigious **organ festival**, Toulouse Les Orgues, t 05 61 22 20 44, in October, and from Oct to June the **Théâtre du Capitole** hosts an **opera and dance** season.

Concerts and exhibitions of dance are also given in the renovated auditorium of the church of **St-Pierre-des-Cuisines**, t 05 61 22 31 44.

The **Sorano Théâtre National**, 35 Allées Jules-Guesde, t 05 34 31 67 16, puts on some of the finest **plays** in Toulouse. For modern French **poetry**, *chanson* and theatre, try **La Cave Poésie**, 71 Rue du Taur, t 05 61 23 62 00.

Cinema

Toulouse likes its fair share of movies as well; the **Cinémathèque**, 69 Rue du Taur, t 05 62 30 30 10, *www.tacinemathequedetoulouse.com*, is the second most important in France, and often shows films in V.O. (*version originale*), as does **ABC**, 13 Rue St-Bernard, t 05 61 29 81 00.

Clubs

L'Aposia, 9 bis Rue Jean Rodier, t 05 05 71 84 11. A huge club, playing groove, techno, disco and more to a young mixed crowd.

Chez Tonton, 16 Place St-Pierre, t 05 61 21 89 54. A trendy *pastis* hangout.

El Barrio Latino, 144 Av de Muret, t 05 61 59 00 58. A good Latin venue with a restaurant. *Closed Mon–Wed.*

Havana Café, Av des Crêtes, Ramonville, t 05 62 88 34 94. A happening place with regular live music.

Puerto Habana, 12 Port St-Etienne, t 05 61 54 45 61. Distinctly lively nights out *à la cubana*, with live salsa.

Language

A working knowledge of French will make your holiday more enjoyable, but is not essential in big cities, where you can always find someone working in a travel office, bank, shop, hotel or restaurant who speaks at least rudimentary English. Venturing into the less-travelled hinterlands may well require an effort to recall your school French; a small travel phrase book and English–French dictionary can come in handy.

Even if your French is brilliant, the soupy southern twang may throw you. Any word with a nasal *in* or *en* becomes something like *aing* (*vaing* for *vin*). The last vowel on many words that are silent in the north get to express themselves in the south (*encore* sounds something like *engcora*).

What remains the same as anywhere else in France is the level of politeness expected: use *monsieur*, *madame* or *mademoiselle* when speaking to everyone (and *garçon* in restaurants only if you add '*s'il vous plaît*'), from your first *bonjour* to your last *au revoir*.

See pp.56–60 for menu vocabulary.

Pronunciation

Vowels
a, à, â between *a* in 'bat' and 'part'
é, er, ez at end of word as *a* in 'plate' but a bit shorter
e at end of word not pronounced
e at end of syllable or in one-syllable word pronounced weakly, like *er* in 'mother'
i as *ee* in 'bee'
o as *o* in 'pot'
ô as *o* in 'go'
u, û between *oo* in 'boot' and *ee* in 'bee'

Vowel Combinations
ai as *a* in 'plate'
aî as *e* in 'bet'
ail as *i* in 'kite'
au, eau as *o* in 'go'
ei as *e* in 'bet'
eu, œu as *er* in 'mother'
oi between *wa* in 'swam' and *u* in 'swum'
oy in middle of words as 'why'; otherwise as 'oi', above
ui as *wee* in 'twee'

Nasal Vowels
Vowels followed by an *n* or an *m* have a nasal sound.
an, en as *o* in 'pot' + nasal sound
ain, ein, in as *a* in 'bat' + nasal sound
on as *aw* in 'paw' + nasal sound
un as *u* in 'nut' + nasal sound

Consonants
Many French consonants are pronounced as in English, but there are some exceptions:
c followed by *e, i* or *y* and *ç* as *s* in 'sit'
c followed by *a, o* or *u* as *c* in 'cat'
g followed by *e, i* or *y* as *s* in 'pleasure'
gn as *ni* in 'opinion'
j as *s* in 'pleasure'
ll as *y* in 'yes'
qu as *k* in 'kite'
s between vowels as *z* in 'zebra'
s otherwise as *s* in 'sit'
w except in English words as *v* in 'vest'
x at end of word as *s* in 'sit'
x otherwise as *x* in 'six'

Stress
The stress usually falls on the last syllable except when the word ends with an unaccented *e*.

Vocabulary

The nouns in the list below are marked as either masculine *(m)* or feminine *(f)*.

If masculine, 'the' is *le*, or *l'* if the word begins with a vowel; and 'a' is *un*. 'Some' or 'any' is *du*. For example, *'A quelle heure part le train pour Montpellier?/Je voudrais un oreiller/du savon.'*

If feminine, 'the' is *la*, or *l'* if the word begins with a vowel; and 'a' is *une*. 'Some' or 'any' is *'de la'*. For example, *'Je cherche la sortie/une pharmacie/Je voudrais de l'aspirine.'*

If plural, 'the' is *les*, and 'some' or 'any' is *des*. For example, *'Où sont les toilettes/Est-ce que vous avez des cartes postales?'*

General

hello *bonjour*
good evening *bonsoir*
good night *bonne nuit*
goodbye *au revoir*
please *s'il vous plaît*
thank you **(very much)** *merci (beaucoup)*
yes *oui*
no *non*
good *bon (bonne)*
bad *mauvais*
excuse me *pardon, excusez-moi*
Can you help me? *Pourriez-vous m'aider?*

My name is... *Je m'appelle...*
What is your name? *Comment t'appelles-tu?* (informal), *Comment vous appelez-vous?* (formal)
How are you? *Comment allez-vous?*
Fine *Ça va bien*
I don't understand *Je ne comprends pas*
I don't know *Je ne sais pas*
Speak more slowly *Pourriez-vous parler plus lentement?*
How do you say ... in French? *Comment dit-on ... en français?*
Help! *Au secours!*

Where is (the railway station)? *Où se trouve (la gare)?*
Is it far? *C'est loin?*
left *à gauche*
right *à droite*
straight on *tout droit*

entrance *entrée (f)*
exit *sortie (f)*
open *ouvert(e)*
closed *fermé(e)*
WC *toilettes (fpl)*
men *hommes*
ladies *dames* or *femmes*

doctor *médecin (m)*
hospital *hôpital (m)*
emergency room/A&E *salle des urgences (f)*
police station *commissariat de police (m)*
tourist information office *office de tourisme (m)*
How much is it? *C'est combien?*
Do you have...? *Est-ce que vous avez...?*
It's too expensive *C'est trop cher*
bank *banque (f)*
money *argent (m)*
change *monnaie (f)*
credit card *carte de crédit (f)*
traveller's cheque *chèque de voyage (m)*
post office *la poste*
stamp *timbre (m)*
postcard *carte postale (f)*
public phone *cabine téléphonique (f)*
shop *magasin (m)*
central food market *halles (fpl)*
tobacconist *tabac (m)*
pharmacy *pharmacie (f)*
aspirin *aspirine (f)*
condoms *préservatifs (mpl)*
insect repellent *anti-insecte (m)*
sun cream *crème solaire (f)*
tampons *tampons hygiéniques (mpl)*

Transport

airport *aéroport (m)*
aeroplane *avion (m)*
go on foot *aller à pied*
bicycle *bicyclette (f) / vélo (m)*
mountain bike *vélo tout terrain, VTT (m)*
bus *autobus (m)*
bus stop *arrêt d'autobus (m)*
coach station *gare routière (f)*
railway station *gare (f)*
train *train (m)*
platform *quai (m) / voie (f)*
date-stamp machine *composteur (m)*
timetable *horaire (m)*
left-luggage locker *consigne automatique (f)*

car *voiture (f)*
taxi *taxi (m)*
underground/subway *métro (m)*
ticket office *guichet (m)*
ticket *billet (m)*
single to... *un aller (or aller simple) pour...*
return/round trip to... *un aller et retour pour...*
What time does the ... leave?
A quelle heure part...?
delayed *en retard*
on time *à l'heure*

Accommodation

single room *chambre pour une personne (f)*
twin room *chambre à deux lits (f)*
double room *chambre pour deux personnes (f) / chambre double (f)*
bed *lit (m)*
blanket *couverture (f)*
cot (child's bed) *lit d'enfant (m)*
pillow *oreiller (m)*
soap *savon (m)*
towel *serviette (f)*
booking *réservation (f)*
I would like to book a room *Je voudrais réserver une chambre*

Months

January *janvier*
February *février*
March *mars*
April *avril*
May *mai*
June *juin*
July *juillet*
August *août*
September *septembre*
October *octobre*
November *novembre*
December *décembre*

Days

Monday *lundi*
Tuesday *mardi*
Wednesday *mercredi*
Thursday *jeudi*
Friday *vendredi*
Saturday *samedi*
Sunday *dimanche*

Time

What time is it? *Quelle heure est-il?*
month *mois (m)*
week *semaine (f)*
day *jour (m) / journée (f)*
morning *matin (m)*
afternoon *après-midi (m or f)*
evening *soir (m)*
night *nuit (f)*
today *aujourd'hui*
yesterday *hier*
tomorrow *demain*
day before yesterday *avant-hier*
day after tomorrow *après-demain*

Numbers

one *un*
two *deux*
three *trois*
four *quatre*
five *cinq*
six *six*
seven *sept*
eight *huit*
nine *neuf*
ten *dix*
eleven *onze*
twelve *douze*
thirteen *treize*
fourteen *quatorze*
fifteen *quinze*
sixteen *seize*
seventeen *dix-sept*
eighteen *dix-huit*
nineteen *dix-neuf*
twenty *vingt*
twenty-one *vingt et un*
twenty-two *vingt-deux*
thirty *trente*
forty *quarante*
fifty *cinquante*
sixty *soixante*
seventy *soixante-dix*
seventy-one *soixante et onze*
eighty *quatre-vingts*
eighty-one *quatre-vingt-un*
ninety *quatre-vingt-dix*
hundred *cent*
two hundred *deux cents*
thousand *mille*

Glossary

abbaye abbey
ambulatory a passage behind the choir of a church, often with radiating chapels
anse cove
arrondissement a city district
auberge inn
aven natural well
bastide taller, more elaborate version of a *mas*, with balconies, wrought-ironwork, reliefs, etc; also a medieval new town, fortified and laid out in a grid
beffroi tower with a town's bell
borie dry-stone shepherd's hut with a corbelled roof
buffet d'eau in French gardens, a fountain built into a wall with water falling through levels of urns or basins
cabane simple weekend or holiday retreat, usually near the sea; a *cabane de gardian* is a thatched cowboy's abode in the Camargue
calanque narrow coastal creek, like a miniature fjord
capitelle the name for *borie* in Languedoc
cardo the main north–south street in a Roman *castrum* or town
caryatid column or pillar carved in the figure of a woman
castrum rectangular Roman army camp, which often grew into a permanent settlement
causse rocky, arid limestone plateau, north of Hérault and in the lower Languedoc
cave (wine) cellar
château mansion, manor house or castle
château fort castle
chemin path
chevet eastern end of a church, including the apse
cirque round natural depression created by erosion at the loop of a river
cloître cloister
clue rocky cleft or transverse valley

col mountain pass
commune in the Middle Ages, the government of a free town or city; today, the smallest unit of local government, encompassing a town or village
côte coast; on wine labels, *côtes, coteaux* and *costières* mean 'hills' or 'slopes'
cours wide main street, like an elongated main square
couvent convent or monastery
crèche Christmas crib with *santons*
donjon castle keep
écluse canal lock
église church
étang lagoon or swamp
Félibre member of the movement to bring back the use of the Provençal language
ferrade cattle branding
gardian a cowboy of the Camargue
gare train station (SNCF)
gare routière coach station
garrigues irregular limestone hills pitted with caves, especially those north of Nîmes and Montpellier
gisant sculpted prone effigy on a tomb
gîte shelter
gîte d'étape basic shelter for walkers
grande randonnée (GR) long-distance hiking path
grau a narrowing, of a canyon or a river
halles covered market
hôtel particulier originally the town residence of the nobility; by the 18th century the word became more generally used for any large, private residence
hôtel de ville city hall
lavoir communal fountain, usually covered, for the washing of clothes
mairie town hall
manade a *gardian*'s farm in the Camargue
maquis Mediterranean scrub. Also used as a term for the French Resistance during the Second World War

marché market

mas a farmhouse and its outbuildings

mascaron ornamental mask, usually one carved on the keystone of an arch

modillon stone projecting from the cornice of a church, carved with a face or animal figure

motte hammock, or a raised area in a swamp

oppidum pre-Roman fortified settlement

Parlement French juridical body, with members appointed by the king; by the late *ancien régime, parlements* exercised a great deal of influence over political affairs

pays region or village

pont bridge

porte gateway

predella small paintings beneath the main subject of a retable

presqu'île peninsula

puy hill

restanques vine or olive terraces

retable carved or painted altarpiece, often consisting of a number of scenes or sculpted ensembles

rez-de-chaussée (RC) ground floor (US first floor)

santon figure in a Christmas nativity scene, usually made of terracotta and dressed in 18th-century Provençal costume

source spring

tour tower

transi on a tomb, a relief of the decomposing cadaver

tympanum sculpted semicircular panel over a church door

vieille ville historic, old quarter of town

village perché hilltop village

Further Reading

Ardagh, John, *France In the New Century: Portrait of a Changing Society* (Penguin, 2000). One of Penguin's informative paperback series on contemporary Europe.

Barber, Malcolm, *The Cathars: Dualist Heretics in Languedoc in the High Middle Ages* (Medieval World Series, Longman, 2000). A solid history, and good for debunking occultist theories.

Bonner, Anthony, *Songs of the Troubadours* (Allen & Unwin, 1973). An introduction to the life and times of the troubadours, with translations of best-known verses.

Davis, Natalie Zemon, *The Return of Martin Guerre* (Harvard, 1983). In the tradition of Ladurie's 'microhistory', the true story (earlier made into a film with Gérard Dépardieu) of a lost son who reappears in a 16th-century Languedoc village – but turns out to be an impostor.

Holt, Mack P., *The French Wars of Religion, 1562–1629* (Cambridge University Press, 1995).

Hugo, Victor, *Les Misérables*, many editions. Injustice among the galley-slaves and basis for the hit musical.

Johnson, Christopher, *The Rise and Fall of Industrial Languedoc, 1700–1920* (Oxford, 1995). An interesting historical lesson: everyone writes about industrialization; here's the story of how a region de-industrializes itself.

Ladurie, Emmanuel Leroi, *Montaillou: The Promised Land of Error* (Vintage, 1979). The classic work of French 'microhistory', a fascinating and rigorous account of everything about life and work in a village of the Ariège in 1300, taken from copious local records. Montaillou was the last surviving community of Cathars. Ladurie expanded his work in

The Peasants of Languedoc (University of Illinois, 1977) and *Love, Death and Money in the Pays d'Oc* (Scholar, 1982).

Lugand, Jacques, Robert St-Jean and Jean Nougaret, *Languedoc Roman* (Zodiaque, 1975). The best of Languedoc's Romanesque architecture, with plans, lots of photos and an English translation.

Moon, Patrick, *Virgile's Vineyard: A Year in the Languedoc Wine Country* (John Murray, 2004). The expat-recounts-the-glories-of-rural-France genre comes to Languedoc, in a tale centered on wine-making.

Oldenbourg, Zoe, *Massacre at Montségur, A History of the Albigensian Crusade* (Phoenix, 2001). Very readable history. The same author also wrote a historical novel on the era, *Destiny of Fire* (Carroll and Graf, 1999).

Petrarch, Francesco, *Songs and Sonnets from Laura's Lifetime* (Anvil Press, 1985).

Strang, Paul, *Languedoc-Roussillon: The Wine and Wine Makers* (Mitchell Beazley, 1979). A complete guide to the region and its recent wine revolution: where to find the bargains and the real surprises.

Strayer, Joseph, *The Albigensian Crusades* (University of Michigan, 1992). One of the best works on the subject, on both the heresy and the consequences of the 'crusade' for Occitania.

Whitfield, Sarah, *Fauvism* (Thames and Hudson, 1991). A good introduction to the movement that changed art history.

Wright, Rupert, *Notes from the Languedoc* (Ebury Press, 2005). A *Times* journalist's affectionate and insightful account of Languedoc today, as well as its history and culture.

Index

Main page references are in **bold**. Page references to maps are in *italics*.

2nd edition published 2008

Cadogan Guides is an imprint of
New Holland Publishers (UK) Ltd
London • Cape Town • Sydney • Auckland

New Holland Publishers (UK) Ltd	80 McKenzie Street	Unit 1, 66 Gibbes Street	218 Lake Road
Garfield House	Cape Town 8001	Chatswood, NSW 2067	Northcote
86–88 Edgware Road	South Africa	Australia	Auckland
London W2 2EA			New Zealand

Cadogan@nhpub.co.uk
www.cadoganguides.com
t 44 (0)20 7724 7773

Distributed in the United States by Globe Pequot, Connecticut

Copyright © Dana Facaros and Michael Pauls 2006, 2008
© 2008 New Holland Publishers (UK) Ltd

Cover photographs: © Bruno Barbier/CORBIS, © Massimo Borchi/CORBIS
Photo essay photographs © Alys Tomlinson
Maps © Cadogan Guides, drawn by Maidenhead Cartographic Services Ltd
Cover and photo essay design: Sarah Rianhard-Gardner
Editor: Linda McQueen
Proofreading: Susannah Wight
Indexing: Isobel McLean

Printed in Italy by Legoprint
A catalogue record for this book is available from the British Library

ISBN: 978-1-86011-392-5

Languedoc-Roussillon touring atlas

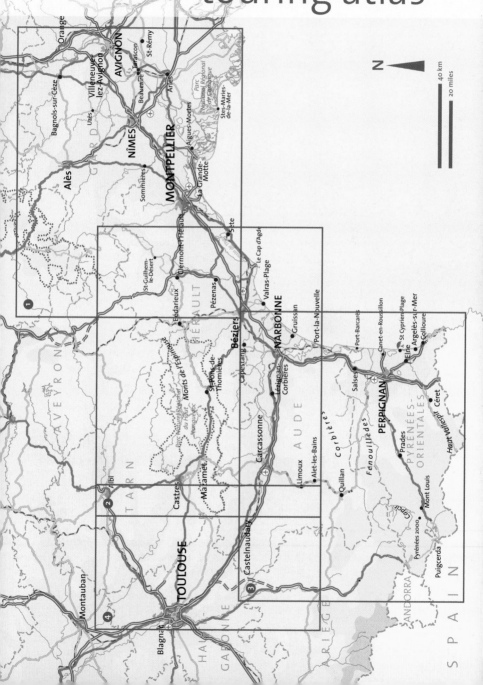

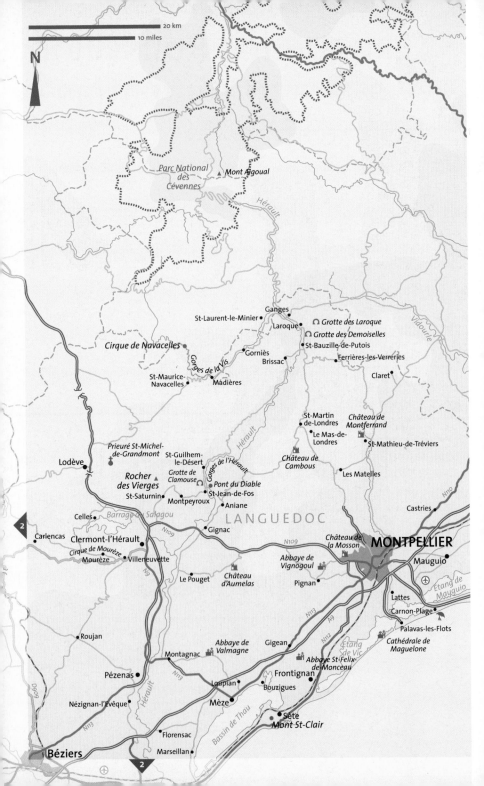

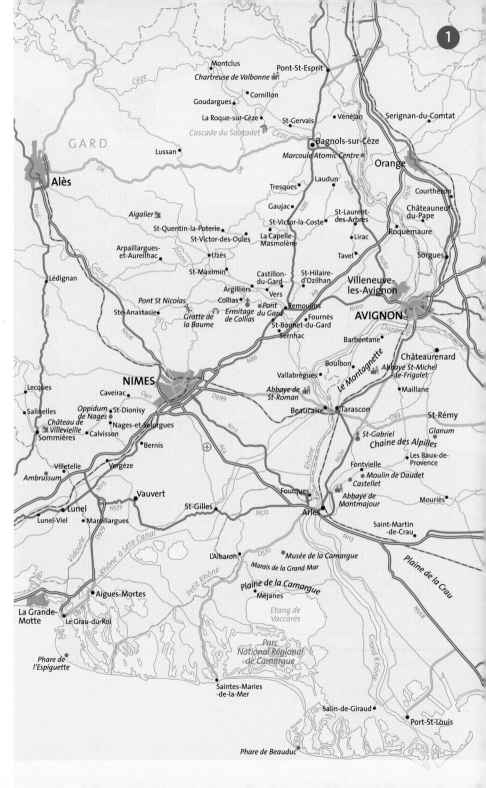

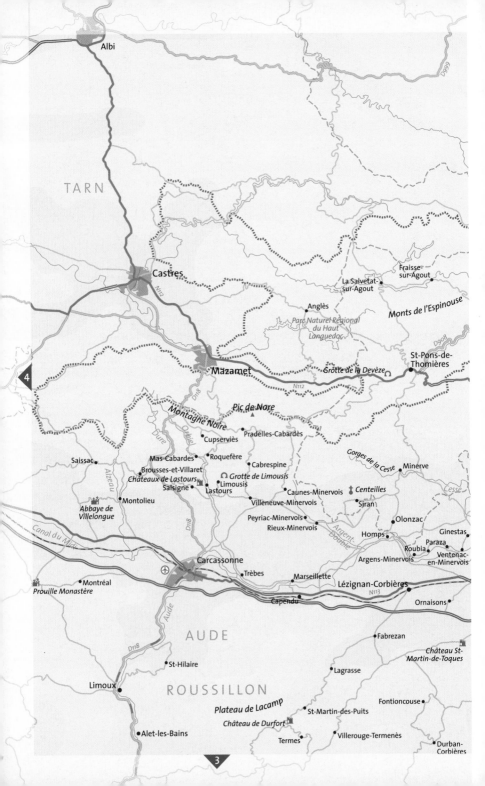

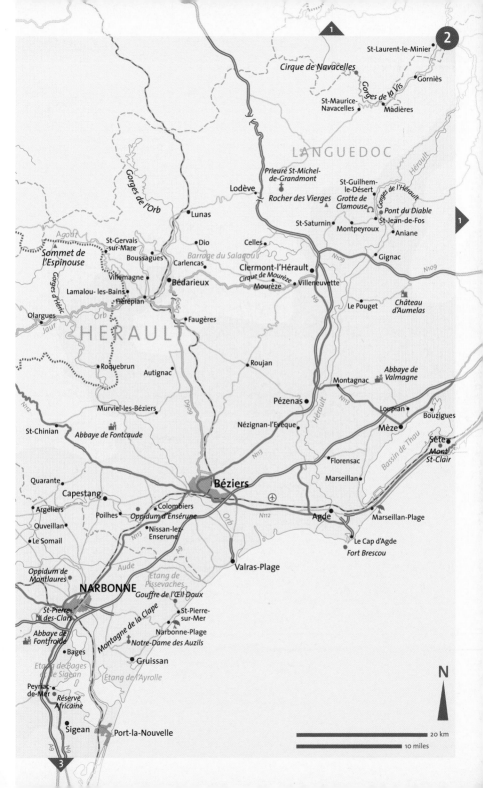

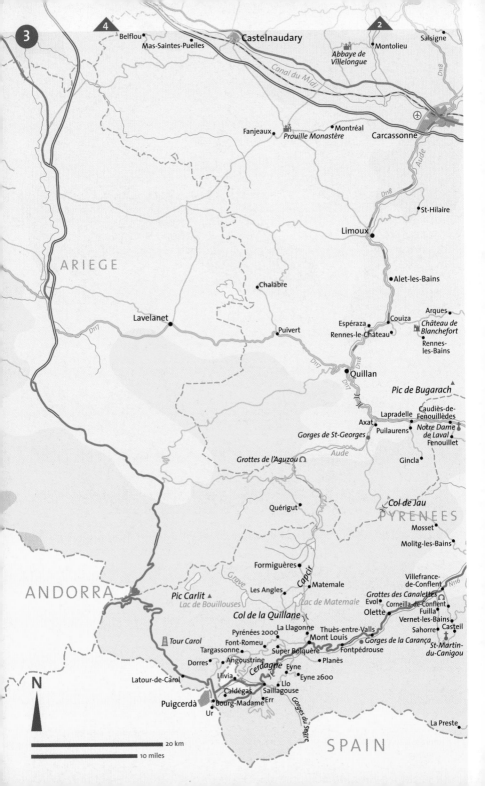

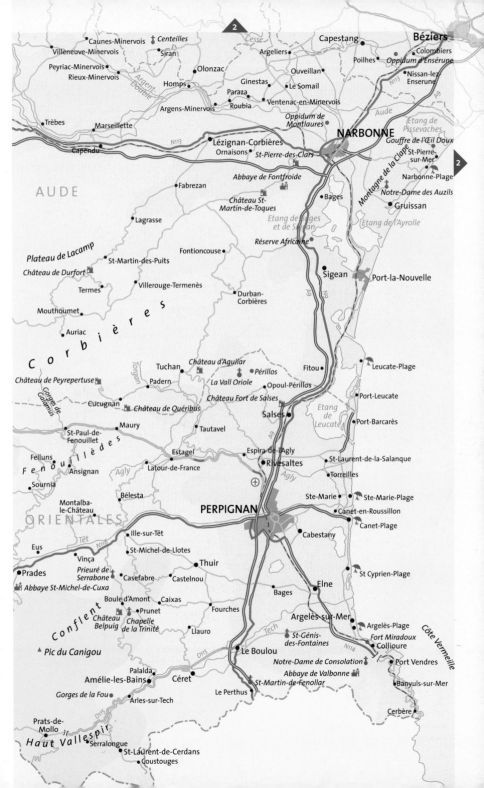

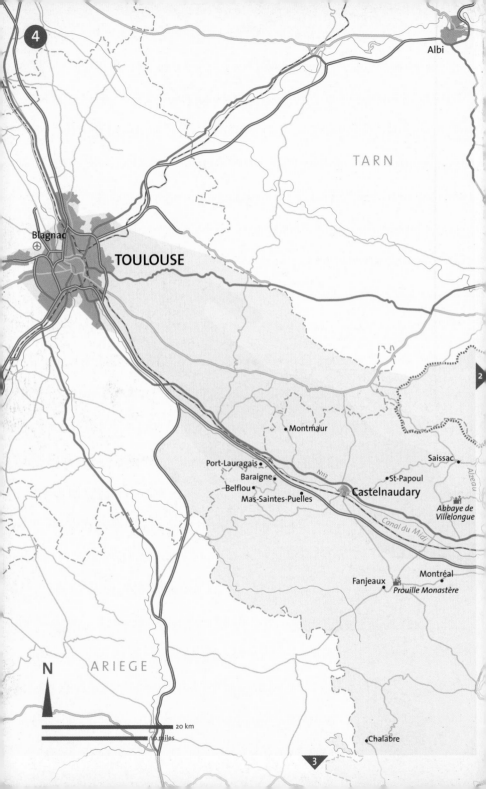